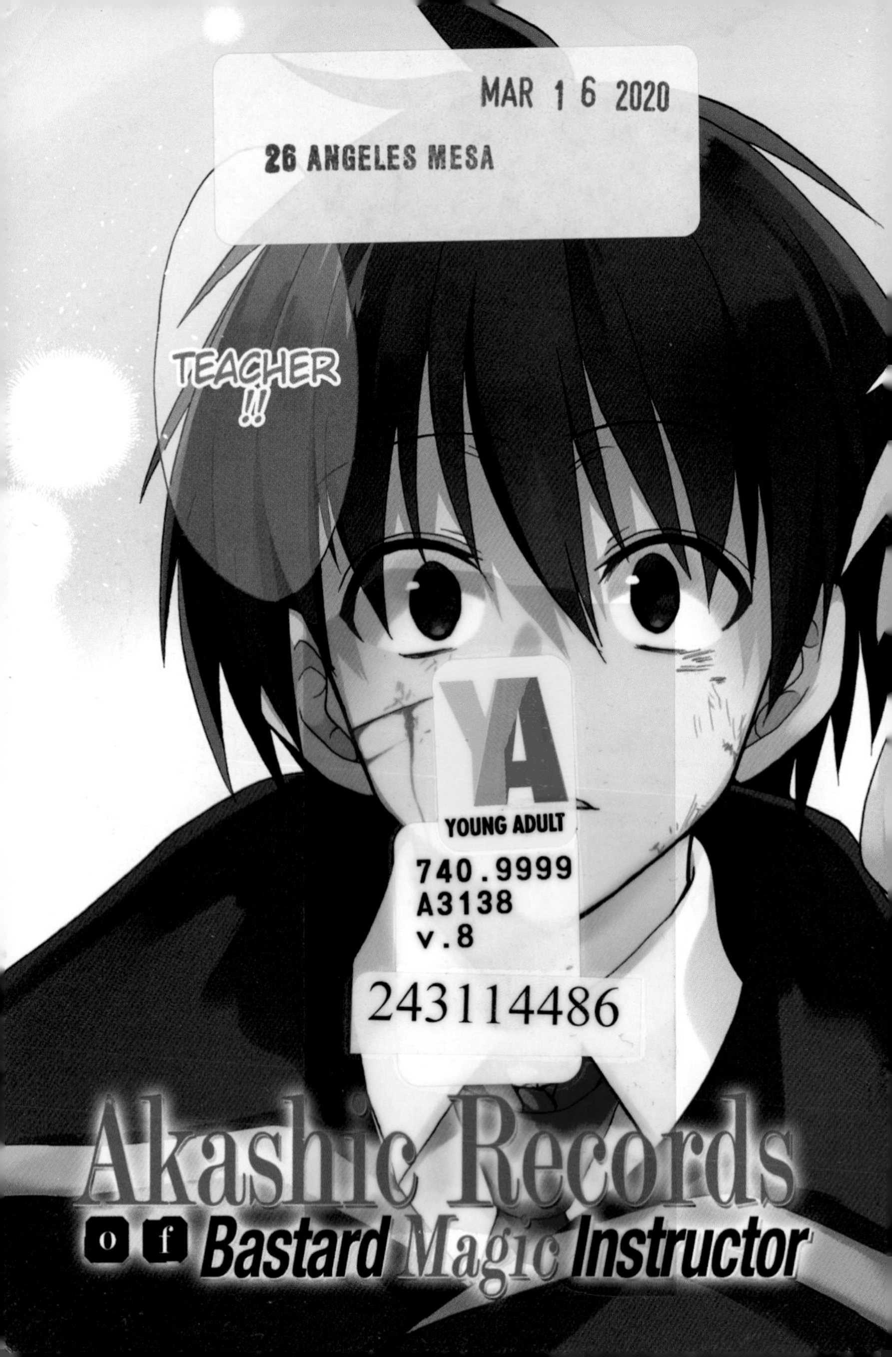
TEACHER
!!
Akashic Records
of Bastard Magic Instructor

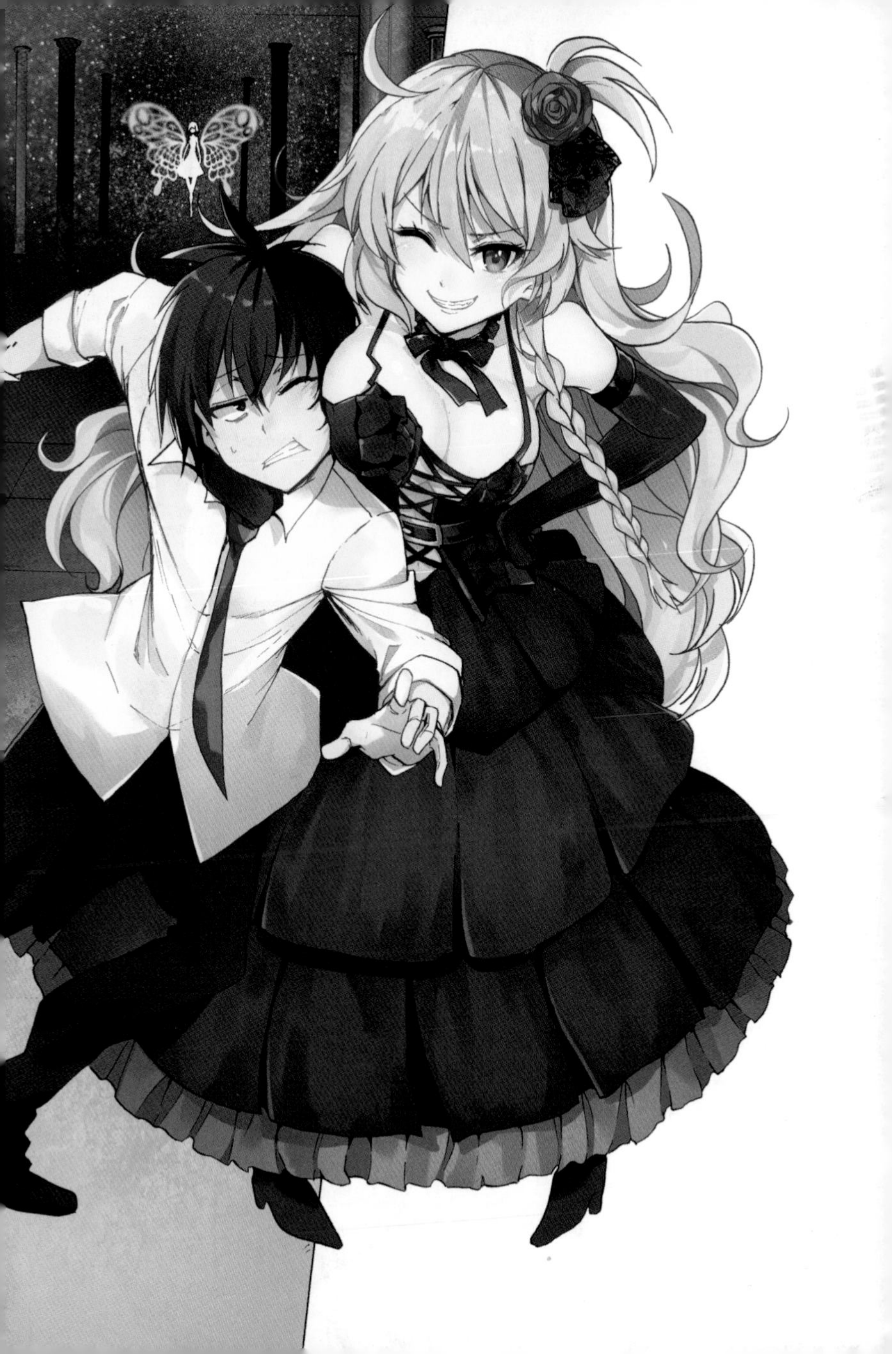

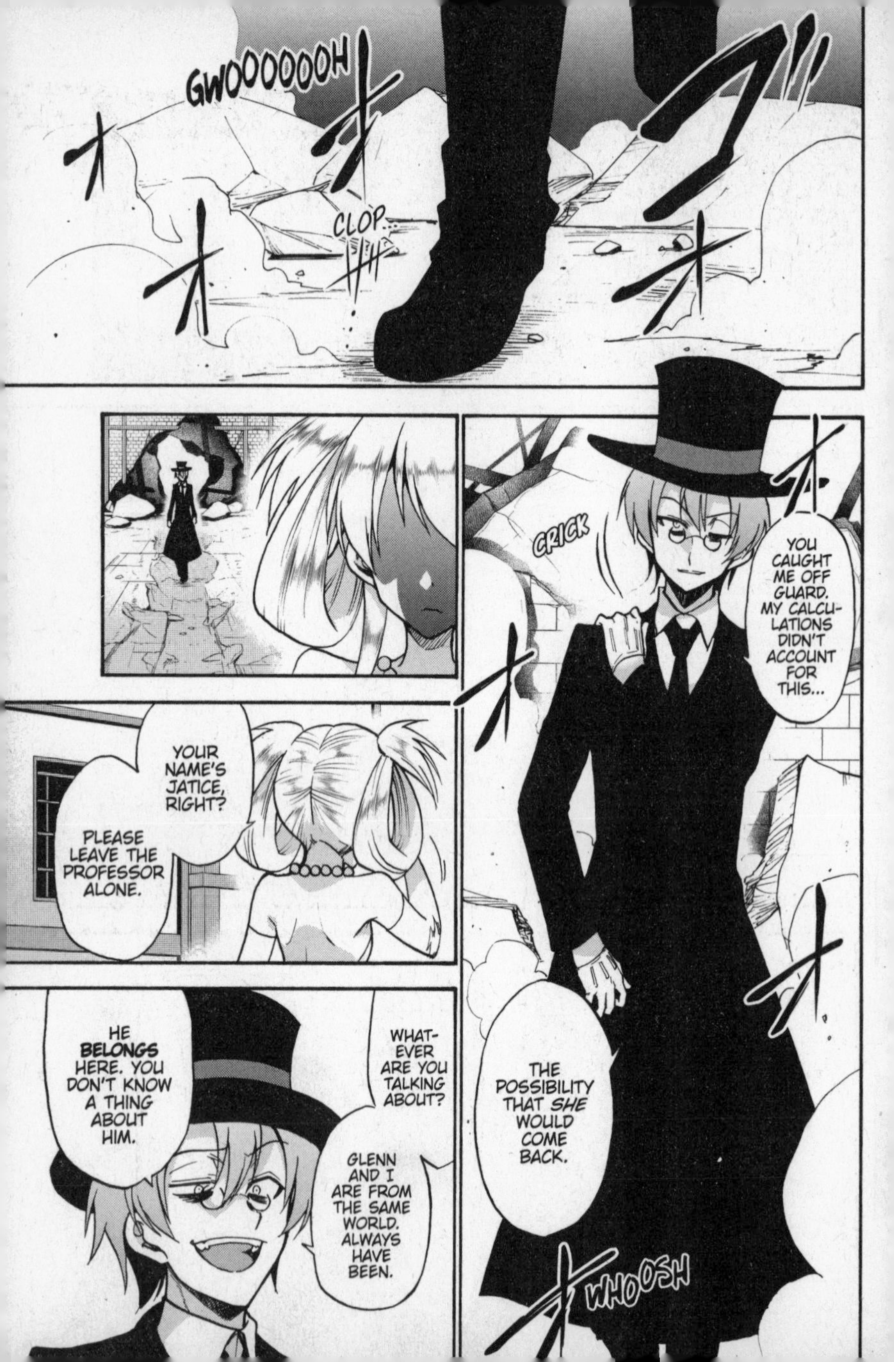
GWOOOOOH
CLOP...
CRICK
YOU CAUGHT ME OFF GUARD. MY CALCULATIONS DIDN'T ACCOUNT FOR THIS...
THE POSSIBILITY THAT *SHE* WOULD COME BACK.
WHOOSH
YOUR NAME'S JATICE, RIGHT?
PLEASE LEAVE THE PROFESSOR ALONE.
WHATEVER ARE YOU TALKING ABOUT?
GLENN AND I ARE FROM THE SAME WORLD. ALWAYS HAVE BEEN.
HE **BELONGS** HERE. YOU DON'T KNOW A THING ABOUT HIM.

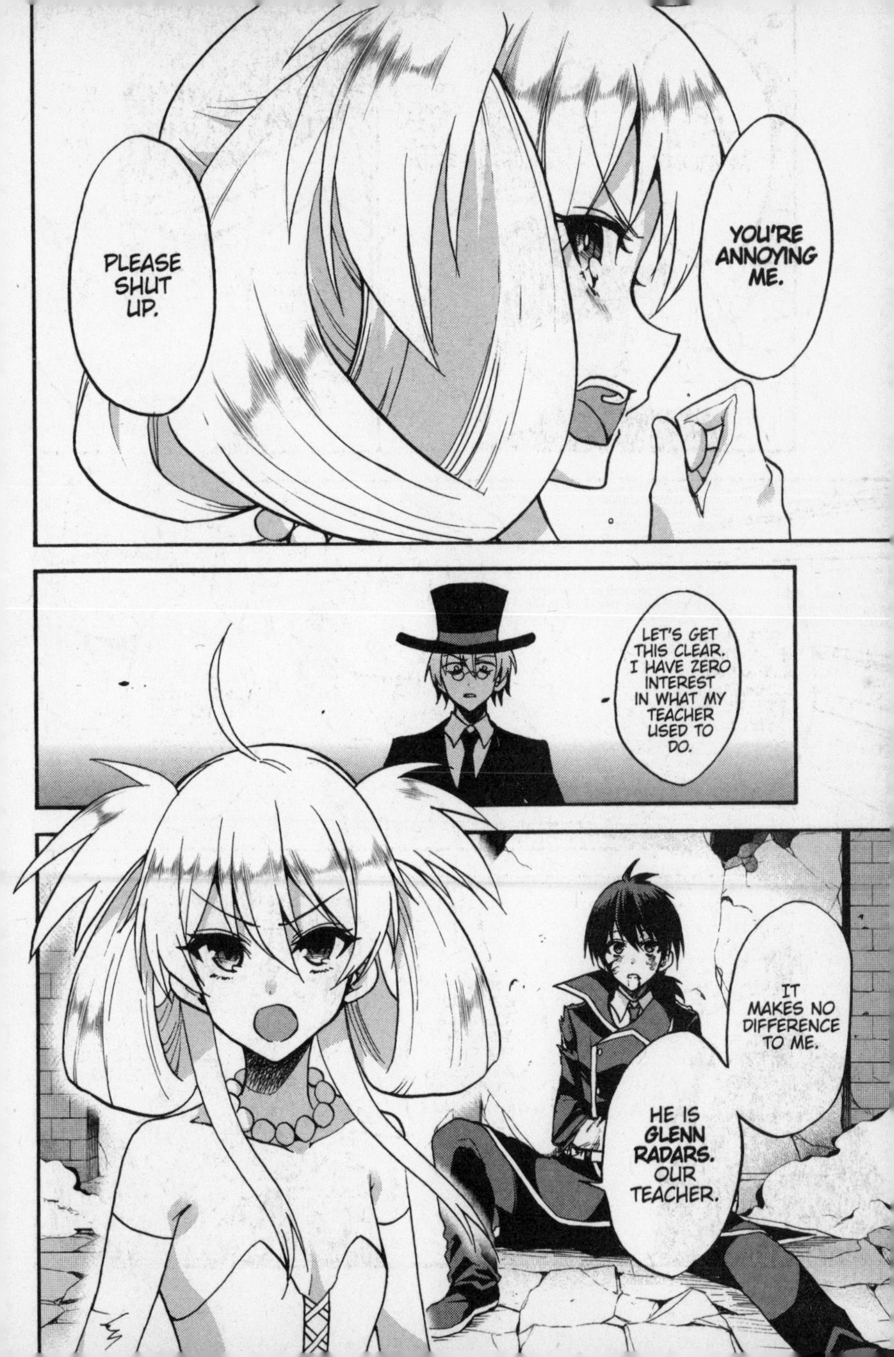
YOU'RE ANNOYING ME.
PLEASE SHUT UP.
LET'S GET THIS CLEAR. I HAVE ZERO INTEREST IN WHAT MY TEACHER USED TO DO.
IT MAKES NO DIFFERENCE TO ME.
HE IS GLENN RADARS. OUR TEACHER.

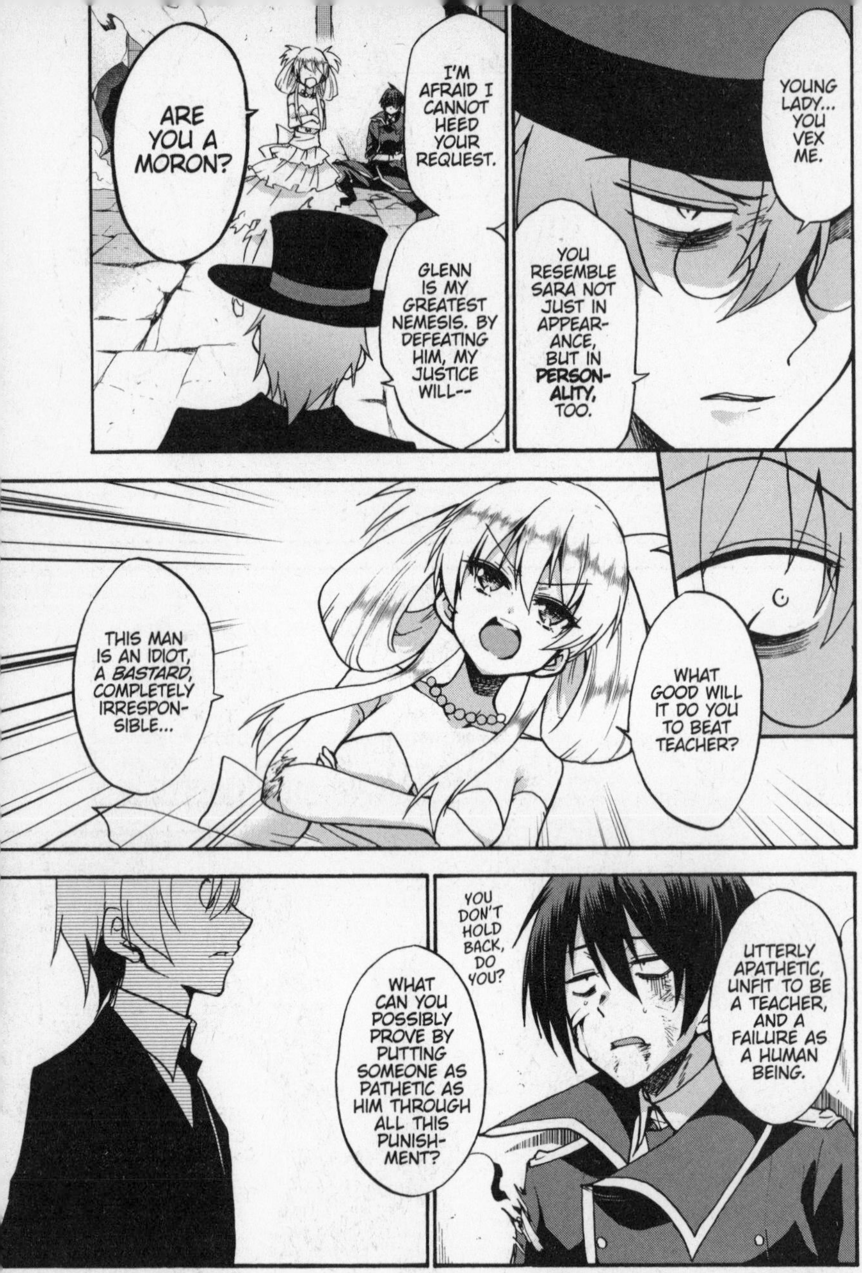
YOUNG LADY... YOU VEX ME.
YOU RESEMBLE SARA NOT JUST IN APPEARANCE, BUT IN **PERSONALITY**, TOO.
I'M AFRAID I CANNOT HEED YOUR REQUEST.
GLENN IS MY GREATEST NEMESIS. BY DEFEATING HIM, MY JUSTICE WILL--
ARE YOU A MORON?
WHAT GOOD WILL IT DO YOU TO BEAT TEACHER?
THIS MAN IS AN IDIOT, A *BASTARD*, COMPLETELY IRRESPONSIBLE...
UTTERLY APATHETIC, UNFIT TO BE A TEACHER, AND A FAILURE AS A HUMAN BEING.
YOU DON'T HOLD BACK, DO YOU?
WHAT CAN YOU POSSIBLY PROVE BY PUTTING SOMEONE AS PATHETIC AS HIM THROUGH ALL THIS PUNISHMENT?

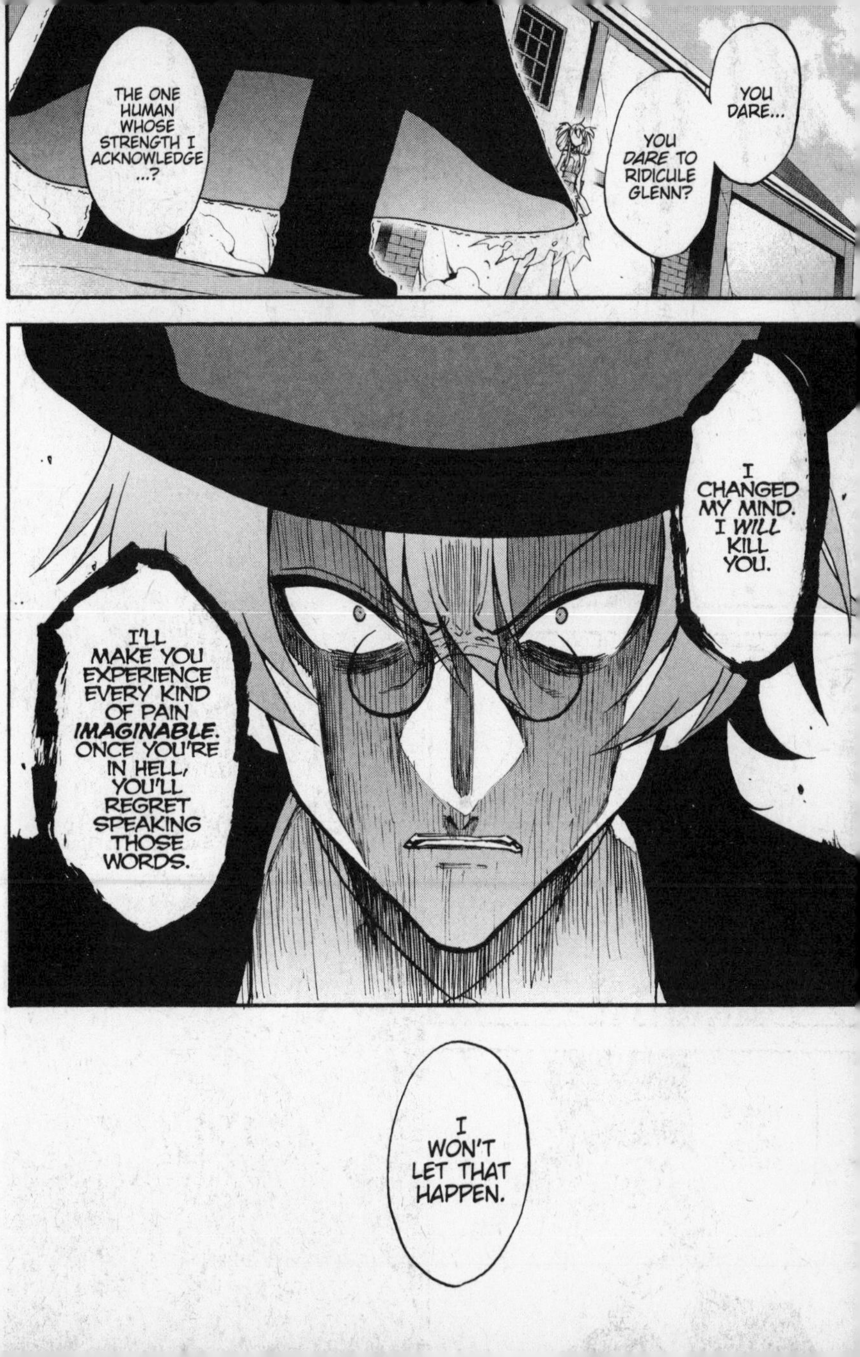
YOU DARE...
YOU *DARE* TO RIDICULE GLENN?
THE ONE HUMAN WHOSE STRENGTH I ACKNOWLEDGE ...?
I CHANGED MY MIND. I *WILL* KILL YOU.
I'LL MAKE YOU EXPERIENCE EVERY KIND OF PAIN ***IMAGINABLE***. ONCE YOU'RE IN HELL, YOU'LL REGRET SPEAKING THOSE WORDS.
I WON'T LET THAT HAPPEN.

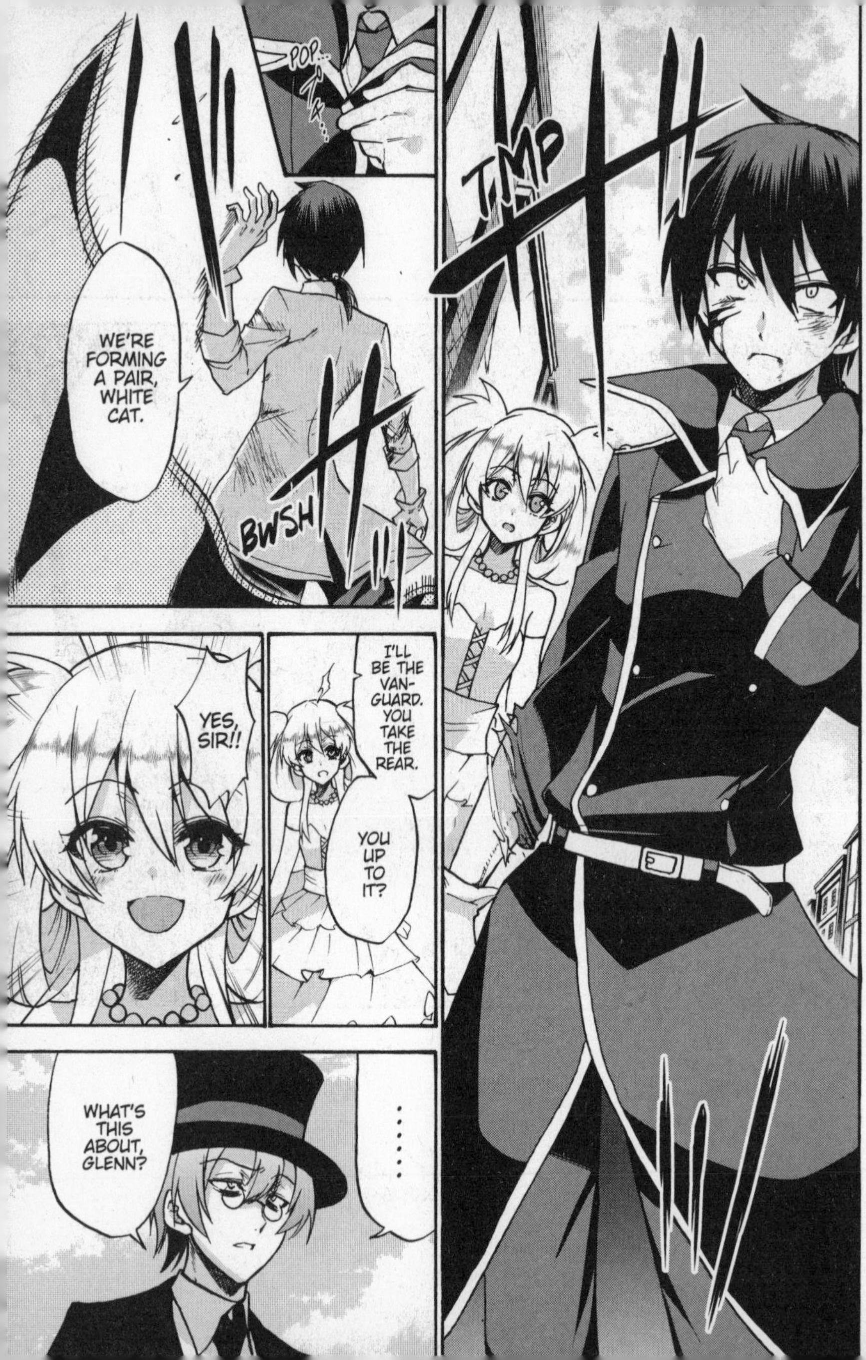
TMP
POP...
WE'RE FORMING A PAIR, WHITE CAT.
BWSH
I'LL BE THE VAN-GUARD. YOU TAKE THE REAR.
YOU UP TO IT?
YES, SIR!!
......
WHAT'S THIS ABOUT, GLENN?

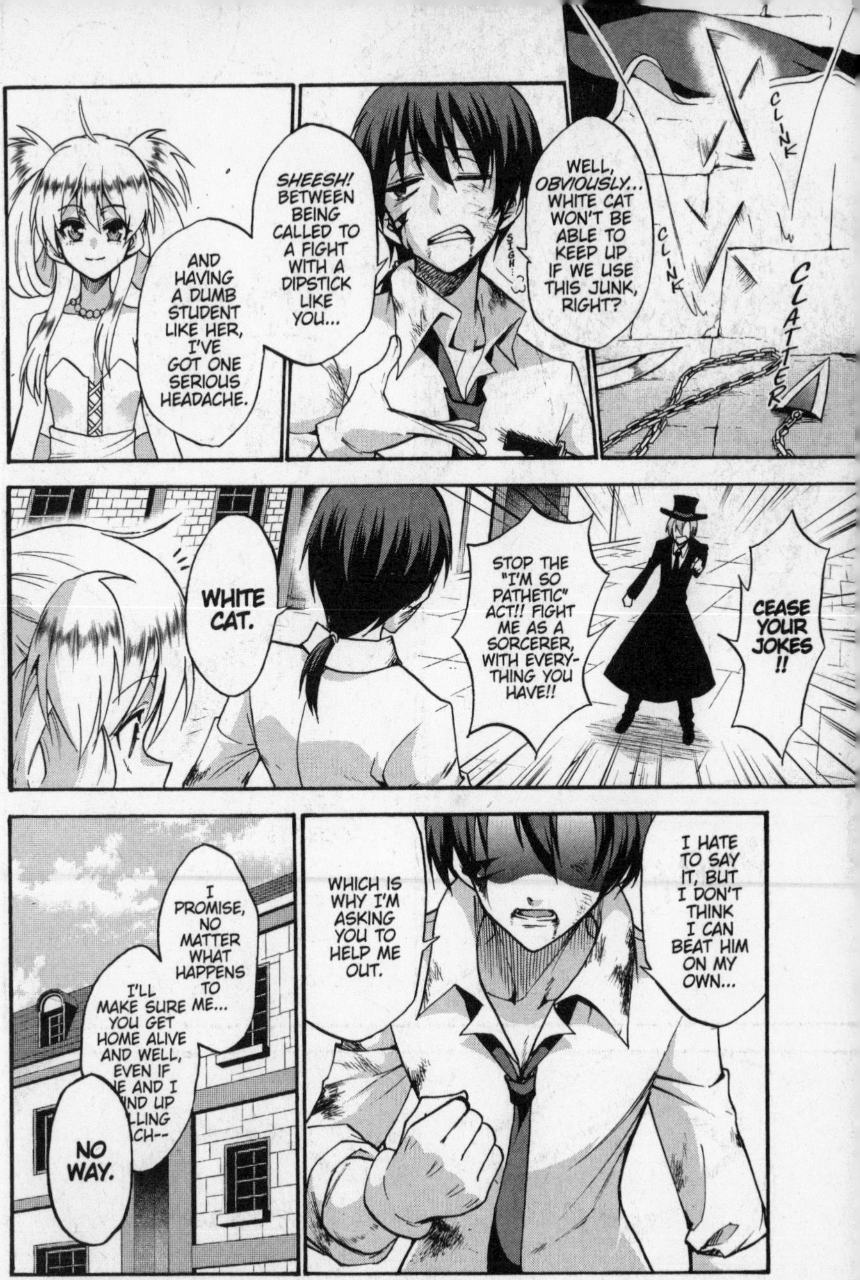
CLINK
CLINK
CLATTER
WELL, OBVIOUSLY... WHITE CAT WON'T BE ABLE TO KEEP UP IF WE USE THIS JUNK, RIGHT?
SIGH...
SHEESH! BETWEEN BEING CALLED TO A FIGHT WITH A DIPSTICK LIKE YOU...
AND HAVING A DUMB STUDENT LIKE HER, I'VE GOT ONE SERIOUS HEADACHE.
CEASE YOUR JOKES!!
STOP THE "I'M SO PATHETIC" ACT!! FIGHT ME AS A SORCERER, WITH EVERYTHING YOU HAVE!!
WHITE CAT.
I HATE TO SAY IT, BUT I DON'T THINK I CAN BEAT HIM ON MY OWN...
WHICH IS WHY I'M ASKING YOU TO HELP ME OUT.
I PROMISE, NO MATTER WHAT HAPPENS TO ME...
I'LL MAKE SURE YOU GET HOME ALIVE AND WELL, EVEN IF E AND I IND UP LLING CH--
NO WAY.

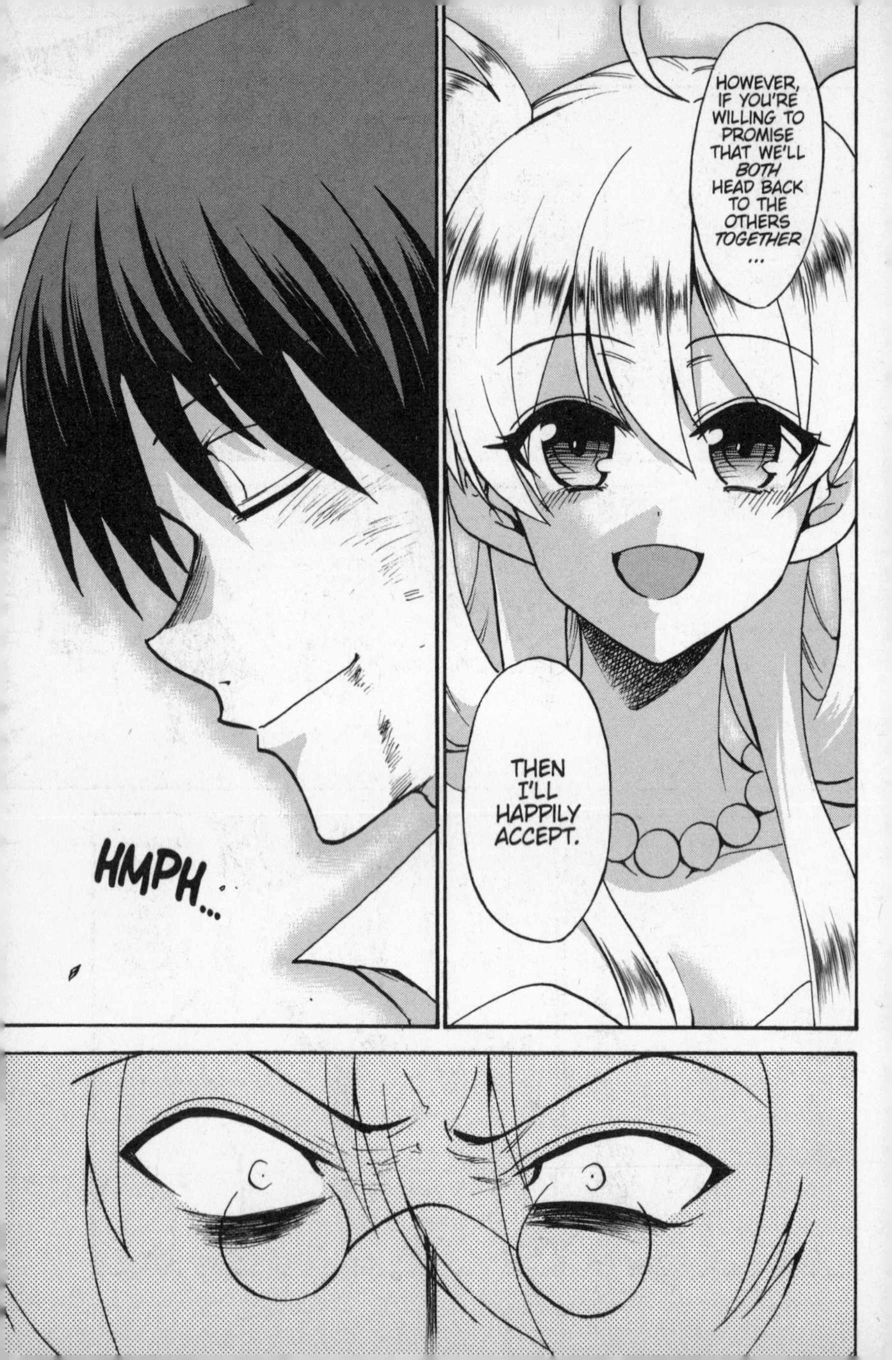
HOWEVER, IF YOU'RE WILLING TO PROMISE THAT WE'LL *BOTH* HEAD BACK TO THE OTHERS *TOGETHER* ...
THEN I'LL HAPPILY ACCEPT.
HMPH...

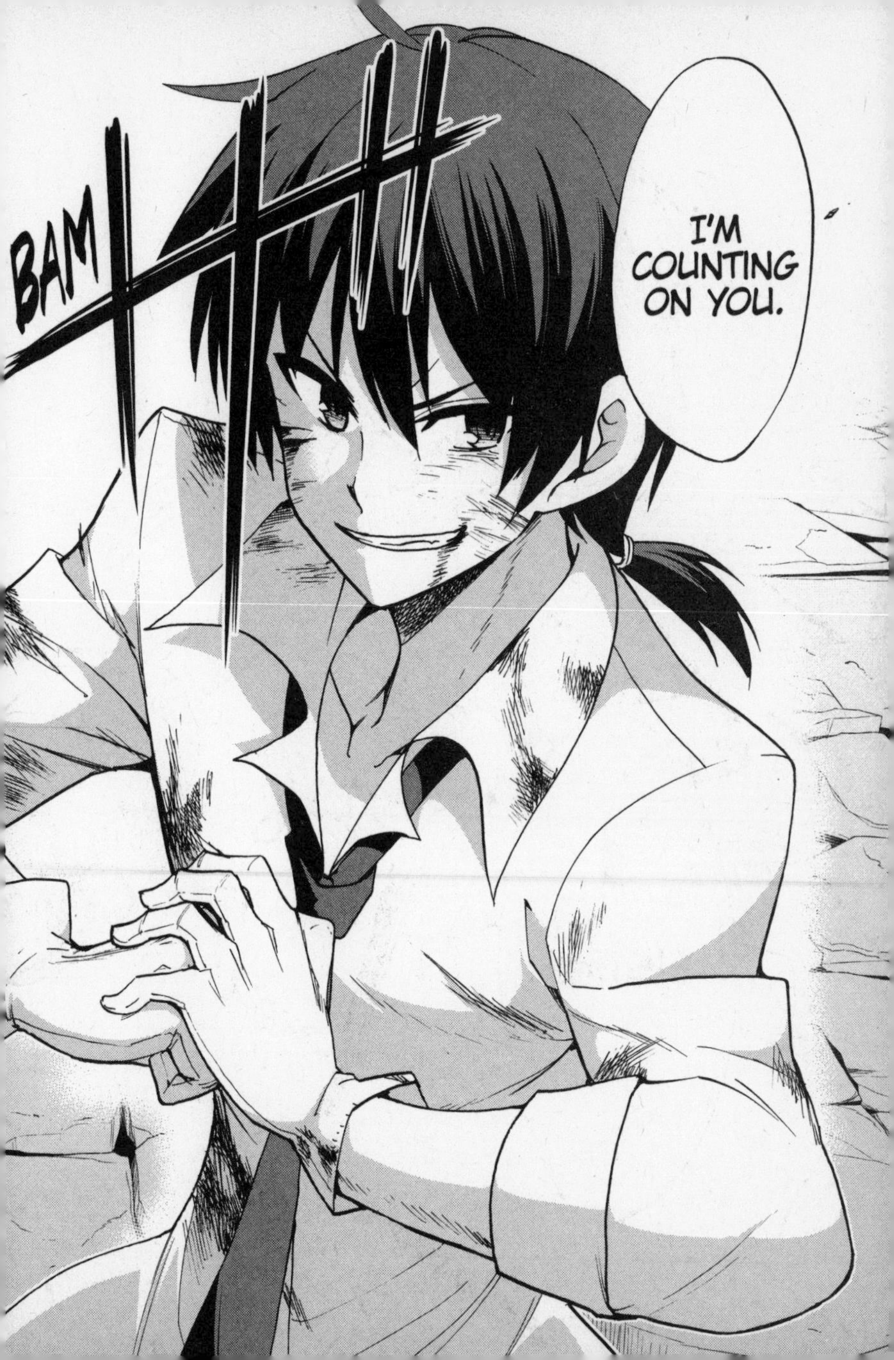
I'M COUNTING ON YOU.
BAM

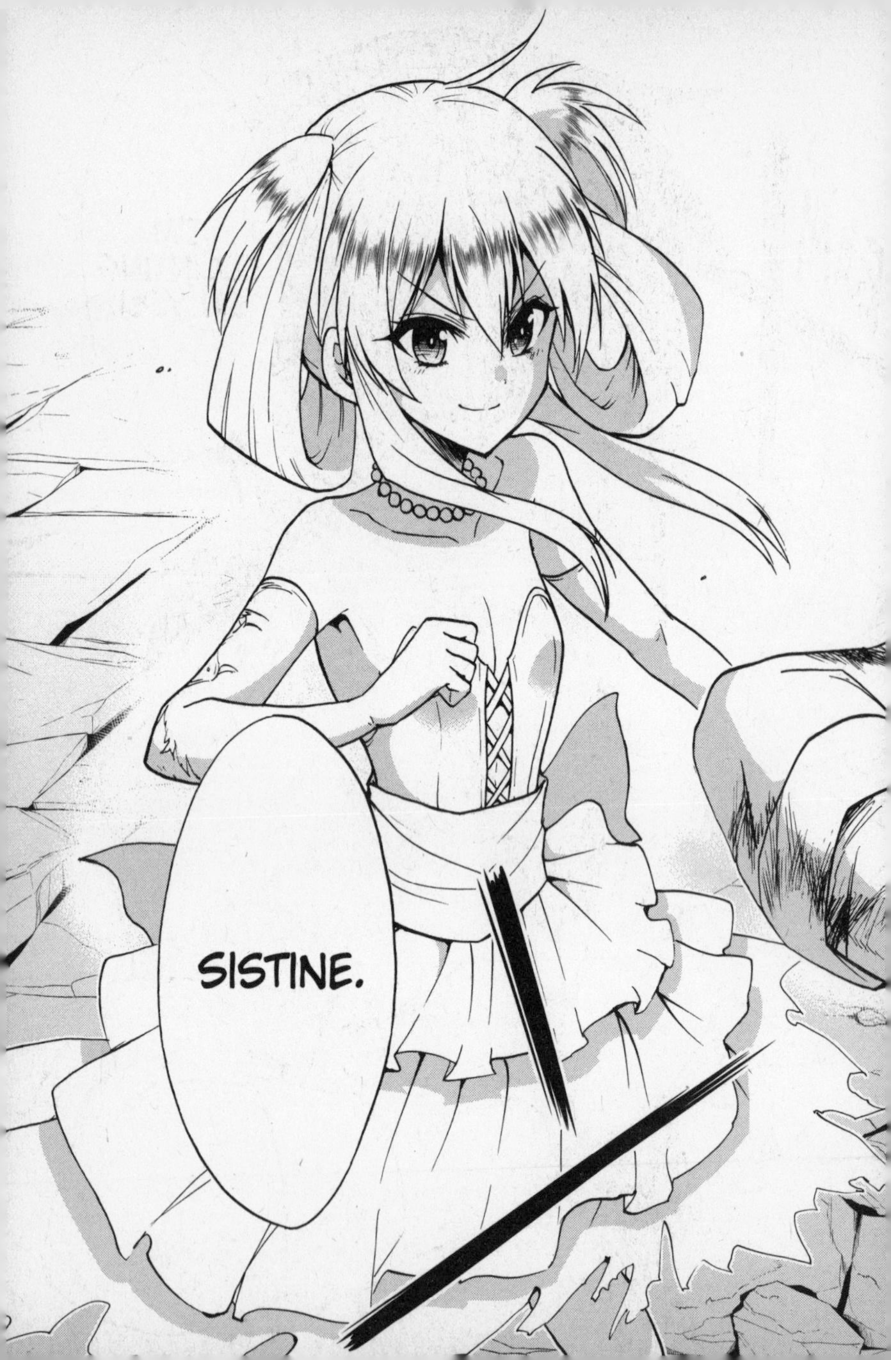
SISTINE.

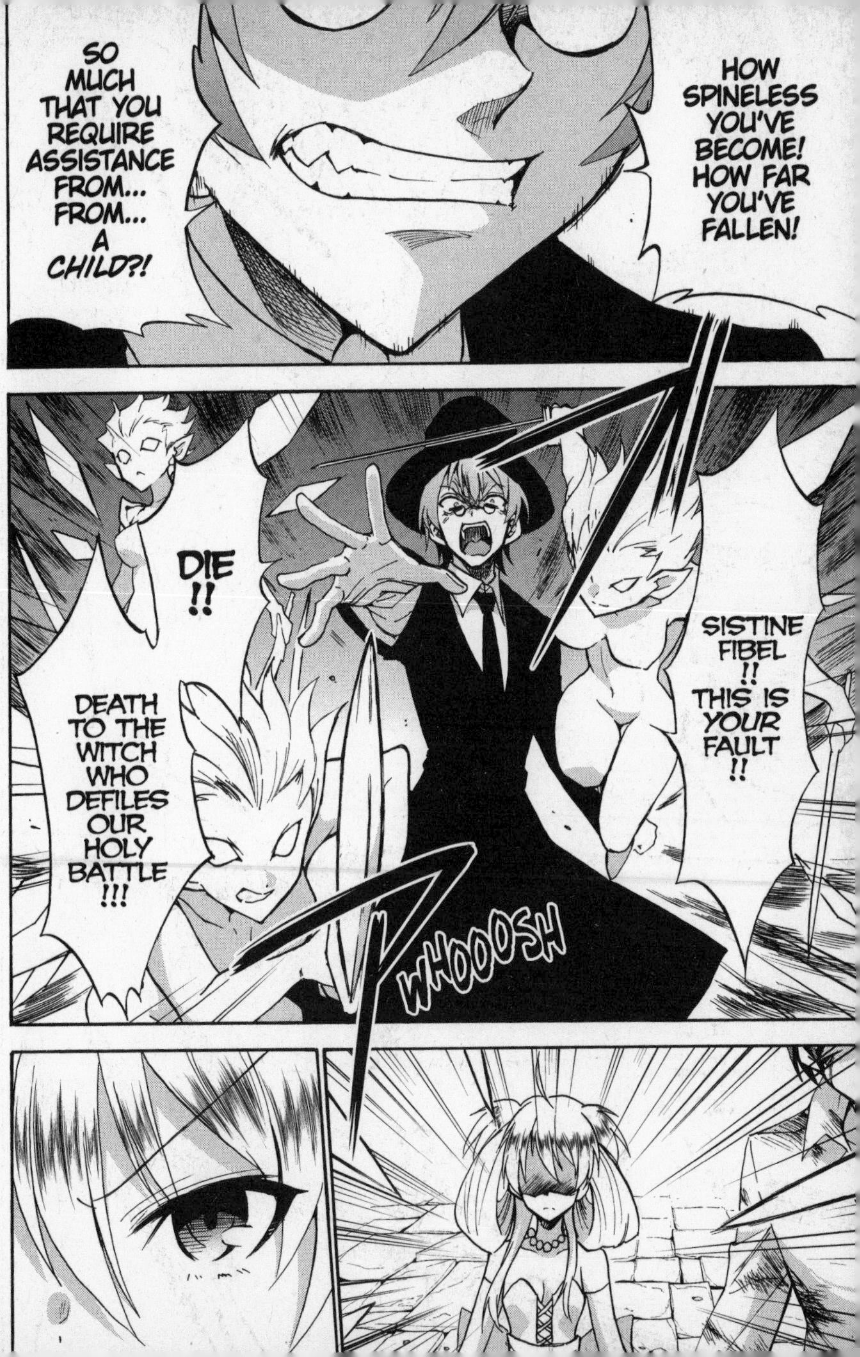
HOW SPINELESS YOU'VE BECOME! HOW FAR YOU'VE FALLEN!
SO MUCH THAT YOU REQUIRE ASSISTANCE FROM... FROM... A CHILD?!
SISTINE FIBEL!! THIS IS YOUR FAULT!!
DIE!!
DEATH TO THE WITCH WHO DEFILES OUR HOLY BATTLE!!!
WHOOOSH

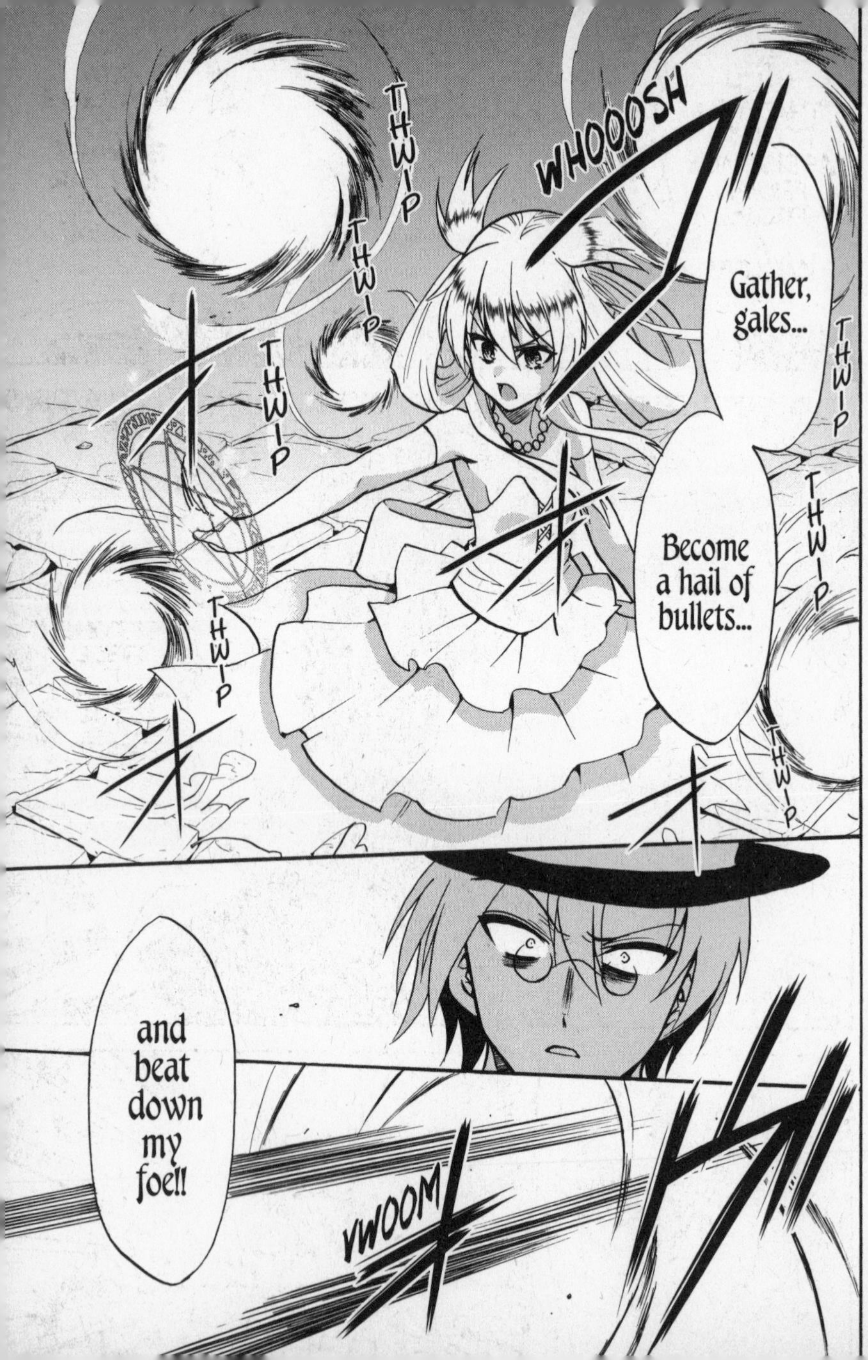
THWIP
Gather, gales...
THWIP
Become a hail of bullets...
THWIP
WHOOOSH
THWIP
THWIP
THWIP
THWIP
and beat down my foe!!
VWOOM

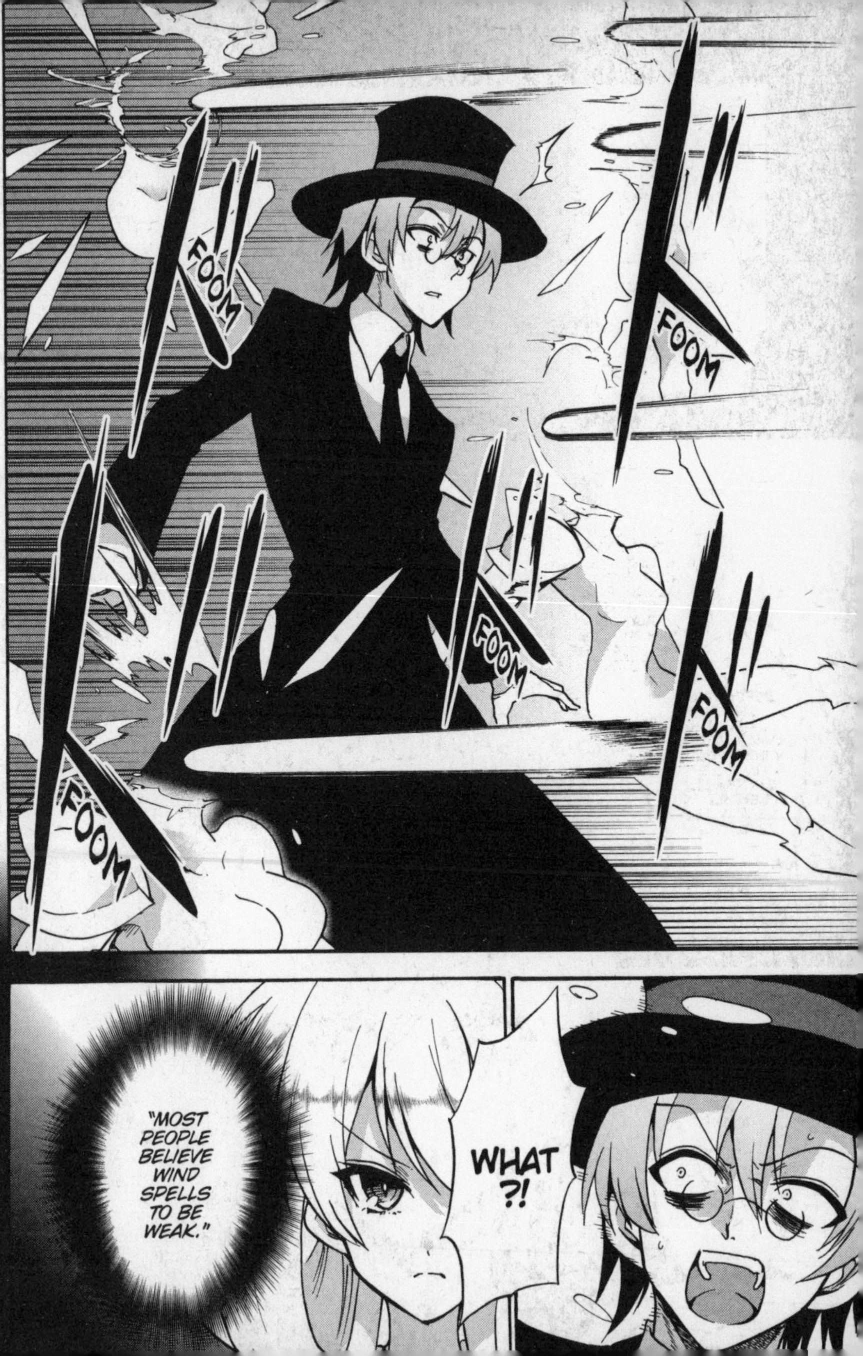
FOOM
FOOM
FOOM
FOOM
FOOM
WHAT ?!
"MOST PEOPLE BELIEVE WIND SPELLS TO BE WEAK."

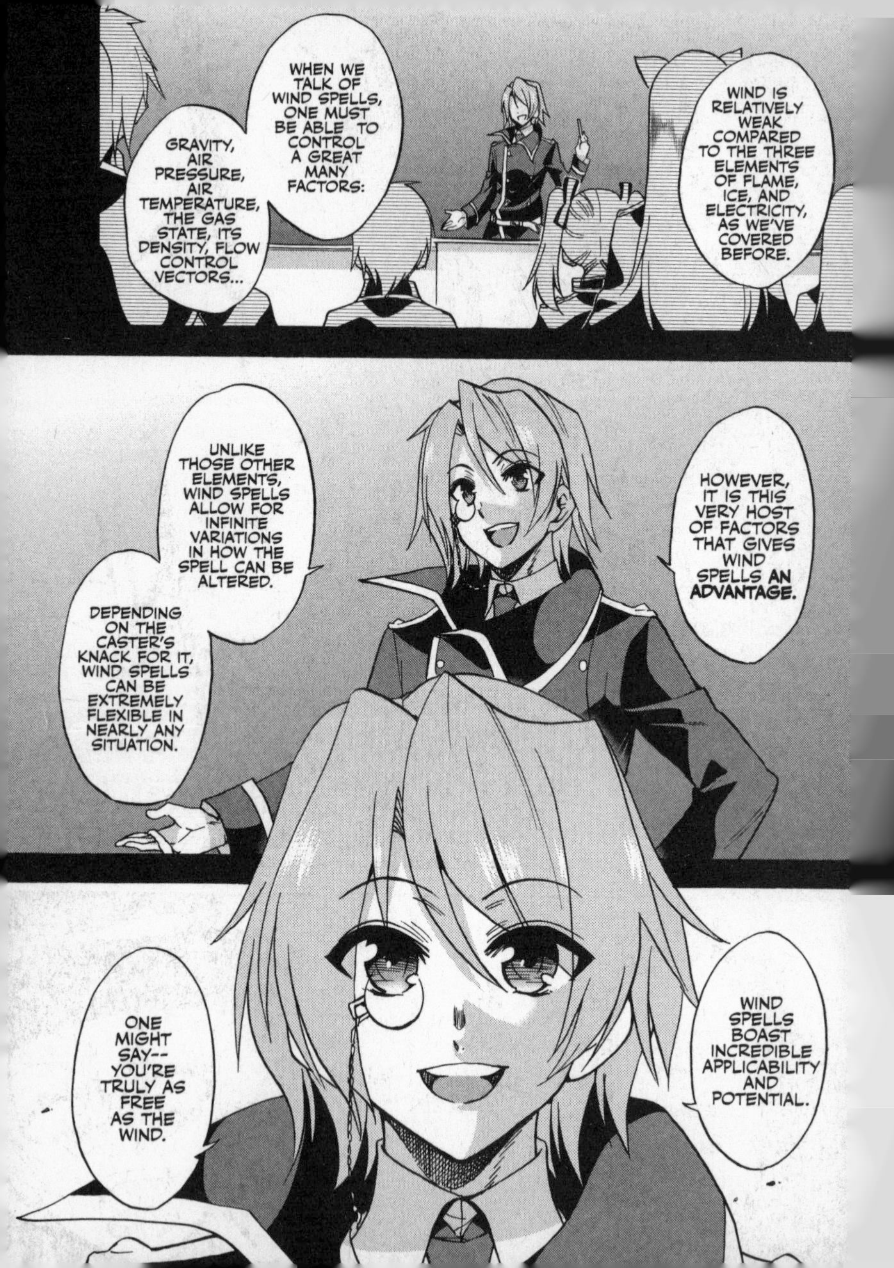
WIND IS RELATIVELY WEAK COMPARED TO THE THREE ELEMENTS OF FLAME, ICE, AND ELECTRICITY, AS WE'VE COVERED BEFORE.
WHEN WE TALK OF WIND SPELLS, ONE MUST BE ABLE TO CONTROL A GREAT MANY FACTORS:
GRAVITY, AIR PRESSURE, AIR TEMPERATURE, THE GAS STATE, ITS DENSITY, FLOW CONTROL VECTORS...
HOWEVER, IT IS THIS VERY HOST OF FACTORS THAT GIVES WIND SPELLS **AN ADVANTAGE.**
UNLIKE THOSE OTHER ELEMENTS, WIND SPELLS ALLOW FOR INFINITE VARIATIONS IN HOW THE SPELL CAN BE ALTERED.
DEPENDING ON THE CASTER'S KNACK FOR IT, WIND SPELLS CAN BE EXTREMELY FLEXIBLE IN NEARLY ANY SITUATION.
WIND SPELLS BOAST INCREDIBLE APPLICABILITY AND POTENTIAL.
ONE MIGHT SAY-- YOU'RE TRULY AS FREE AS THE WIND.

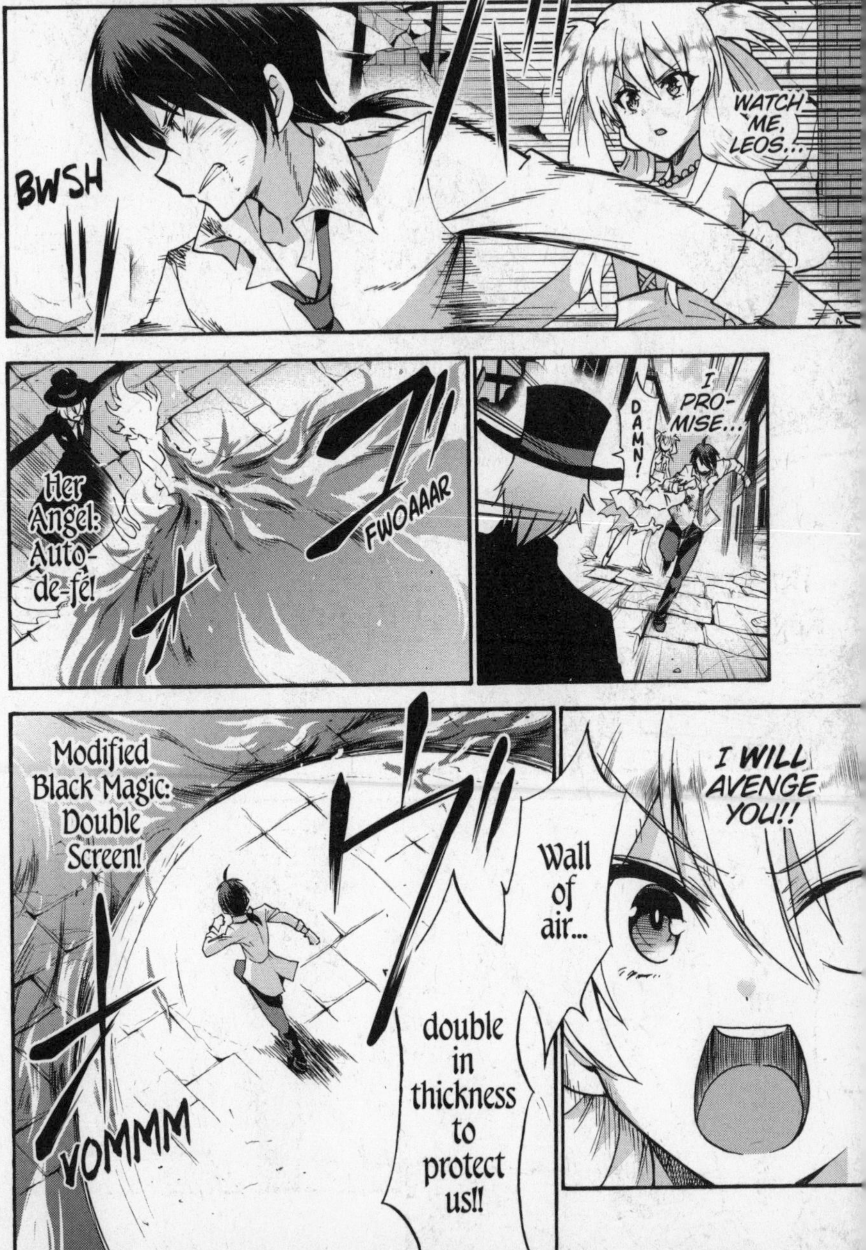
WATCH ME, LEOS...
BWSH
I PROMISE...
DAMN!
Her Angel: Auto-de-fé!
FWOAAAR
I WILL AVENGE YOU!!
Modified Black Magic: Double Screen!
Wall of air...
double in thickness to protect us!!
VOMMM

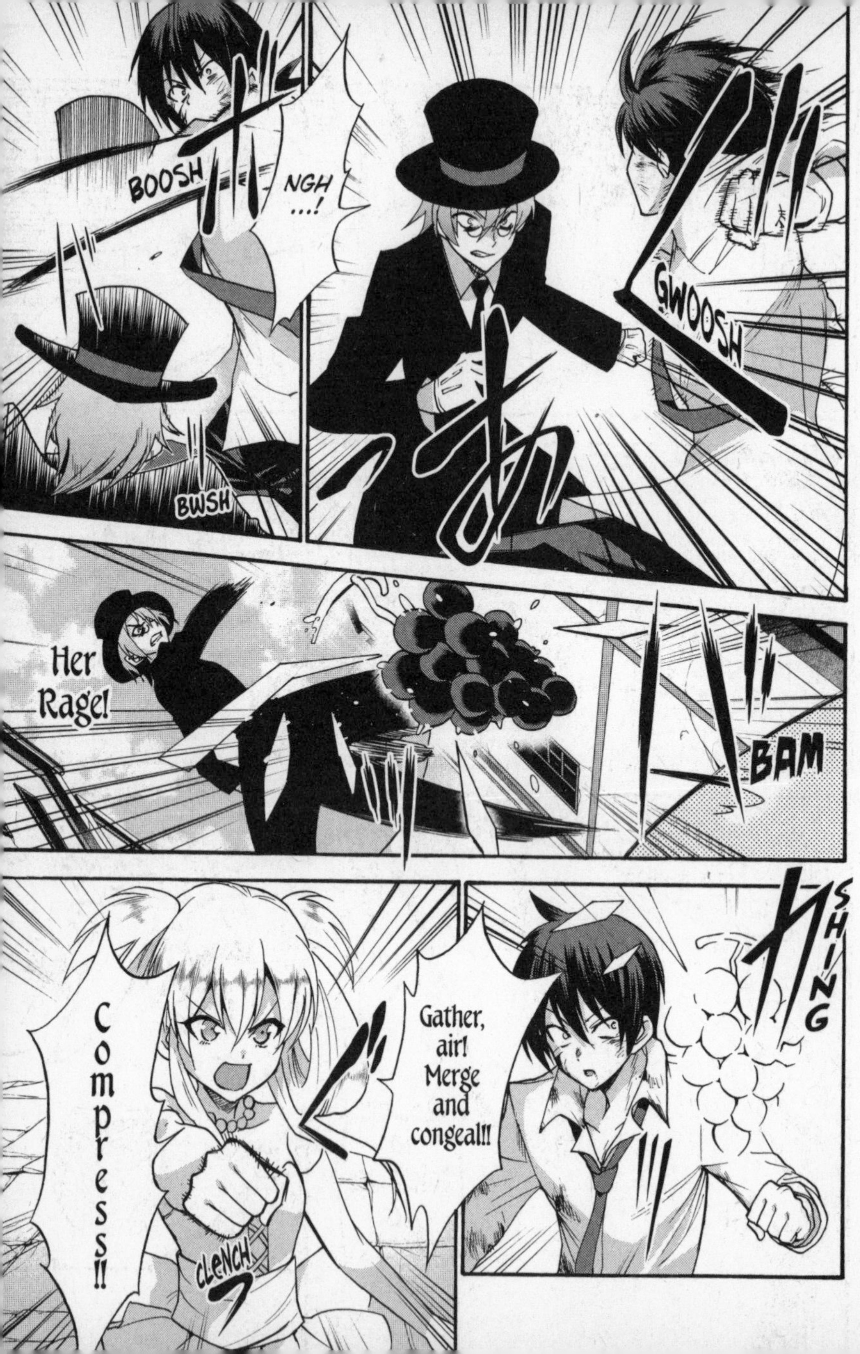
GWOOSH
BOOSH
NGH ...!
BWSH
BAM
Her Rage!
SHING
Gather, air! Merge and congeal!!
Compress!!
CLENCH

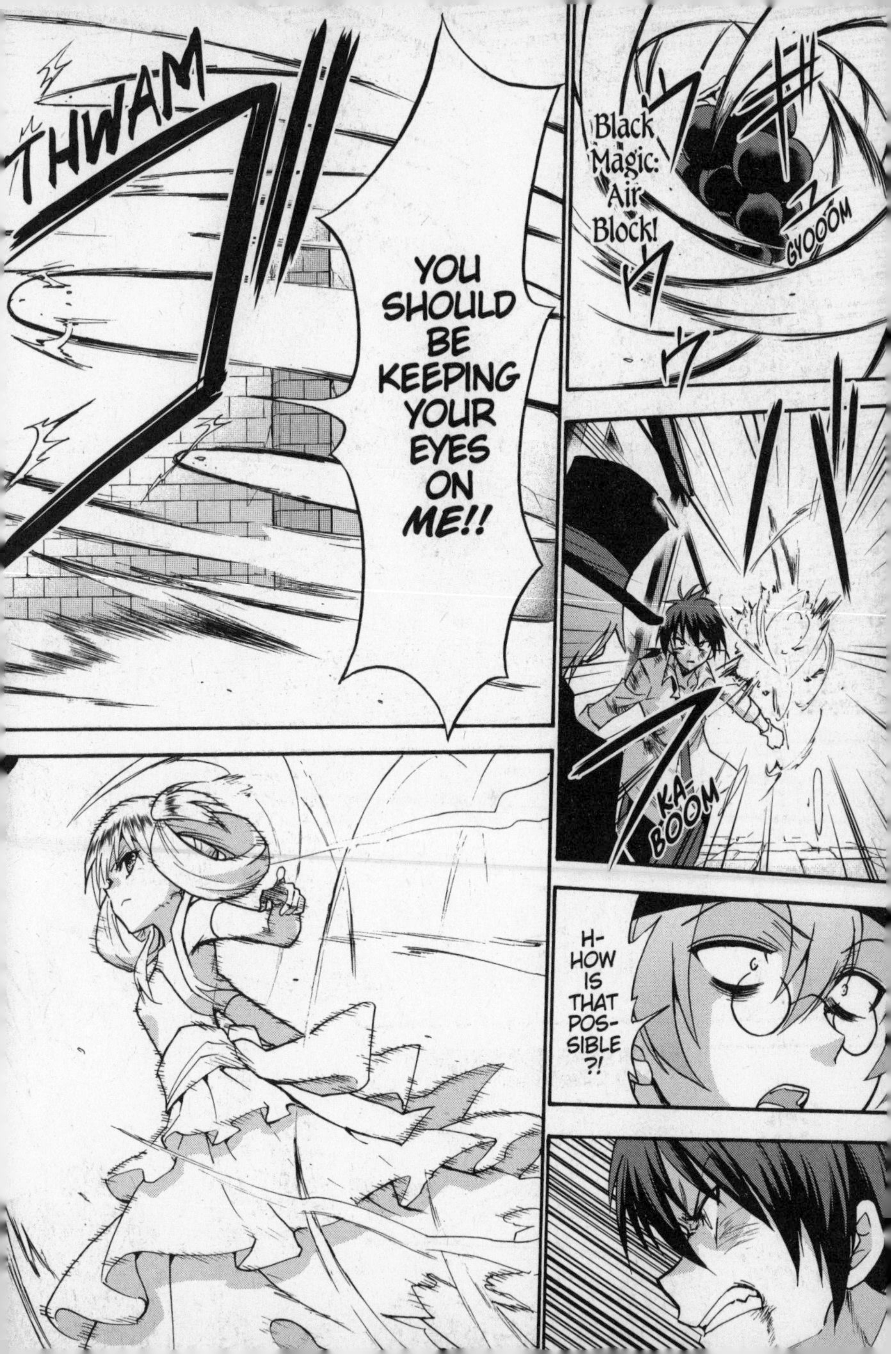

Black Magic: Air Block!
GYOOOM
THWAM
YOU SHOULD BE KEEPING YOUR EYES ON *ME!!*
KA-BOOM
H-HOW IS THAT POS-SIBLE?!

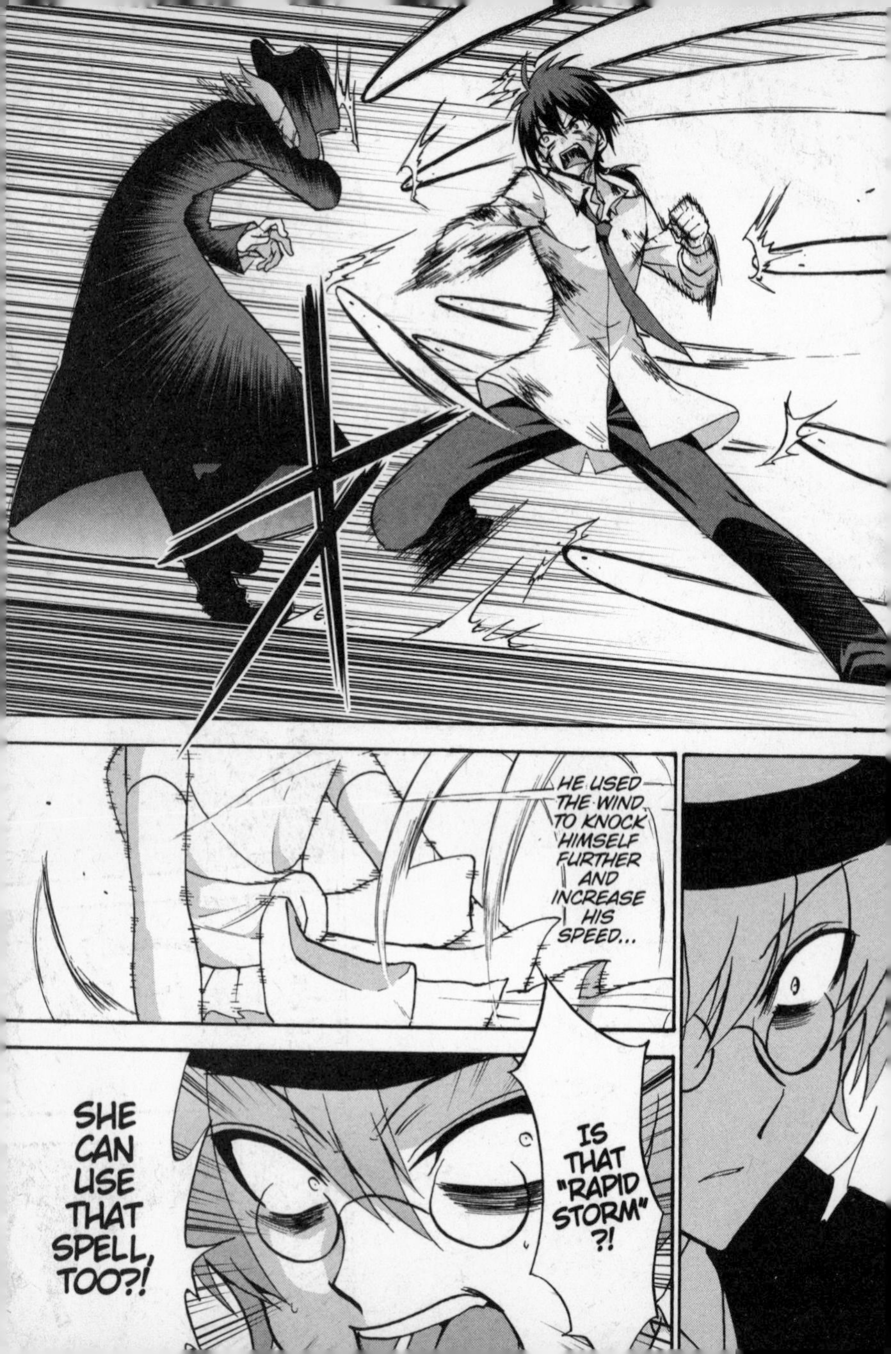
HE USED THE WIND TO KNOCK HIMSELF FURTHER AND INCREASE HIS SPEED...
IS THAT "RAPID STORM"?!
SHE CAN USE THAT SPELL, TOO?!

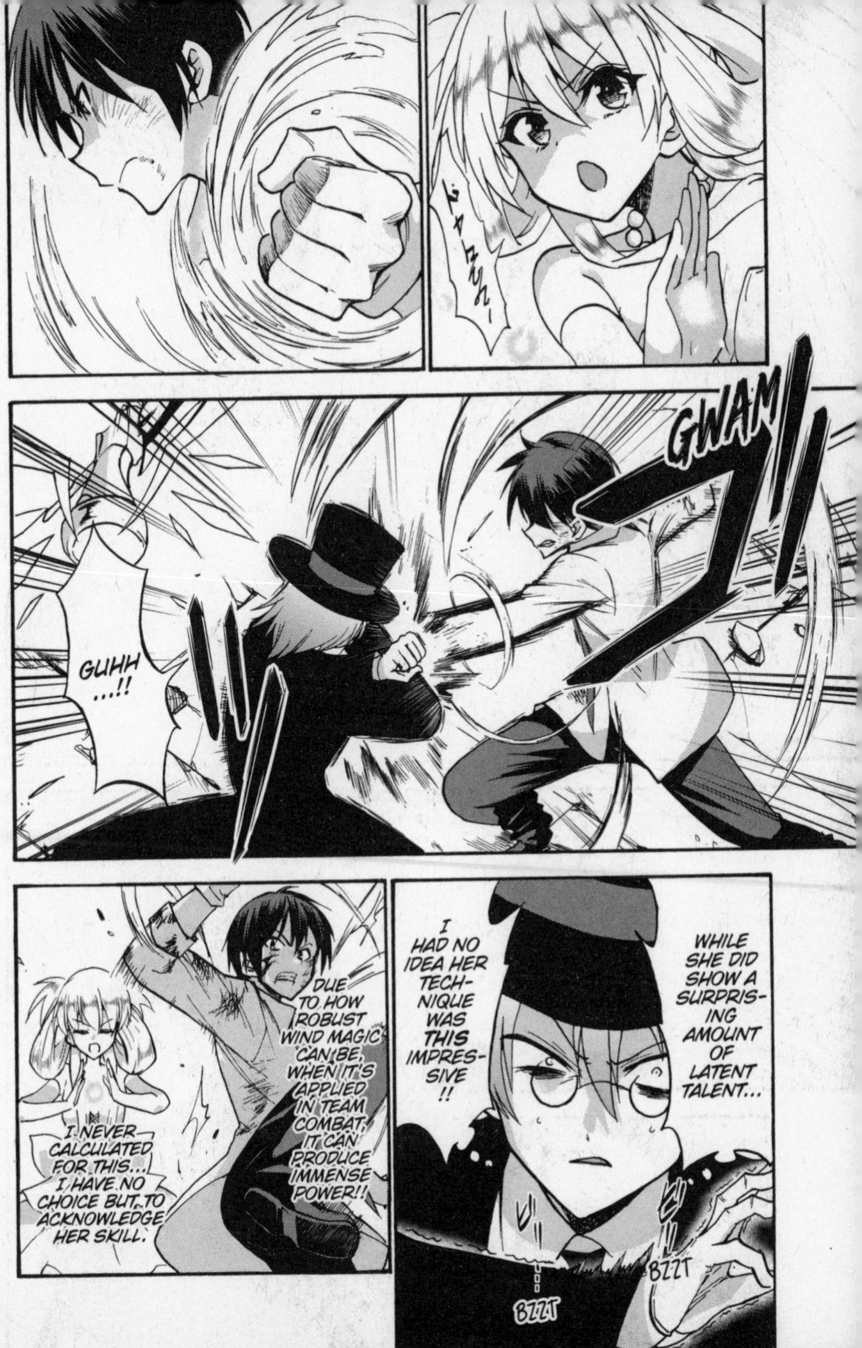
GWAM
GUHH ...!!
WHILE SHE DID SHOW A SURPRISING AMOUNT OF LATENT TALENT...
I HAD NO IDEA HER TECHNIQUE WAS THIS IMPRESSIVE!!
BZZT
BZZT
DUE TO HOW ROBUST WIND MAGIC CAN BE, WHEN IT'S APPLIED IN TEAM COMBAT, IT CAN PRODUCE IMMENSE POWER!!
I NEVER CALCULATED FOR THIS... I HAVE NO CHOICE BUT TO ACKNOWLEDGE HER SKILL.

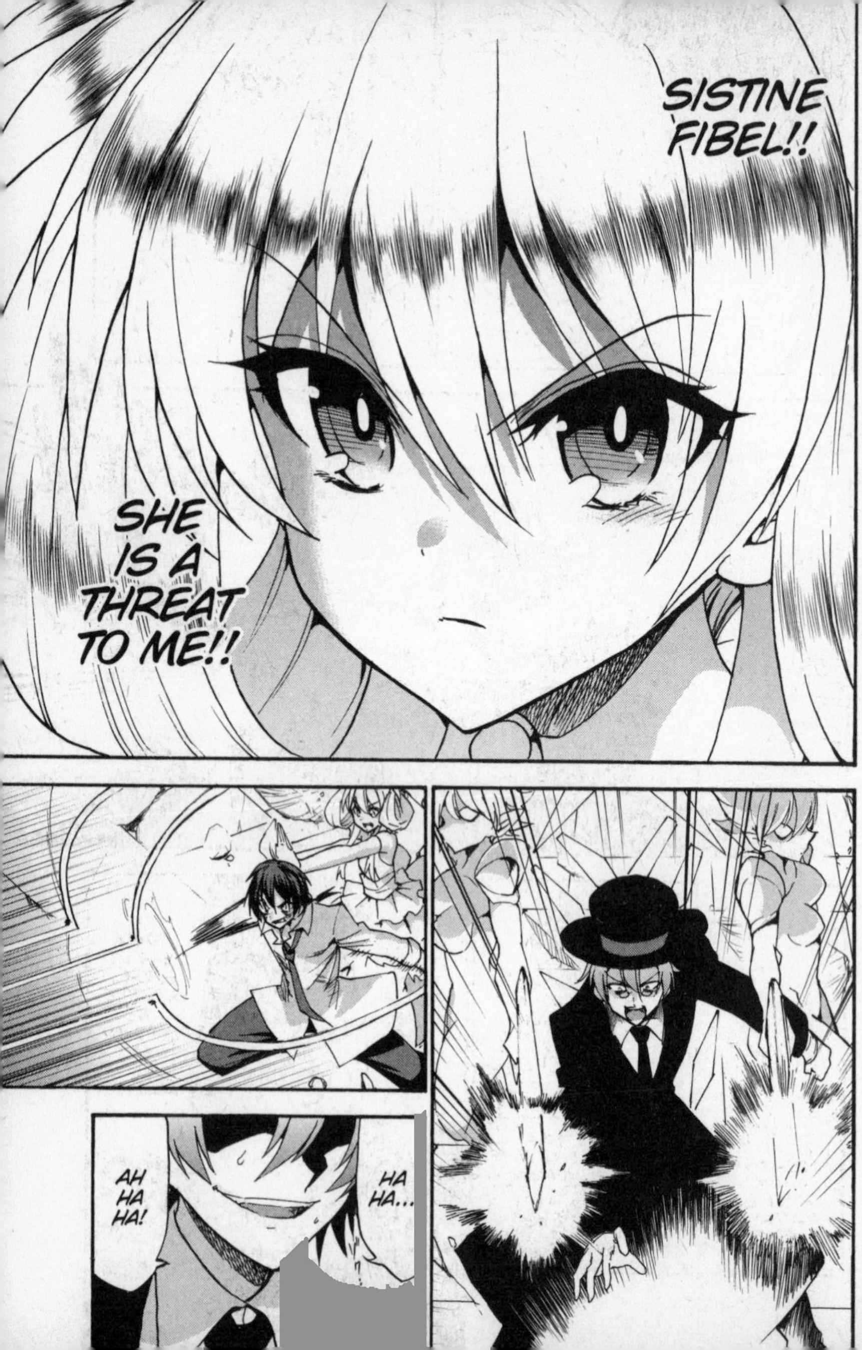
SISTINE FIBEL!!
SHE IS A THREAT TO ME!!
AH HA HA!
HA HA...

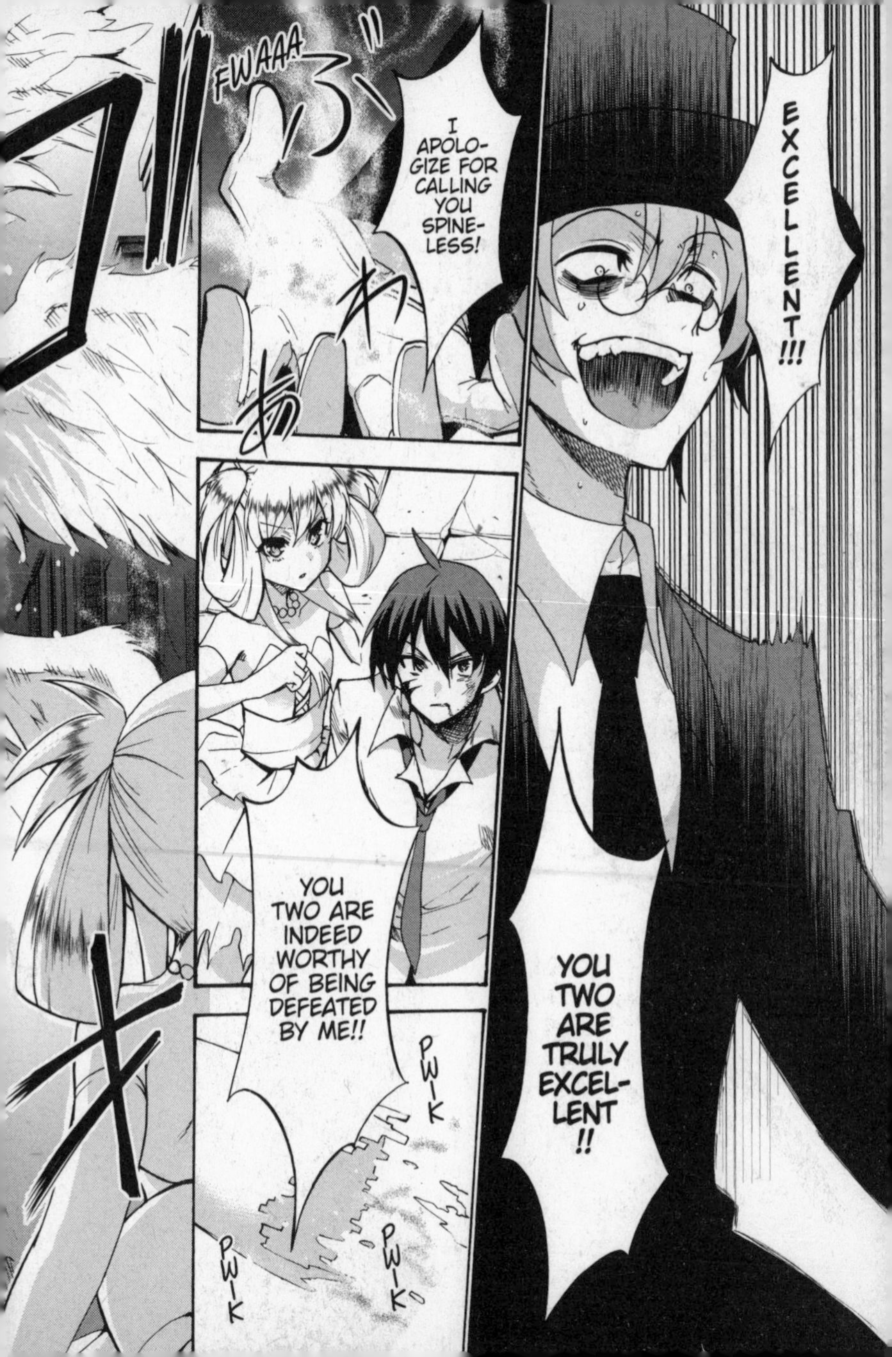
EXCELLENT!!!
YOU TWO ARE TRULY EXCEL-LENT!!
FWAAA
I APOLO-GIZE FOR CALLING YOU SPINE-LESS!
YOU TWO ARE INDEED WORTHY OF BEING DEFEATED BY ME!!
PWIK
PWIK
PWIK

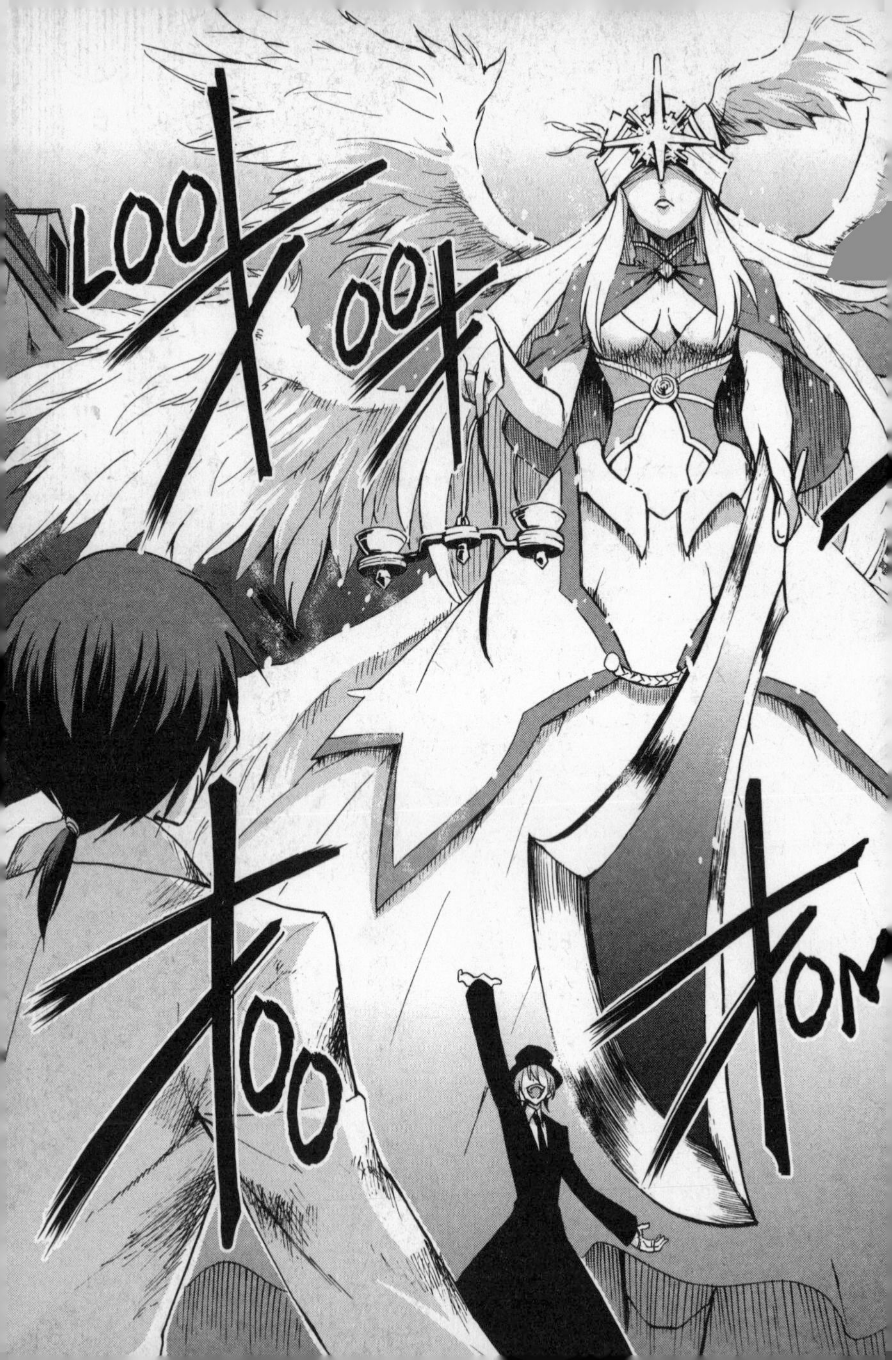
LOOOO
OOOM

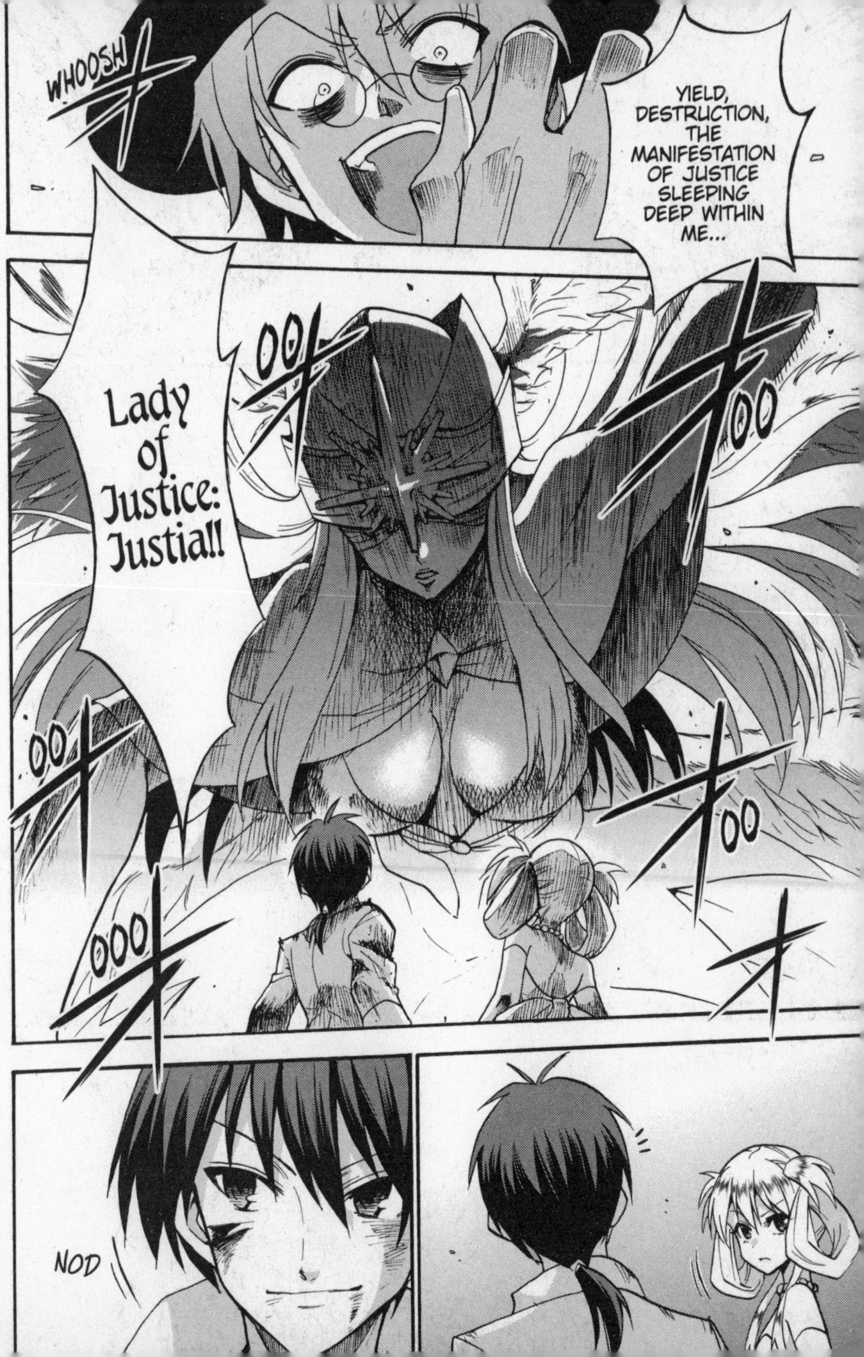
WHOOSH
YIELD, DESTRUCTION, THE MANIFESTATION OF JUSTICE SLEEPING DEEP WITHIN ME...
OO
OO
Lady of Justice: Justia!!
OO
OO
OOO
NOD

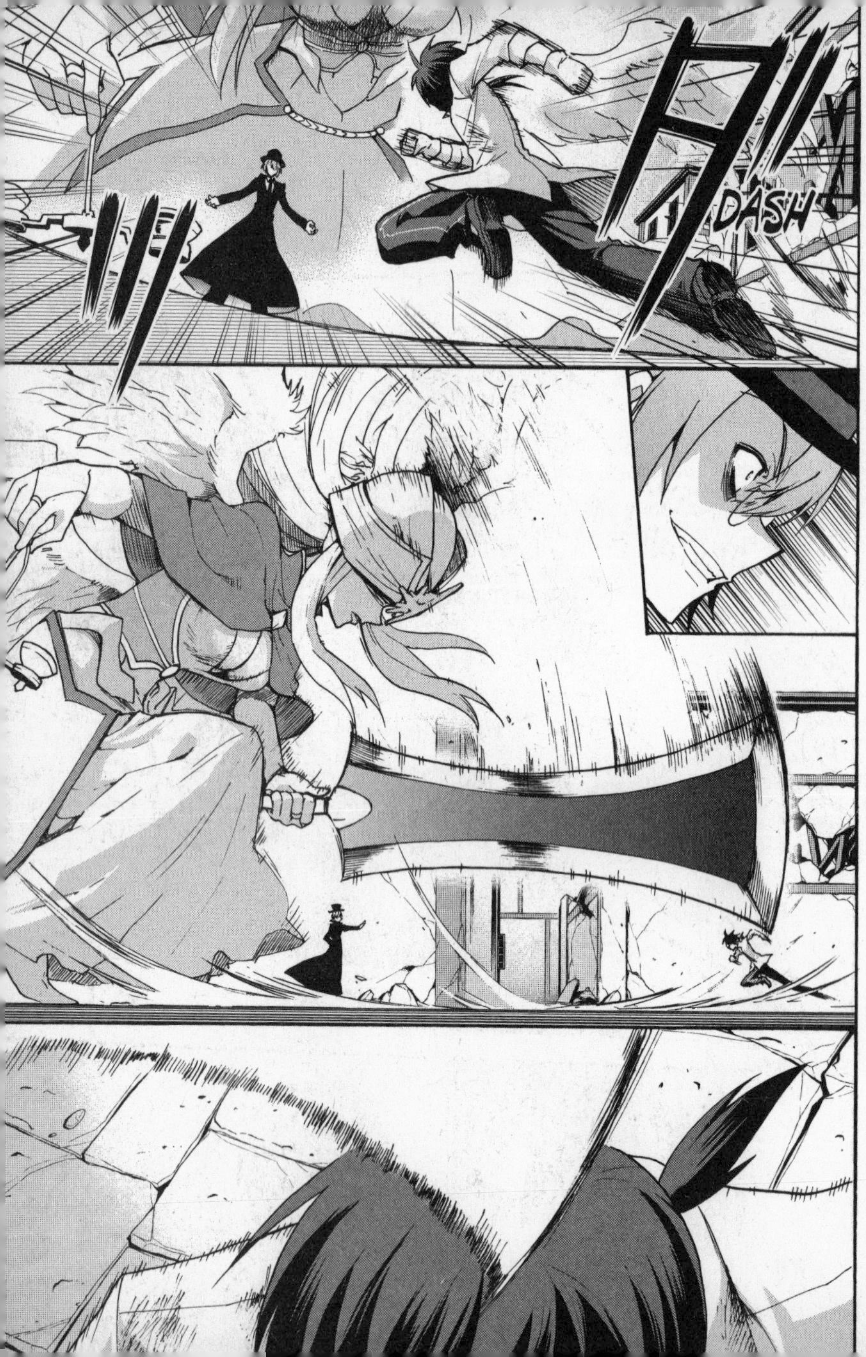
DASH

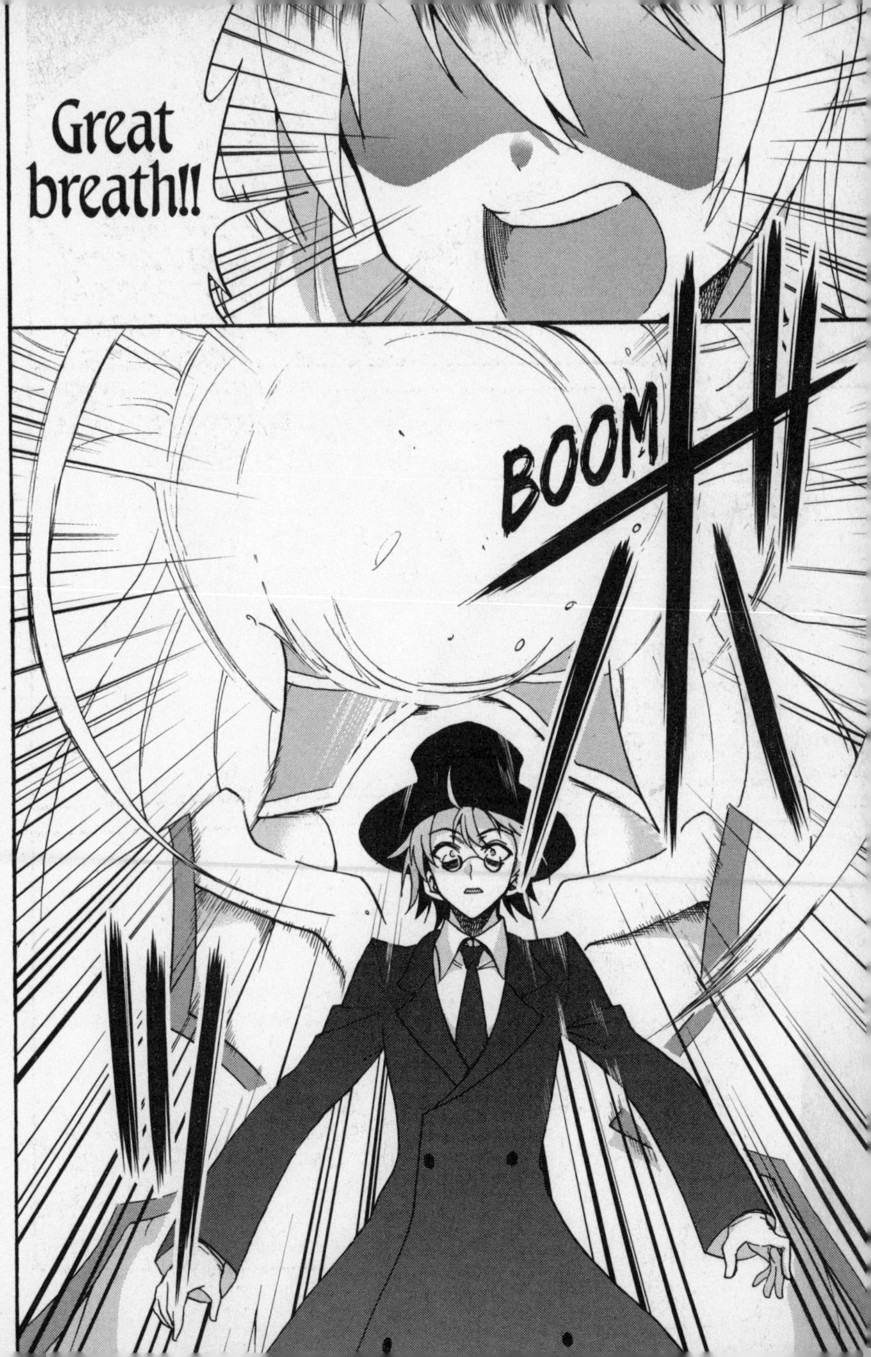
Great breath!!
BOOM

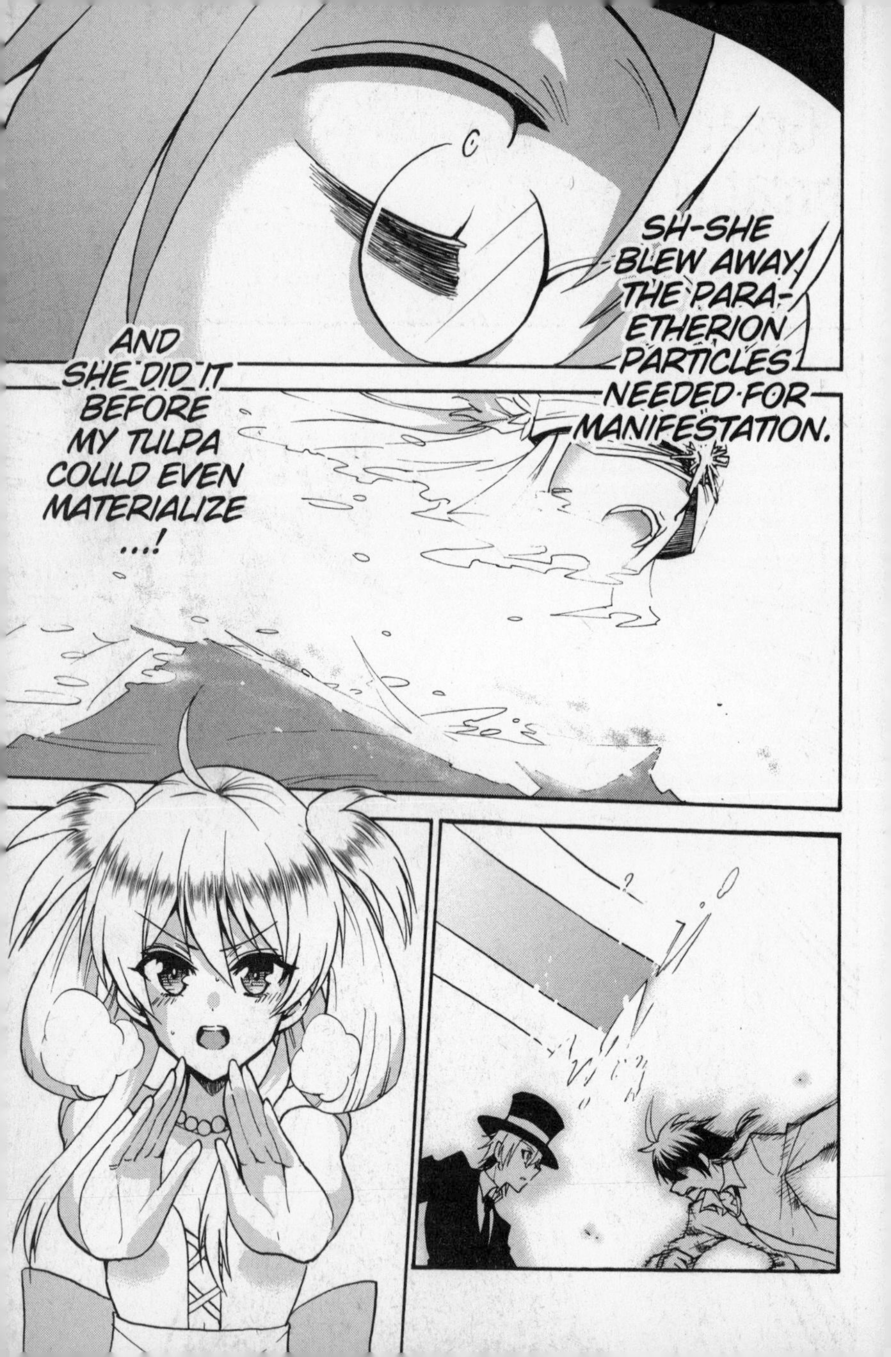
SH-SHE BLEW AWAY THE PARA-ETHERION PARTICLES NEEDED FOR MANIFESTATION.
AND SHE DID IT BEFORE MY TULPA COULD EVEN MATERIALIZE ...!

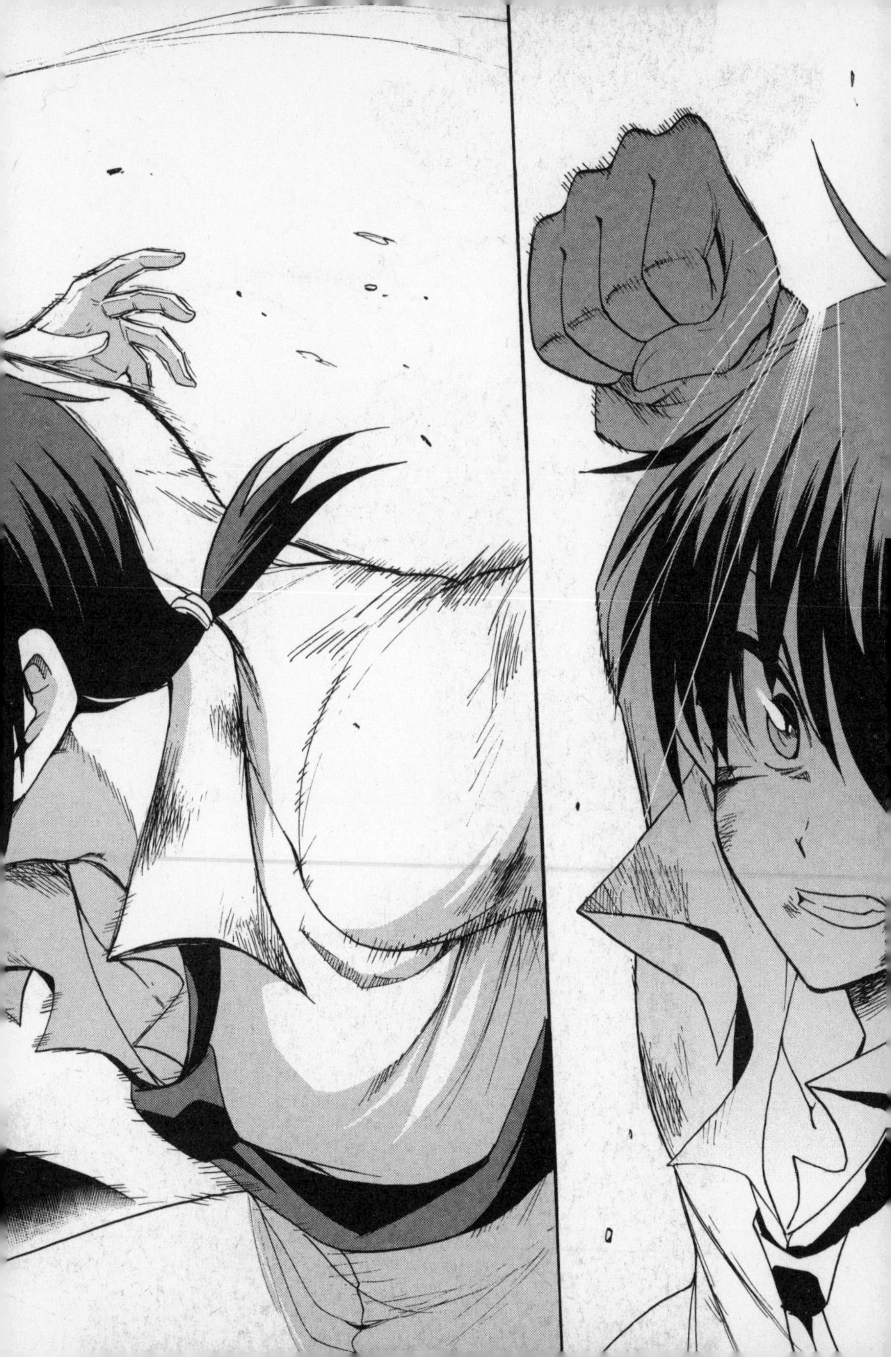

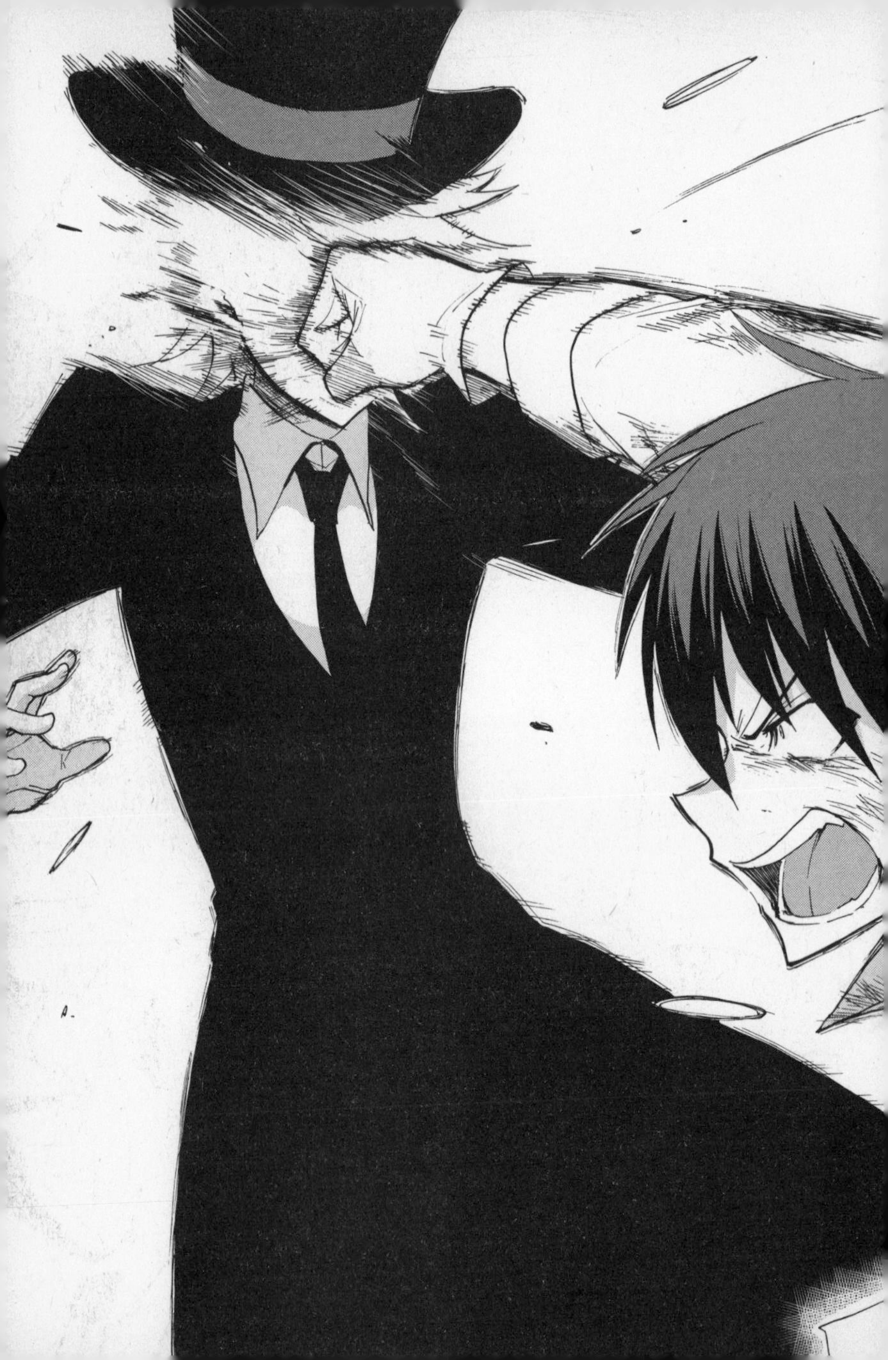

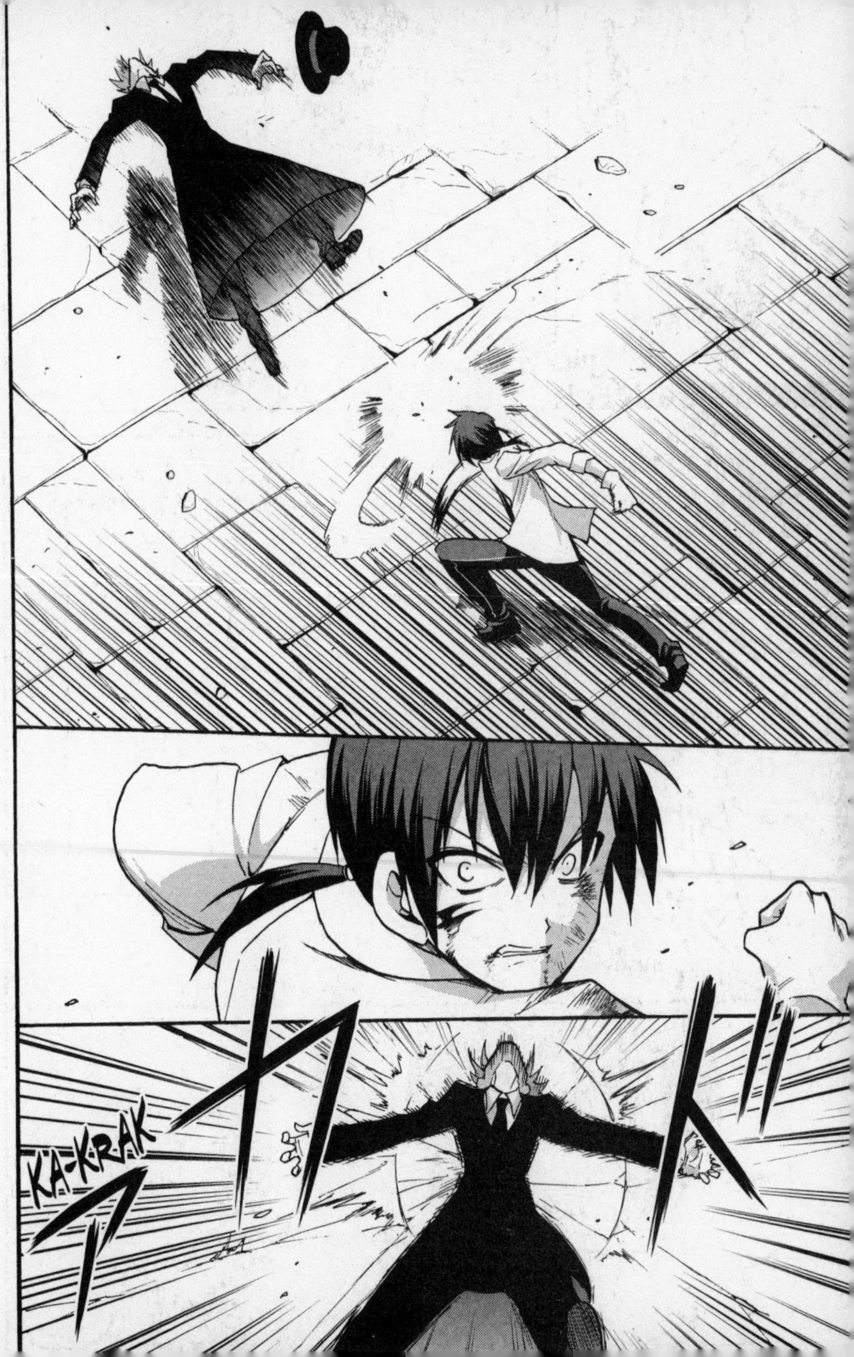
KA-KRAK

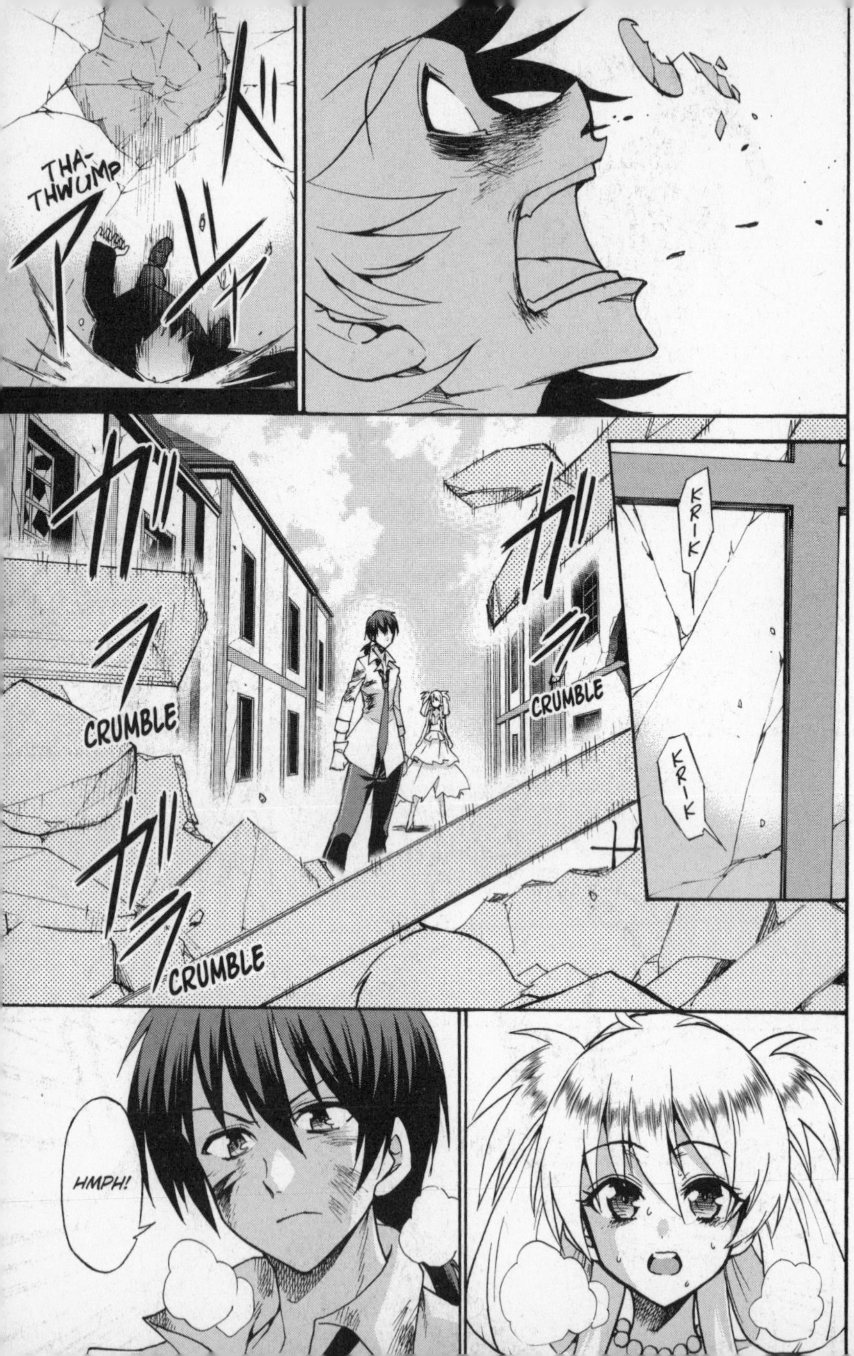
THA-THWUMP
KRIK
KRIK
CRUMBLE
CRUMBLE
CRUMBLE
HMPH!

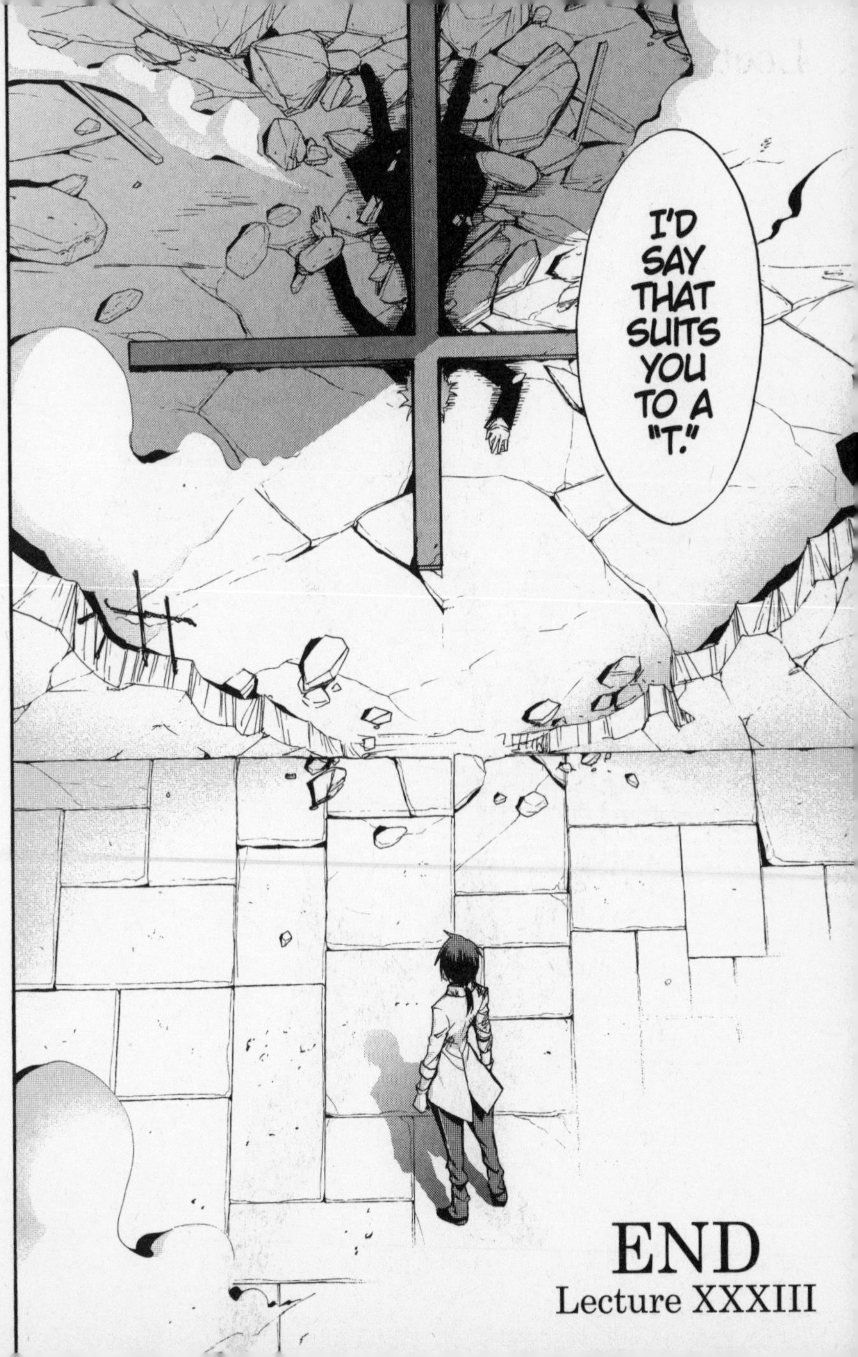
I'D SAY THAT SUITS YOU TO A "T."
END
Lecture XXXIII

# Lecture XXXIV

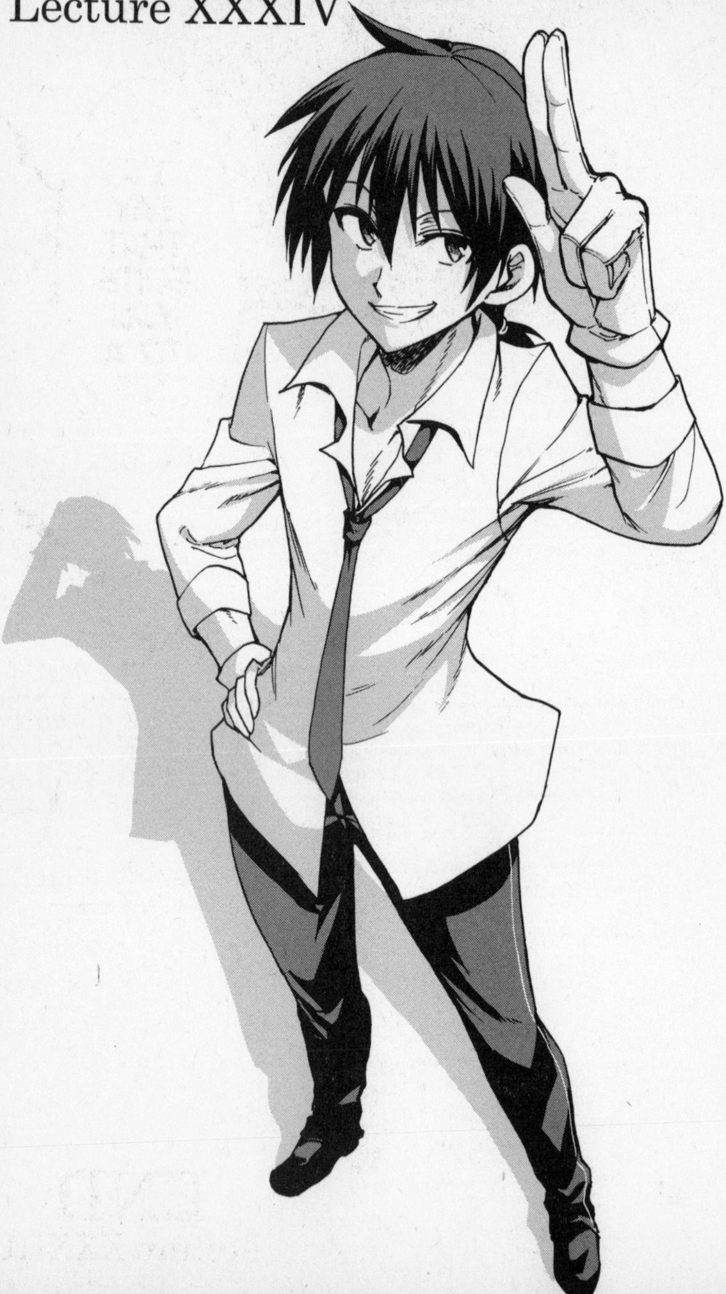

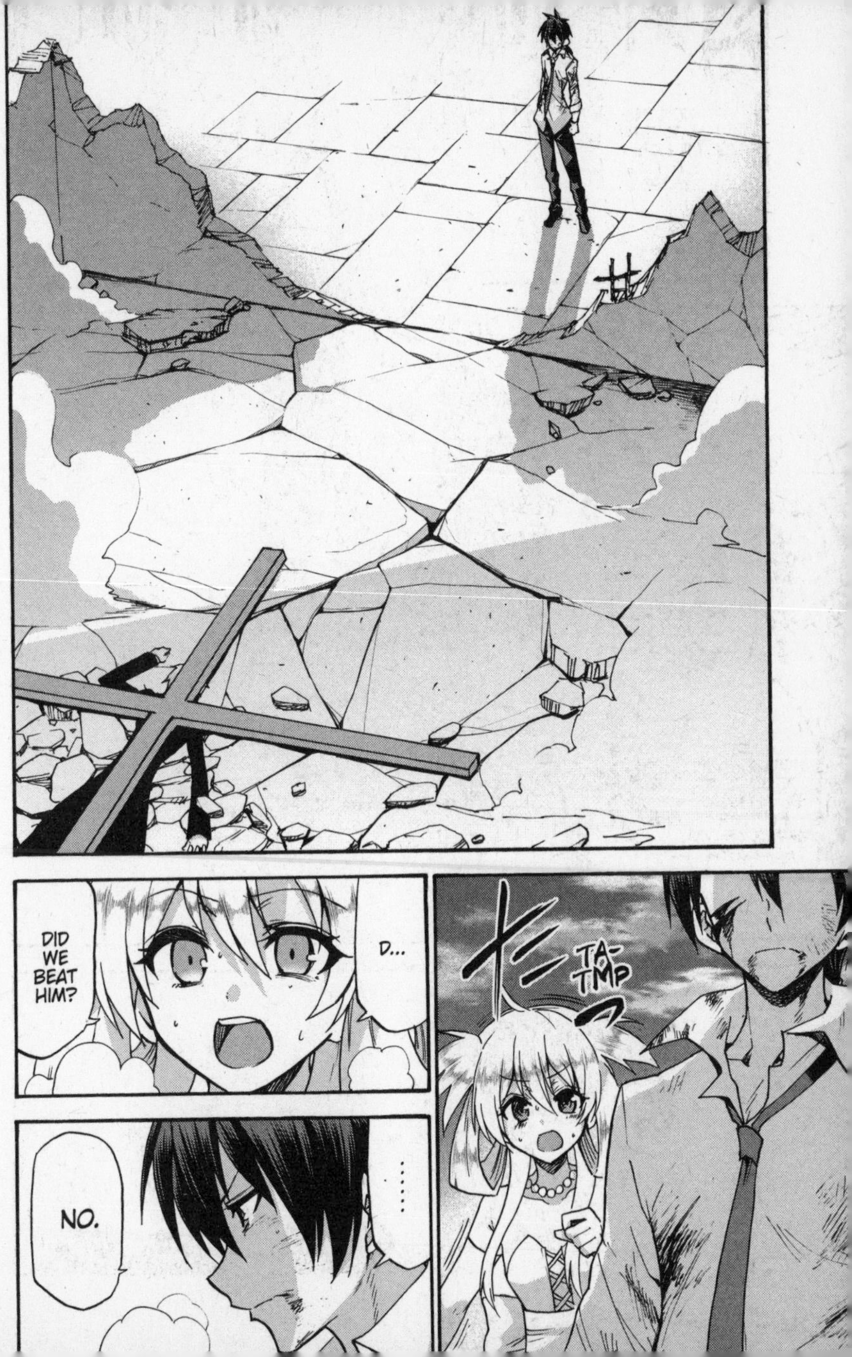
TA-TMP
D...
DID WE BEAT HIM?
......
NO.

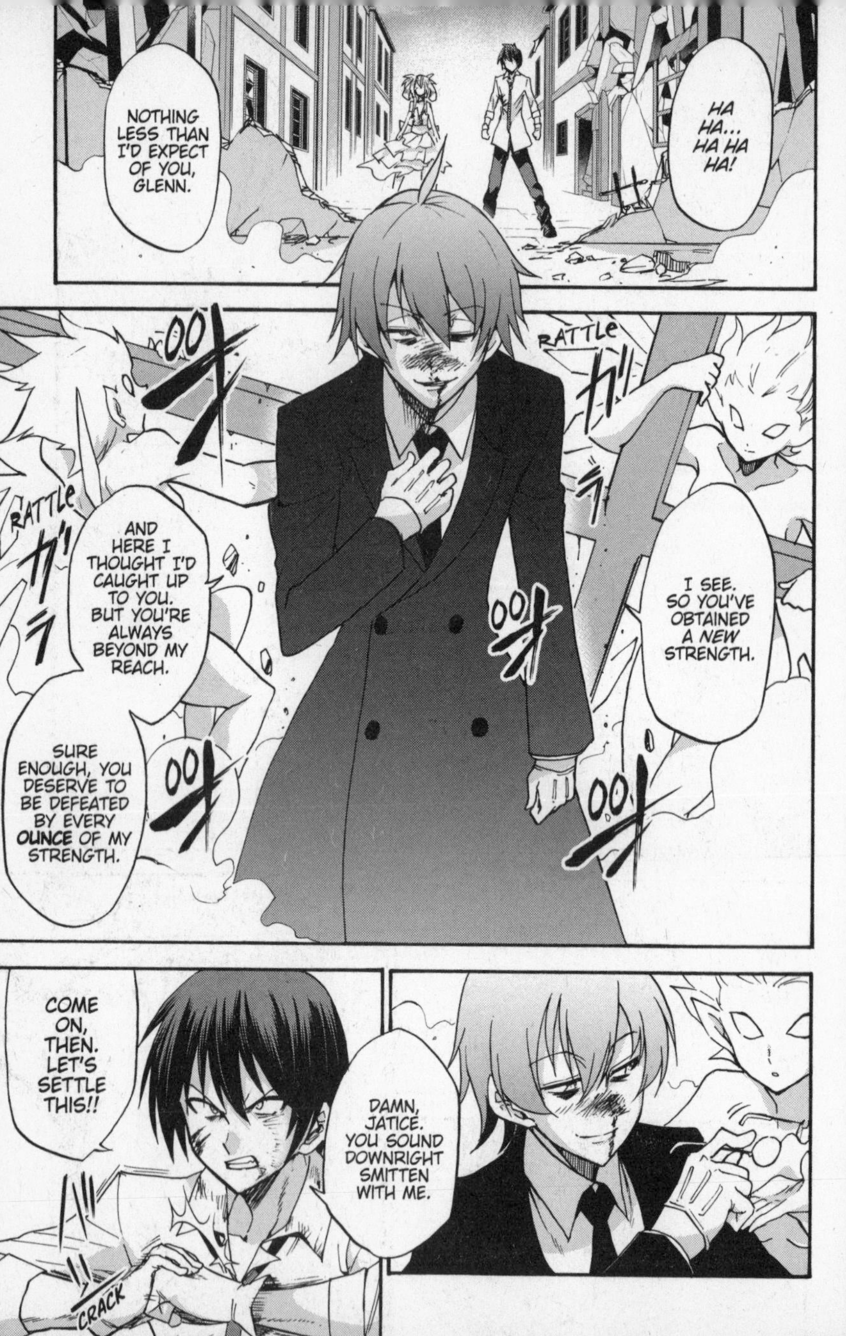
HA HA... HA HA HA!
NOTHING LESS THAN I'D EXPECT OF YOU, GLENN.
RATTLE
I SEE. SO YOU'VE OBTAINED A *NEW* STRENGTH.
RATTLE
AND HERE I THOUGHT I'D CAUGHT UP TO YOU. BUT YOU'RE ALWAYS BEYOND MY REACH.
SURE ENOUGH, YOU DESERVE TO BE DEFEATED BY EVERY **OUNCE** OF MY STRENGTH.
DAMN, JATICE. YOU SOUND DOWNRIGHT SMITTEN WITH ME.
COME ON, THEN. LET'S SETTLE THIS!!
CRACK

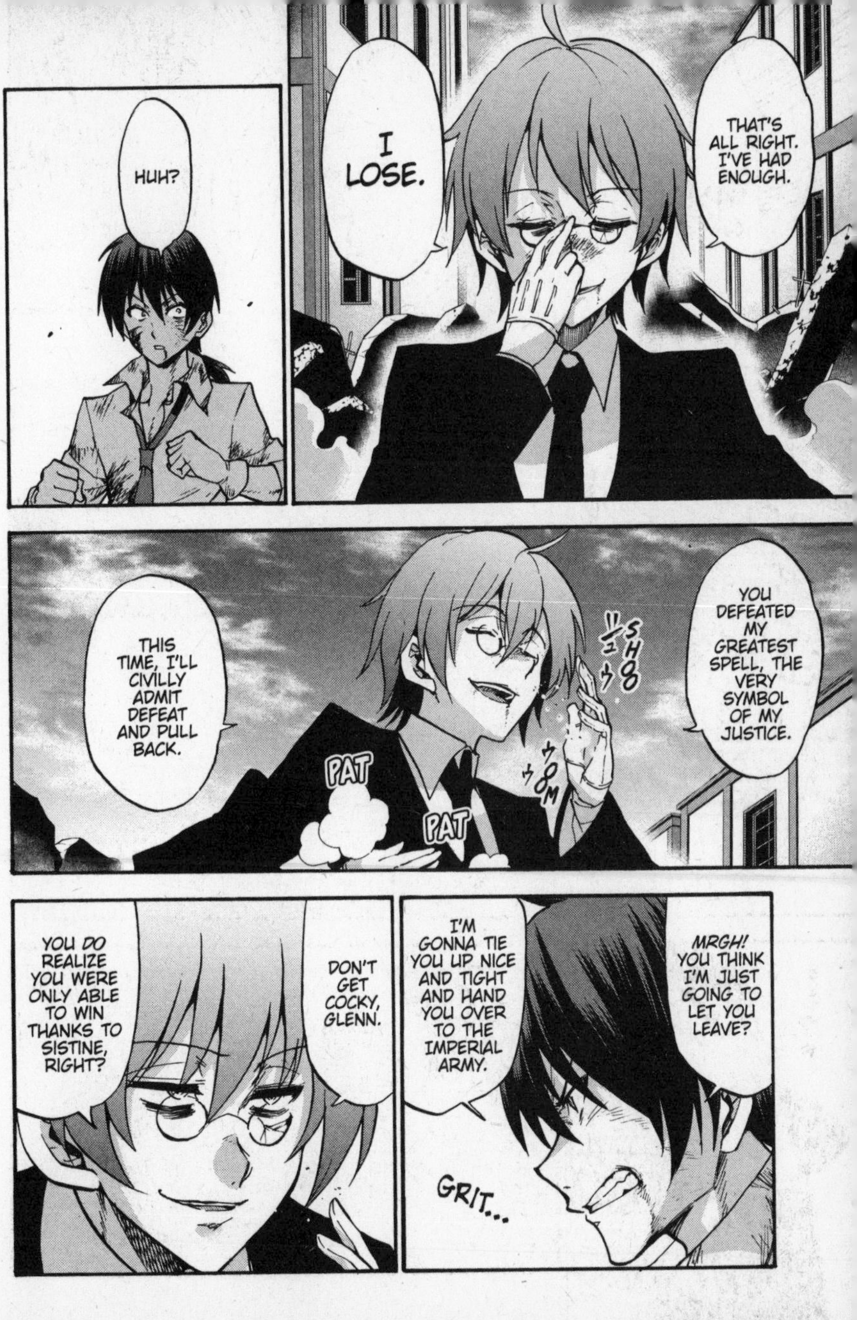
THAT'S ALL RIGHT. I'VE HAD ENOUGH.
I LOSE.
HUH?
YOU DEFEATED MY GREATEST SPELL, THE VERY SYMBOL OF MY JUSTICE.
SHOO
OOM
PAT
PAT
THIS TIME, I'LL CIVILLY ADMIT DEFEAT AND PULL BACK.
MRGH! YOU THINK I'M JUST GOING TO LET YOU LEAVE?
I'M GONNA TIE YOU UP NICE AND TIGHT AND HAND YOU OVER TO THE IMPERIAL ARMY.
GRIT...
DON'T GET COCKY, GLENN.
YOU DO REALIZE YOU WERE ONLY ABLE TO WIN THANKS TO SISTINE, RIGHT?

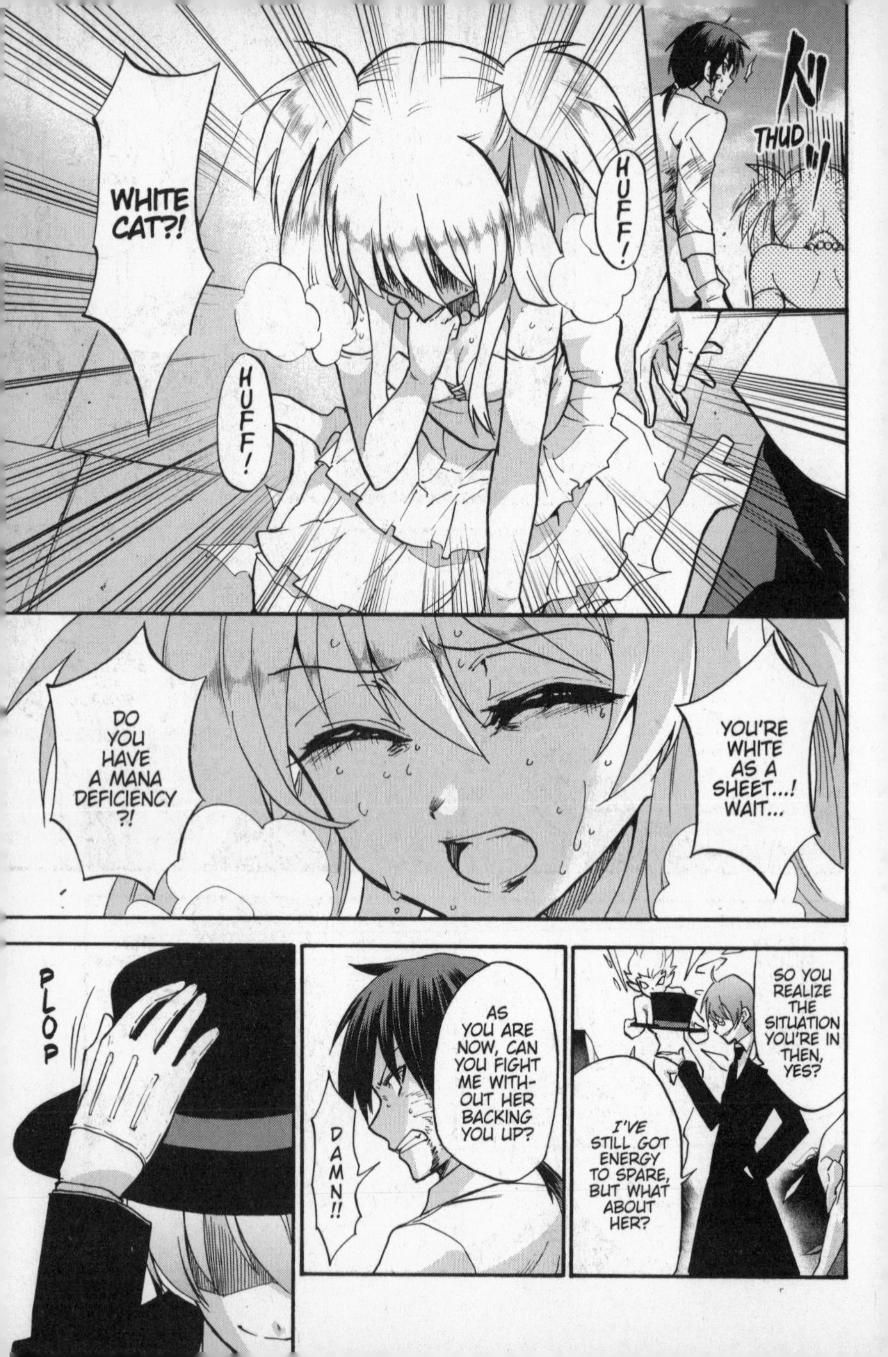
THUD
HUFF!
WHITE CAT?!
HUFF!
YOU'RE WHITE AS A SHEET...! WAIT...
DO YOU HAVE A MANA DEFICIENCY?!
SO YOU REALIZE THE SITUATION YOU'RE IN THEN, YES?
I'VE STILL GOT ENERGY TO SPARE, BUT WHAT ABOUT HER?
AS YOU ARE NOW, CAN YOU FIGHT ME WITH-OUT HER BACKING YOU UP?
DAMN!!
PLOP

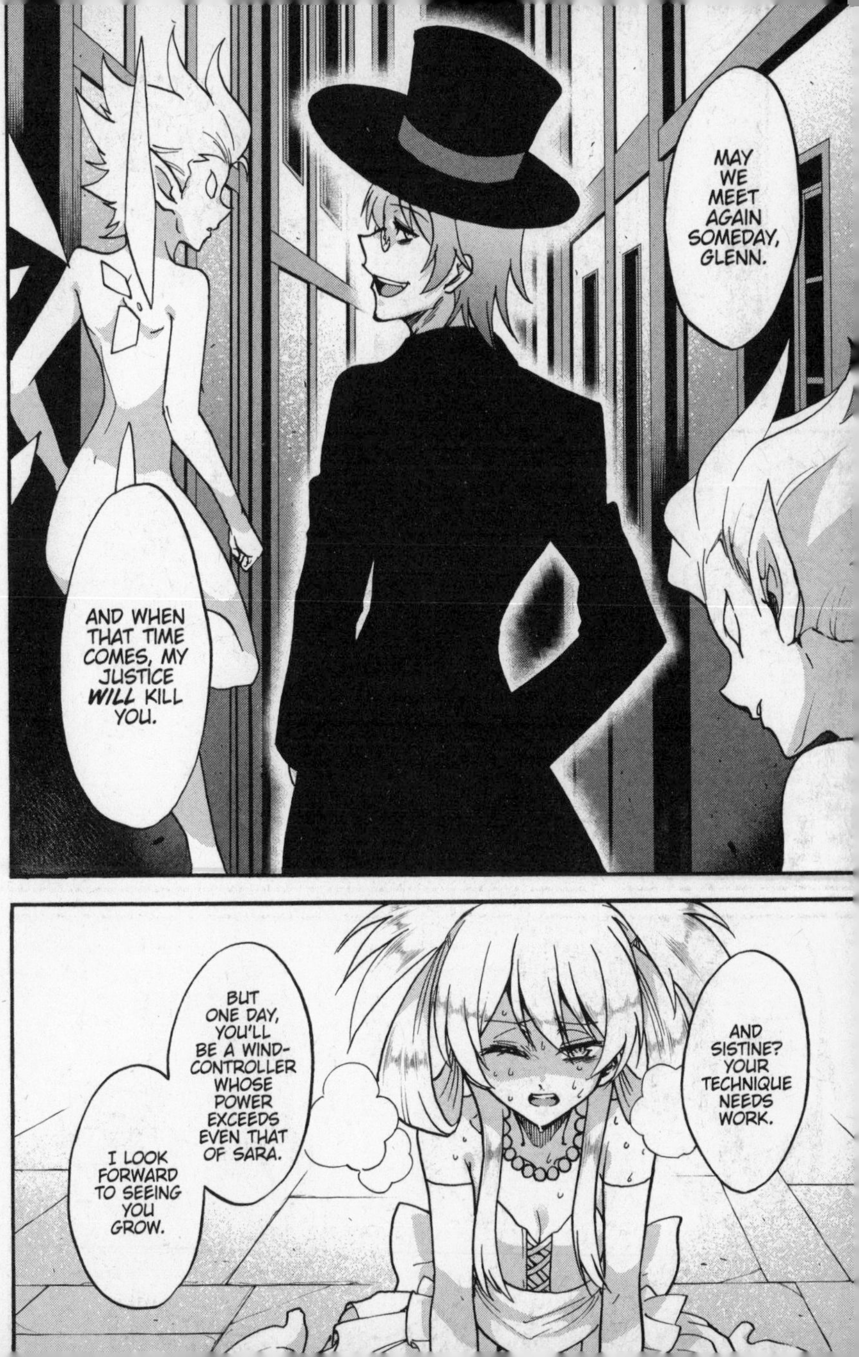
MAY WE MEET AGAIN SOMEDAY, GLENN.
AND WHEN THAT TIME COMES, MY JUSTICE *WILL* KILL YOU.
AND SISTINE? YOUR TECHNIQUE NEEDS WORK.
BUT ONE DAY, YOU'LL BE A WIND-CONTROLLER WHOSE POWER EXCEEDS EVEN THAT OF SARA.
I LOOK FORWARD TO SEEING YOU GROW.

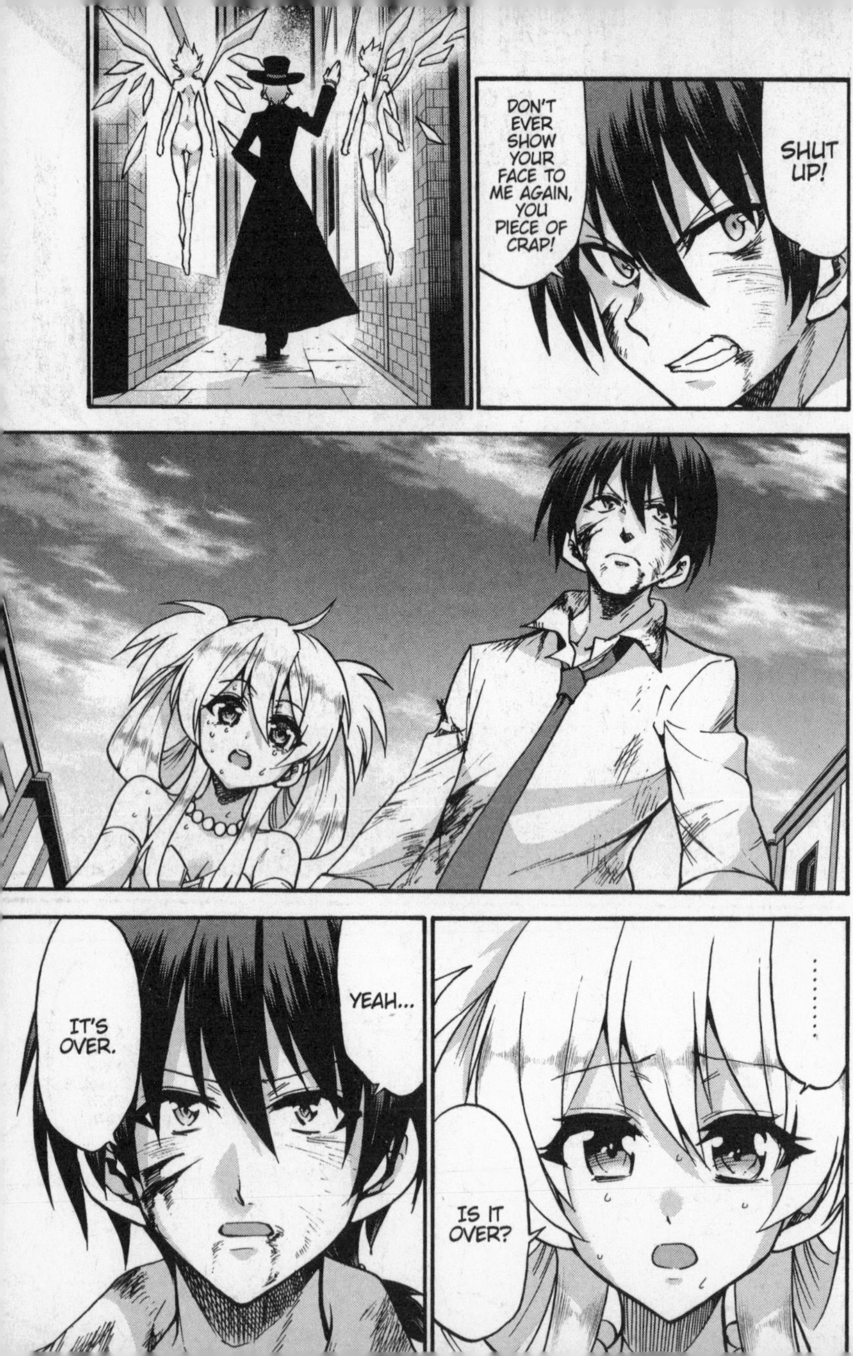
SHUT UP!
DON'T EVER SHOW YOUR FACE TO ME AGAIN, YOU PIECE OF CRAP!
........
IS IT OVER?
YEAH...
IT'S OVER.

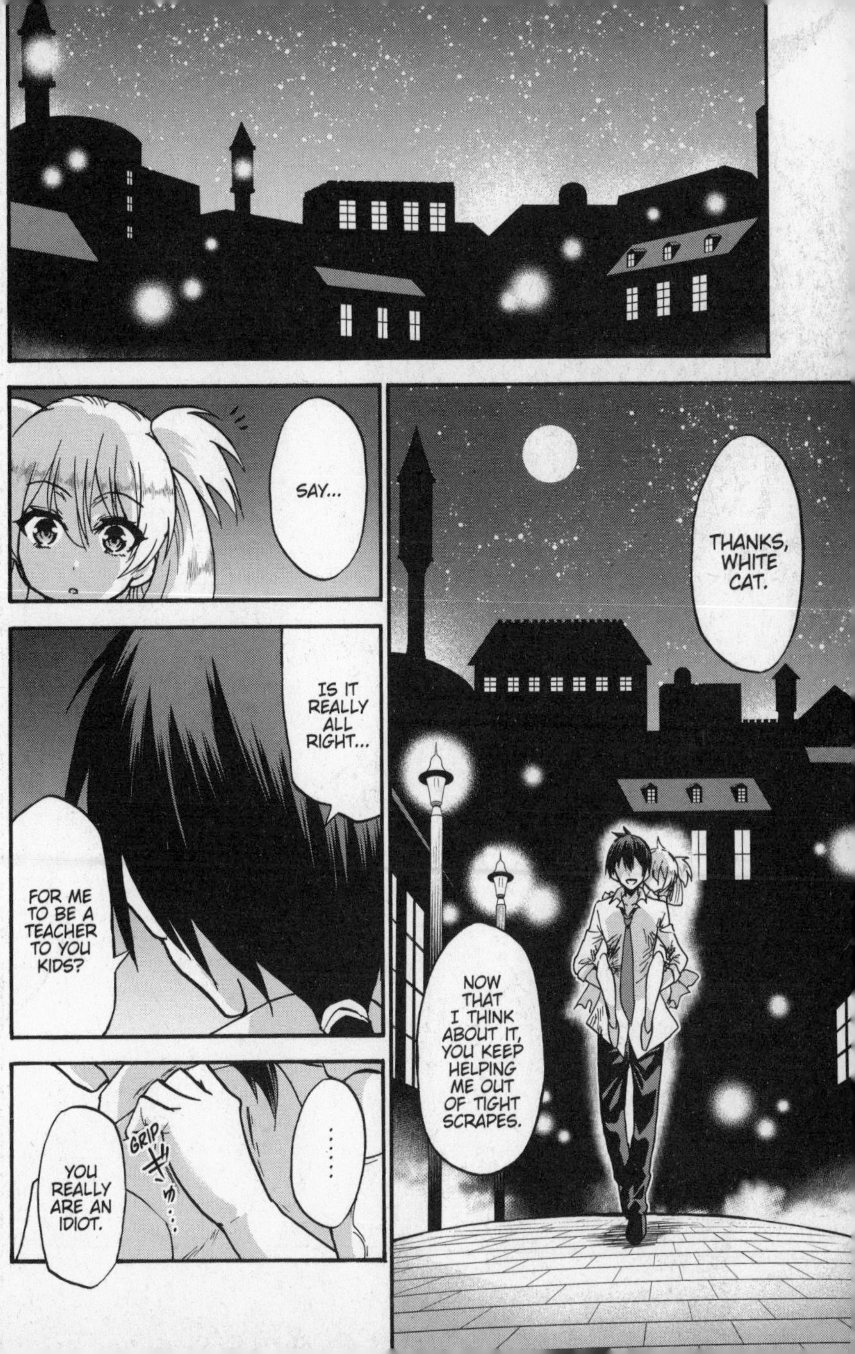
THANKS, WHITE CAT.
NOW THAT I THINK ABOUT IT, YOU KEEP HELPING ME OUT OF TIGHT SCRAPES.
SAY...
IS IT REALLY ALL RIGHT...
FOR ME TO BE A TEACHER TO YOU KIDS?
......
GRIP
YOU REALLY ARE AN IDIOT.

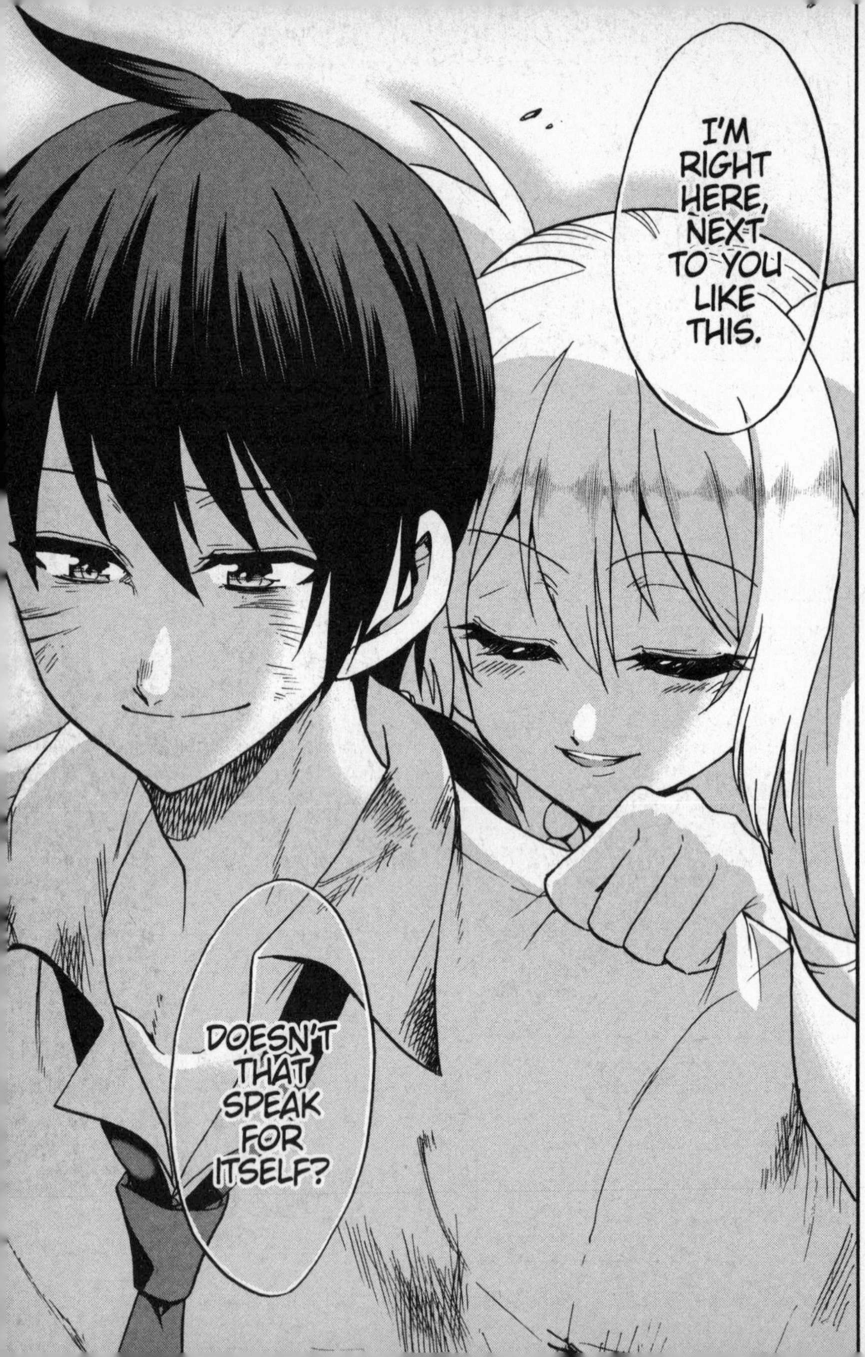
I'M RIGHT HERE, NEXT TO YOU LIKE THIS.
DOESN'T THAT SPEAK FOR ITSELF?

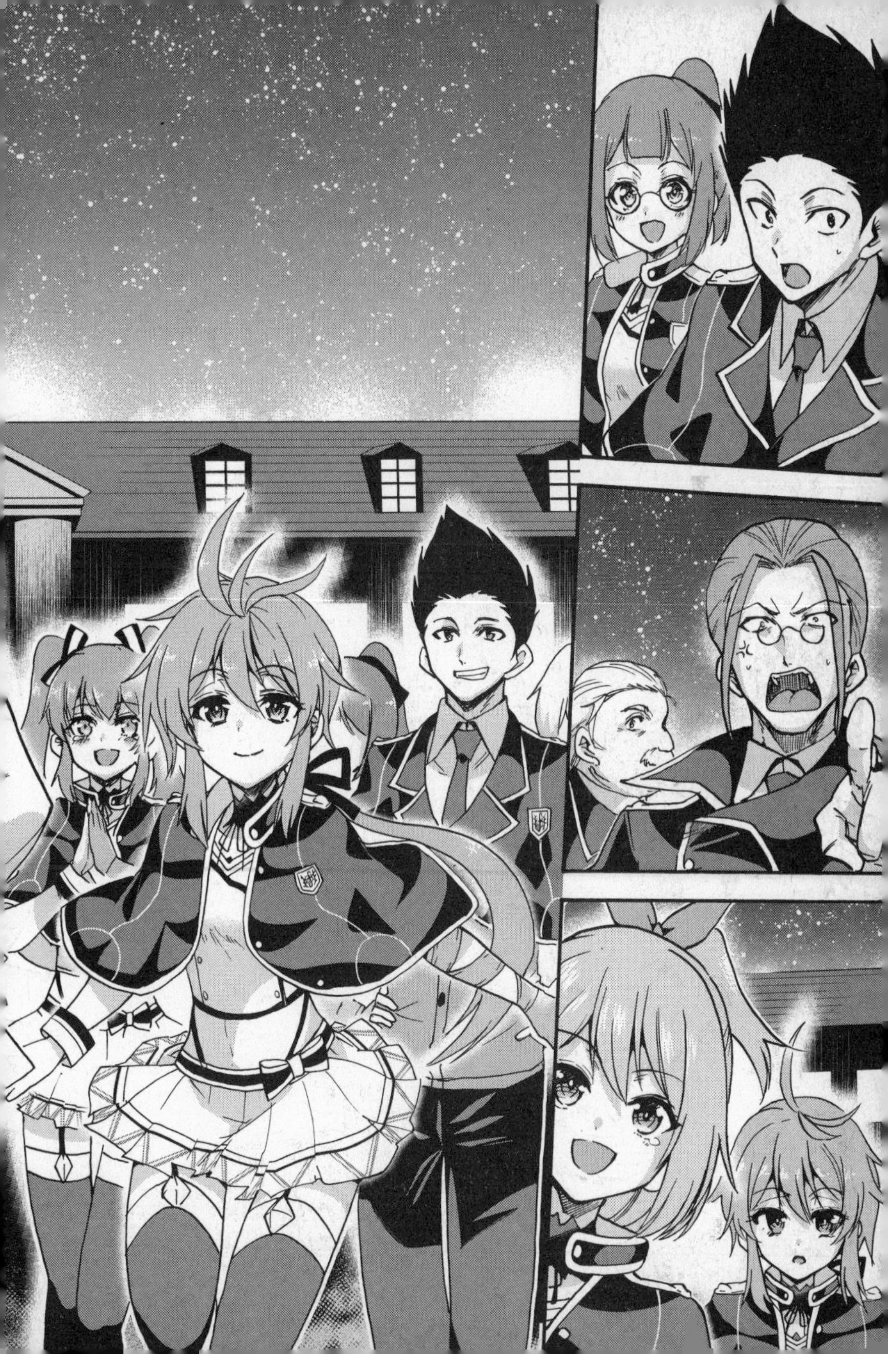

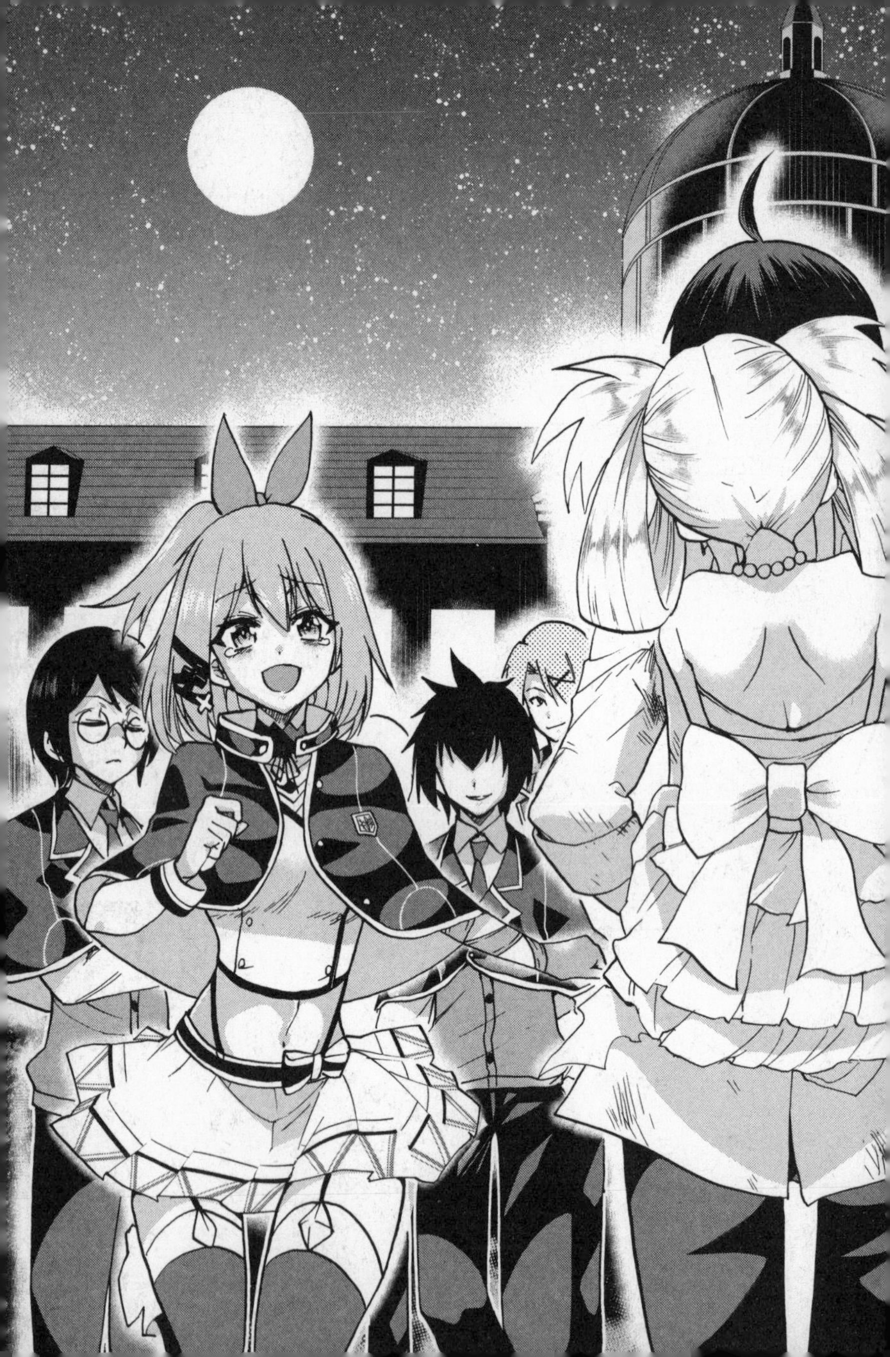

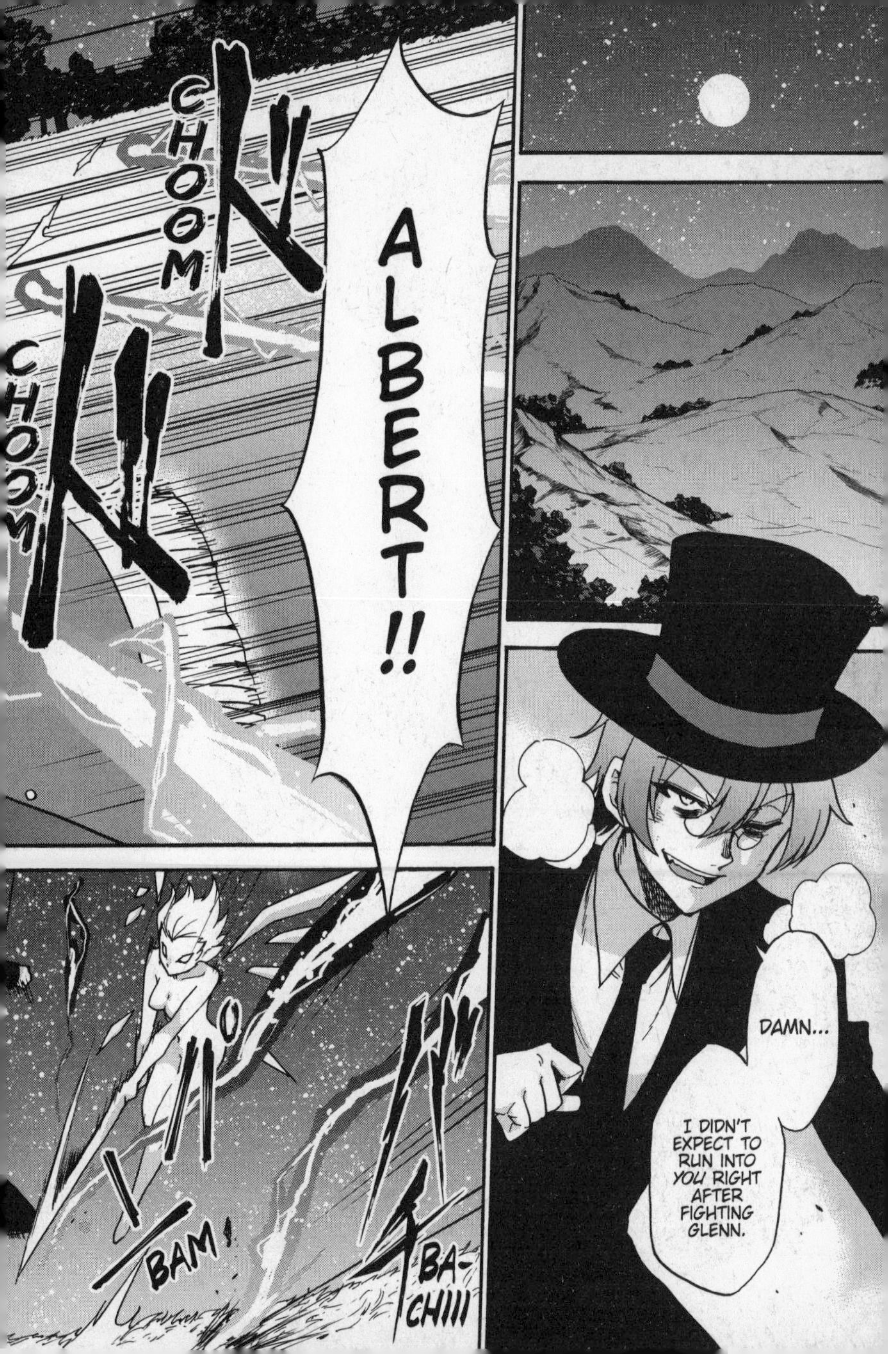

DAMN...
I DIDN'T EXPECT TO RUN INTO *YOU* RIGHT AFTER FIGHTING GLENN.
ALBERT!!
CHOOM
CHOOM
BAM
BA-CHIIII

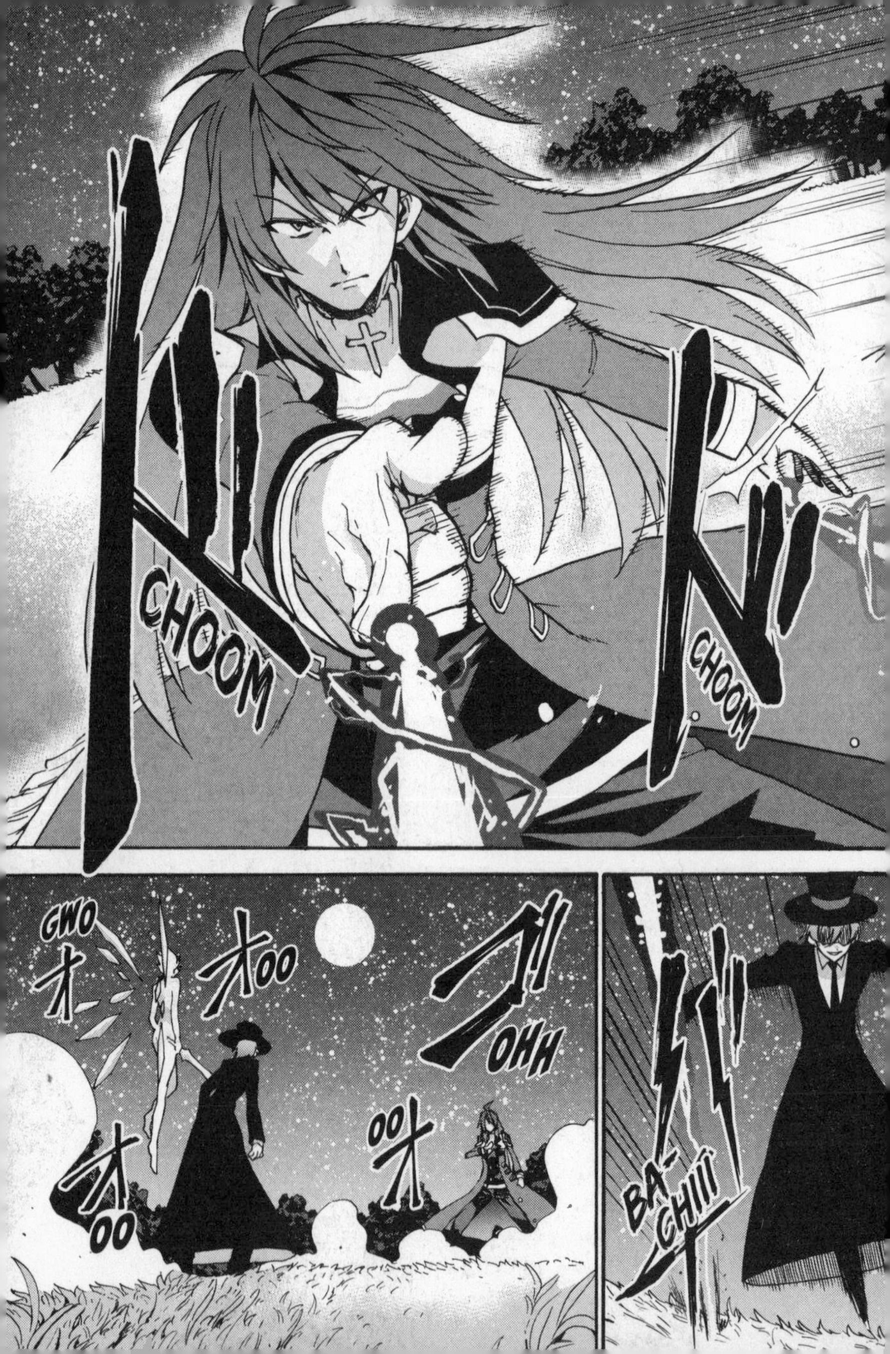
CHOOM
CHOOM
BA-CHIII
GWO
OOO
OHH
OOO
OOO

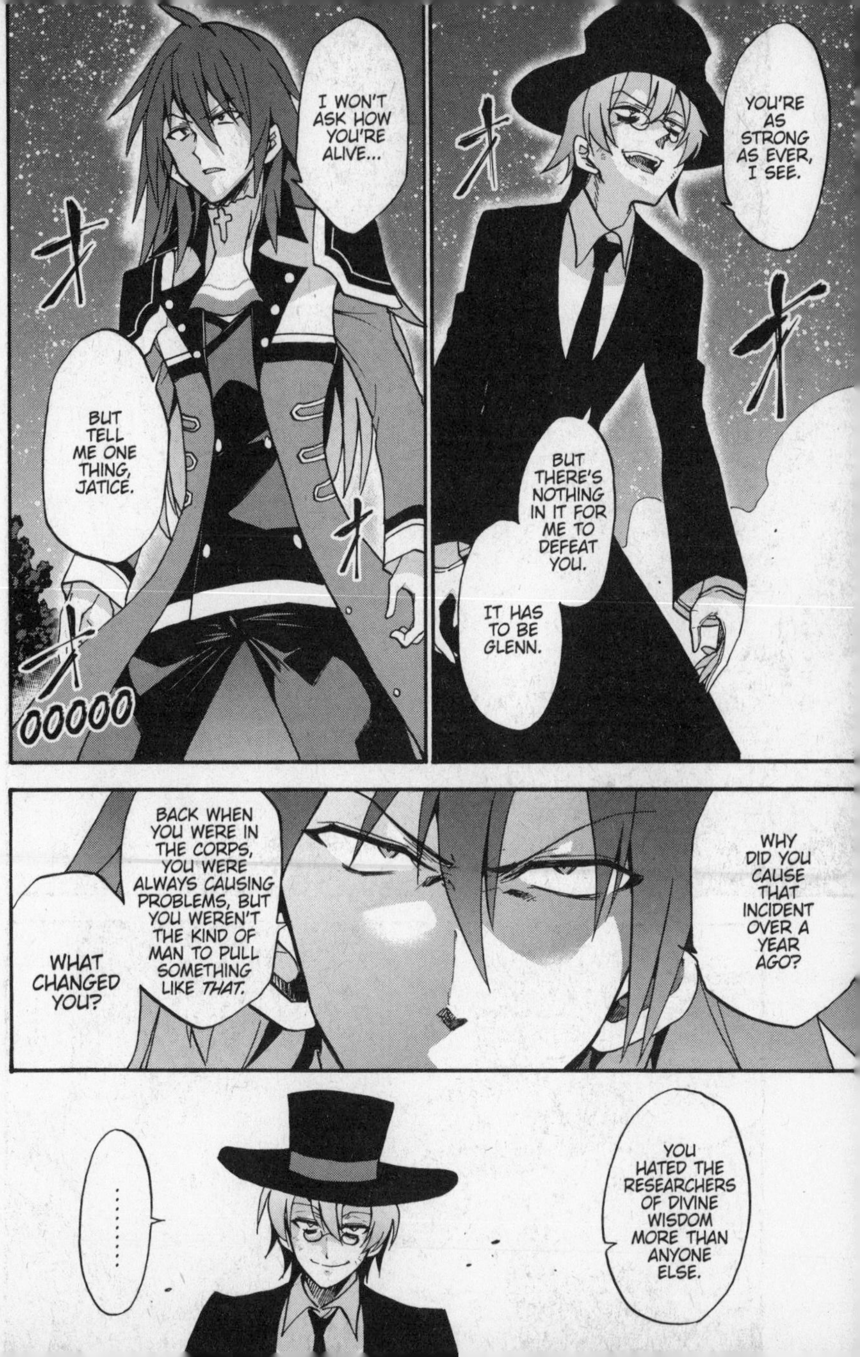
YOU'RE AS STRONG AS EVER, I SEE.
BUT THERE'S NOTHING IN IT FOR ME TO DEFEAT YOU.
IT HAS TO BE GLENN.
I WON'T ASK HOW YOU'RE ALIVE...
BUT TELL ME ONE THING, JATICE.
OOOOO
WHY DID YOU CAUSE THAT INCIDENT OVER A YEAR AGO?
BACK WHEN YOU WERE IN THE CORPS, YOU WERE ALWAYS CAUSING PROBLEMS, BUT YOU WEREN'T THE KIND OF MAN TO PULL SOMETHING LIKE *THAT*.
WHAT CHANGED YOU?
YOU HATED THE RESEARCHERS OF DIVINE WISDOM MORE THAN ANYONE ELSE.
......

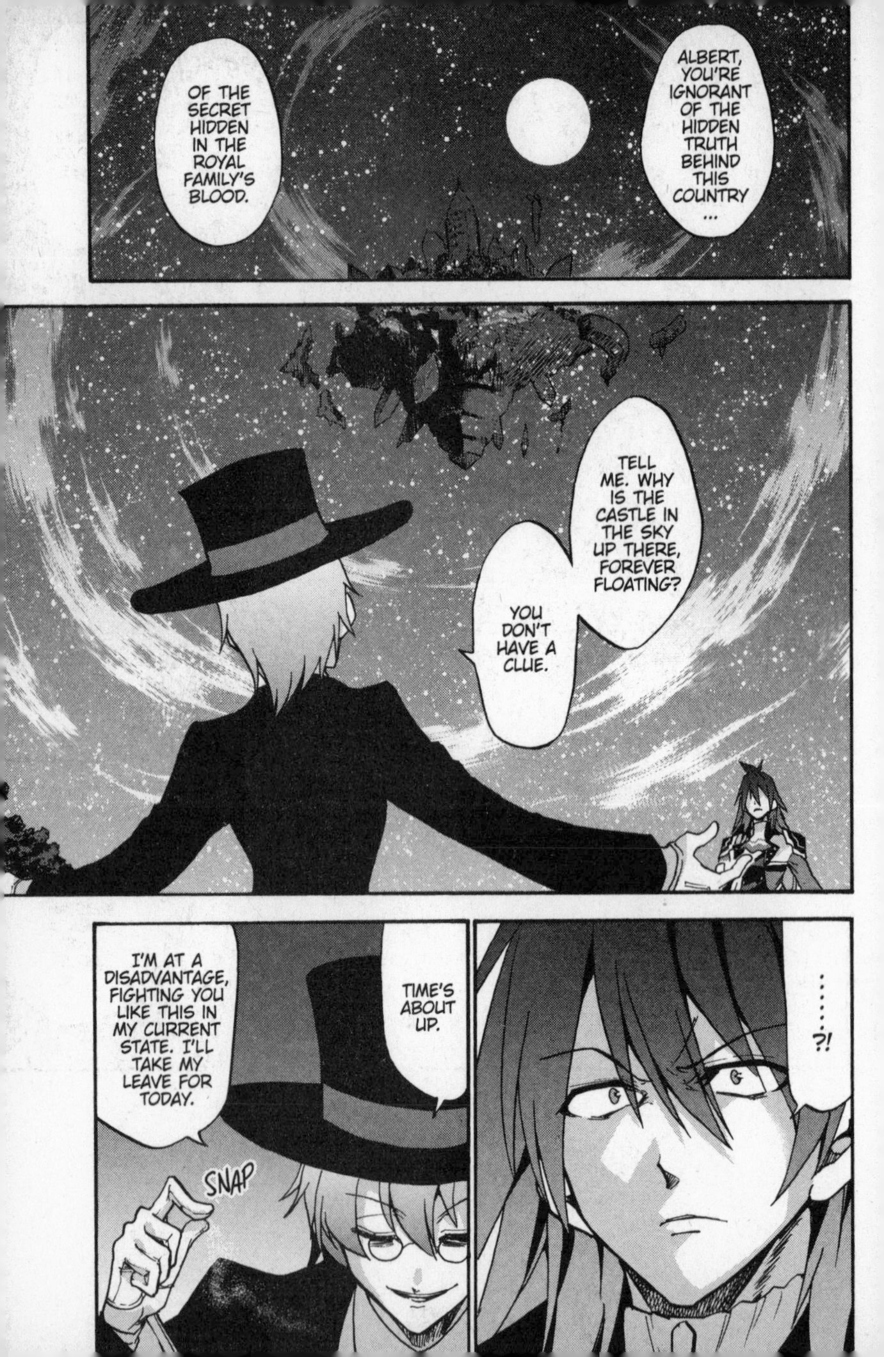
ALBERT, YOU'RE IGNORANT OF THE HIDDEN TRUTH BEHIND THIS COUNTRY ...
OF THE SECRET HIDDEN IN THE ROYAL FAMILY'S BLOOD.
TELL ME. WHY IS THE CASTLE IN THE SKY UP THERE, FOREVER FLOATING?
YOU DON'T HAVE A CLUE.
......?!
TIME'S ABOUT UP.
I'M AT A DISADVANTAGE, FIGHTING YOU LIKE THIS IN MY CURRENT STATE. I'LL TAKE MY LEAVE FOR TODAY.
SNAP

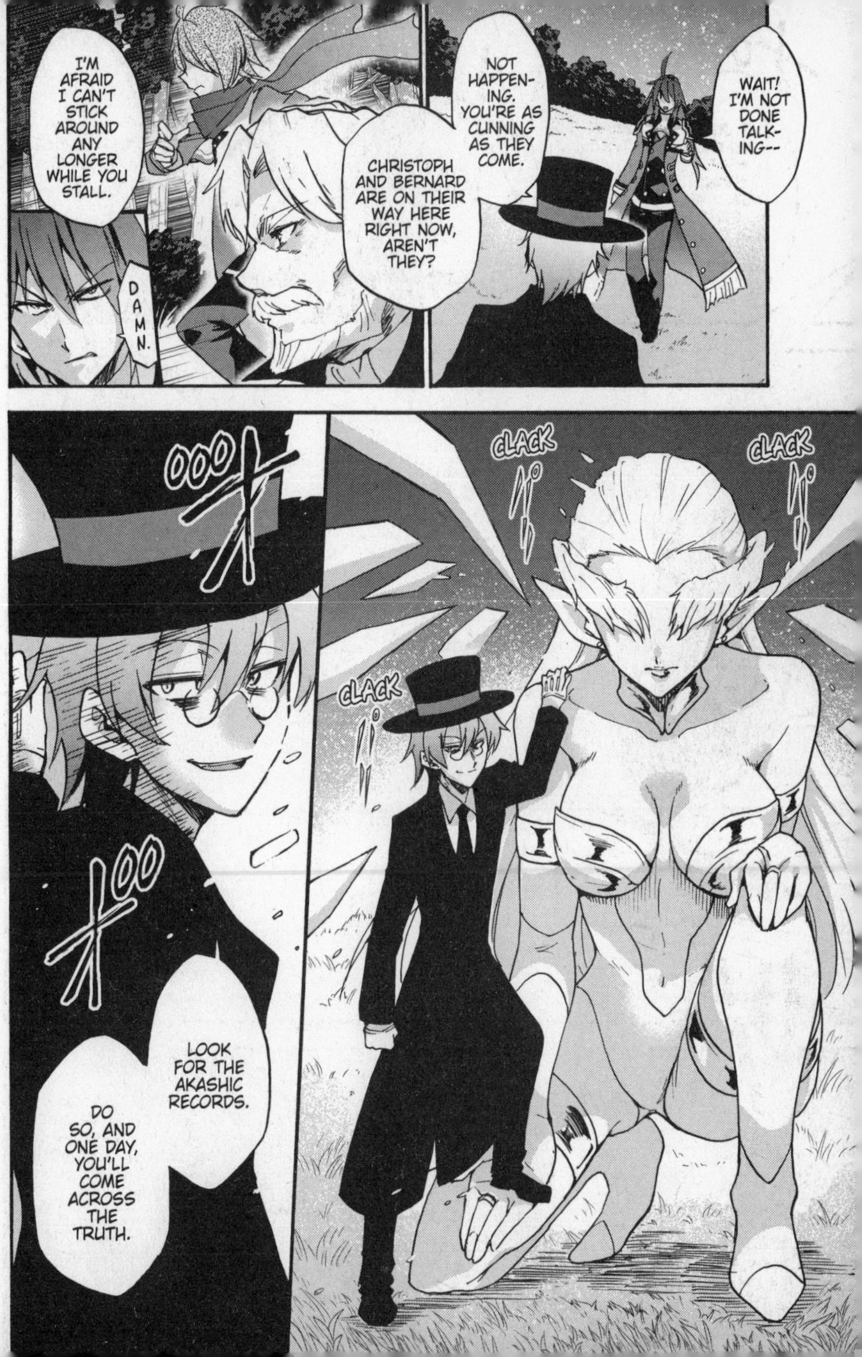
WAIT! I'M NOT DONE TALKING--
NOT HAPPENING. YOU'RE AS CUNNING AS THEY COME.
CHRISTOPH AND BERNARD ARE ON THEIR WAY HERE RIGHT NOW, AREN'T THEY?
I'M AFRAID I CAN'T STICK AROUND ANY LONGER WHILE YOU STALL.
DAMN.
CLACK
CLACK
CLACK
OOO
OO
LOOK FOR THE AKASHIC RECORDS.
DO SO, AND ONE DAY, YOU'LL COME ACROSS THE TRUTH.

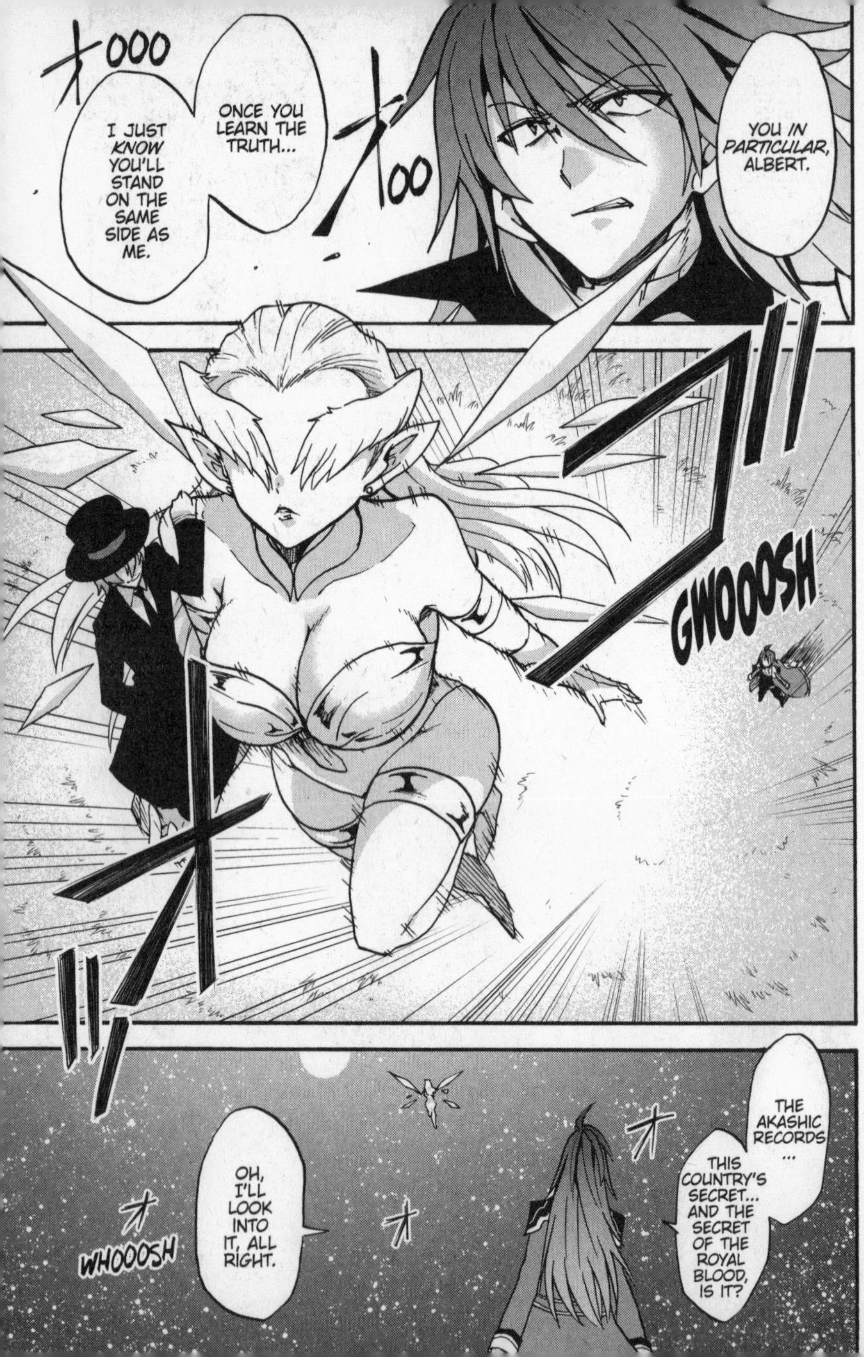
YOU IN PARTICULAR, ALBERT.
ONCE YOU LEARN THE TRUTH...
I JUST KNOW YOU'LL STAND ON THE SAME SIDE AS ME.
GWOOOSH
THE AKASHIC RECORDS ... THIS COUNTRY'S SECRET... AND THE SECRET OF THE ROYAL BLOOD, IS IT?
OH, I'LL LOOK INTO IT, ALL RIGHT.
WHOOOSH

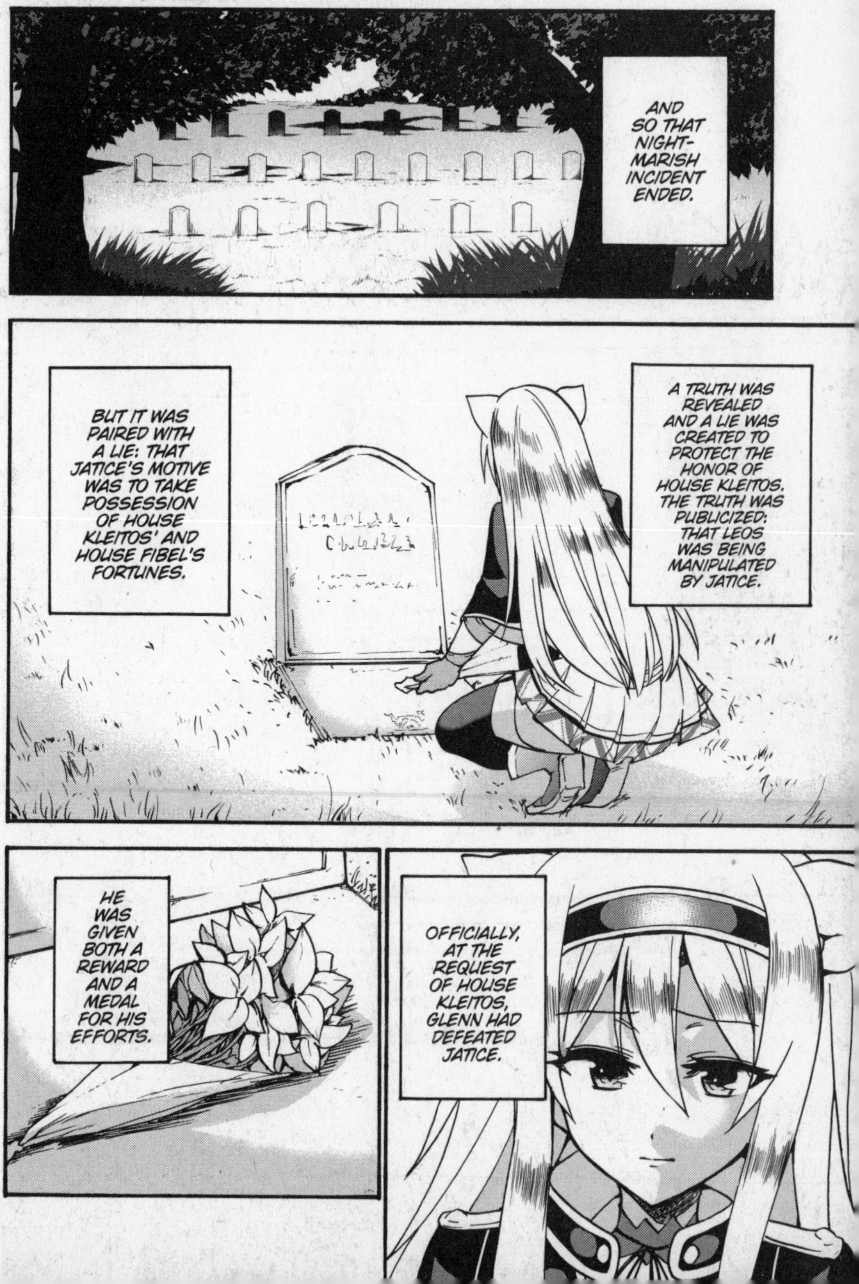
AND SO THAT NIGHT-MARISH INCIDENT ENDED.
A TRUTH WAS REVEALED AND A LIE WAS CREATED TO PROTECT THE HONOR OF HOUSE KLEITOS. THE TRUTH WAS PUBLICIZED: THAT LEOS WAS BEING MANIPULATED BY JATICE.
BUT IT WAS PAIRED WITH A LIE: THAT JATICE'S MOTIVE WAS TO TAKE POSSESSION OF HOUSE KLEITOS' AND HOUSE FIBEL'S FORTUNES.
OFFICIALLY, AT THE REQUEST OF HOUSE KLEITOS, GLENN HAD DEFEATED JATICE.
HE WAS GIVEN BOTH A REWARD AND A MEDAL FOR HIS EFFORTS.

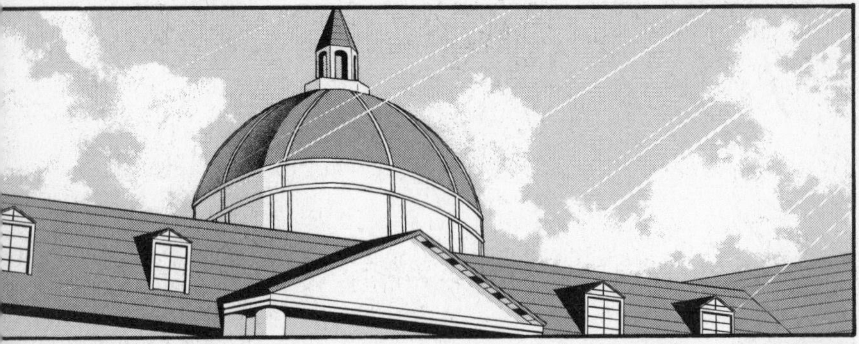
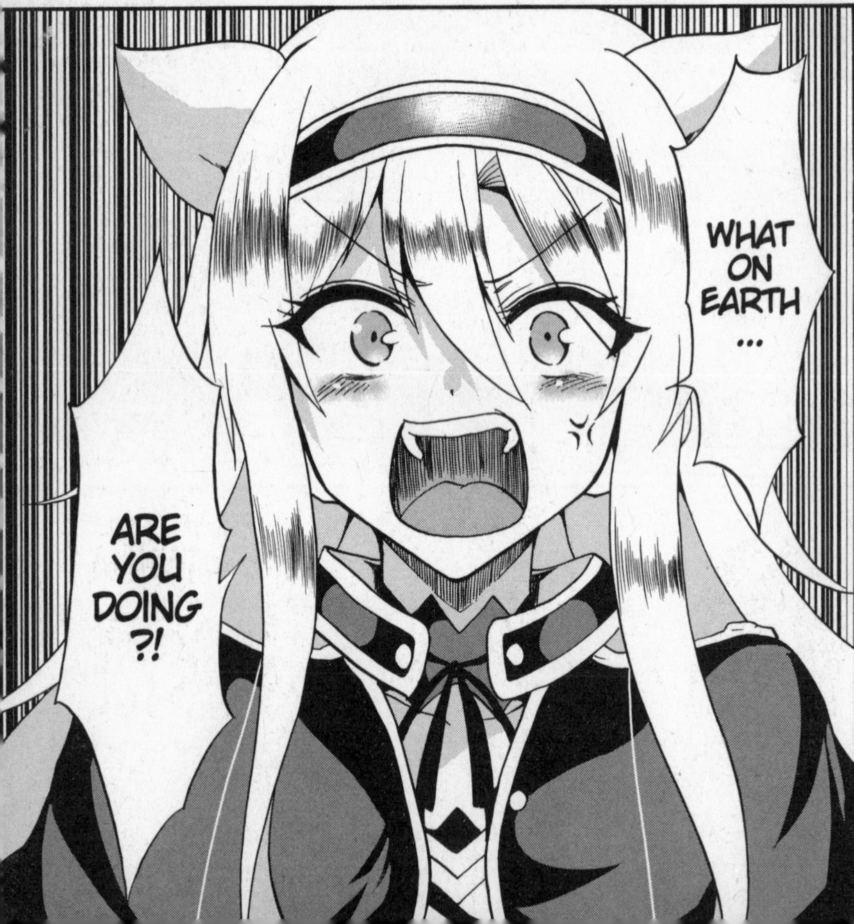
WHAT ON EARTH ...
ARE YOU DOING ?!

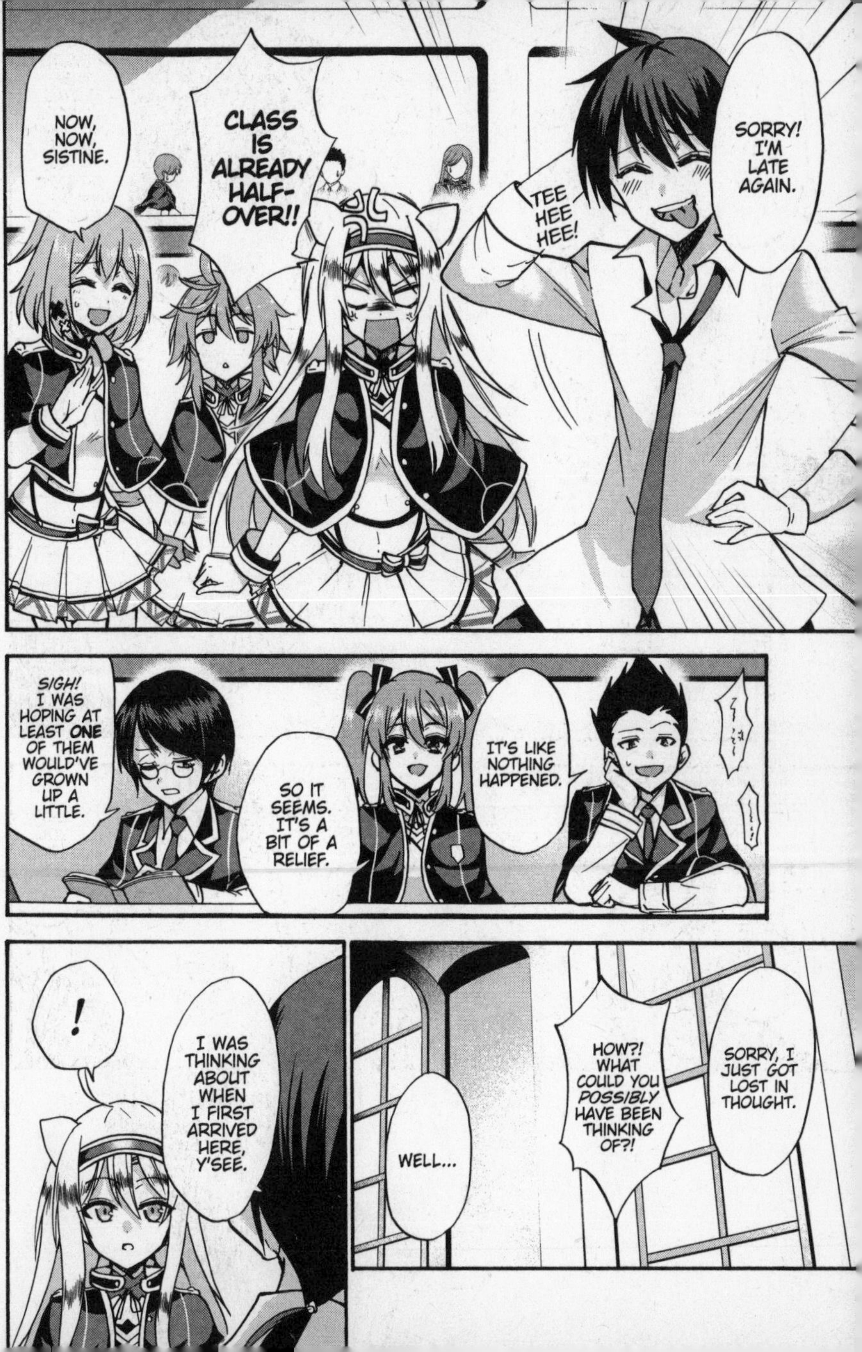
SORRY! I'M LATE AGAIN.
TEE HEE HEE!
CLASS IS ALREADY HALF-OVER!!
NOW, NOW, SISTINE.
IT'S LIKE NOTHING HAPPENED.
SO IT SEEMS. IT'S A BIT OF A RELIEF.
*SIGH!* I WAS HOPING AT LEAST **ONE** OF THEM WOULD'VE GROWN UP A LITTLE.
SORRY, I JUST GOT LOST IN THOUGHT.
HOW?! WHAT COULD YOU *POSSIBLY* HAVE BEEN THINKING OF?!
WELL...
I WAS THINKING ABOUT WHEN I FIRST ARRIVED HERE, Y'SEE.
!

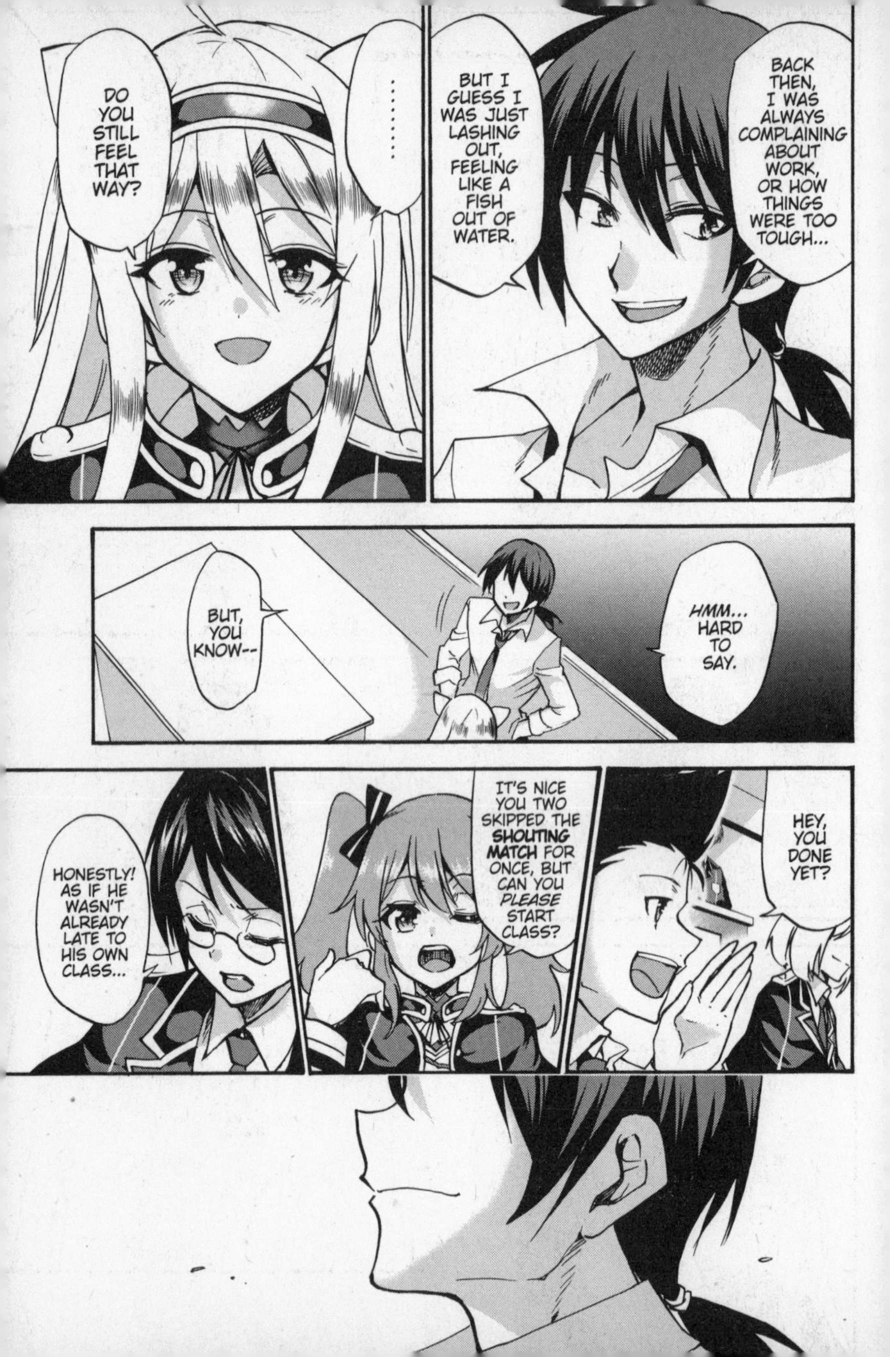
BACK THEN, I WAS ALWAYS COMPLAINING ABOUT WORK, OR HOW THINGS WERE TOO TOUGH...
BUT I GUESS I WAS JUST LASHING OUT, FEELING LIKE A FISH OUT OF WATER.
......
DO YOU STILL FEEL THAT WAY?
HMM... HARD TO SAY.
BUT, YOU KNOW--
HEY, YOU DONE YET?
IT'S NICE YOU TWO SKIPPED THE SHOUTING MATCH FOR ONCE, BUT CAN YOU PLEASE START CLASS?
HONESTLY! AS IF HE WASN'T ALREADY LATE TO HIS OWN CLASS...

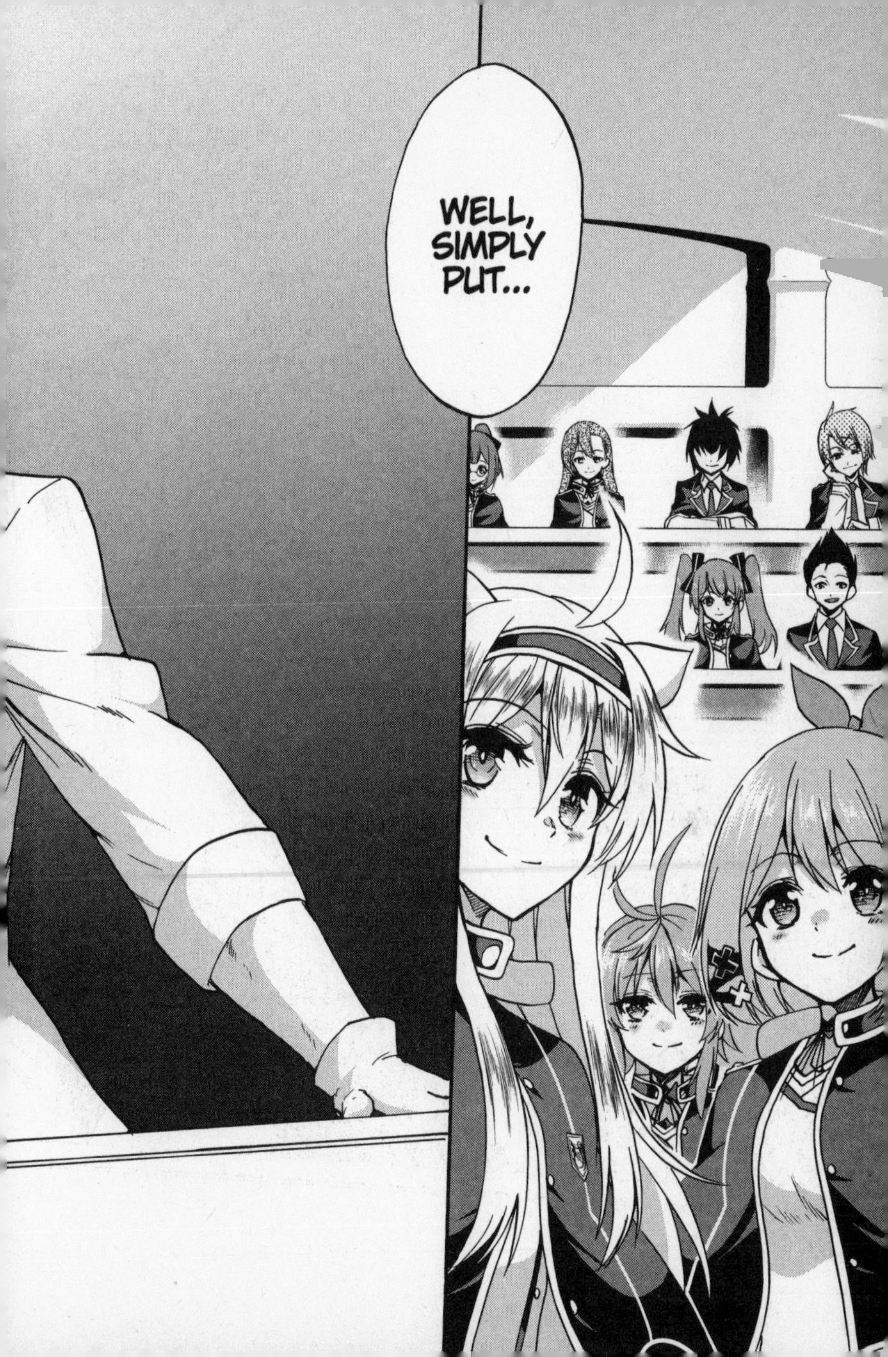
WELL, SIMPLY PUT...

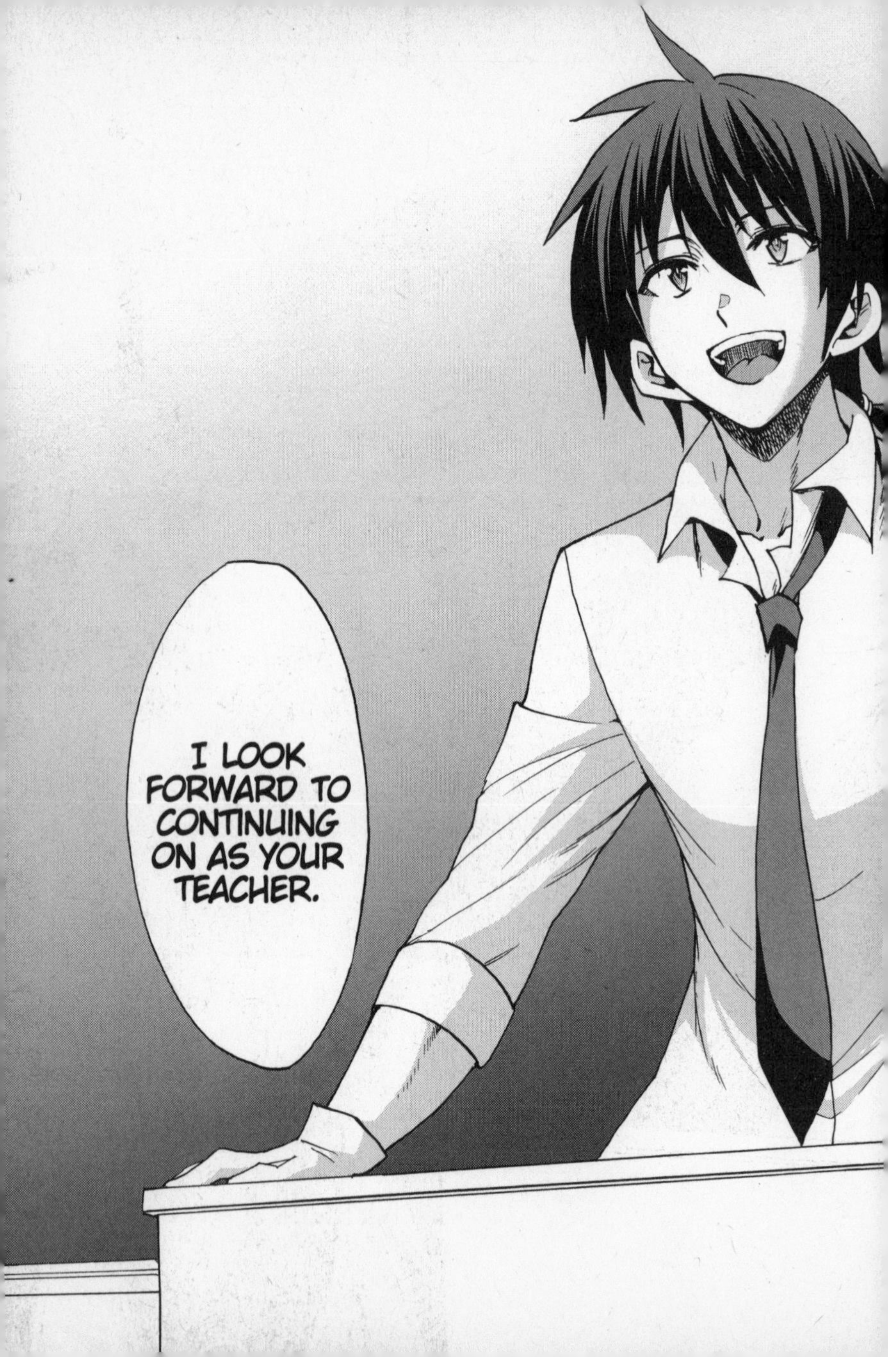
I LOOK FORWARD TO CONTINUING ON AS YOUR TEACHER.

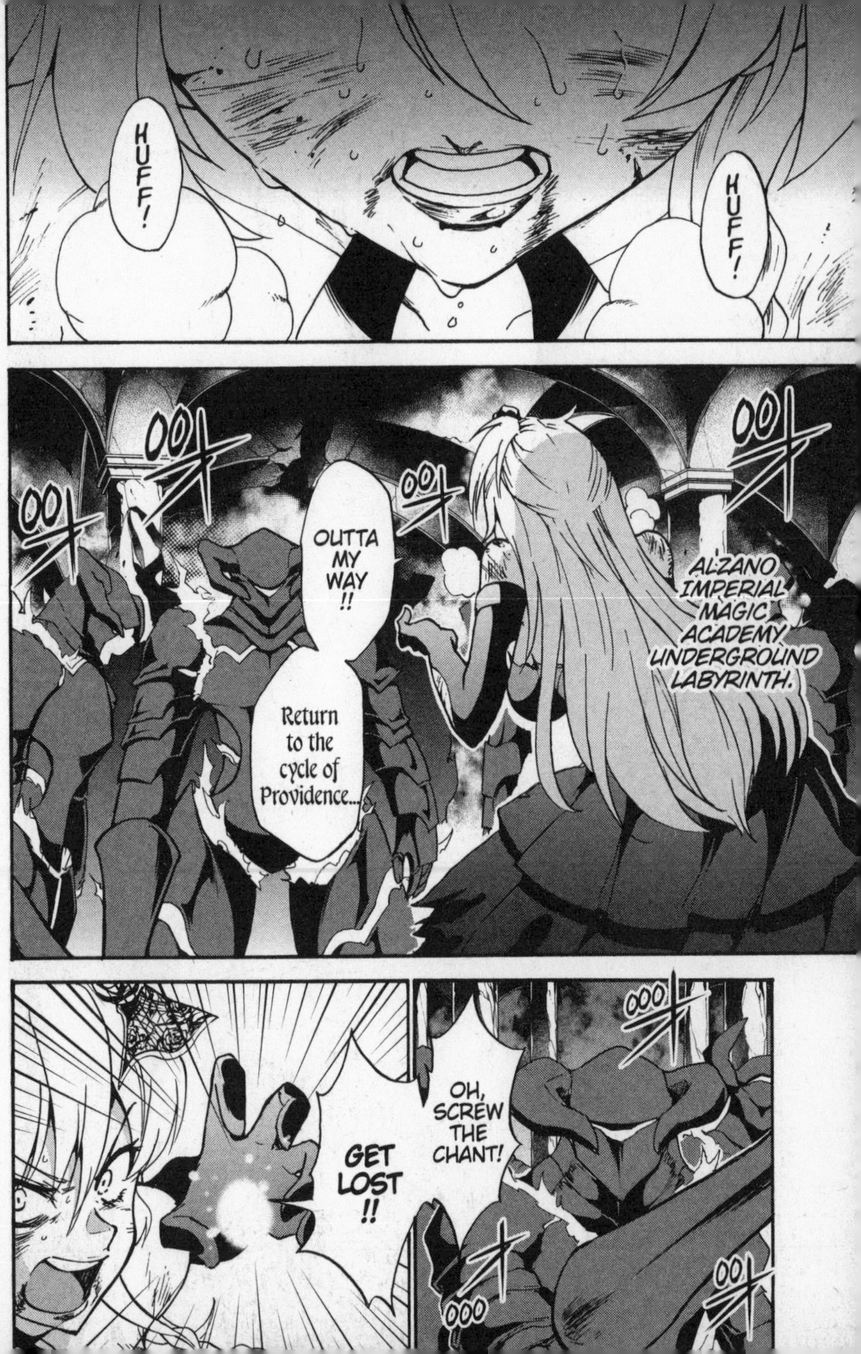
HUFF!
HUFF!
OO
ALZANO IMPERIAL MAGIC ACADEMY UNDERGROUND LABYRINTH.
OO
OUTTA MY WAY!!
Return to the cycle of Providence...
OO
OO
OOO
OH, SCREW THE CHANT!
GET LOST!!
OO
OOO

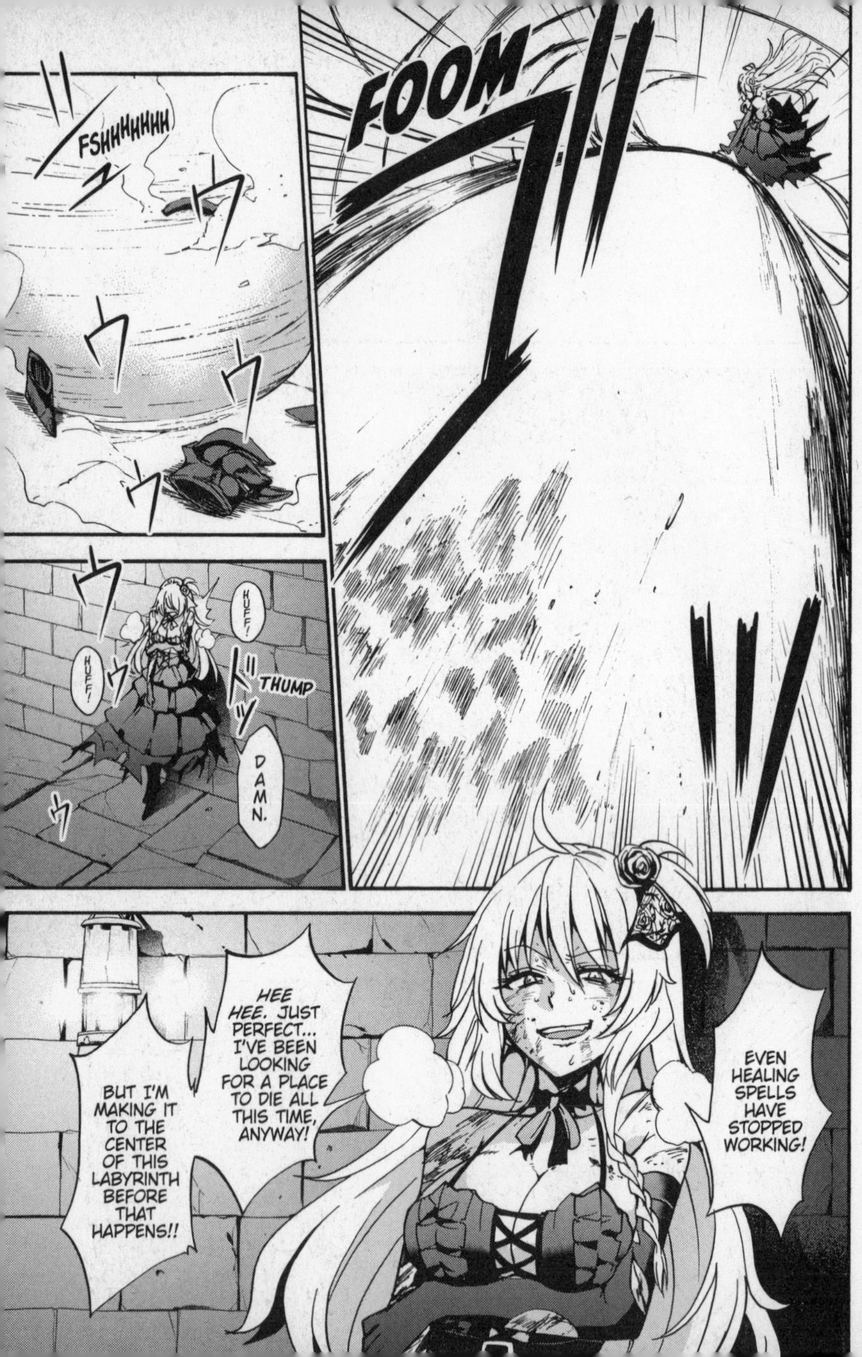

FOOM
FSHHHHHHH
HUFF!
HUFF!
THUMP
DAMN.
EVEN HEALING SPELLS HAVE STOPPED WORKING!
HEE HEE. JUST PERFECT... I'VE BEEN LOOKING FOR A PLACE TO DIE ALL THIS TIME, ANYWAY!
BUT I'M MAKING IT TO THE CENTER OF THIS LABYRINTH BEFORE THAT HAPPENS!!

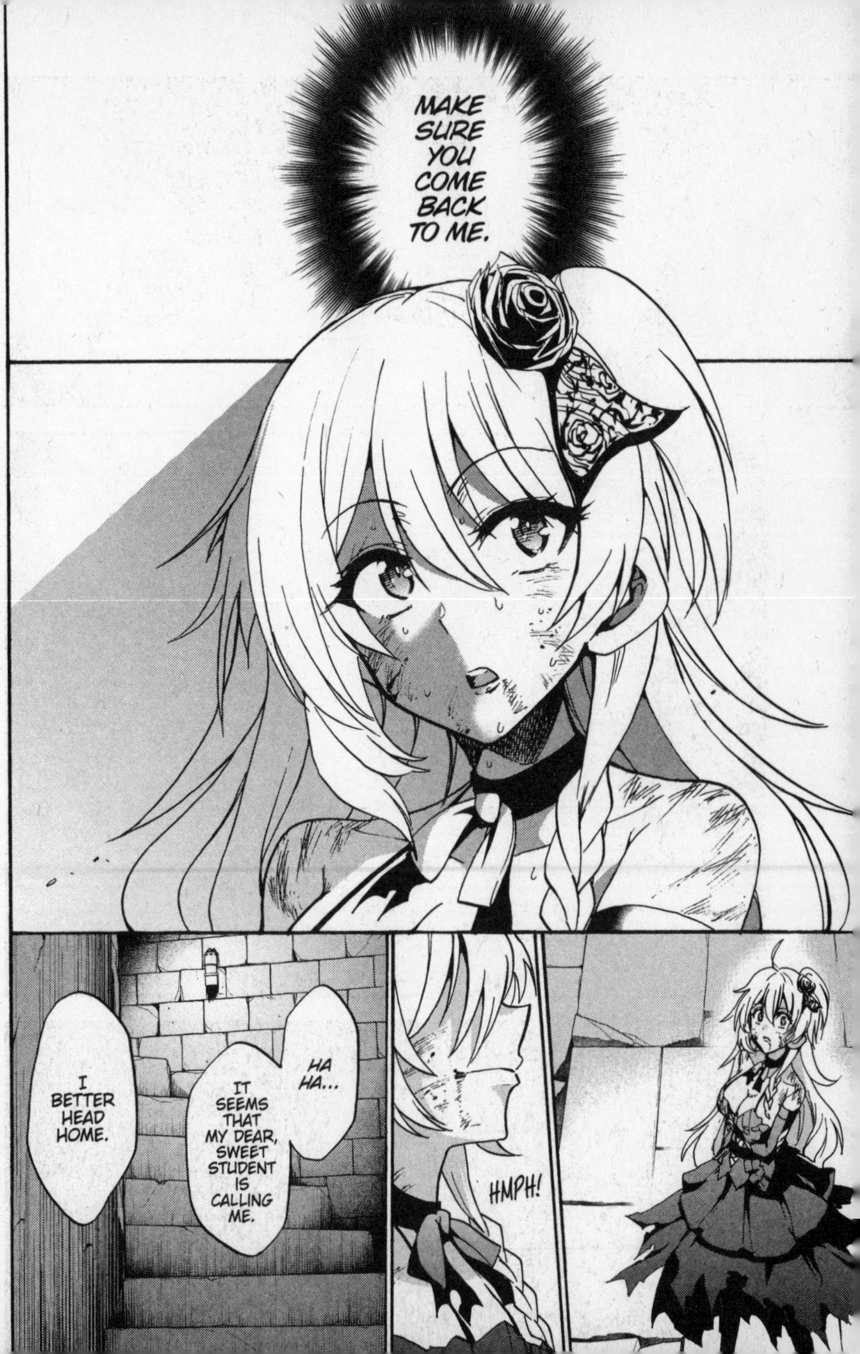
MAKE SURE YOU COME BACK TO ME.
HMPH!
HA HA...
IT SEEMS THAT MY DEAR, SWEET STUDENT IS CALLING ME.
I BETTER HEAD HOME.

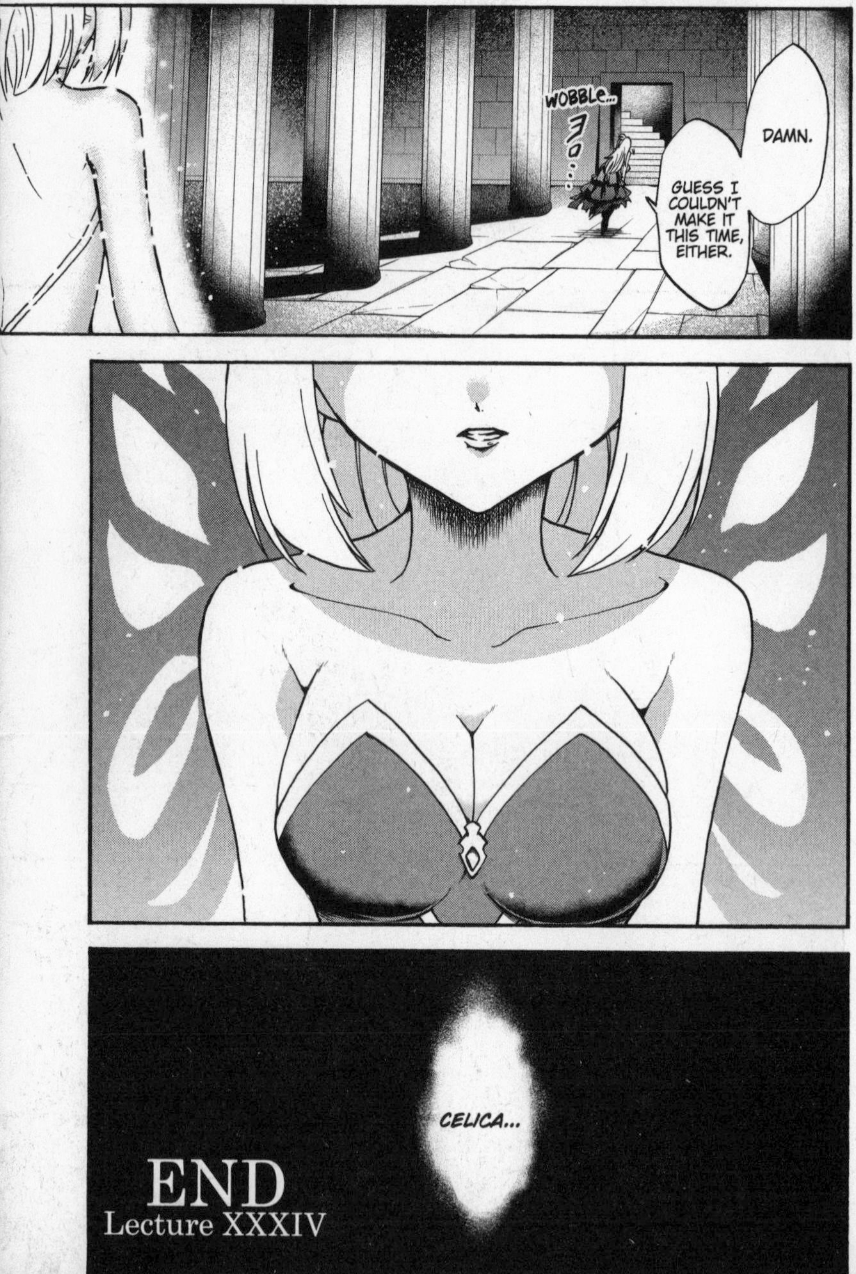
DAMN.
GUESS I COULDN'T MAKE IT THIS TIME, EITHER.
WOBBLE...
ヨロ…
CELICA...
END
Lecture XXXIV

# Akashic Records
o  f  *Bastard* Magic *Instructor*

# Lecture XXXV

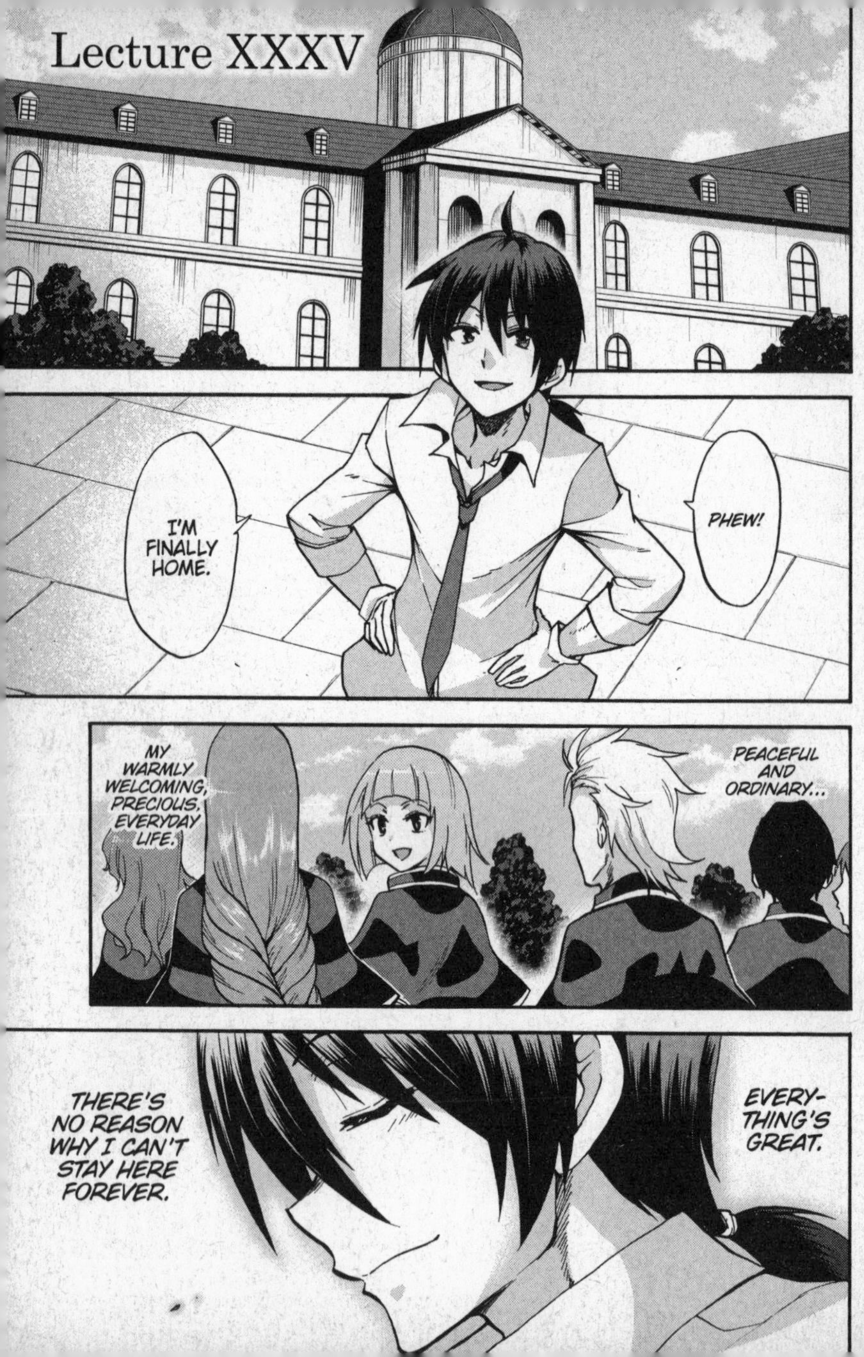
PHEW!
I'M FINALLY HOME.
PEACEFUL AND ORDINARY...
MY WARMLY WELCOMING, PRECIOUS, EVERYDAY LIFE.
EVERYTHING'S GREAT.
THERE'S NO REASON WHY I CAN'T STAY HERE FOREVER.

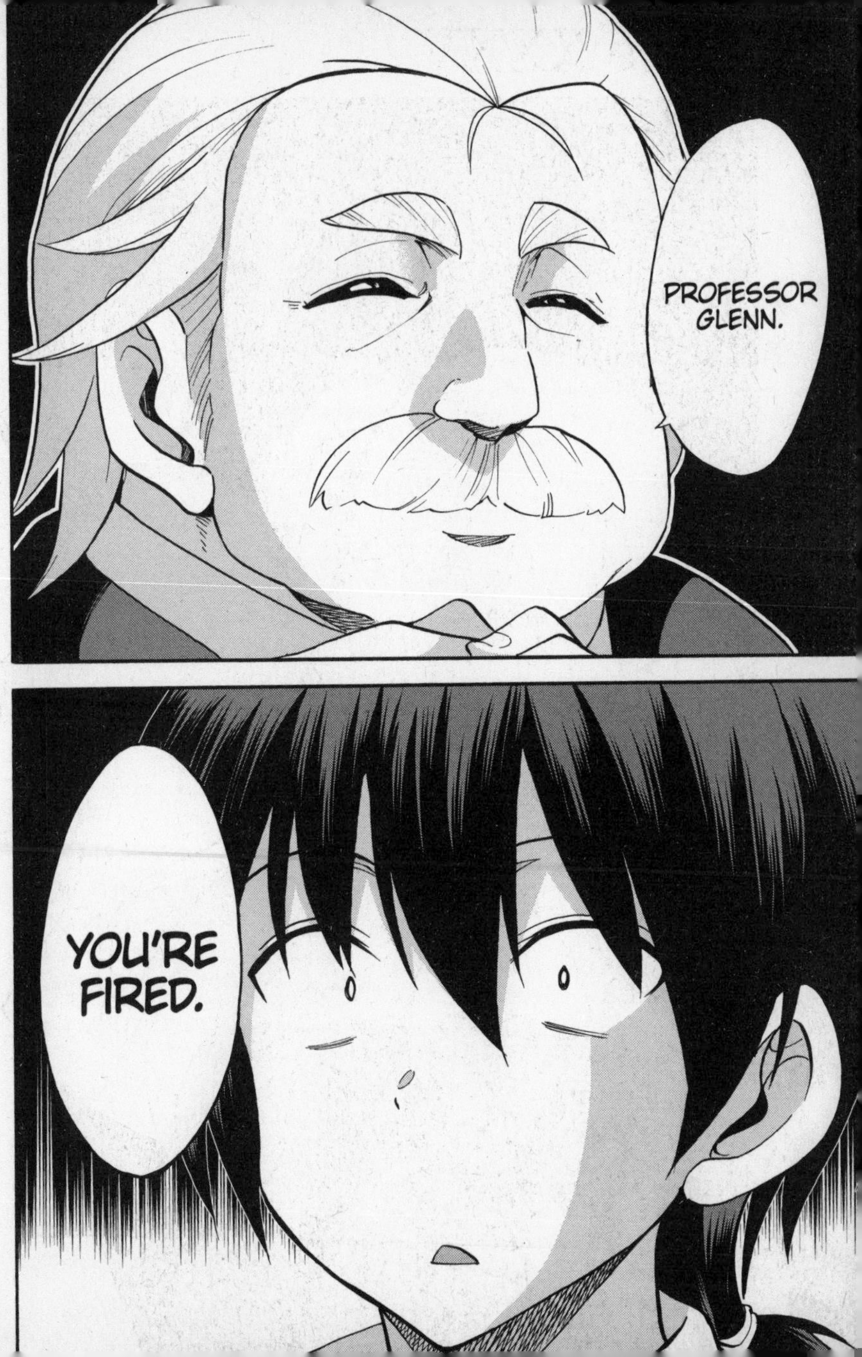
PROFESSOR GLENN.
YOU'RE FIRED.

# Lecture XXXV

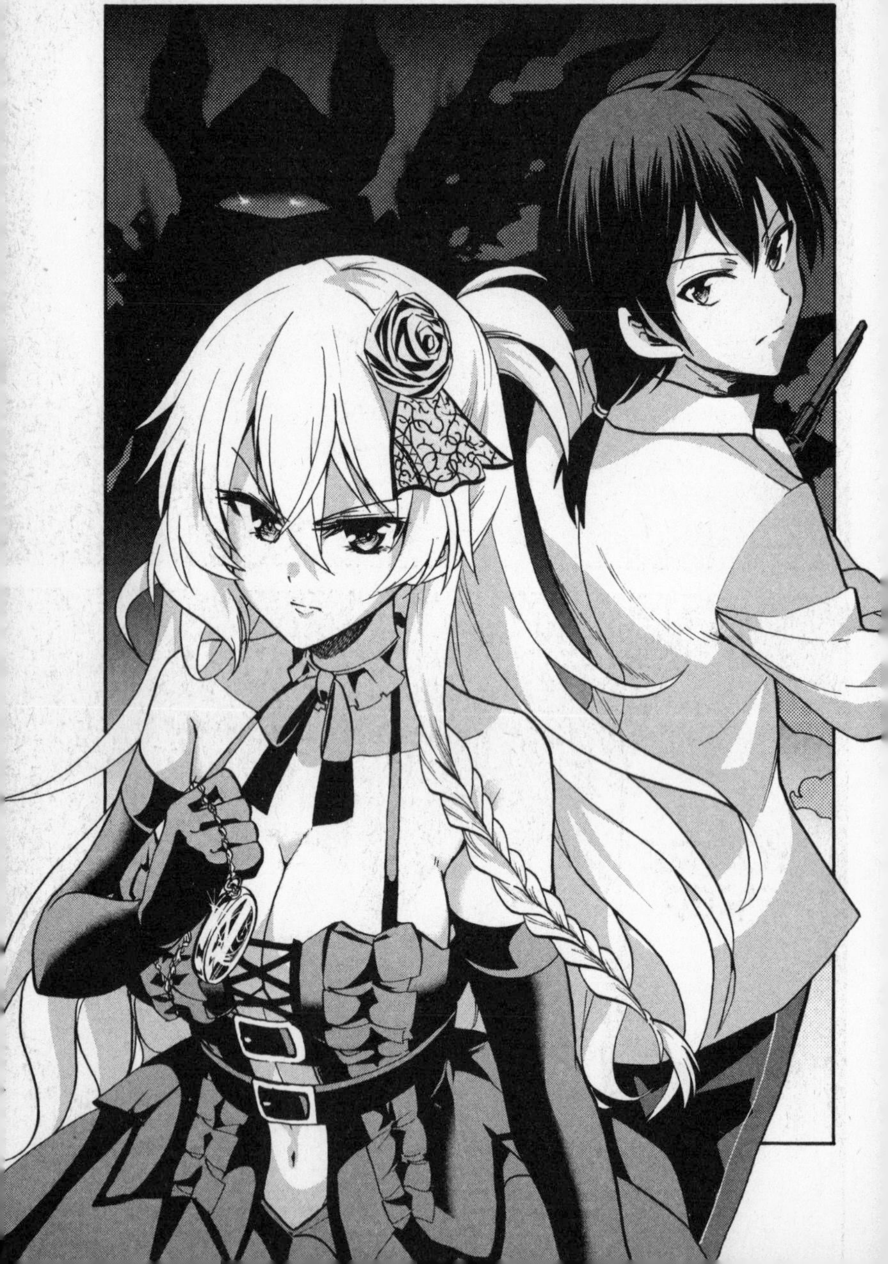

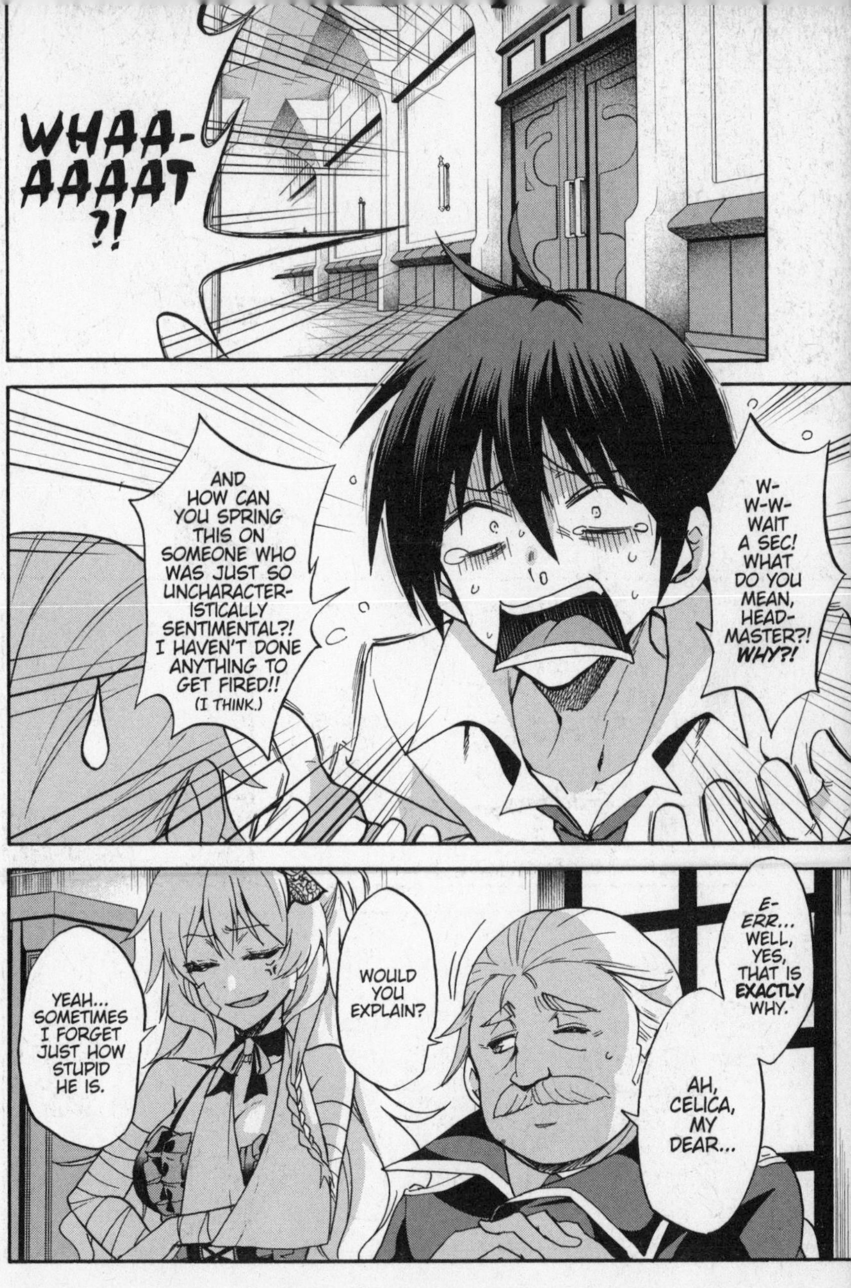
WHAA-AAAAT?!
W-W-W-WAIT A SEC! WHAT DO YOU MEAN, HEAD-MASTER?! **WHY?!**
AND HOW CAN YOU SPRING THIS ON SOMEONE WHO WAS JUST SO UNCHARACTER-ISTICALLY SENTIMENTAL?! I HAVEN'T DONE ANYTHING TO GET FIRED!! (I THINK.)
E-ERR... WELL, YES, THAT IS **EXACTLY** WHY.
AH, CELICA, MY DEAR...
WOULD YOU EXPLAIN?
YEAH... SOMETIMES I FORGET JUST HOW STUPID HE IS.

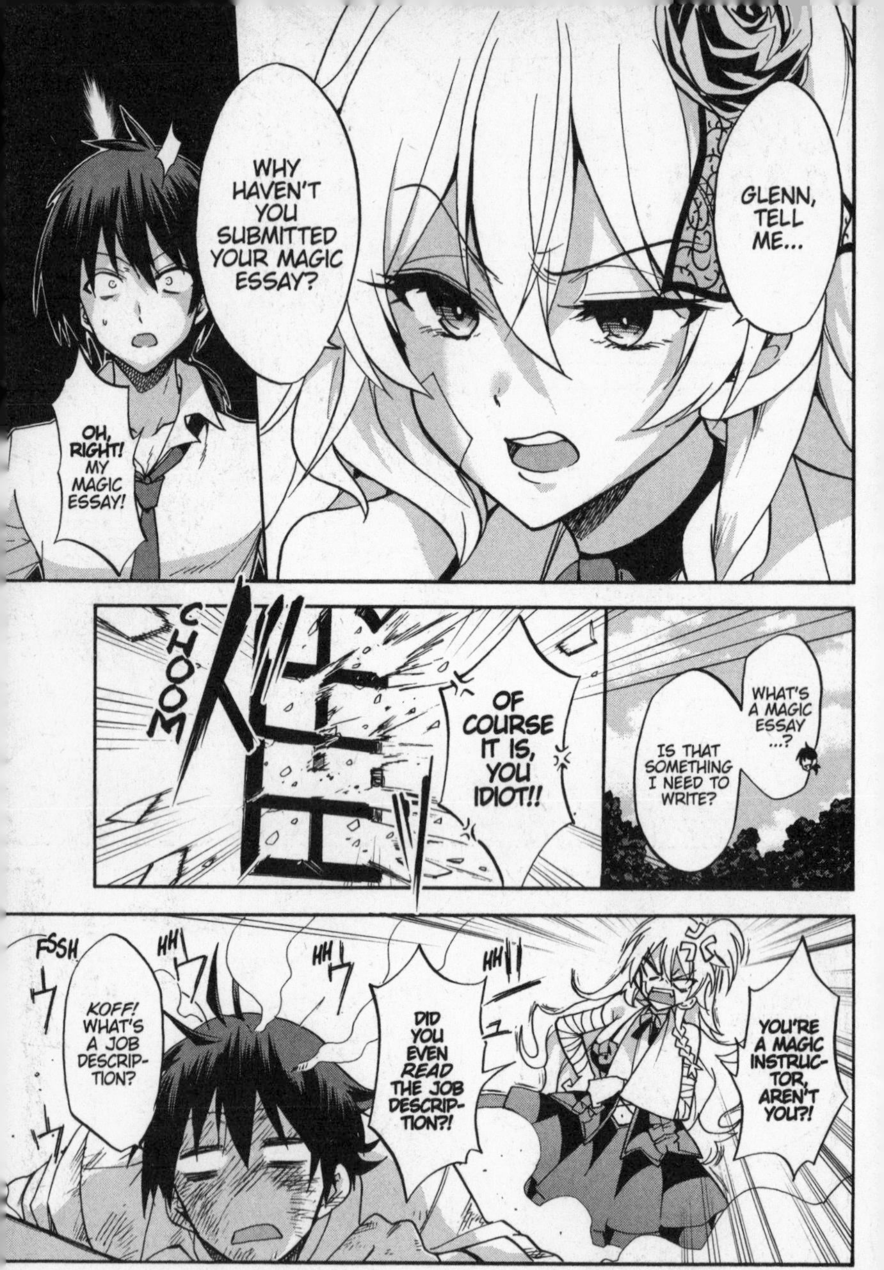
GLENN, TELL ME...
WHY HAVEN'T YOU SUBMITTED YOUR MAGIC ESSAY?
OH, RIGHT! MY MAGIC ESSAY!
WHAT'S A MAGIC ESSAY ...?
IS THAT SOMETHING I NEED TO WRITE?
OF COURSE IT IS, YOU IDIOT!!
CHOOM
YOU'RE A MAGIC INSTRUCTOR, AREN'T YOU?!
HH
DID YOU EVEN *READ* THE JOB DESCRIPTION?!
HH
HH
*KOFF!* WHAT'S A JOB DESCRIPTION?
FSSH

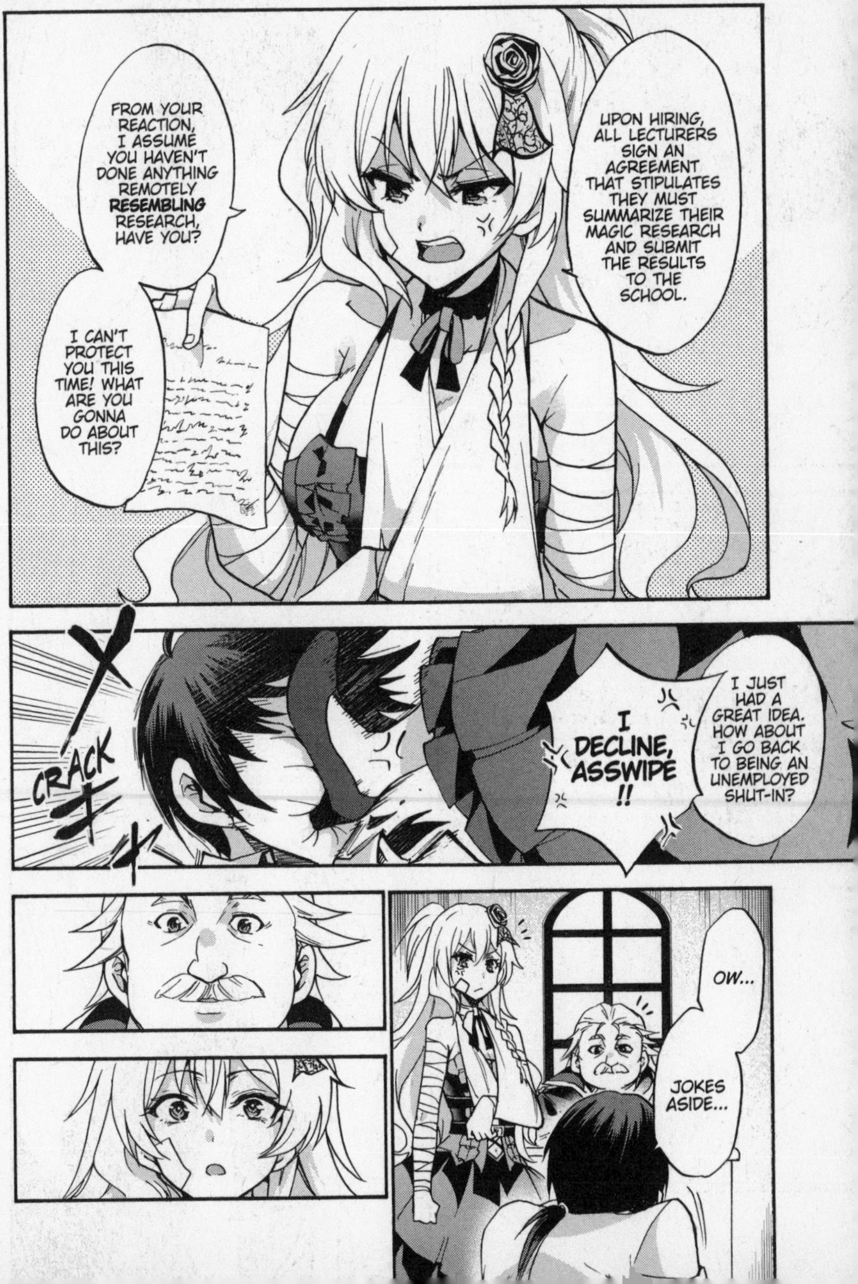
UPON HIRING, ALL LECTURERS SIGN AN AGREEMENT THAT STIPULATES THEY MUST SUMMARIZE THEIR MAGIC RESEARCH AND SUBMIT THE RESULTS TO THE SCHOOL.
FROM YOUR REACTION, I ASSUME YOU HAVEN'T DONE ANYTHING REMOTELY **RESEMBLING** RESEARCH, HAVE YOU?
I CAN'T PROTECT YOU THIS TIME! WHAT ARE YOU GONNA DO ABOUT THIS?
I JUST HAD A GREAT IDEA. HOW ABOUT I GO BACK TO BEING AN UNEMPLOYED SHUT-IN?
**I DECLINE, ASSWIPE !!**
CRACK
OW...
JOKES ASIDE...

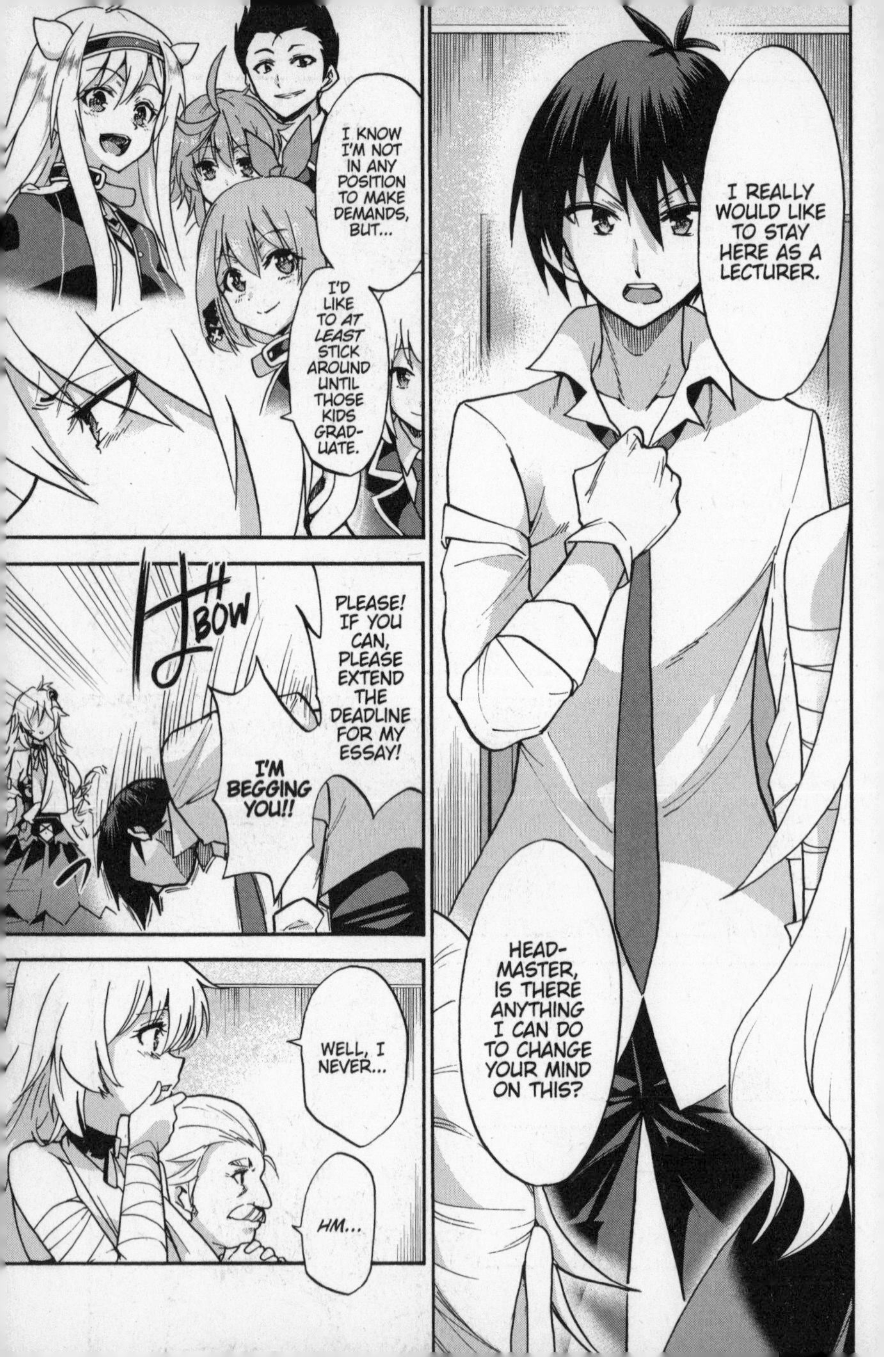

I REALLY WOULD LIKE TO STAY HERE AS A LECTURER.
HEAD-MASTER, IS THERE ANYTHING I CAN DO TO CHANGE YOUR MIND ON THIS?
I KNOW I'M NOT IN ANY POSITION TO MAKE DEMANDS, BUT...
I'D LIKE TO AT LEAST STICK AROUND UNTIL THOSE KIDS GRAD-UATE.
PLEASE! IF YOU CAN, PLEASE EXTEND THE DEADLINE FOR MY ESSAY!
BOW
I'M BEGGING YOU!!
WELL, I NEVER...
HM...

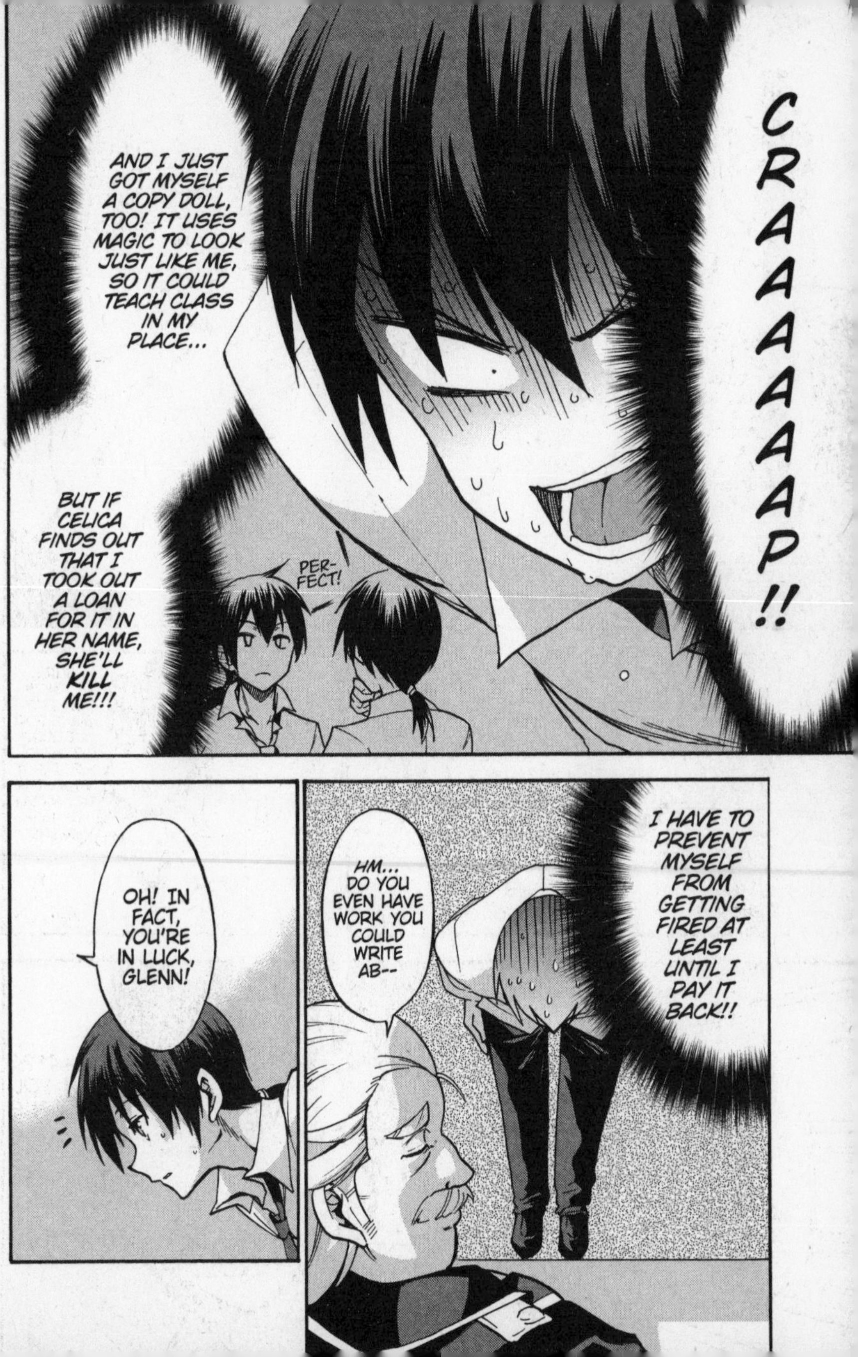
CRAAAAAAP!!
AND I JUST GOT MYSELF A COPY DOLL, TOO! IT USES MAGIC TO LOOK JUST LIKE ME, SO IT COULD TEACH CLASS IN MY PLACE...
BUT IF CELICA FINDS OUT THAT I TOOK OUT A LOAN FOR IT IN HER NAME, SHE'LL KILL ME!!!
PER-FECT!
I HAVE TO PREVENT MYSELF FROM GETTING FIRED AT LEAST UNTIL I PAY IT BACK!!
HM... DO YOU EVEN HAVE WORK YOU COULD WRITE AB--
OH! IN FACT, YOU'RE IN LUCK, GLENN!

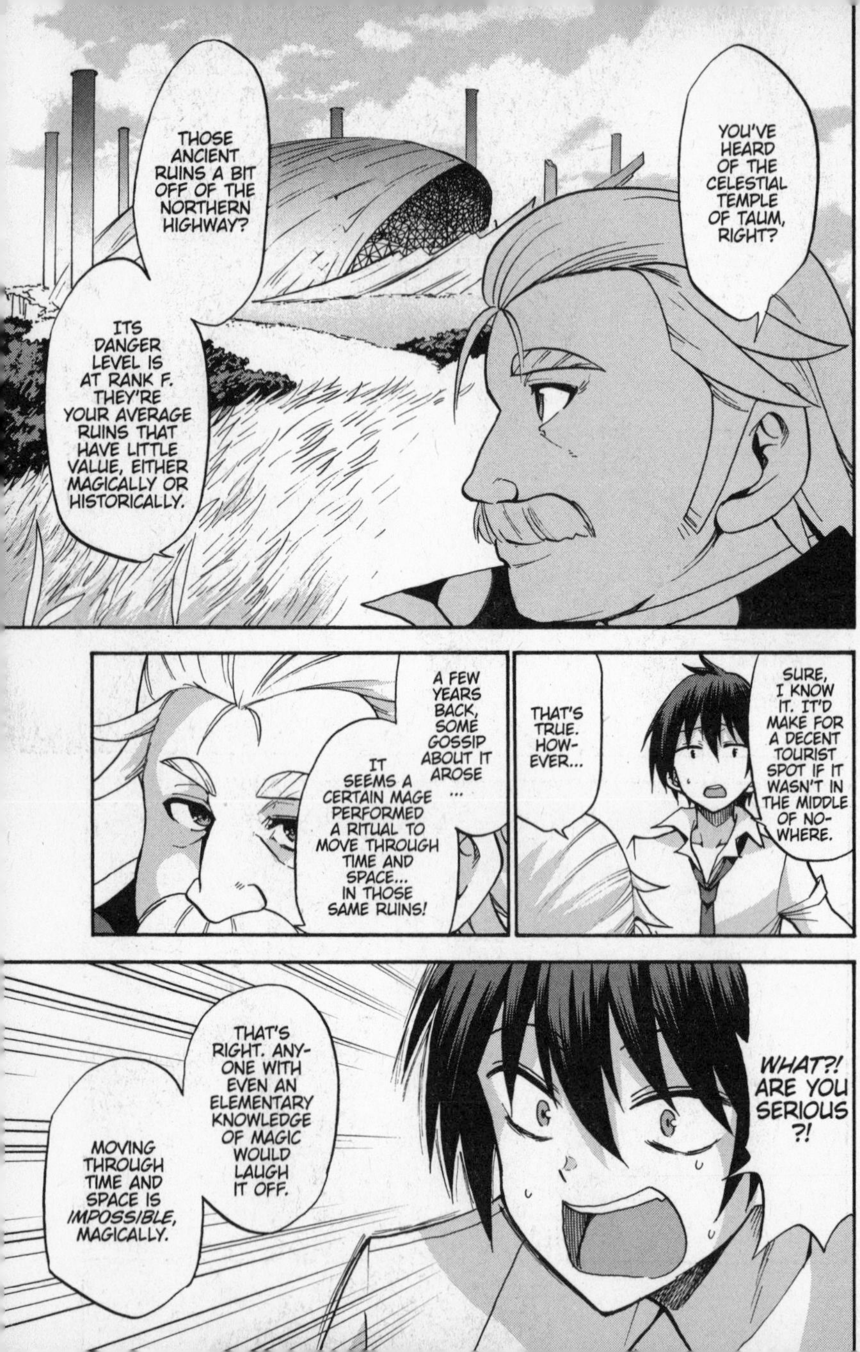
YOU'VE HEARD OF THE CELESTIAL TEMPLE OF TAUM, RIGHT?
THOSE ANCIENT RUINS A BIT OFF OF THE NORTHERN HIGHWAY?
ITS DANGER LEVEL IS AT RANK F. THEY'RE YOUR AVERAGE RUINS THAT HAVE LITTLE VALUE, EITHER MAGICALLY OR HISTORICALLY.
SURE, I KNOW IT. IT'D MAKE FOR A DECENT TOURIST SPOT IF IT WASN'T IN THE MIDDLE OF NO-WHERE.
THAT'S TRUE. HOW-EVER...
A FEW YEARS BACK, SOME GOSSIP ABOUT IT AROSE ...
IT SEEMS A CERTAIN MAGE PERFORMED A RITUAL TO MOVE THROUGH TIME AND SPACE... IN THOSE SAME RUINS!
WHAT?! ARE YOU SERIOUS ?!
THAT'S RIGHT. ANY-ONE WITH EVEN AN ELEMENTARY KNOWLEDGE OF MAGIC WOULD LAUGH IT OFF.
MOVING THROUGH TIME AND SPACE IS IMPOSSIBLE, MAGICALLY.

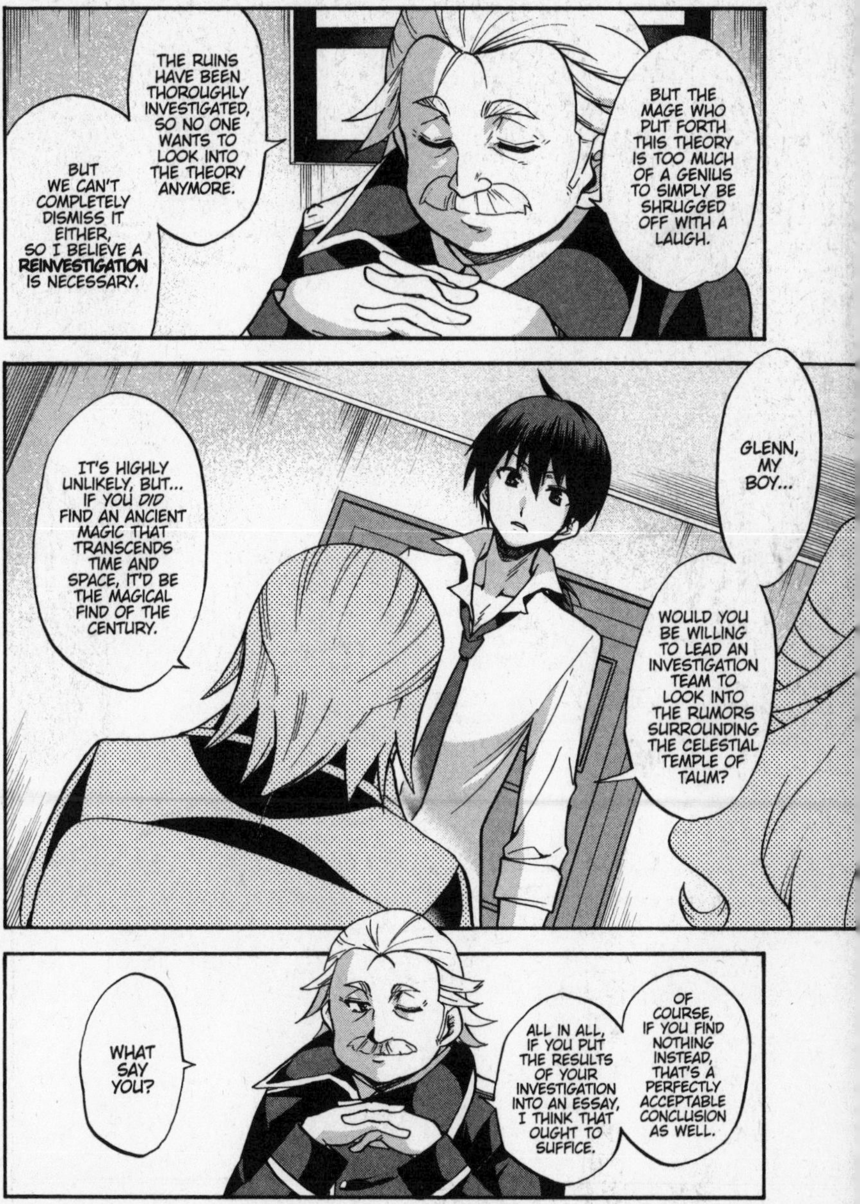
BUT THE MAGE WHO PUT FORTH THIS THEORY IS TOO MUCH OF A GENIUS TO SIMPLY BE SHRUGGED OFF WITH A LAUGH.
THE RUINS HAVE BEEN THOROUGHLY INVESTIGATED, SO NO ONE WANTS TO LOOK INTO THE THEORY ANYMORE.
BUT WE CAN'T COMPLETELY DISMISS IT EITHER, SO I BELIEVE A **REINVESTIGATION** IS NECESSARY.
GLENN, MY BOY...
WOULD YOU BE WILLING TO LEAD AN INVESTIGATION TEAM TO LOOK INTO THE RUMORS SURROUNDING THE CELESTIAL TEMPLE OF TAUM?
IT'S HIGHLY UNLIKELY, BUT... IF YOU *DID* FIND AN ANCIENT MAGIC THAT TRANSCENDS TIME AND SPACE, IT'D BE THE MAGICAL FIND OF THE CENTURY.
OF COURSE, IF YOU FIND NOTHING INSTEAD, THAT'S A PERFECTLY ACCEPTABLE CONCLUSION AS WELL.
ALL IN ALL, IF YOU PUT THE RESULTS OF YOUR INVESTIGATION INTO AN ESSAY, I THINK THAT OUGHT TO SUFFICE.
WHAT SAY YOU?

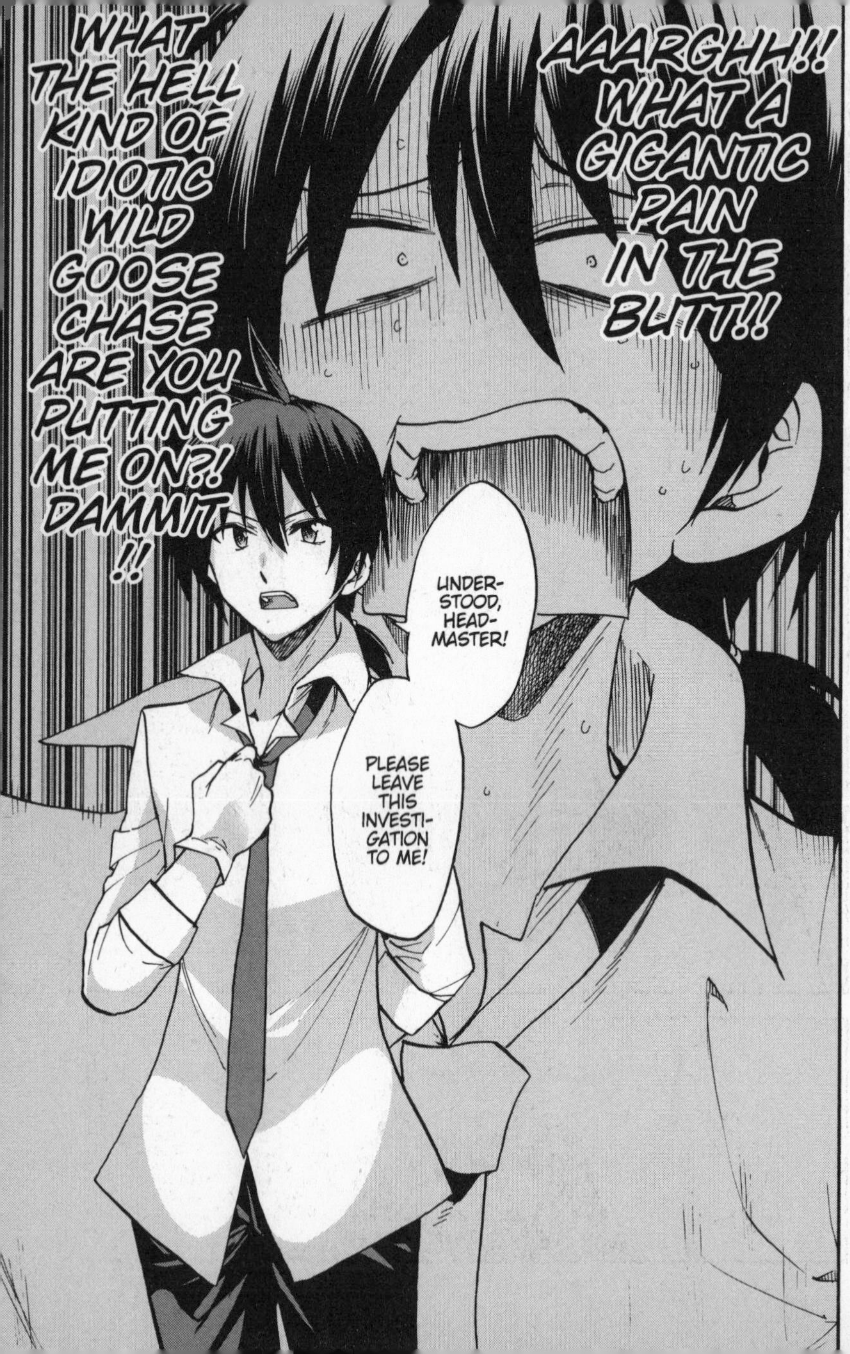
AAARGHH!! WHAT A GIGANTIC PAIN IN THE BUTT!!
WHAT THE HELL KIND OF IDIOTIC WILD GOOSE CHASE ARE YOU PUTTING ME ON?! DAMMIT!!
UNDER-STOOD, HEAD-MASTER!
PLEASE LEAVE THIS INVESTI-GATION TO ME!

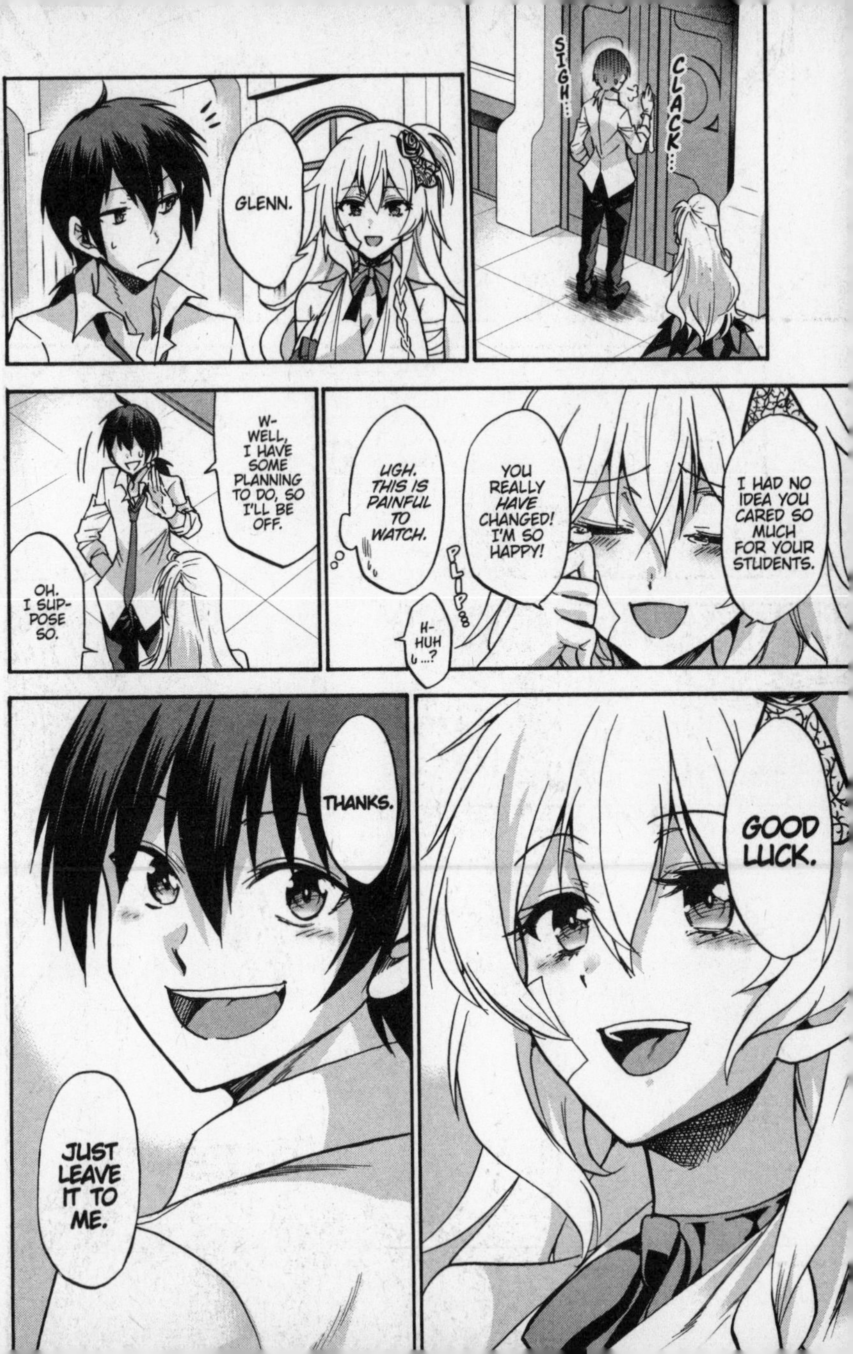
CLACK...
SIGH...
GLENN.
I HAD NO IDEA YOU CARED SO MUCH FOR YOUR STUDENTS.
YOU REALLY HAVE CHANGED! I'M SO HAPPY!
PLIP
UGH. THIS IS PAINFUL TO WATCH.
H-HUH...?
W-WELL, I HAVE SOME PLANNING TO DO, SO I'LL BE OFF.
OH. I SUPPOSE SO.
GOOD LUCK.
THANKS.
JUST LEAVE IT TO ME.

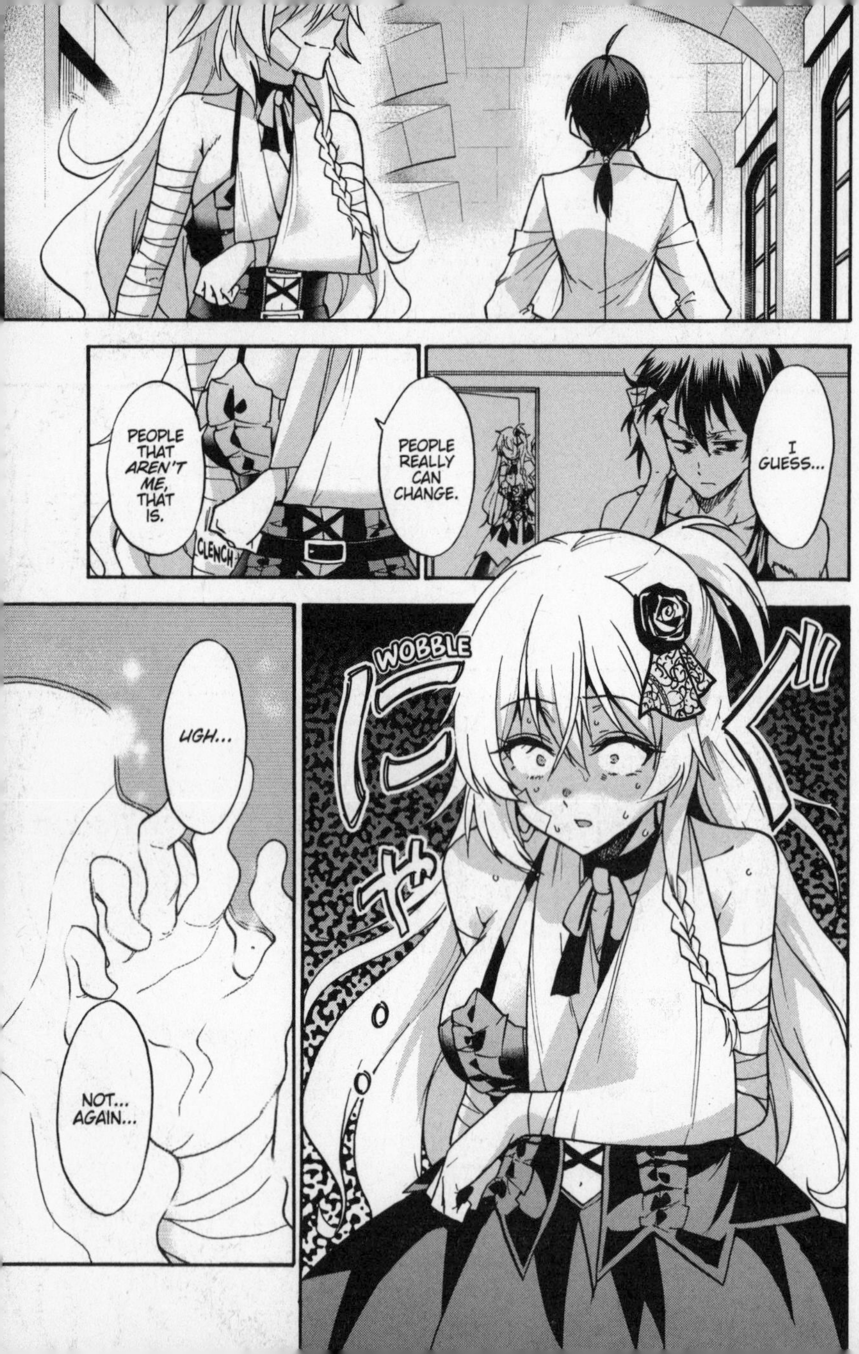
I GUESS...
PEOPLE REALLY CAN CHANGE.
PEOPLE THAT AREN'T ME, THAT IS.
CLENCH
WOBBLE
UGH...
NOT... AGAIN...

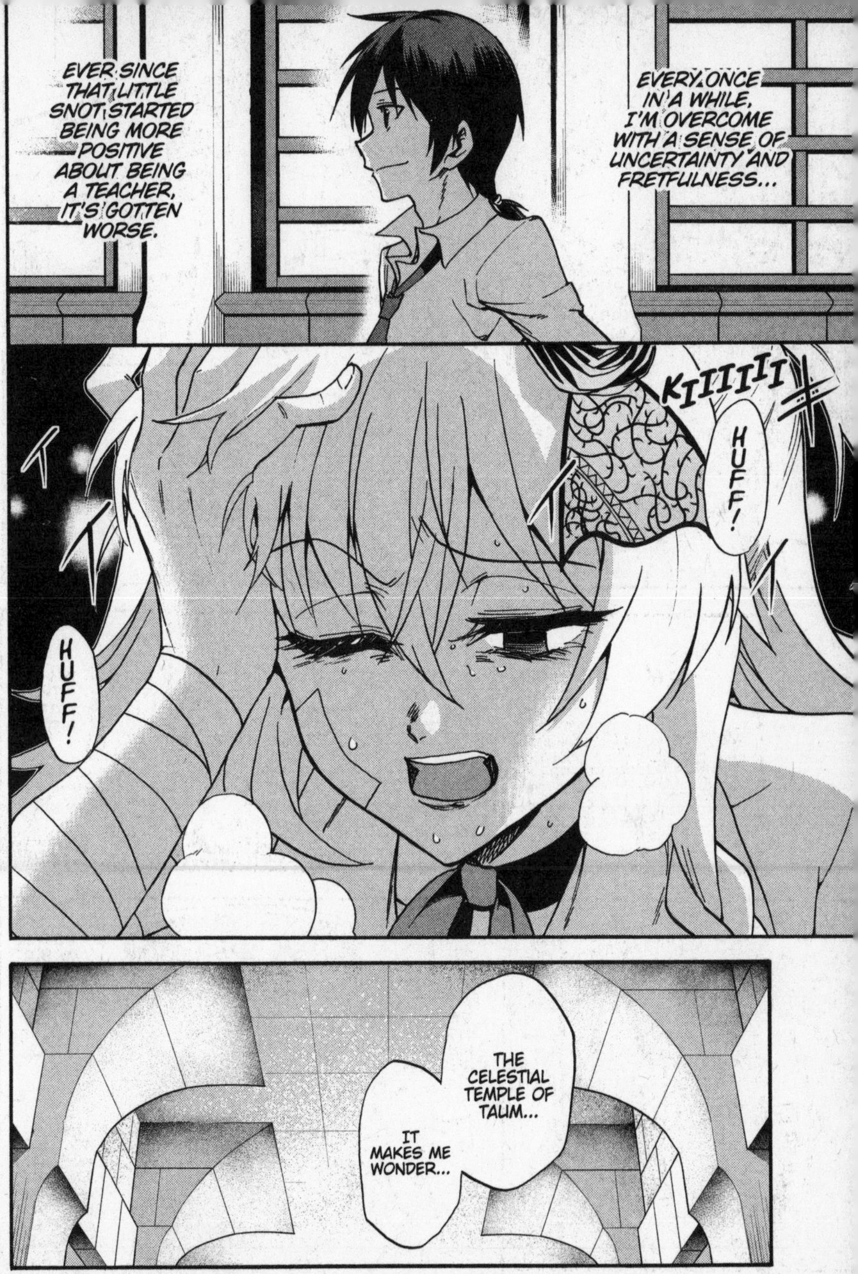
EVERY ONCE IN A WHILE, I'M OVERCOME WITH A SENSE OF UNCERTAINTY AND FRETFULNESS...
EVER SINCE THAT LITTLE SNOT STARTED BEING MORE POSITIVE ABOUT BEING A TEACHER, IT'S GOTTEN WORSE.
KIIIIII
HUFF!
HUFF!
THE CELESTIAL TEMPLE OF TAUM...
IT MAKES ME WONDER...

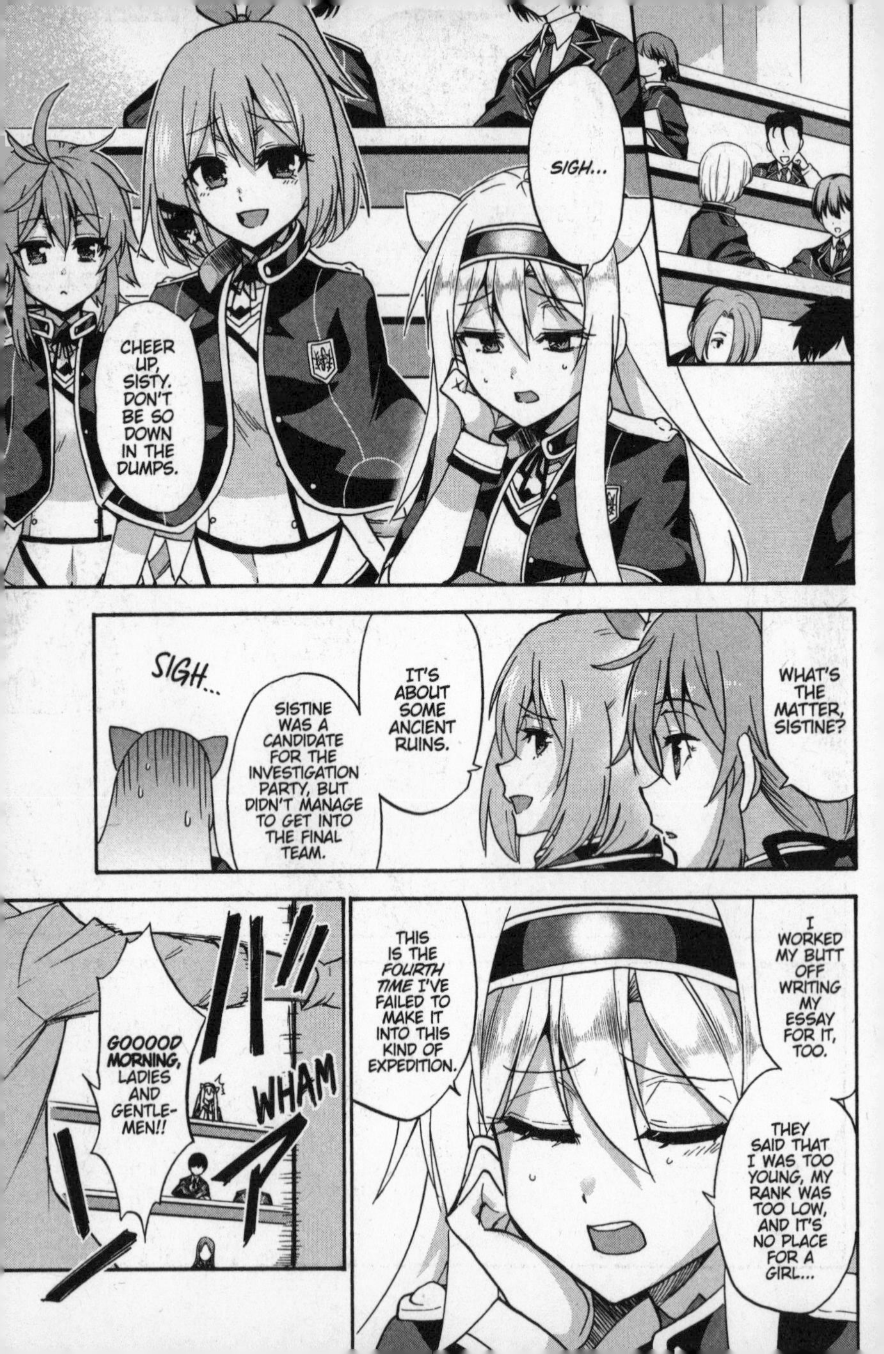
SIGH...
CHEER UP, SISTY. DON'T BE SO DOWN IN THE DUMPS.
WHAT'S THE MATTER, SISTINE?
IT'S ABOUT SOME ANCIENT RUINS.
SISTINE WAS A CANDIDATE FOR THE INVESTIGATION PARTY, BUT DIDN'T MANAGE TO GET INTO THE FINAL TEAM.
SIGH...
I WORKED MY BUTT OFF WRITING MY ESSAY FOR IT, TOO.
THIS IS THE *FOURTH TIME* I'VE FAILED TO MAKE IT INTO THIS KIND OF EXPEDITION.
THEY SAID THAT I WAS TOO YOUNG, MY RANK WAS TOO LOW, AND IT'S NO PLACE FOR A GIRL...
GOOOOD MORNING, LADIES AND GENTLE-MEN!!
WHAM

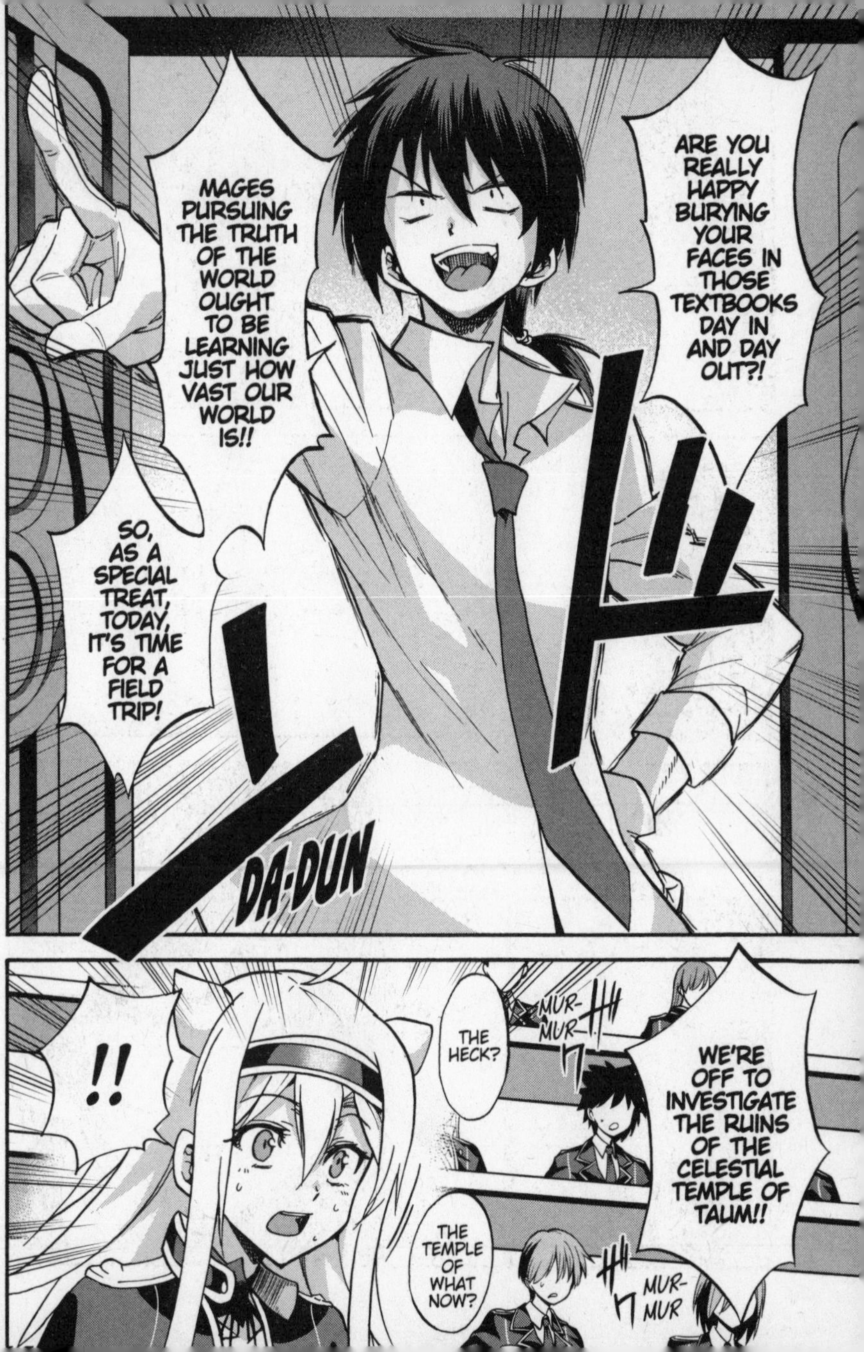

ARE YOU REALLY HAPPY BURYING YOUR FACES IN THOSE TEXTBOOKS DAY IN AND DAY OUT?!
MAGES PURSUING THE TRUTH OF THE WORLD OUGHT TO BE LEARNING JUST HOW VAST OUR WORLD IS!!
SO, AS A SPECIAL TREAT, TODAY, IT'S TIME FOR A FIELD TRIP!
DA-DUN
WE'RE OFF TO INVESTIGATE THE RUINS OF THE CELESTIAL TEMPLE OF TAUM!!
MUR-MUR
THE HECK?
!!
THE TEMPLE OF WHAT NOW?
MUR-MUR

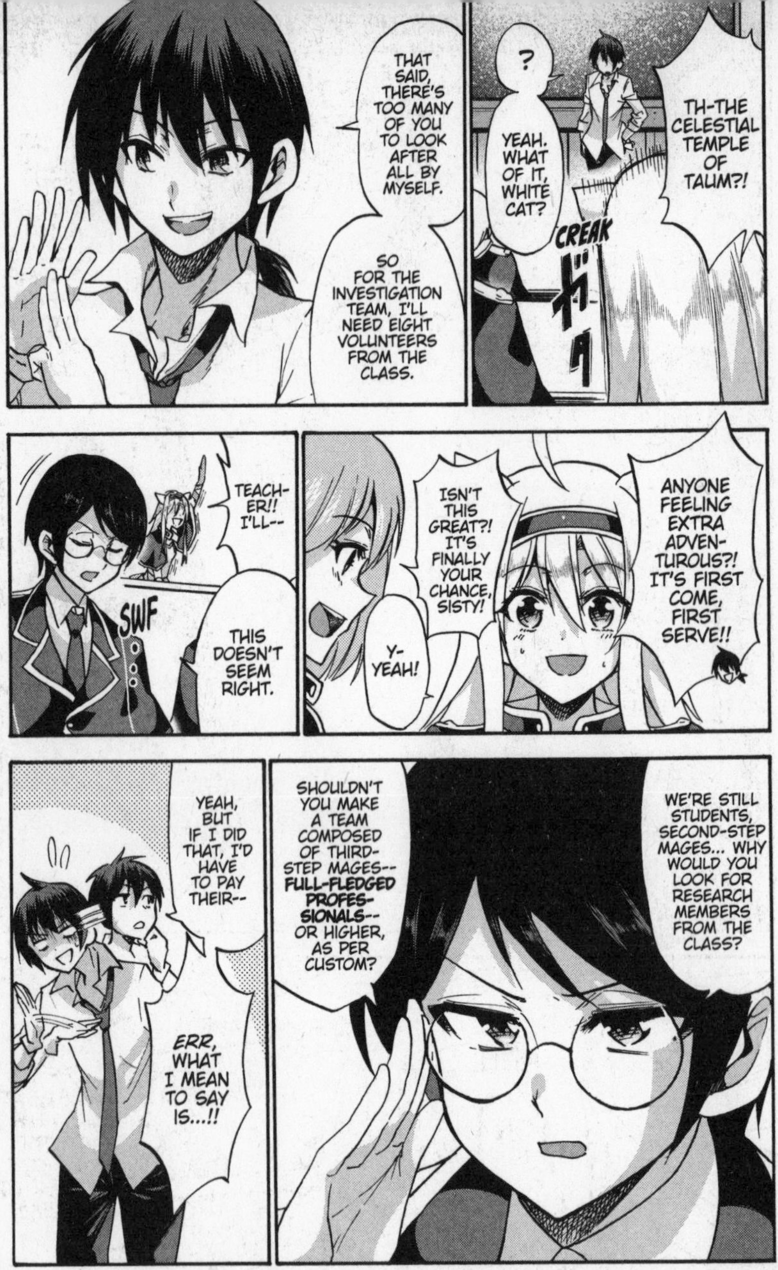
TH-THE CELESTIAL TEMPLE OF TAUM?!
?
YEAH. WHAT OF IT, WHITE CAT?
CREAK
THAT SAID, THERE'S TOO MANY OF YOU TO LOOK AFTER ALL BY MYSELF.
SO FOR THE INVESTIGATION TEAM, I'LL NEED EIGHT VOLUNTEERS FROM THE CLASS.
ANYONE FEELING EXTRA ADVENTUROUS?! IT'S FIRST COME, FIRST SERVE!!
ISN'T THIS GREAT?! IT'S FINALLY YOUR CHANCE, SISTY!
Y-YEAH!
TEACHER!! I'LL--
SWF
THIS DOESN'T SEEM RIGHT.
WE'RE STILL STUDENTS, SECOND-STEP MAGES... WHY WOULD YOU LOOK FOR RESEARCH MEMBERS FROM THE CLASS?
SHOULDN'T YOU MAKE A TEAM COMPOSED OF THIRD-STEP MAGES-- **FULL-FLEDGED PROFESSIONALS**-- OR HIGHER, AS PER CUSTOM?
YEAH, BUT IF I DID THAT, I'D HAVE TO PAY THEIR--
*ERR, WHAT I MEAN TO SAY IS...!!*

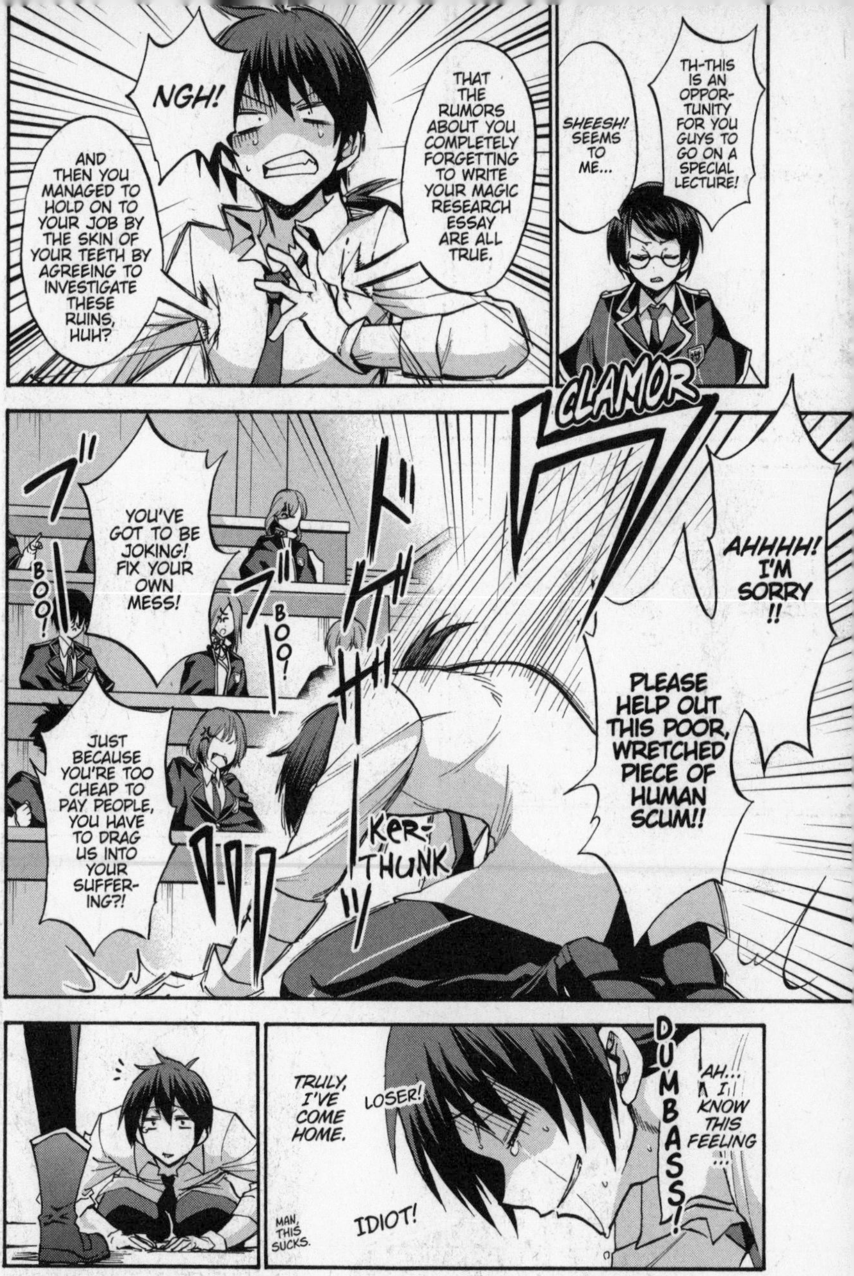
TH-THIS IS AN OPPOR-TUNITY FOR YOU GUYS TO GO ON A SPECIAL LECTURE!
SHEESH! SEEMS TO ME...
THAT THE RUMORS ABOUT YOU COMPLETELY FORGETTING TO WRITE YOUR MAGIC RESEARCH ESSAY ARE ALL TRUE.
NGH!
AND THEN YOU MANAGED TO HOLD ON TO YOUR JOB BY THE SKIN OF YOUR TEETH BY AGREEING TO INVESTIGATE THESE RUINS, HUH?
CLAMOR
AHHHH! I'M SORRY!!
PLEASE HELP OUT THIS POOR, WRETCHED PIECE OF HUMAN SCUM!!
KER-THUNK
YOU'VE GOT TO BE JOKING! FIX YOUR OWN MESS!
BOO!
BOO!
JUST BECAUSE YOU'RE TOO CHEAP TO PAY PEOPLE, YOU HAVE TO DRAG US INTO YOUR SUFFER-ING?!
DUMBASS!
AH... I KNOW THIS FEELING...
LOSER!
TRULY, I'VE COME HOME.
IDIOT!
MAN, THIS SUCKS.

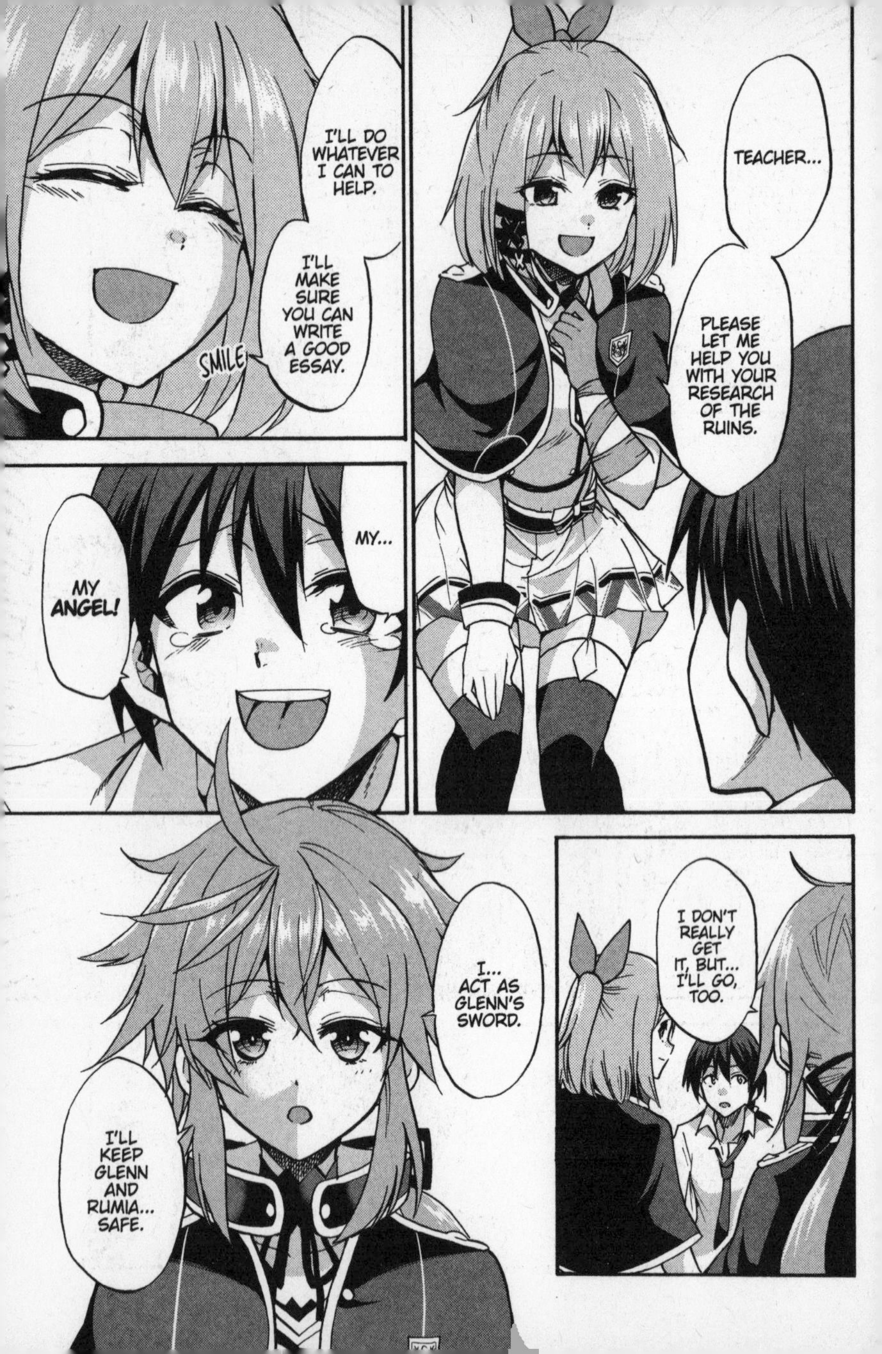
TEACHER...
PLEASE LET ME HELP YOU WITH YOUR RESEARCH OF THE RUINS.
I'LL DO WHATEVER I CAN TO HELP.
I'LL MAKE SURE YOU CAN WRITE A GOOD ESSAY.
SMILE
MY...
MY ANGEL!
I DON'T REALLY GET IT, BUT... I'LL GO, TOO.
I... ACT AS GLENN'S SWORD.
I'LL KEEP GLENN AND RUMIA... SAFE.

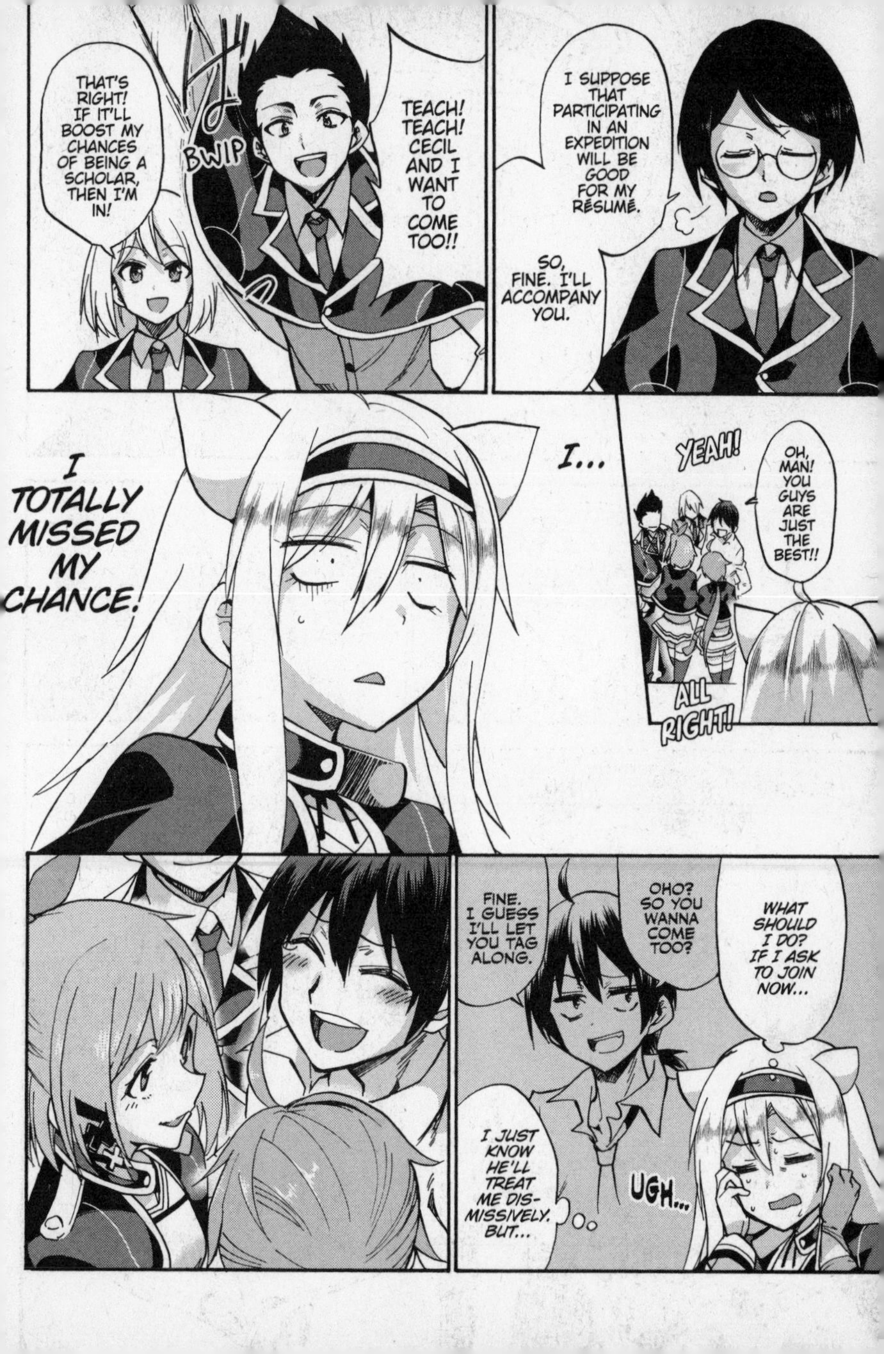
I SUPPOSE THAT PARTICIPATING IN AN EXPEDITION WILL BE GOOD FOR MY RÉSUMÉ.
SO, FINE. I'LL ACCOMPANY YOU.
TEACH! TEACH! CECIL AND I WANT TO COME TOO!!
BWIP
THAT'S RIGHT! IF IT'LL BOOST MY CHANCES OF BEING A SCHOLAR, THEN I'M IN!
YEAH!
OH, MAN! YOU GUYS ARE JUST THE BEST!!
ALL RIGHT!
I...
I TOTALLY MISSED MY CHANCE.
WHAT SHOULD I DO? IF I ASK TO JOIN NOW...
OHO? SO YOU WANNA COME TOO?
FINE. I GUESS I'LL LET YOU TAG ALONG.
I JUST KNOW HE'LL TREAT ME DIS-MISSIVELY. BUT...
UGH...

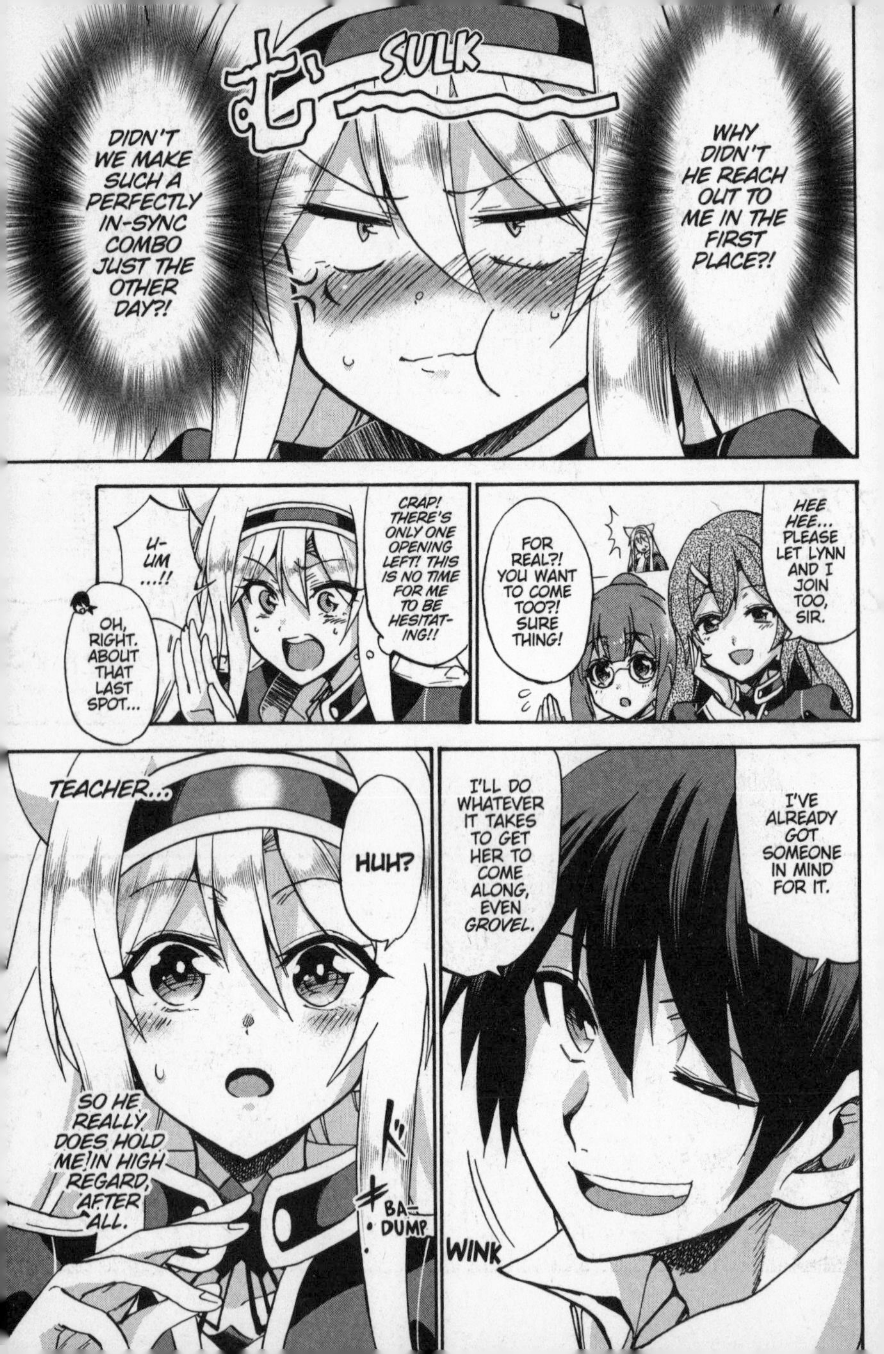
SULK
WHY DIDN'T HE REACH OUT TO ME IN THE FIRST PLACE?!
DIDN'T WE MAKE SUCH A PERFECTLY IN-SYNC COMBO JUST THE OTHER DAY?!
HEE HEE... PLEASE LET LYNN AND I JOIN TOO, SIR.
FOR REAL?! YOU WANT TO COME TOO?! SURE THING!
CRAP! THERE'S ONLY ONE OPENING LEFT! THIS IS NO TIME FOR ME TO BE HESITATING!!
U-UM ...!!
OH, RIGHT. ABOUT THAT LAST SPOT...
I'VE ALREADY GOT SOMEONE IN MIND FOR IT.
I'LL DO WHATEVER IT TAKES TO GET HER TO COME ALONG, EVEN GROVEL.
WINK
HUH?
TEACHER...
SO HE REALLY DOES HOLD ME IN HIGH REGARD, AFTER ALL.
BA-DUMP

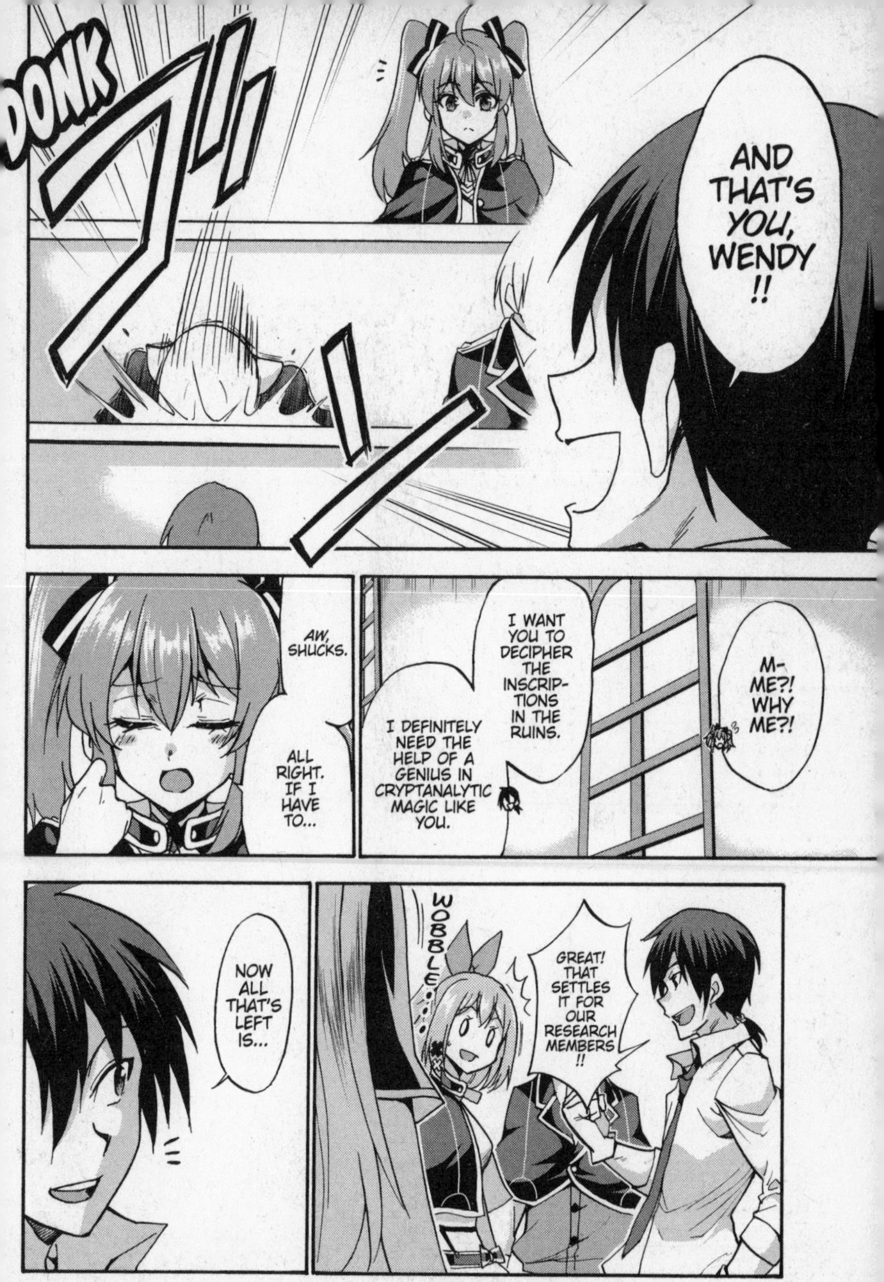
AND THAT'S YOU, WENDY!!
DONK
M-ME?! WHY ME?!
I WANT YOU TO DECIPHER THE INSCRIPTIONS IN THE RUINS.
I DEFINITELY NEED THE HELP OF A GENIUS IN CRYPTANALYTIC MAGIC LIKE YOU.
AW, SHUCKS.
ALL RIGHT. IF I HAVE TO...
GREAT! THAT SETTLES IT FOR OUR RESEARCH MEMBERS!!
WOBBLE
NOW ALL THAT'S LEFT IS...

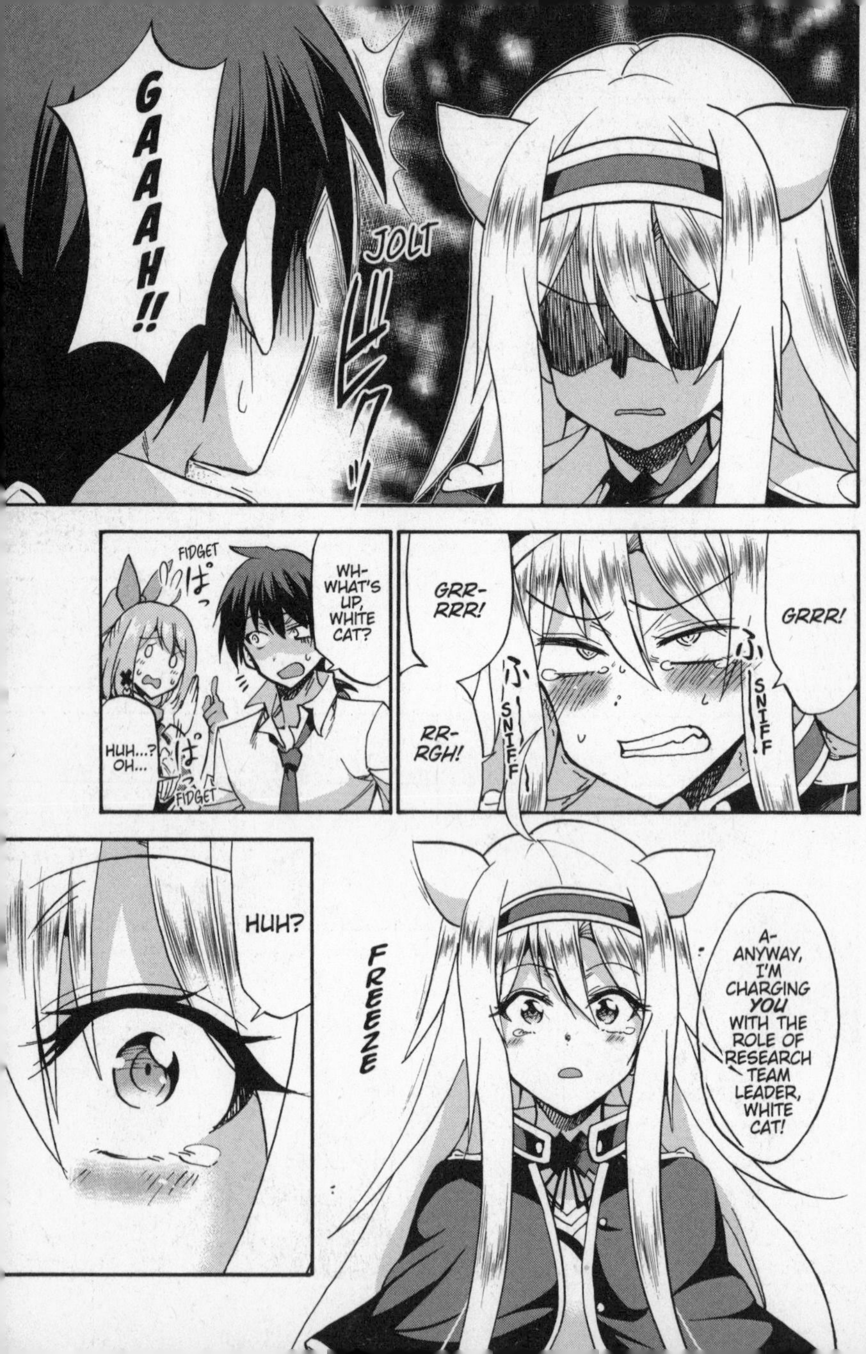
GAAAAH!!
JOLT
GRRR!
SNIFF
GRR-RRR!
SNIFF
RR-RGH!
WH-WHAT'S UP, WHITE CAT?
FIDGET
HUH...? OH...
FIDGET
A-ANYWAY, I'M CHARGING *YOU* WITH THE ROLE OF RESEARCH TEAM LEADER, WHITE CAT!
FREEZE
HUH?

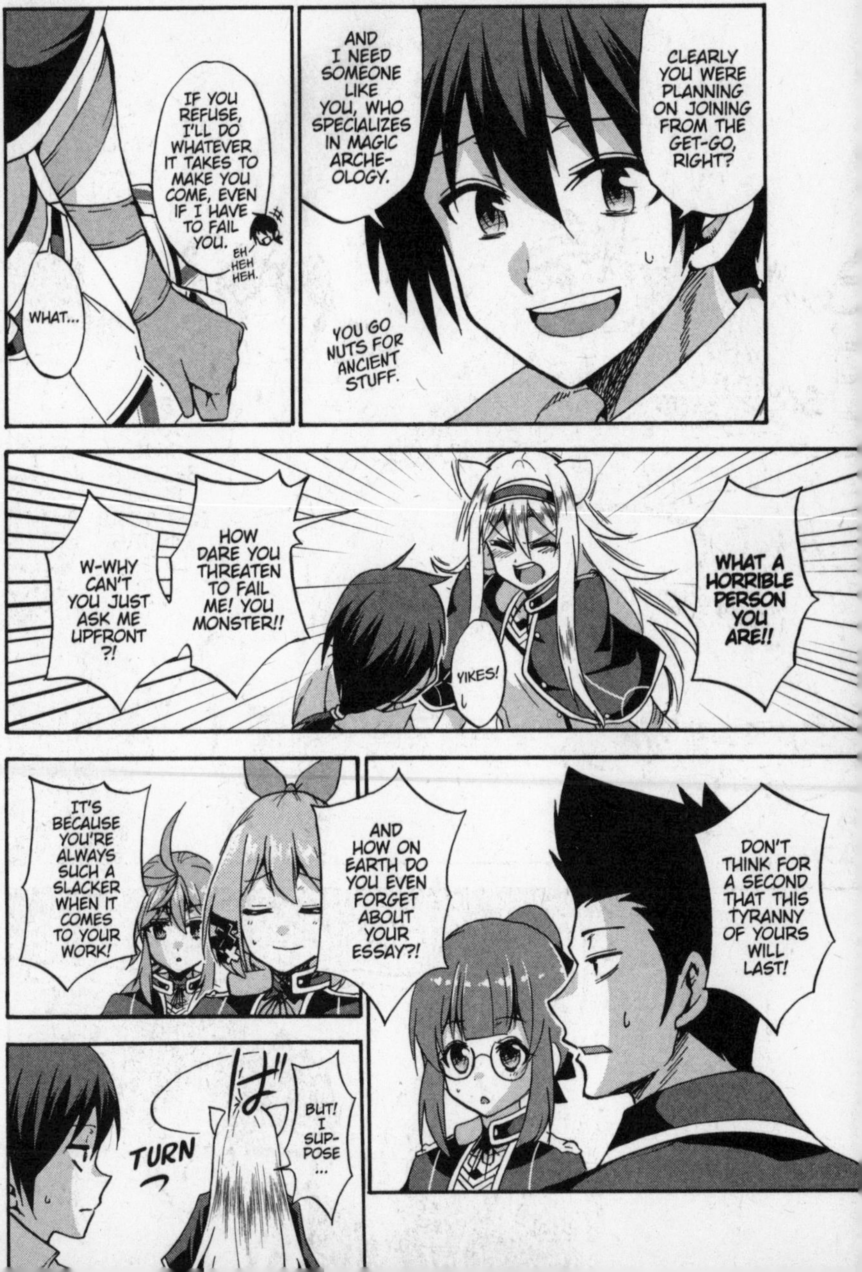

CLEARLY YOU WERE PLANNING ON JOINING FROM THE GET-GO, RIGHT?
AND I NEED SOMEONE LIKE YOU, WHO SPECIALIZES IN MAGIC ARCHE-OLOGY.
YOU GO NUTS FOR ANCIENT STUFF.
IF YOU REFUSE, I'LL DO WHATEVER IT TAKES TO MAKE YOU COME, EVEN IF I HAVE TO FAIL YOU.
EH HEH HEH.
WHAT...
WHAT A HORRIBLE PERSON YOU ARE!!
YIKES!
HOW DARE YOU THREATEN TO FAIL ME! YOU MONSTER!!
W-WHY CAN'T YOU JUST ASK ME UPFRONT?!
DON'T THINK FOR A SECOND THAT THIS TYRANNY OF YOURS WILL LAST!
AND HOW ON EARTH DO YOU EVEN FORGET ABOUT YOUR ESSAY?!
IT'S BECAUSE YOU'RE ALWAYS SUCH A SLACKER WHEN IT COMES TO YOUR WORK!
ば
BUT! I SUP-POSE...
TURN

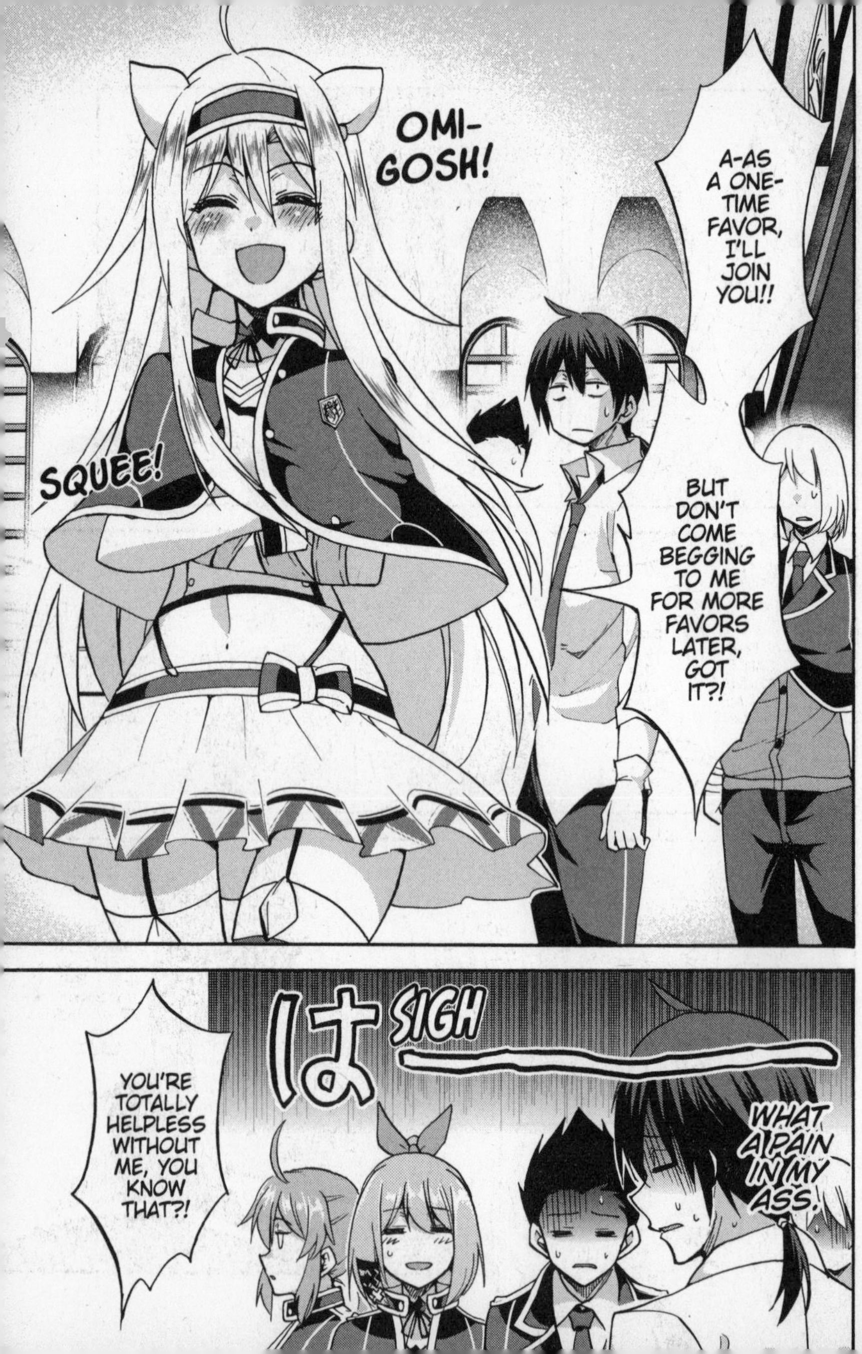
A-AS A ONE-TIME FAVOR, I'LL JOIN YOU!!
BUT DON'T COME BEGGING TO ME FOR MORE FAVORS LATER, GOT IT?!
OMI-GOSH!
SQUEE!
は SIGH
WHAT A PAIN IN MY ASS.
YOU'RE TOTALLY HELPLESS WITHOUT ME, YOU KNOW THAT?!

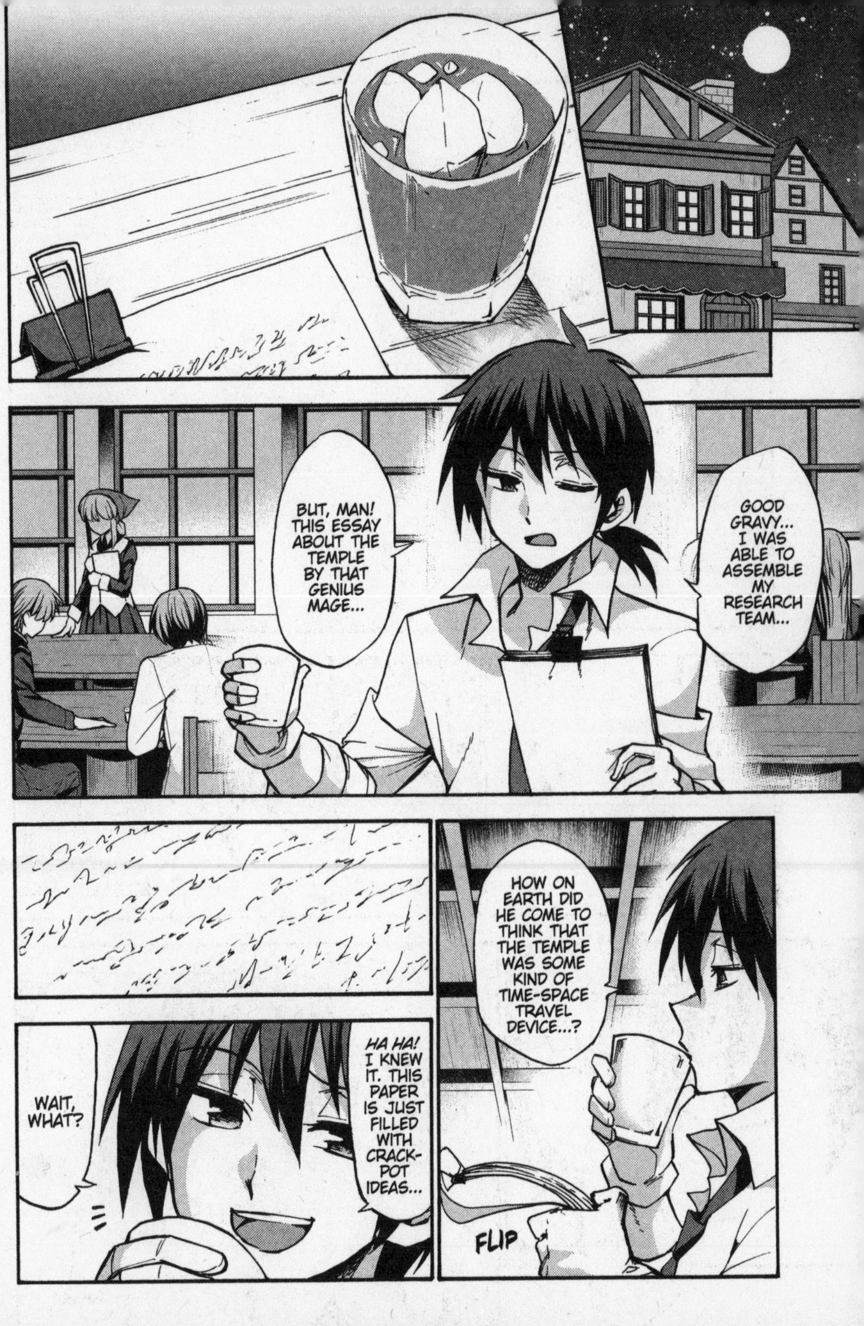
GOOD GRAVY... I WAS ABLE TO ASSEMBLE MY RESEARCH TEAM...
BUT, MAN! THIS ESSAY ABOUT THE TEMPLE BY THAT GENIUS MAGE...
HOW ON EARTH DID HE COME TO THINK THAT THE TEMPLE WAS SOME KIND OF TIME-SPACE TRAVEL DEVICE...?
FLIP
*HA HA!* I KNEW IT. THIS PAPER IS JUST FILLED WITH CRACK-POT IDEAS...
WAIT, WHAT?

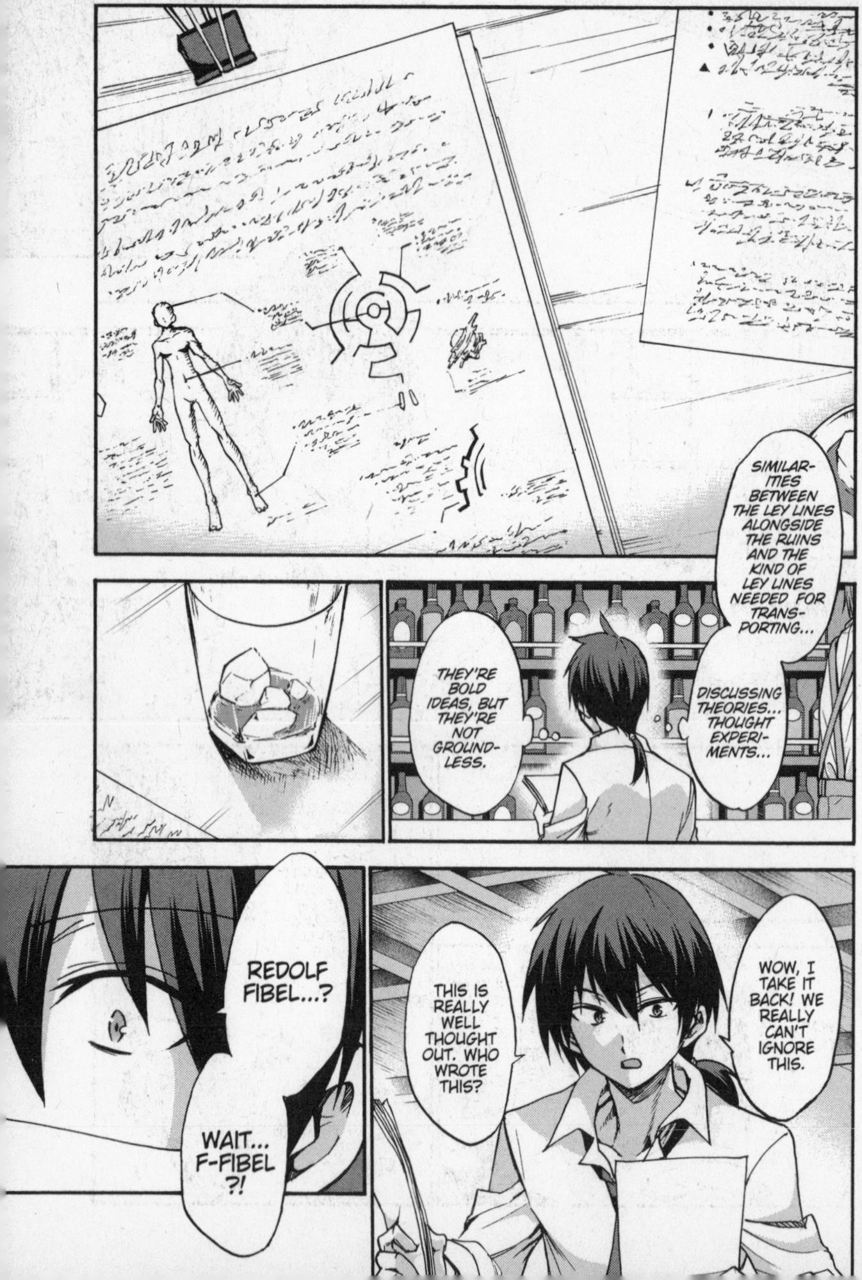
SIMILAR-ITIES BETWEEN THE LEY LINES ALONGSIDE THE RUINS AND THE KIND OF LEY LINES NEEDED FOR TRANS-PORTING...
DISCUSSING THEORIES... THOUGHT EXPERI-MENTS...
THEY'RE BOLD IDEAS, BUT THEY'RE NOT GROUND-LESS.
WOW, I TAKE IT BACK! WE REALLY CAN'T IGNORE THIS.
THIS IS REALLY WELL THOUGHT OUT. WHO WROTE THIS?
REDOLF FIBEL...?
WAIT... F-FIBEL ?!

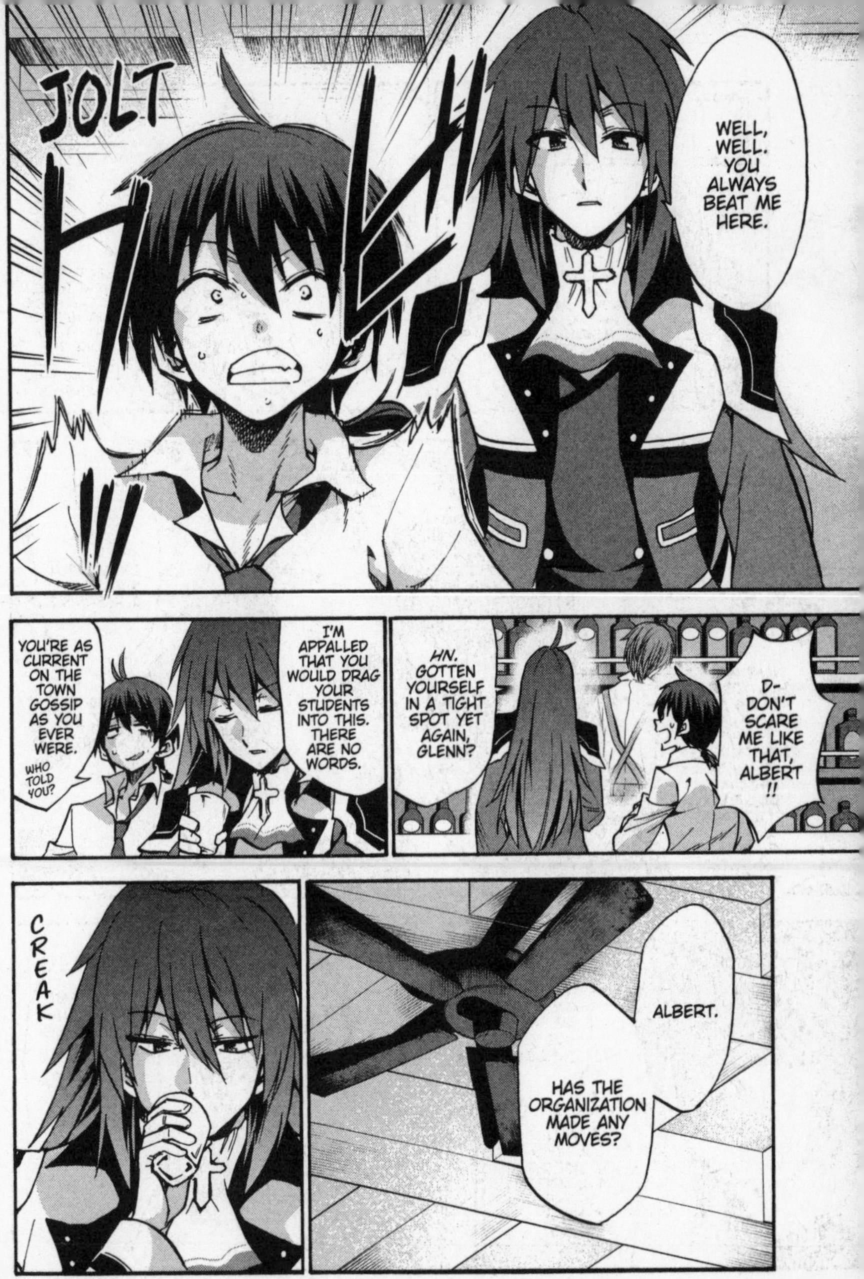
WELL, WELL. YOU ALWAYS BEAT ME HERE.
JOLT
D-DON'T SCARE ME LIKE THAT, ALBERT!!
HN. GOTTEN YOURSELF IN A TIGHT SPOT YET AGAIN, GLENN?
I'M APPALLED THAT YOU WOULD DRAG YOUR STUDENTS INTO THIS. THERE ARE NO WORDS.
YOU'RE AS CURRENT ON THE TOWN GOSSIP AS YOU EVER WERE.
WHO TOLD YOU?
ALBERT.
HAS THE ORGANIZATION MADE ANY MOVES?
CREAK

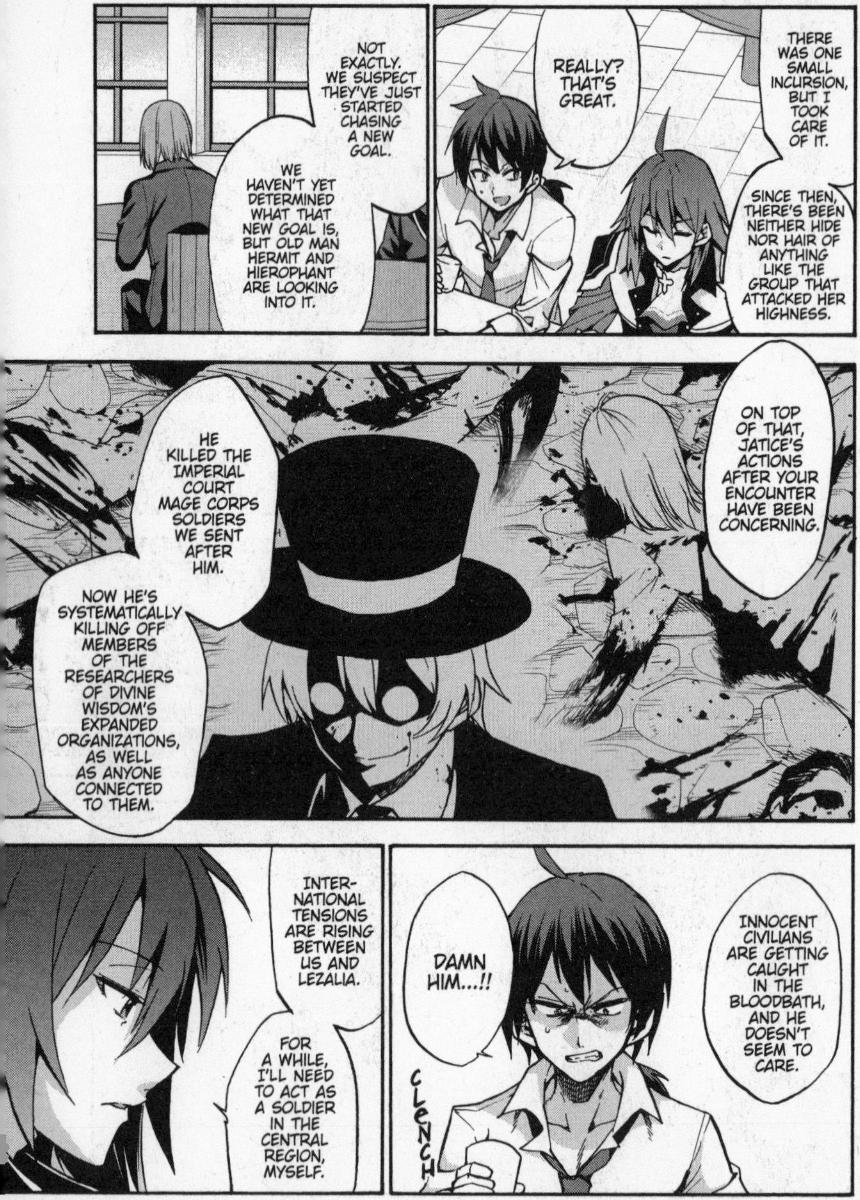
THERE WAS ONE SMALL INCURSION, BUT I TOOK CARE OF IT.
SINCE THEN, THERE'S BEEN NEITHER HIDE NOR HAIR OF ANYTHING LIKE THE GROUP THAT ATTACKED HER HIGHNESS.
REALLY? THAT'S GREAT.
NOT EXACTLY. WE SUSPECT THEY'VE JUST STARTED CHASING A NEW GOAL.
WE HAVEN'T YET DETERMINED WHAT THAT NEW GOAL IS, BUT OLD MAN HERMIT AND HIEROPHANT ARE LOOKING INTO IT.
ON TOP OF THAT, JATICE'S ACTIONS AFTER YOUR ENCOUNTER HAVE BEEN CONCERNING.
HE KILLED THE IMPERIAL COURT MAGE CORPS SOLDIERS WE SENT AFTER HIM.
NOW HE'S SYSTEMATICALLY KILLING OFF MEMBERS OF THE RESEARCHERS OF DIVINE WISDOM'S EXPANDED ORGANIZATIONS, AS WELL AS ANYONE CONNECTED TO THEM.
INNOCENT CIVILIANS ARE GETTING CAUGHT IN THE BLOODBATH, AND HE DOESN'T SEEM TO CARE.
DAMN HIM...!!
CLENCH
INTER-NATIONAL TENSIONS ARE RISING BETWEEN US AND LEZALIA.
FOR A WHILE, I'LL NEED TO ACT AS A SOLDIER IN THE CENTRAL REGION, MYSELF.

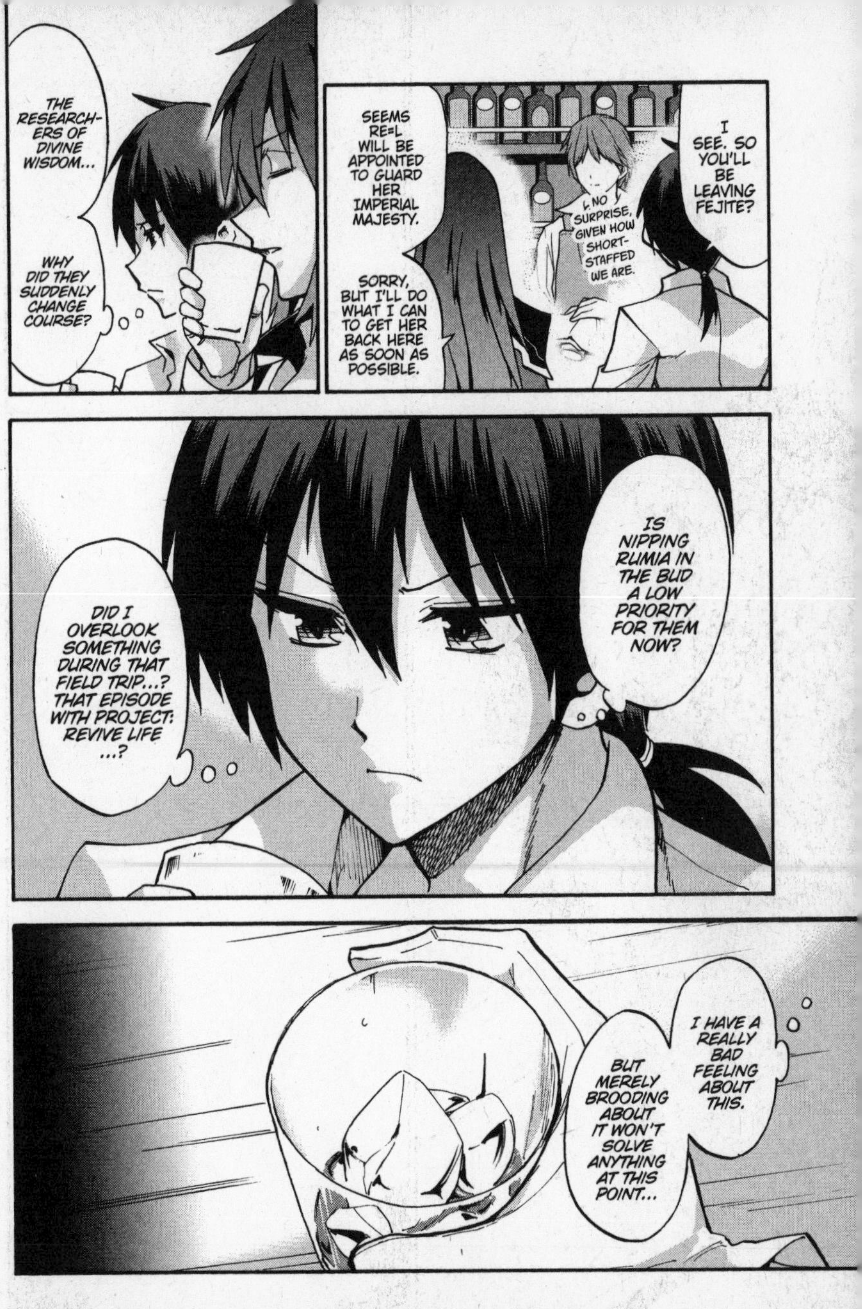
I SEE. SO YOU'LL BE LEAVING FEJITE?
...NO SURPRISE, GIVEN HOW SHORT-STAFFED WE ARE.
SEEMS RE=L WILL BE APPOINTED TO GUARD HER IMPERIAL MAJESTY.
SORRY, BUT I'LL DO WHAT I CAN TO GET HER BACK HERE AS SOON AS POSSIBLE.
THE RESEARCHERS OF DIVINE WISDOM...
WHY DID THEY SUDDENLY CHANGE COURSE?
IS NIPPING RUMIA IN THE BUD A LOW PRIORITY FOR THEM NOW?
DID I OVERLOOK SOMETHING DURING THAT FIELD TRIP...? THAT EPISODE WITH PROJECT: REVIVE LIFE ...?
I HAVE A REALLY BAD FEELING ABOUT THIS.
BUT MERELY BROODING ABOUT IT WON'T SOLVE ANYTHING AT THIS POINT...

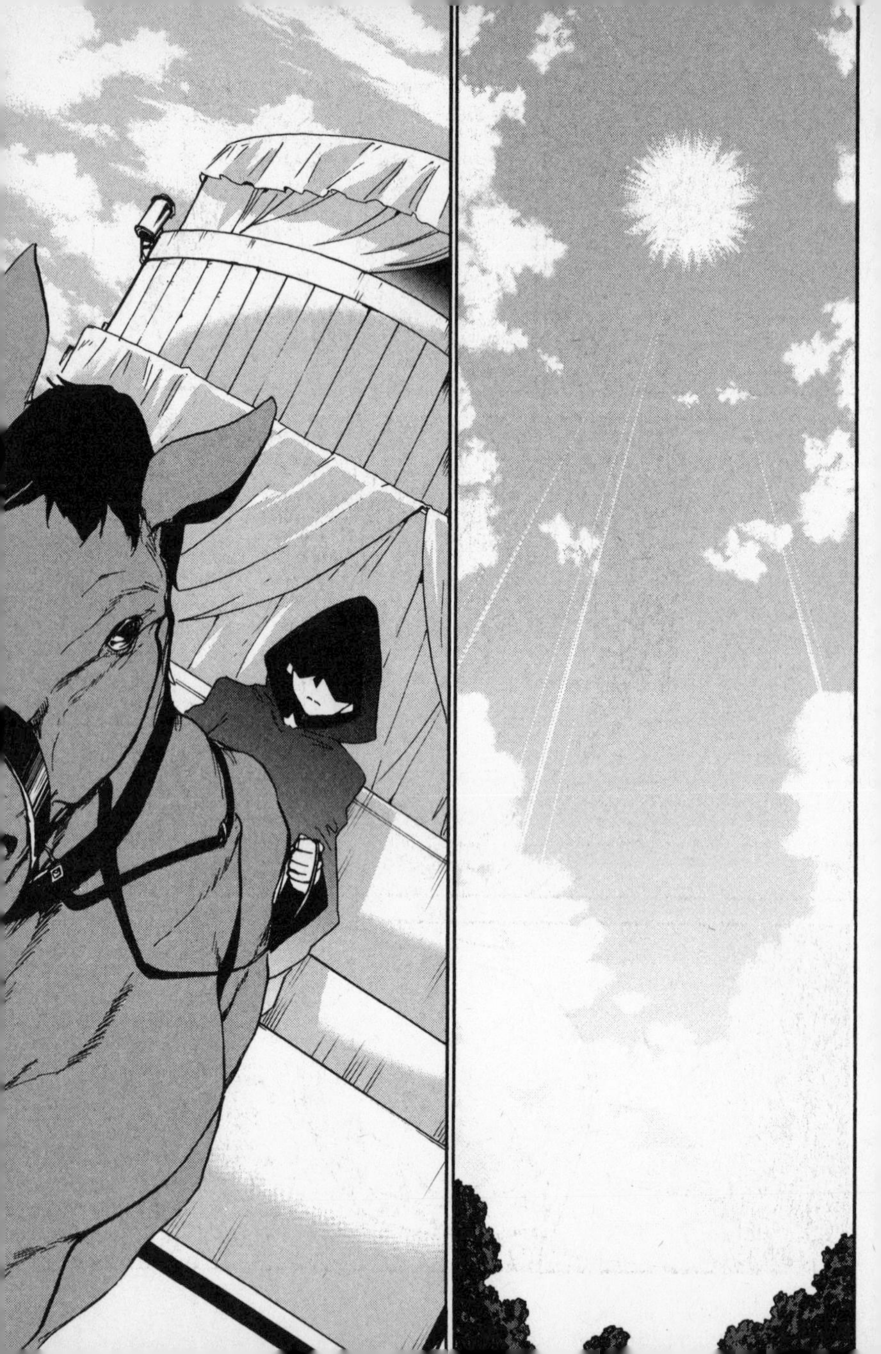

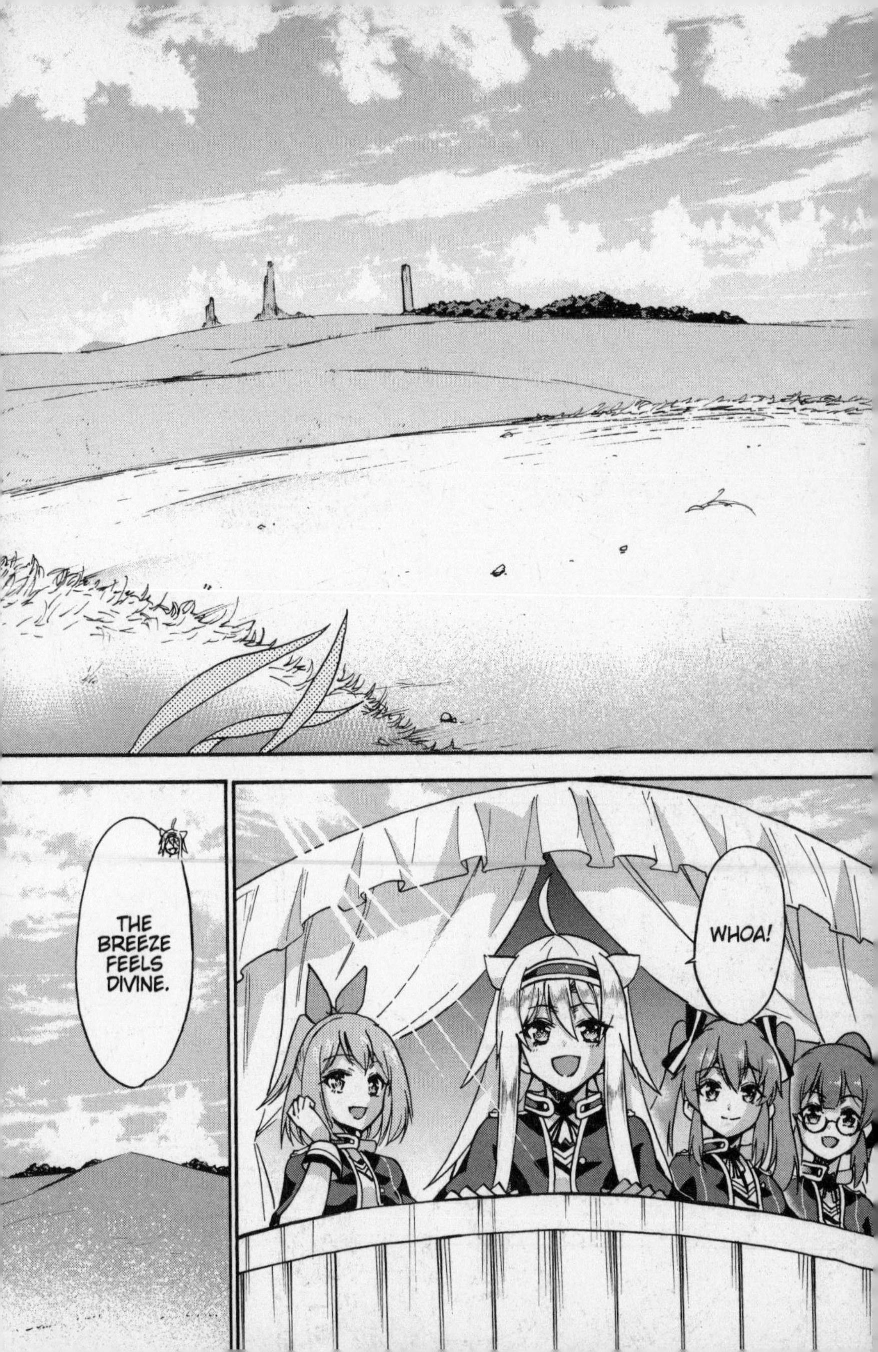
WHOA!
THE BREEZE FEELS DIVINE.

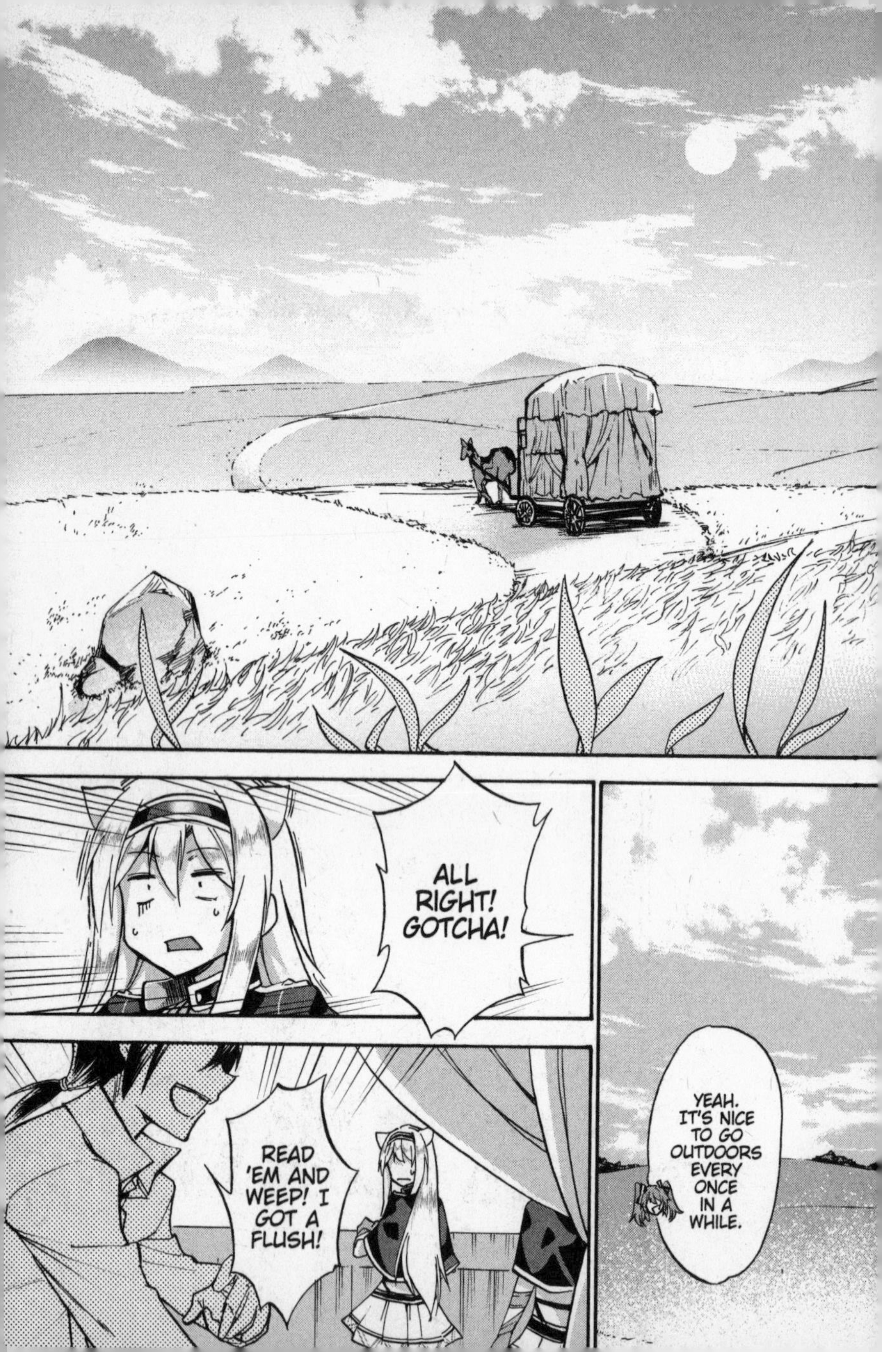
YEAH. IT'S NICE TO GO OUTDOORS EVERY ONCE IN A WHILE.
ALL RIGHT! GOTCHA!
READ 'EM AND WEEP! I GOT A FLUSH!

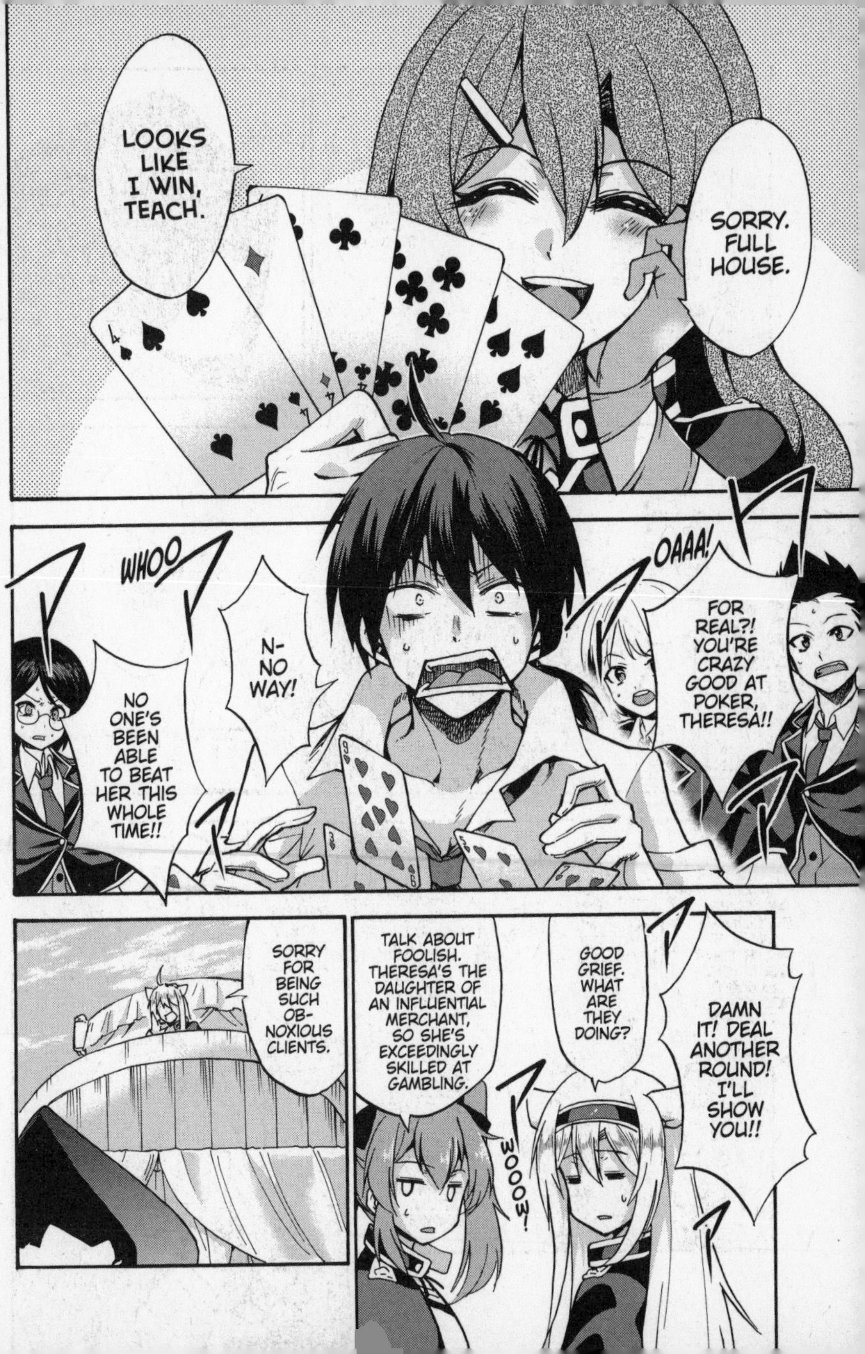
SORRY. FULL HOUSE.
LOOKS LIKE I WIN, TEACH.
OAAA!
FOR REAL?! YOU'RE CRAZY GOOD AT POKER, THERESA!!
N-NO WAY!
WHOO
NO ONE'S BEEN ABLE TO BEAT HER THIS WHOLE TIME!!
DAMN IT! DEAL ANOTHER ROUND! I'LL SHOW YOU!!
GOOD GRIEF. WHAT ARE THEY DOING?
TALK ABOUT FOOLISH. THERESA'S THE DAUGHTER OF AN INFLUENTIAL MERCHANT, SO SHE'S EXCEEDINGLY SKILLED AT GAMBLING.
WOOOW!
SORRY FOR BEING SUCH OB-NOXIOUS CLIENTS.

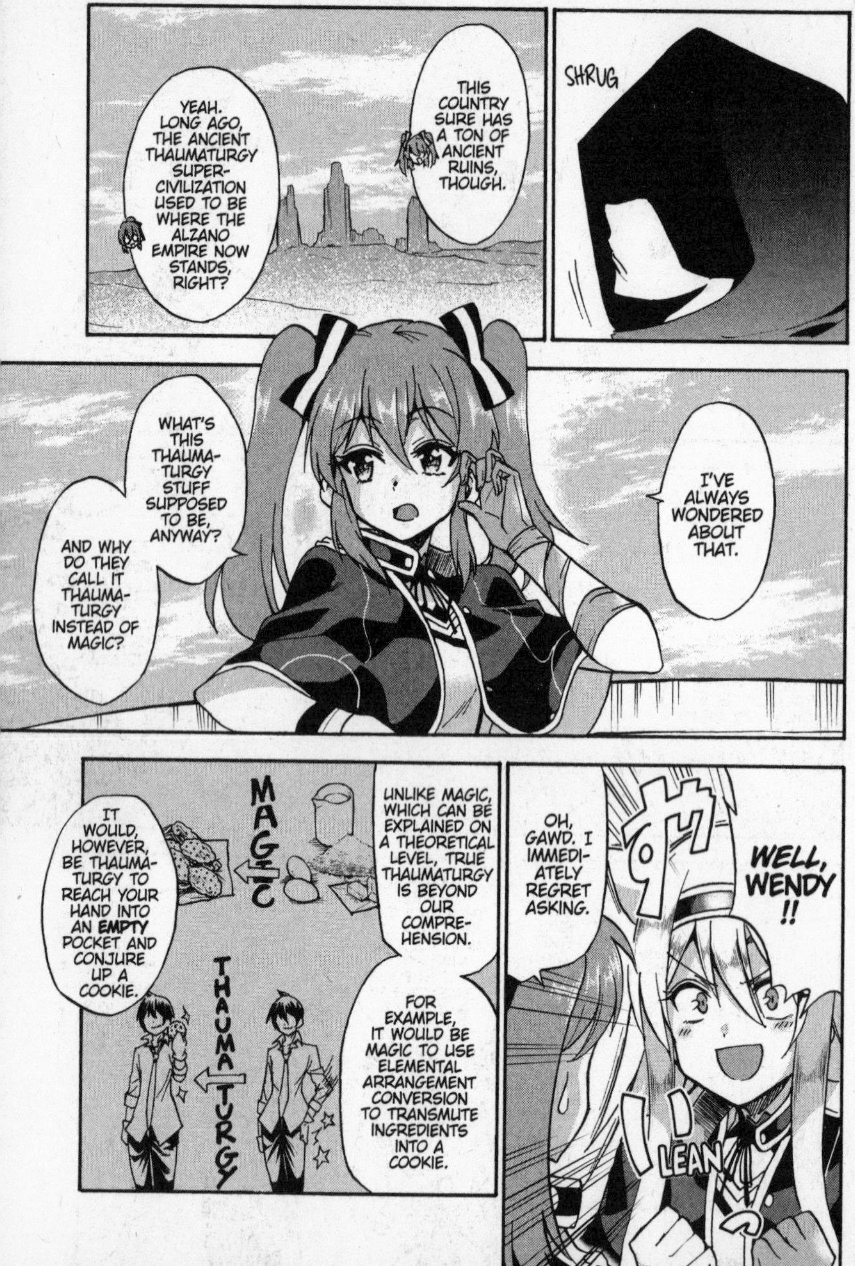
SHRUG
THIS COUNTRY SURE HAS A TON OF ANCIENT RUINS, THOUGH.
YEAH. LONG AGO, THE ANCIENT THAUMATURGY SUPER-CIVILIZATION USED TO BE WHERE THE ALZANO EMPIRE NOW STANDS, RIGHT?
I'VE ALWAYS WONDERED ABOUT THAT.
WHAT'S THIS THAUMATURGY STUFF SUPPOSED TO BE, ANYWAY?
AND WHY DO THEY CALL IT THAUMATURGY INSTEAD OF MAGIC?
WELL, WENDY!!
OH, GAWD. I IMMEDIATELY REGRET ASKING.
LEAN
UNLIKE MAGIC, WHICH CAN BE EXPLAINED ON A THEORETICAL LEVEL, TRUE THAUMATURGY IS BEYOND OUR COMPREHENSION.
MAGIC
IT WOULD, HOWEVER, BE THAUMATURGY TO REACH YOUR HAND INTO AN **EMPTY** POCKET AND CONJURE UP A COOKIE.
FOR EXAMPLE, IT WOULD BE MAGIC TO USE ELEMENTAL ARRANGEMENT CONVERSION TO TRANSMUTE INGREDIENTS INTO A COOKIE.
THAUMATURGY

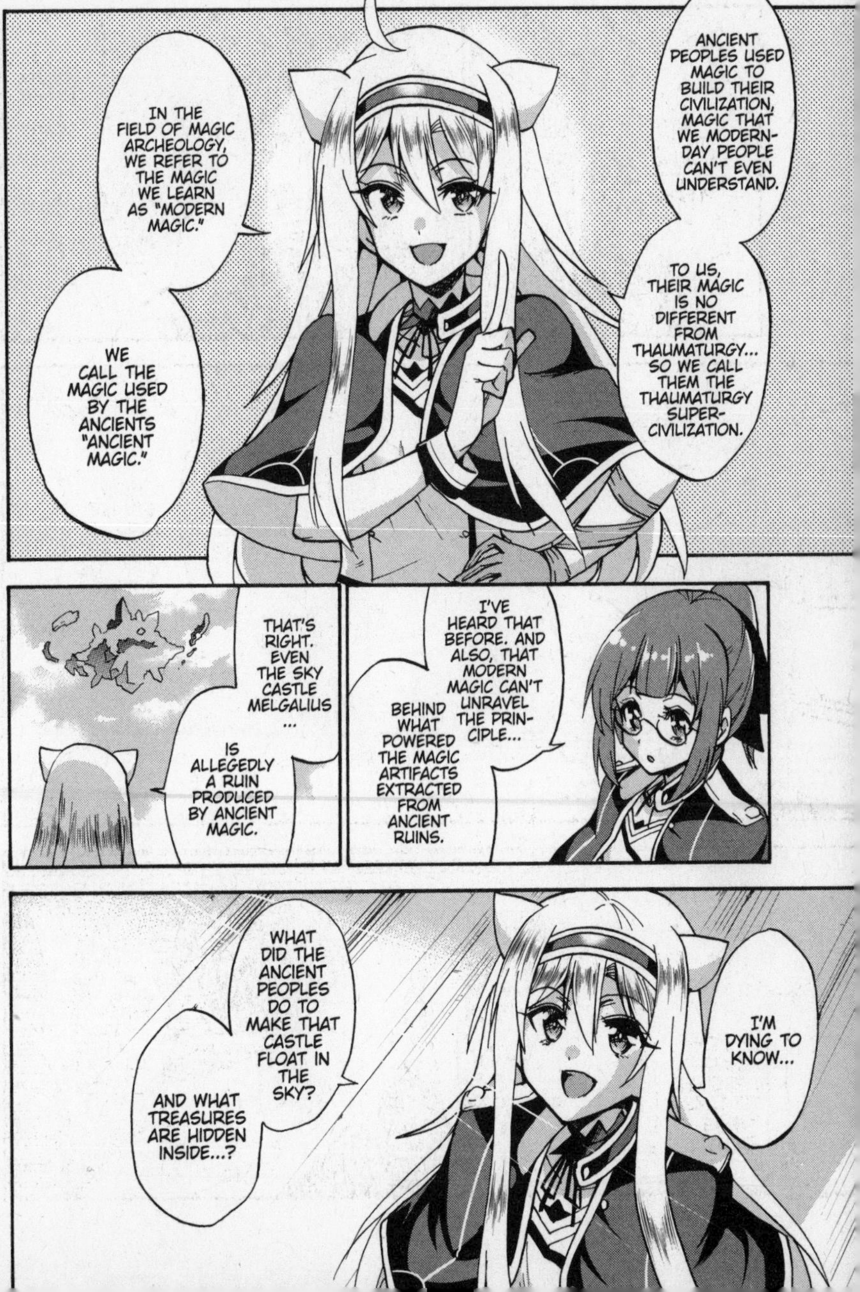
ANCIENT PEOPLES USED MAGIC TO BUILD THEIR CIVILIZATION, MAGIC THAT WE MODERN-DAY PEOPLE CAN'T EVEN UNDERSTAND.
TO US, THEIR MAGIC IS NO DIFFERENT FROM THAUMATURGY... SO WE CALL THEM THE THAUMATURGY SUPER-CIVILIZATION.
IN THE FIELD OF MAGIC ARCHEOLOGY, WE REFER TO THE MAGIC WE LEARN AS "MODERN MAGIC."
WE CALL THE MAGIC USED BY THE ANCIENTS "ANCIENT MAGIC."
I'VE HEARD THAT BEFORE. AND ALSO, THAT MODERN MAGIC CAN'T UNRAVEL THE PRIN-CIPLE...
BEHIND WHAT POWERED THE MAGIC ARTIFACTS EXTRACTED FROM ANCIENT RUINS.
THAT'S RIGHT. EVEN THE SKY CASTLE MELGALIUS...
IS ALLEGEDLY A RUIN PRODUCED BY ANCIENT MAGIC.
I'M DYING TO KNOW...
WHAT DID THE ANCIENT PEOPLES DO TO MAKE THAT CASTLE FLOAT IN THE SKY?
AND WHAT TREASURES ARE HIDDEN INSIDE...?

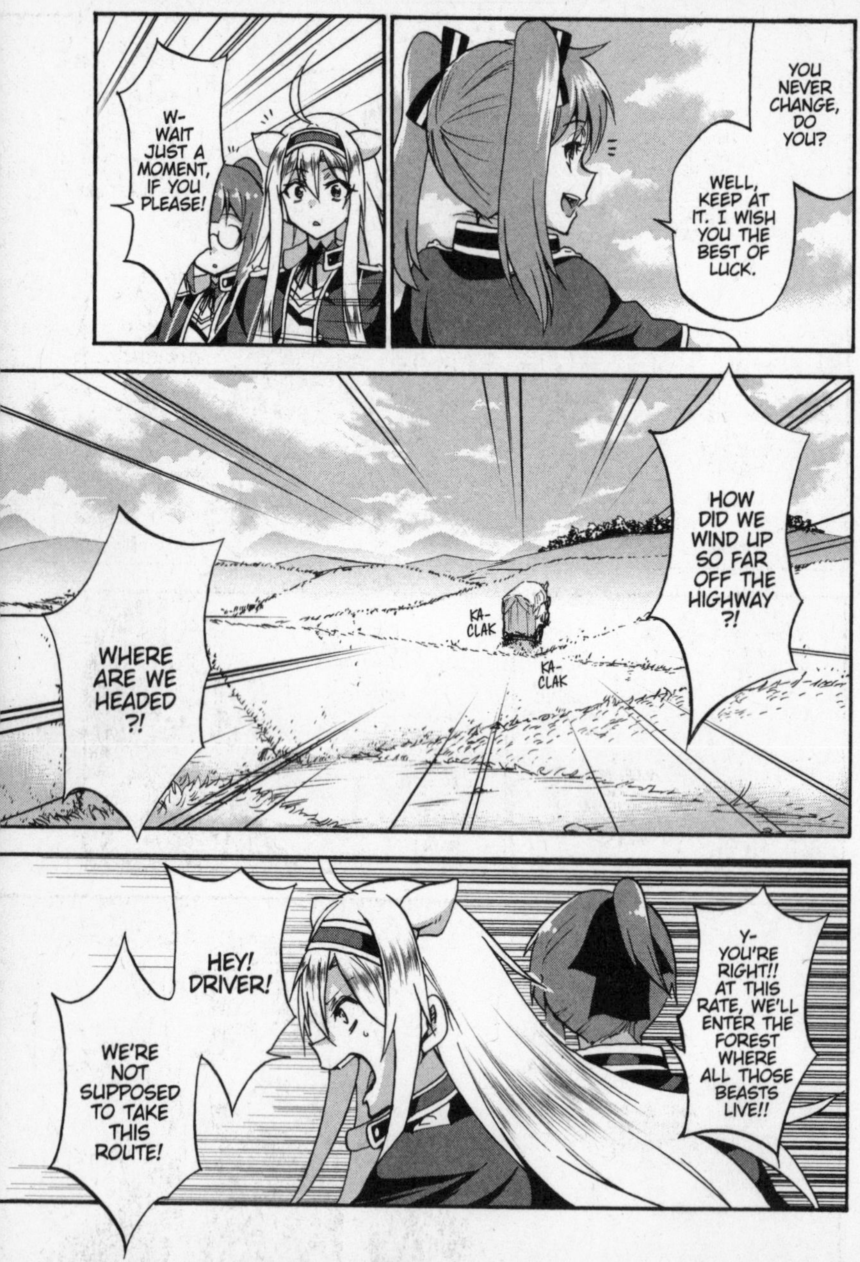
YOU NEVER CHANGE, DO YOU?
WELL, KEEP AT IT. I WISH YOU THE BEST OF LUCK.
W-WAIT JUST A MOMENT, IF YOU PLEASE!
HOW DID WE WIND UP SO FAR OFF THE HIGHWAY ?!
KA-CLAK
KA-CLAK
WHERE ARE WE HEADED ?!
Y-YOU'RE RIGHT!! AT THIS RATE, WE'LL ENTER THE FOREST WHERE ALL THOSE BEASTS LIVE!!
HEY! DRIVER!
WE'RE NOT SUPPOSED TO TAKE THIS ROUTE!

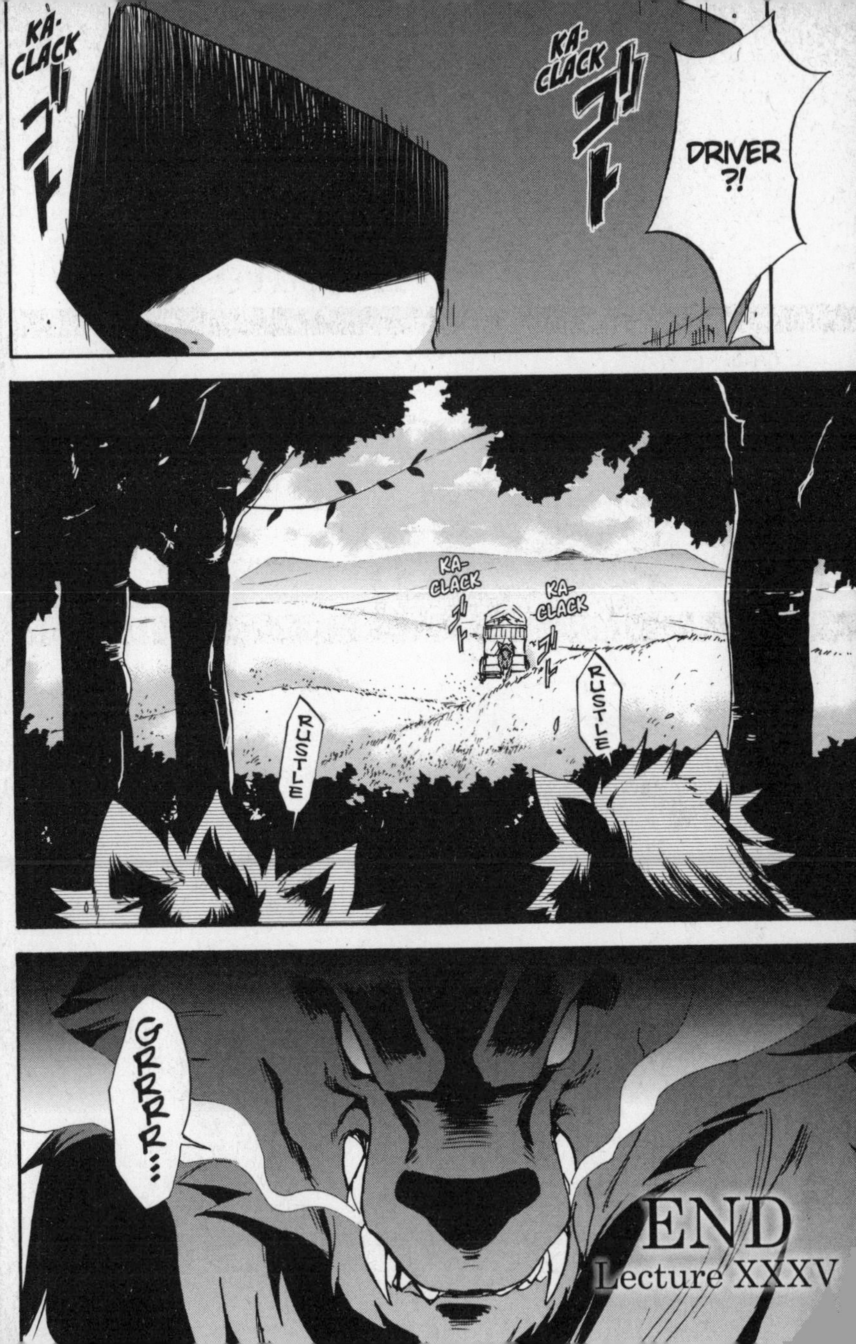
DRIVER ?!
KA-CLACK
KA-CLACK
KA-CLACK
KA-CLACK
RUSTLE
RUSTLE
GRRRR...
END
Lecture XXXV

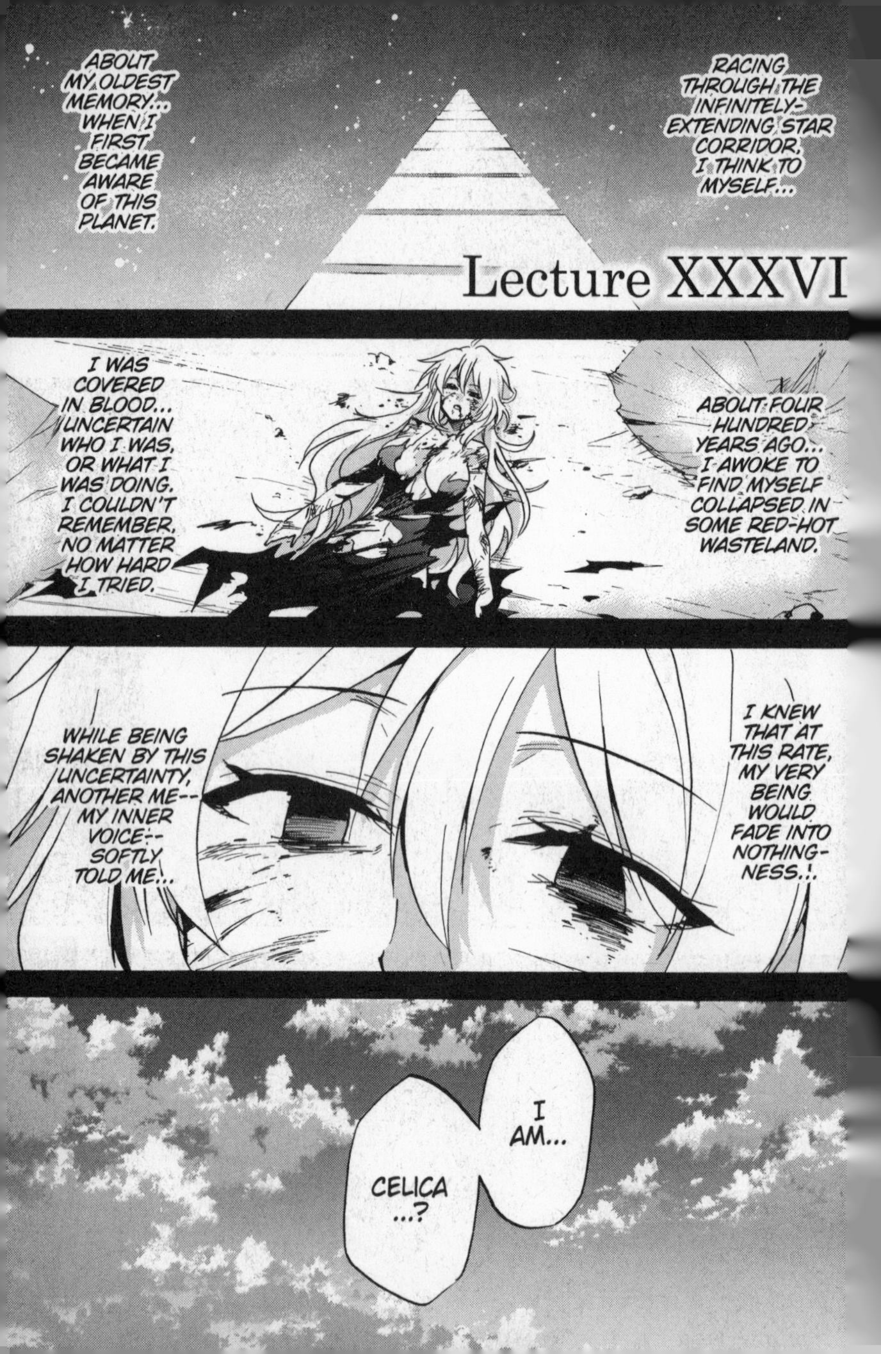
RACING THROUGH THE INFINITELY-EXTENDING STAR CORRIDOR, I THINK TO MYSELF...
ABOUT MY OLDEST MEMORY... WHEN I FIRST BECAME AWARE OF THIS PLANET.
Lecture XXXVI
ABOUT FOUR HUNDRED YEARS AGO... I AWOKE TO FIND MYSELF COLLAPSED IN SOME RED-HOT WASTELAND.
I WAS COVERED IN BLOOD... UNCERTAIN WHO I WAS, OR WHAT I WAS DOING. I COULDN'T REMEMBER, NO MATTER HOW HARD I TRIED.
I KNEW THAT AT THIS RATE, MY VERY BEING WOULD FADE INTO NOTHING-NESS...!
WHILE BEING SHAKEN BY THIS UNCERTAINTY, ANOTHER ME-- MY INNER VOICE-- SOFTLY TOLD ME...
I AM...
CELICA ...?

# Lecture XXXVI

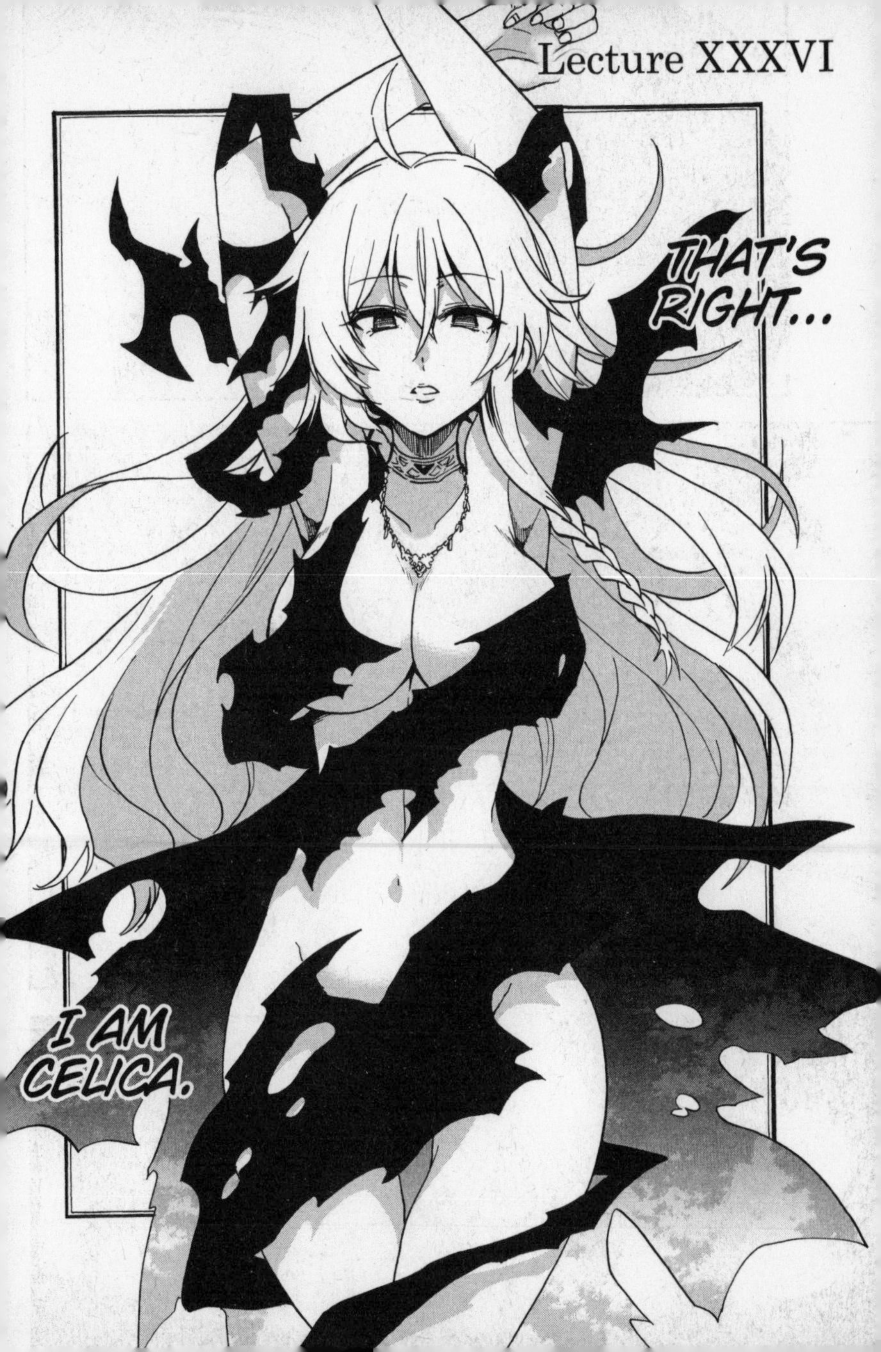
THAT'S RIGHT...
I AM CELICA.

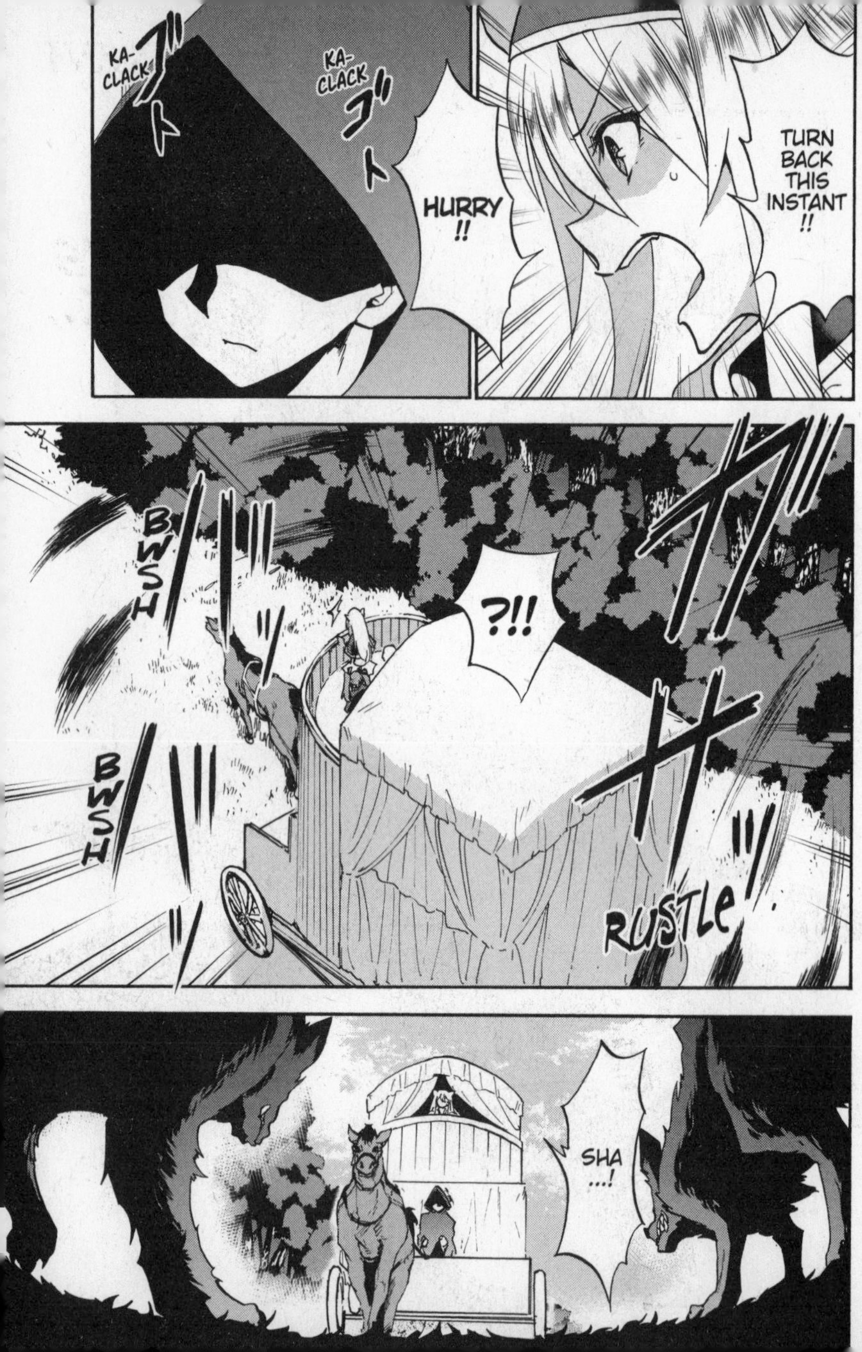
TURN BACK THIS INSTANT!!
KA-CLACK
HURRY!!
KA-CLACK
?!!
RUSTLE
BWSH
BWSH
SHA...!

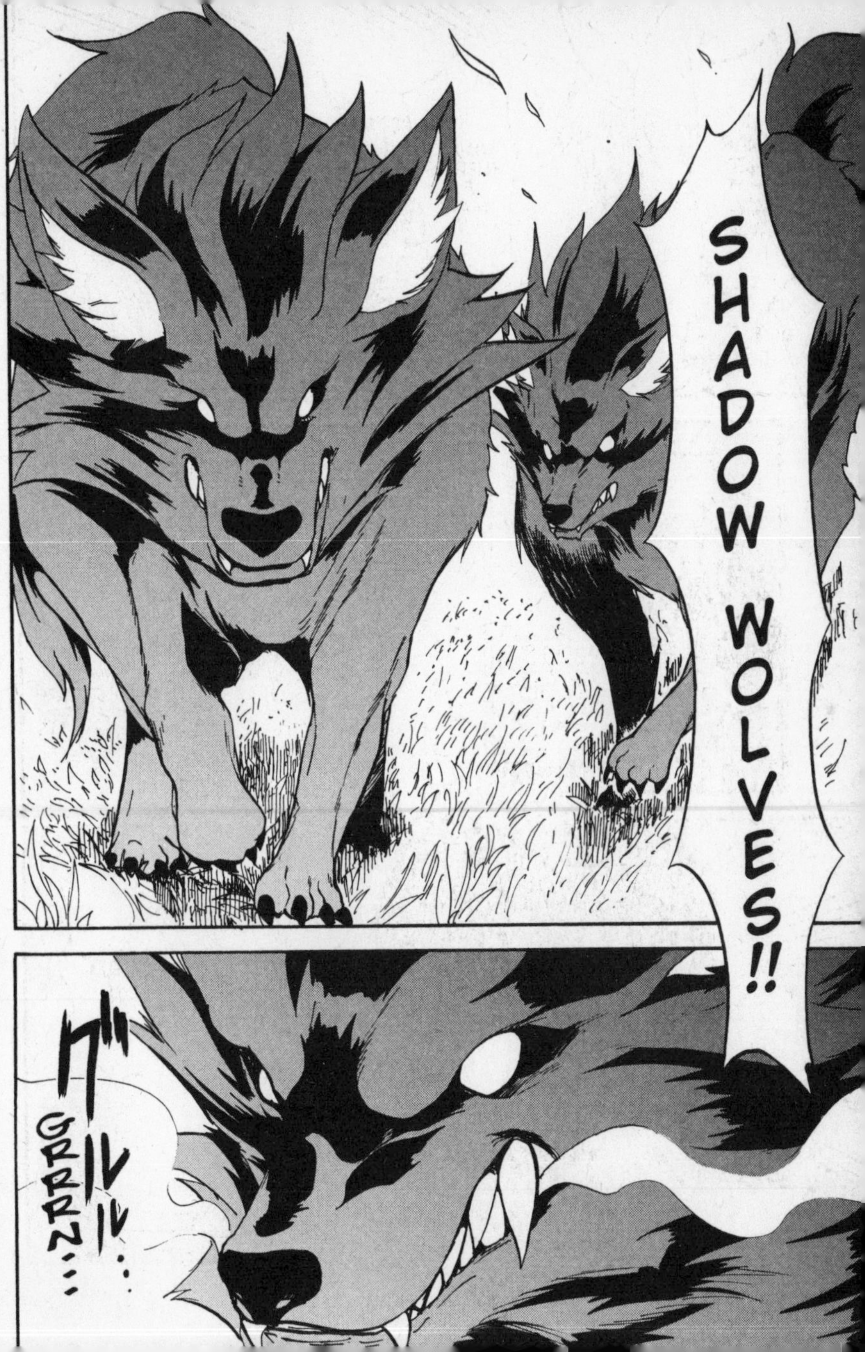
SHADOW WOLVES!!
グルル…
GRRRN...

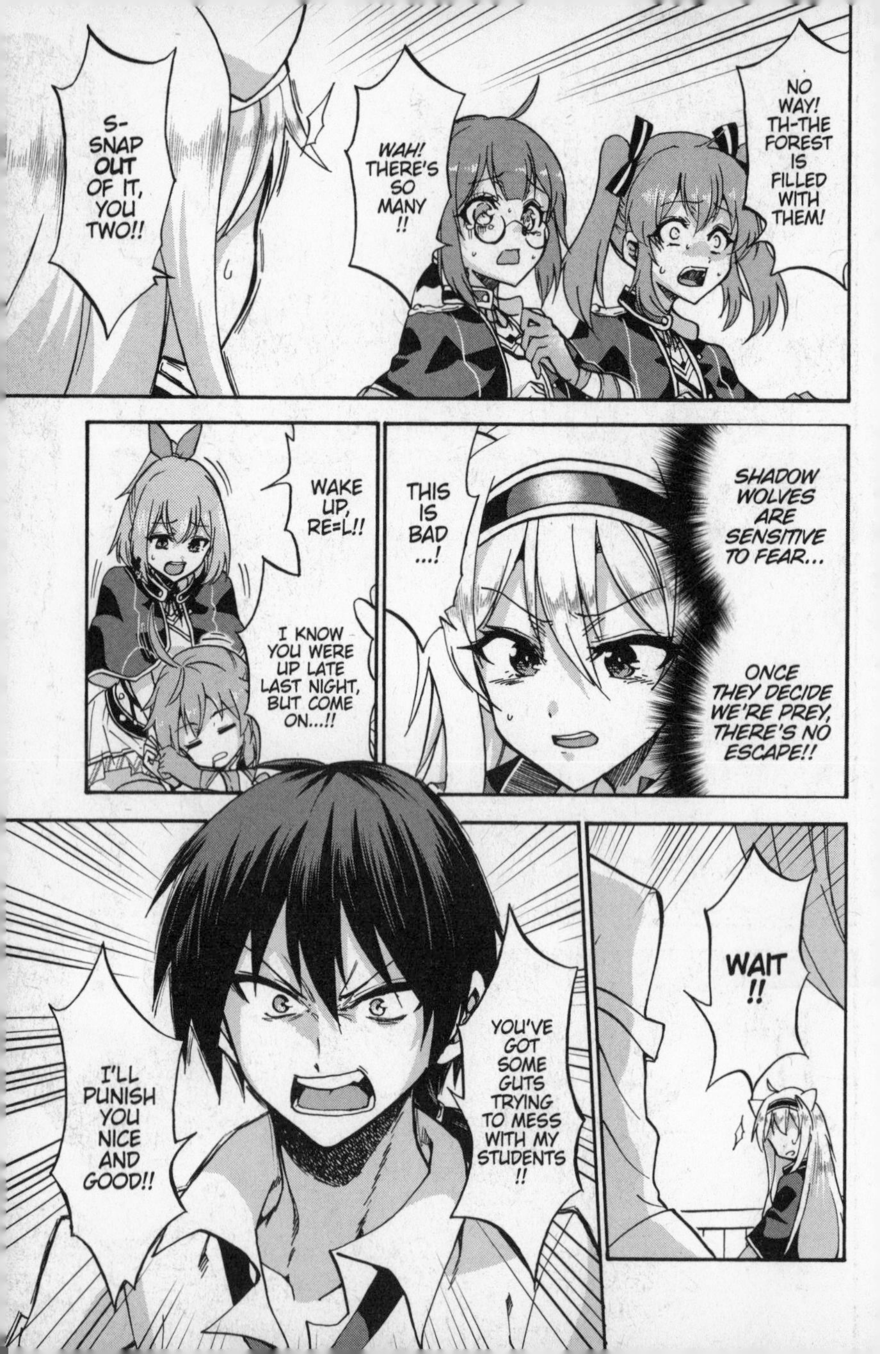
NO WAY! TH-THE FOREST IS FILLED WITH THEM!
WAH! THERE'S SO MANY!!
S-SNAP OUT OF IT, YOU TWO!!
SHADOW WOLVES ARE SENSITIVE TO FEAR...
THIS IS BAD...!
ONCE THEY DECIDE WE'RE PREY, THERE'S NO ESCAPE!!
WAKE UP, RE=L!!
I KNOW YOU WERE UP LATE LAST NIGHT, BUT COME ON...!!
WAIT!!
YOU'VE GOT SOME GUTS TRYING TO MESS WITH MY STUDENTS!!
I'LL PUNISH YOU NICE AND GOOD!!

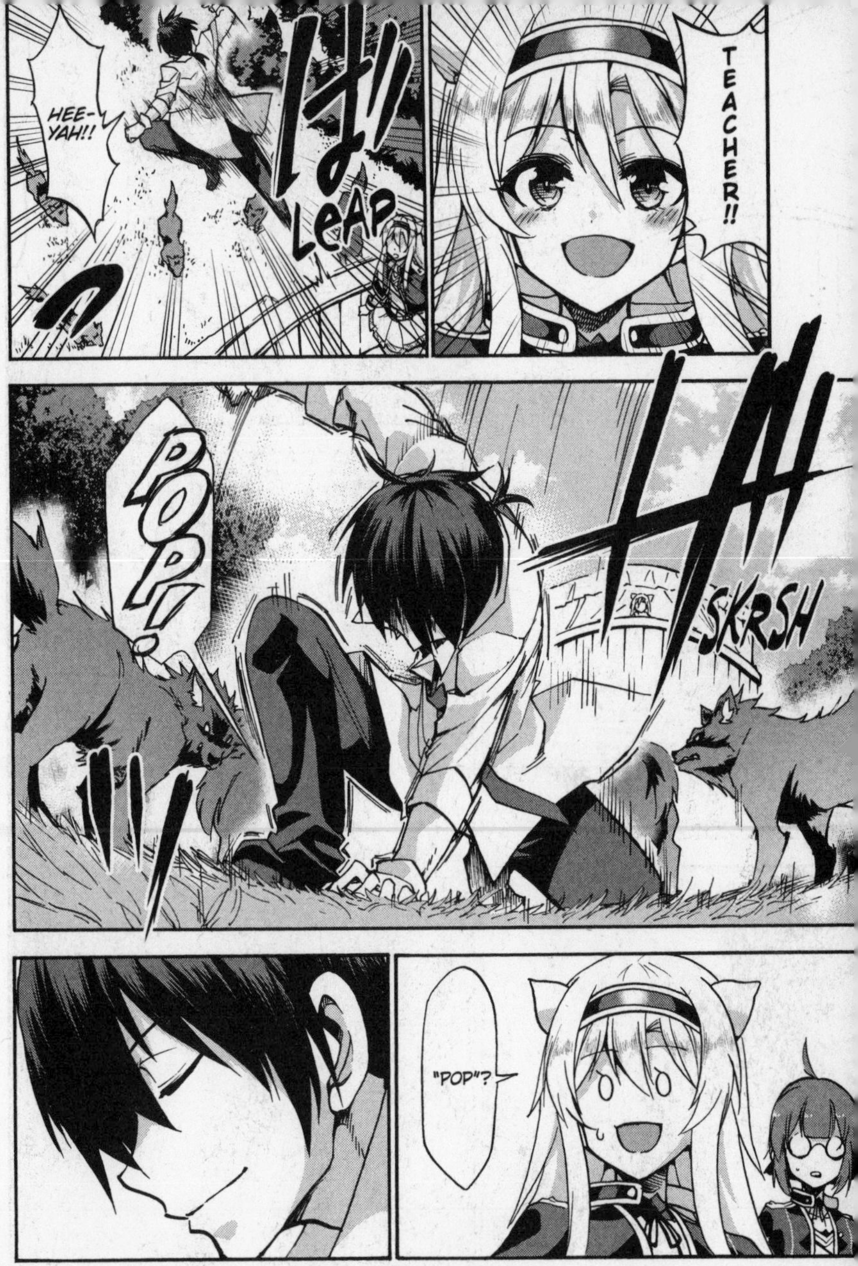
TEACHER!!
HEE-YAH!!
LEAP
SKRSH
POP!
"POP"?

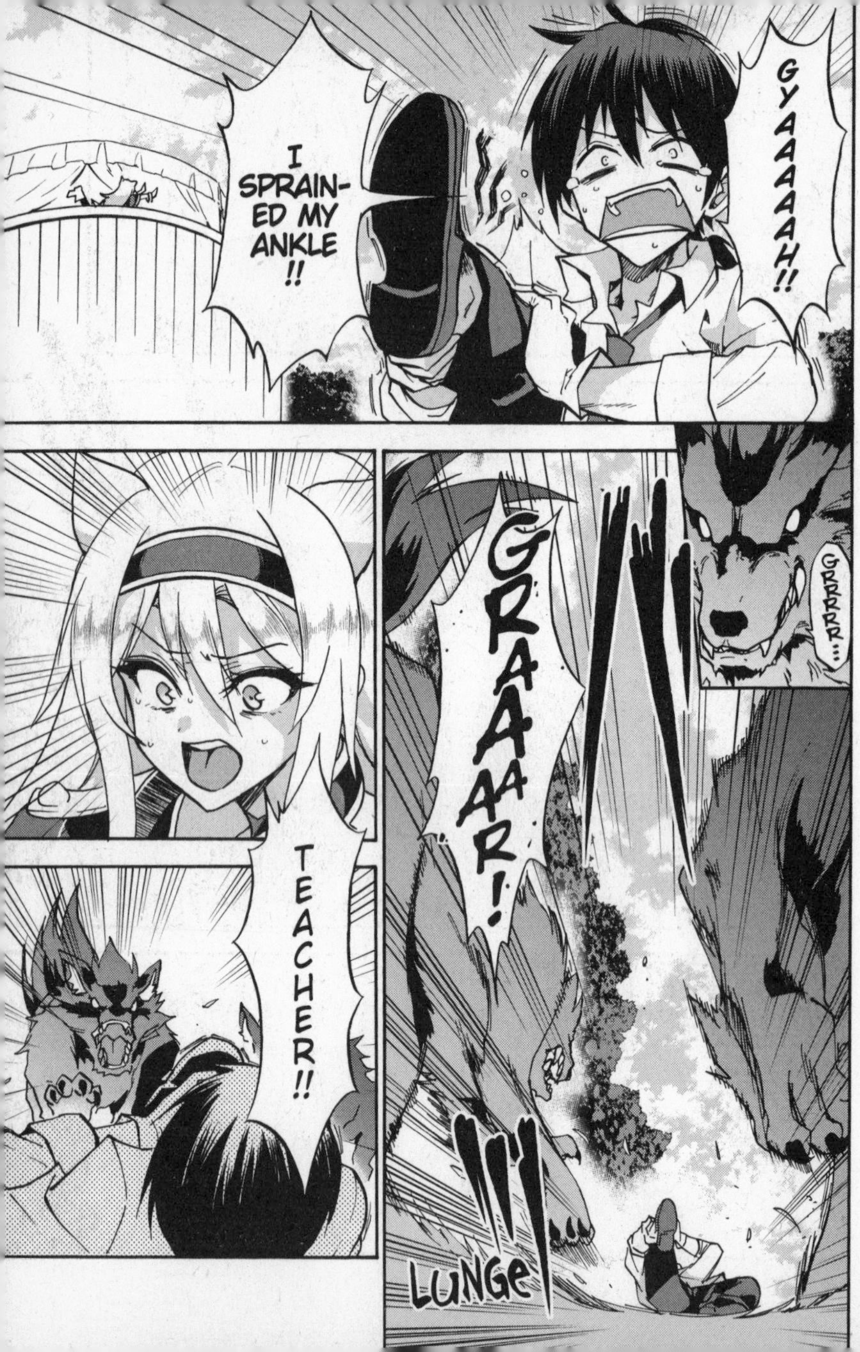
GYAAAAAH!!
I SPRAIN-ED MY ANKLE!!
GRRRRR...
GRAAAAR!
LUNGE
TEACHER!!

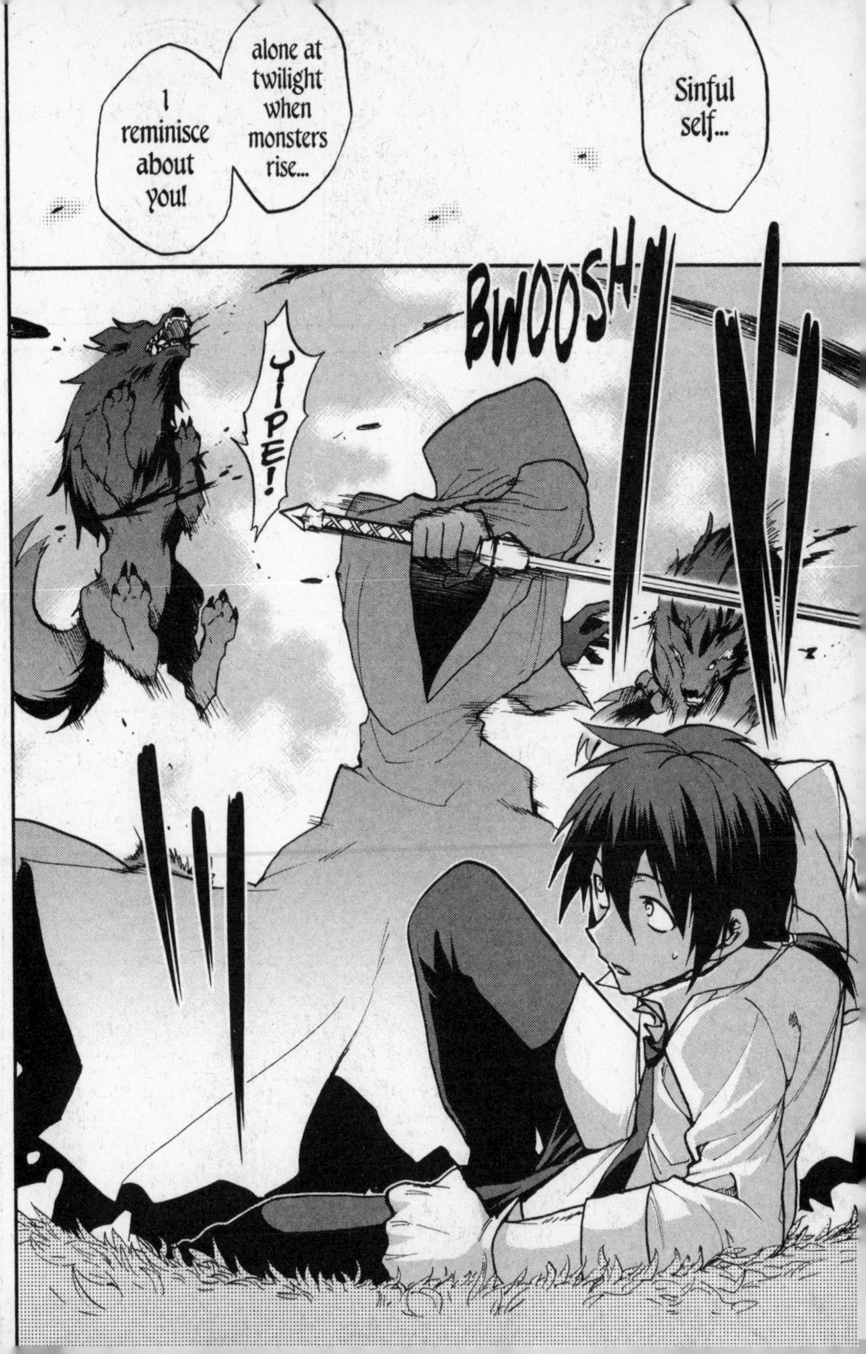
Sinful self...
alone at twilight when monsters rise...
I reminisce about you!
BWOOSH
YIPE!

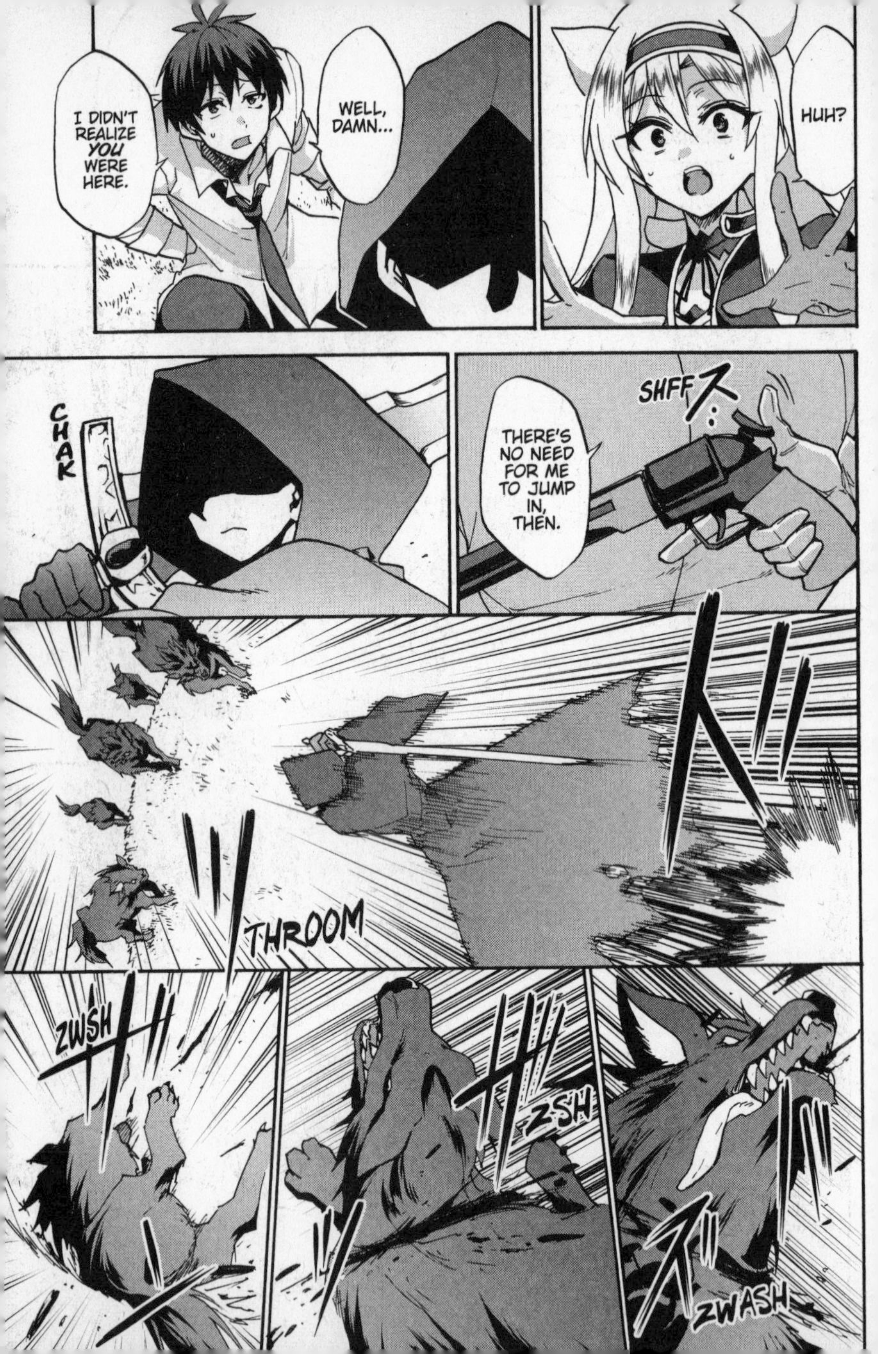
HUH?
WELL, DAMN...
I DIDN'T REALIZE *YOU* WERE HERE.
SHFF
THERE'S NO NEED FOR ME TO JUMP IN, THEN.
CHAK
THROOM
ZWASH
ZSH
ZWSH

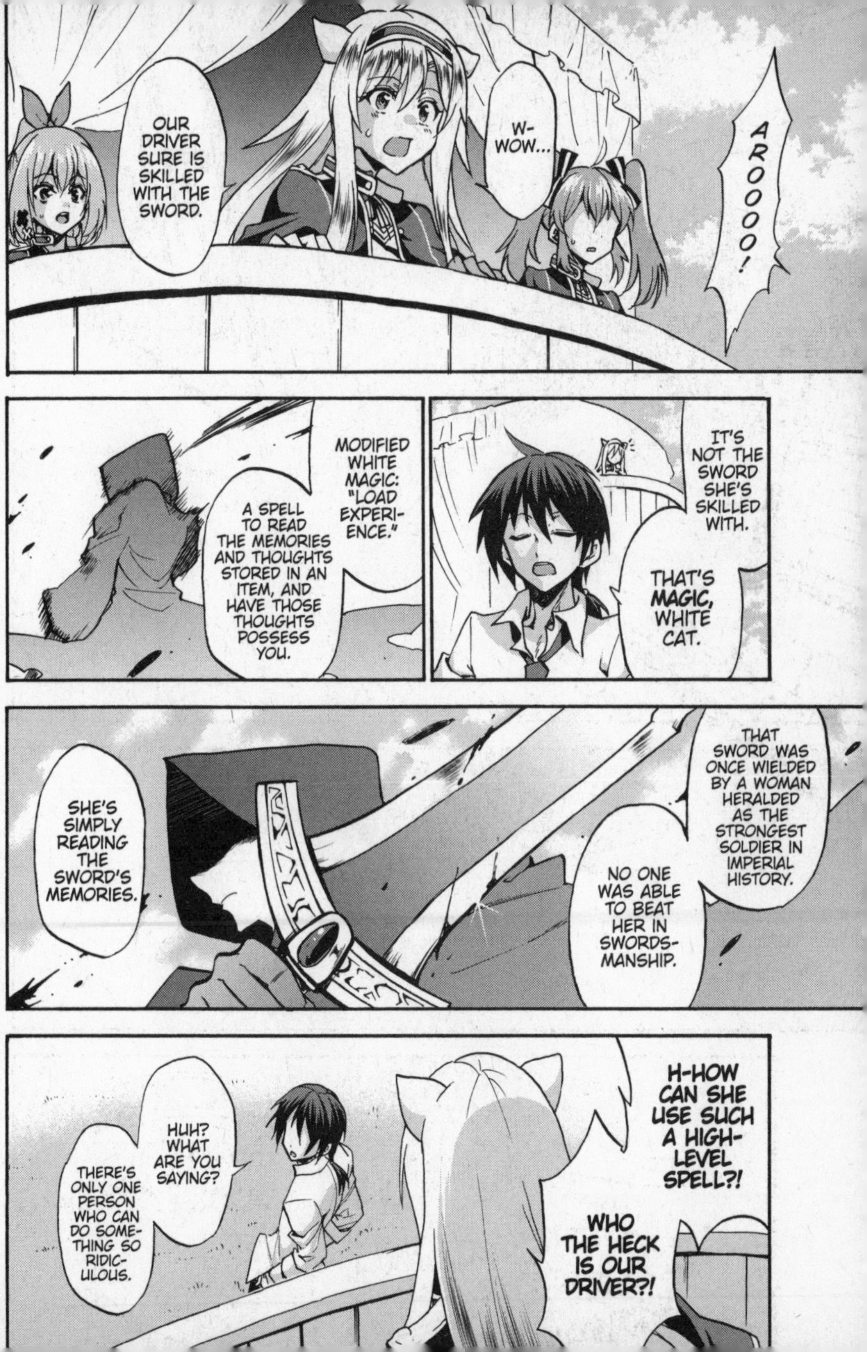
AROOOOO!
W-WOW...
OUR DRIVER SURE IS SKILLED WITH THE SWORD.
IT'S NOT THE SWORD SHE'S SKILLED WITH.
THAT'S MAGIC, WHITE CAT.
MODIFIED WHITE MAGIC: "LOAD EXPERIENCE."
A SPELL TO READ THE MEMORIES AND THOUGHTS STORED IN AN ITEM, AND HAVE THOSE THOUGHTS POSSESS YOU.
THAT SWORD WAS ONCE WIELDED BY A WOMAN HERALDED AS THE STRONGEST SOLDIER IN IMPERIAL HISTORY.
NO ONE WAS ABLE TO BEAT HER IN SWORDSMANSHIP.
SHE'S SIMPLY READING THE SWORD'S MEMORIES.
H-HOW CAN SHE USE SUCH A HIGH-LEVEL SPELL?!
WHO THE HECK IS OUR DRIVER?!
HUH? WHAT ARE YOU SAYING?
THERE'S ONLY ONE PERSON WHO CAN DO SOMETHING SO RIDICULOUS.

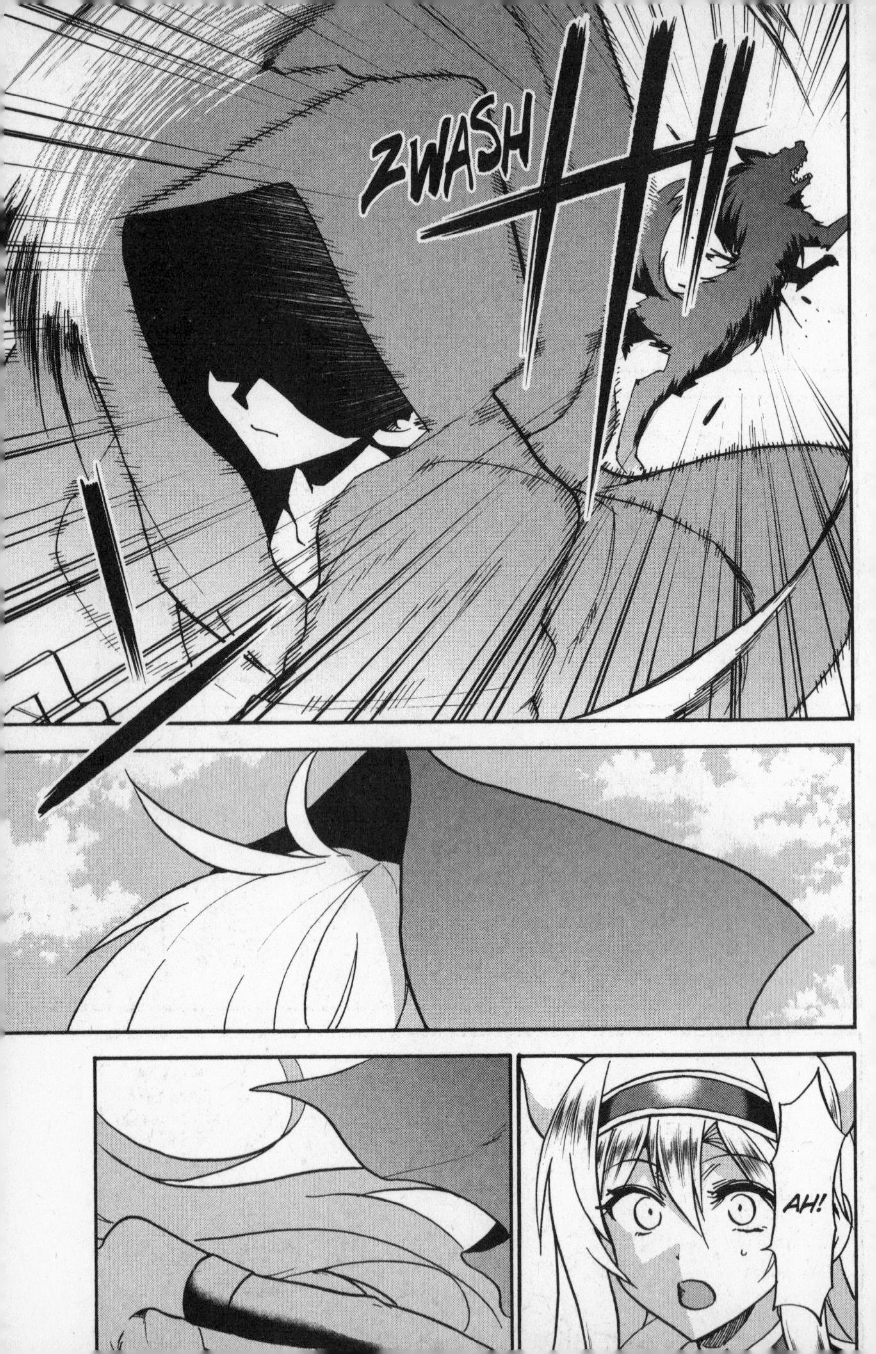
ZWASH
AH!

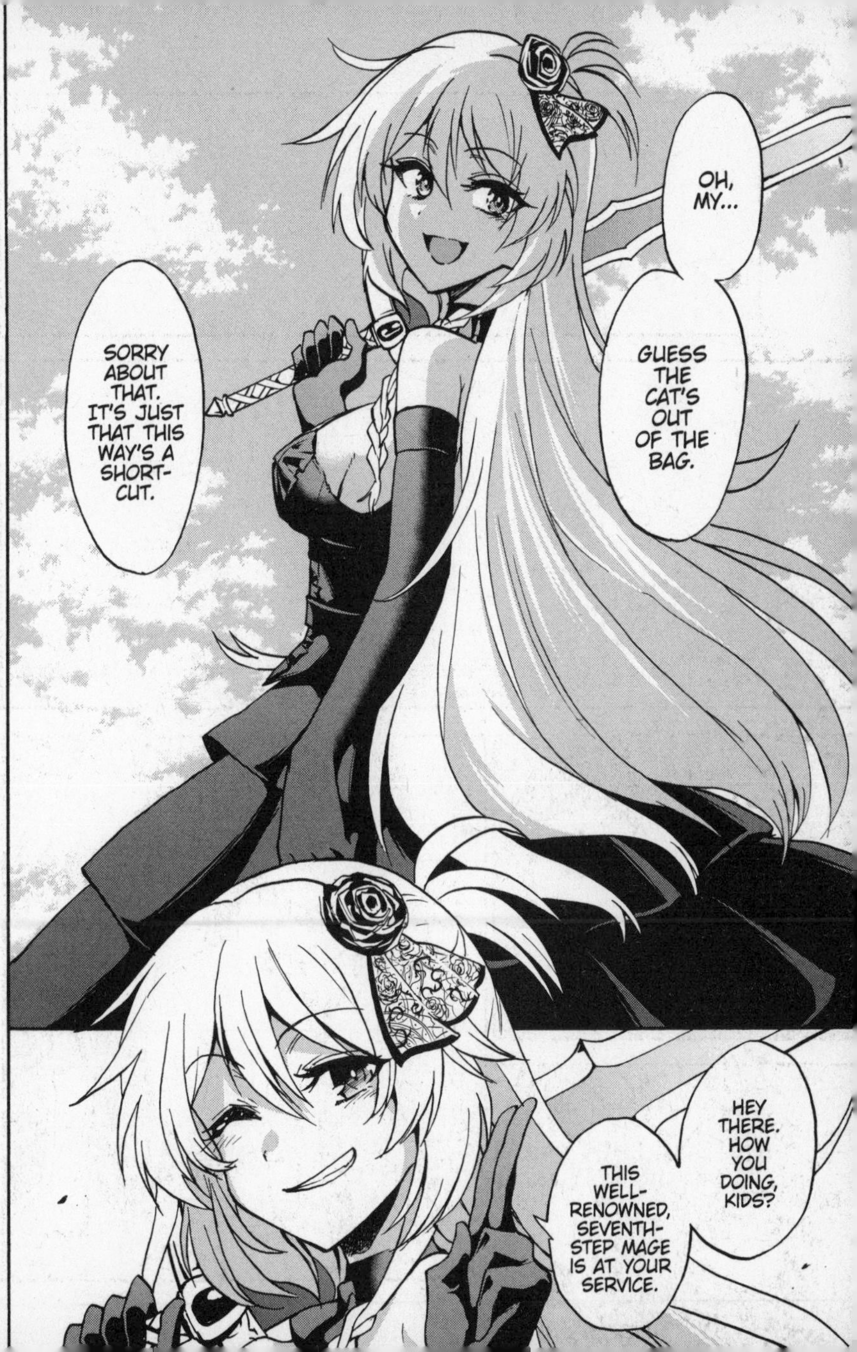
OH, MY...
GUESS THE CAT'S OUT OF THE BAG.
SORRY ABOUT THAT. IT'S JUST THAT THIS WAY'S A SHORT-CUT.
HEY THERE. HOW YOU DOING, KIDS?
THIS WELL-RENOWNED, SEVENTH-STEP MAGE IS AT YOUR SERVICE.

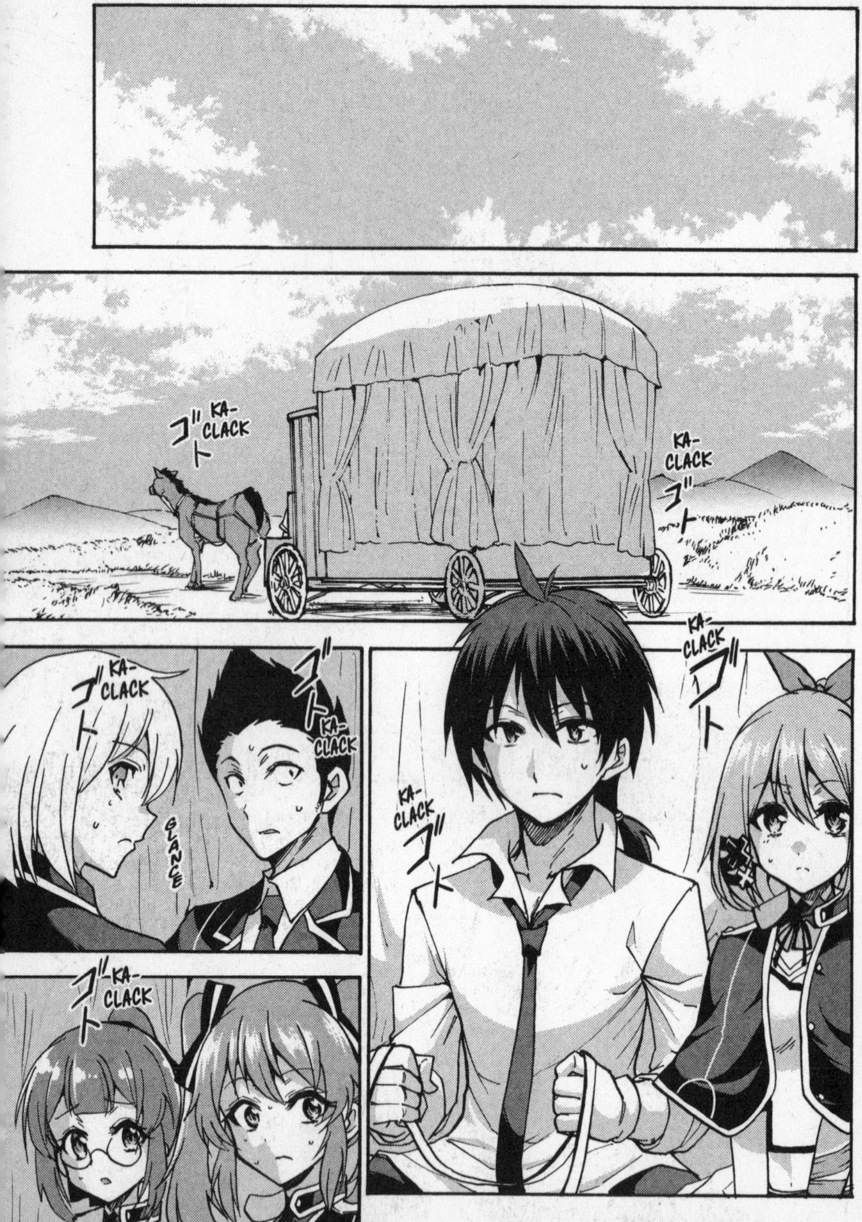
KA-CLACK
ゴト
KA-CLACK
ゴト
KA-CLACK
ゴト
KA-CLACK
ゴト
ゴト
KA-CLACK
KA-CLACK
ゴト
GLANCE
ゴト
KA-CLACK

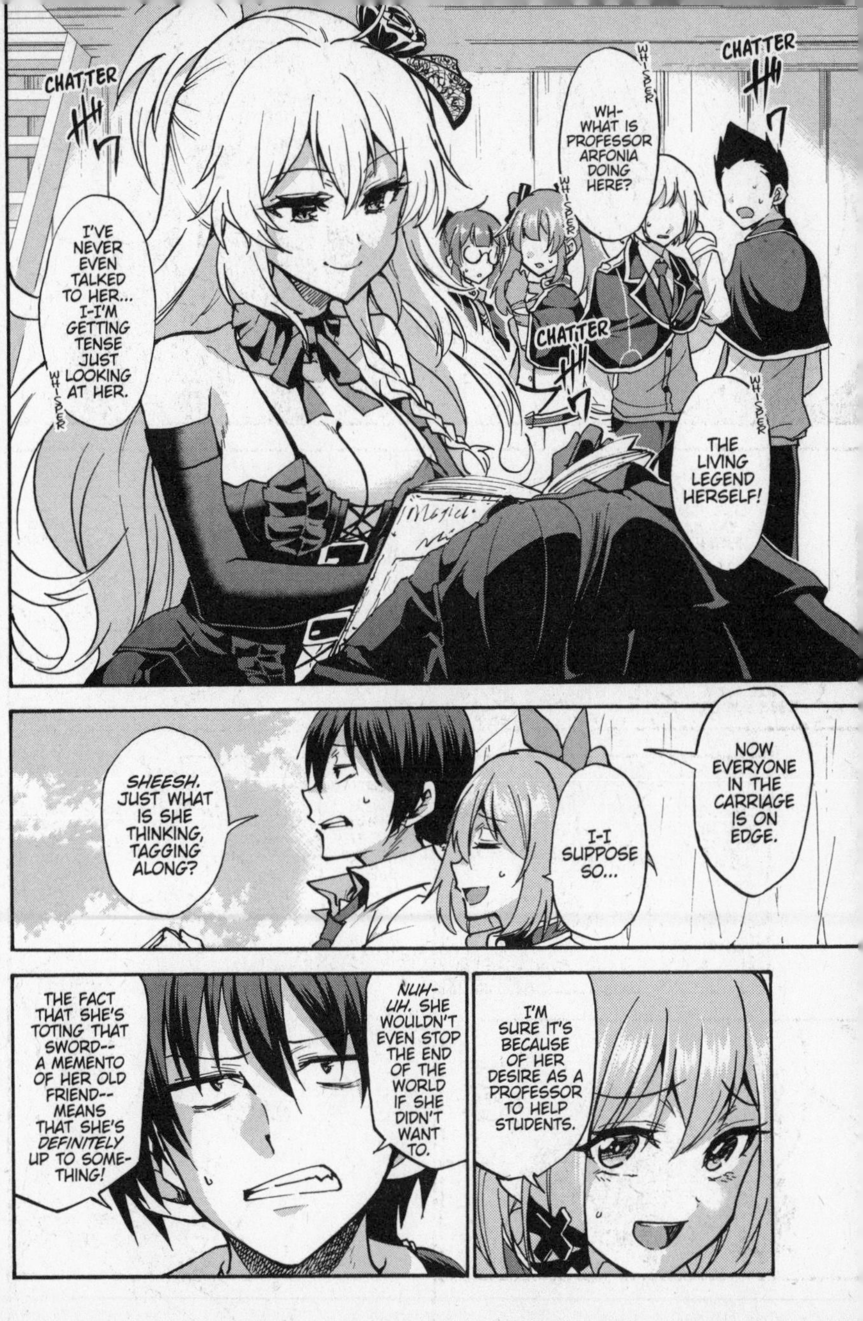
CHATTER
WHISPER
WH- WHAT IS PROFESSOR ARFONIA DOING HERE?
WHISPER
WHISPER
THE LIVING LEGEND HERSELF!
CHATTER
CHATTER
I'VE NEVER EVEN TALKED TO HER... I-I'M GETTING TENSE JUST LOOKING AT HER.
WHISPER
NOW EVERYONE IN THE CARRIAGE IS ON EDGE.
I-I SUPPOSE SO...
*SHEESH.* JUST WHAT IS SHE THINKING, TAGGING ALONG?
I'M SURE IT'S BECAUSE OF HER DESIRE AS A PROFESSOR TO HELP STUDENTS.
*NUH-UH.* SHE WOULDN'T EVEN STOP THE END OF THE WORLD IF SHE DIDN'T WANT TO.
THE FACT THAT SHE'S TOTING THAT SWORD-- A MEMENTO OF HER OLD FRIEND-- MEANS THAT SHE'S *DEFINITELY* UP TO SOME-THING!

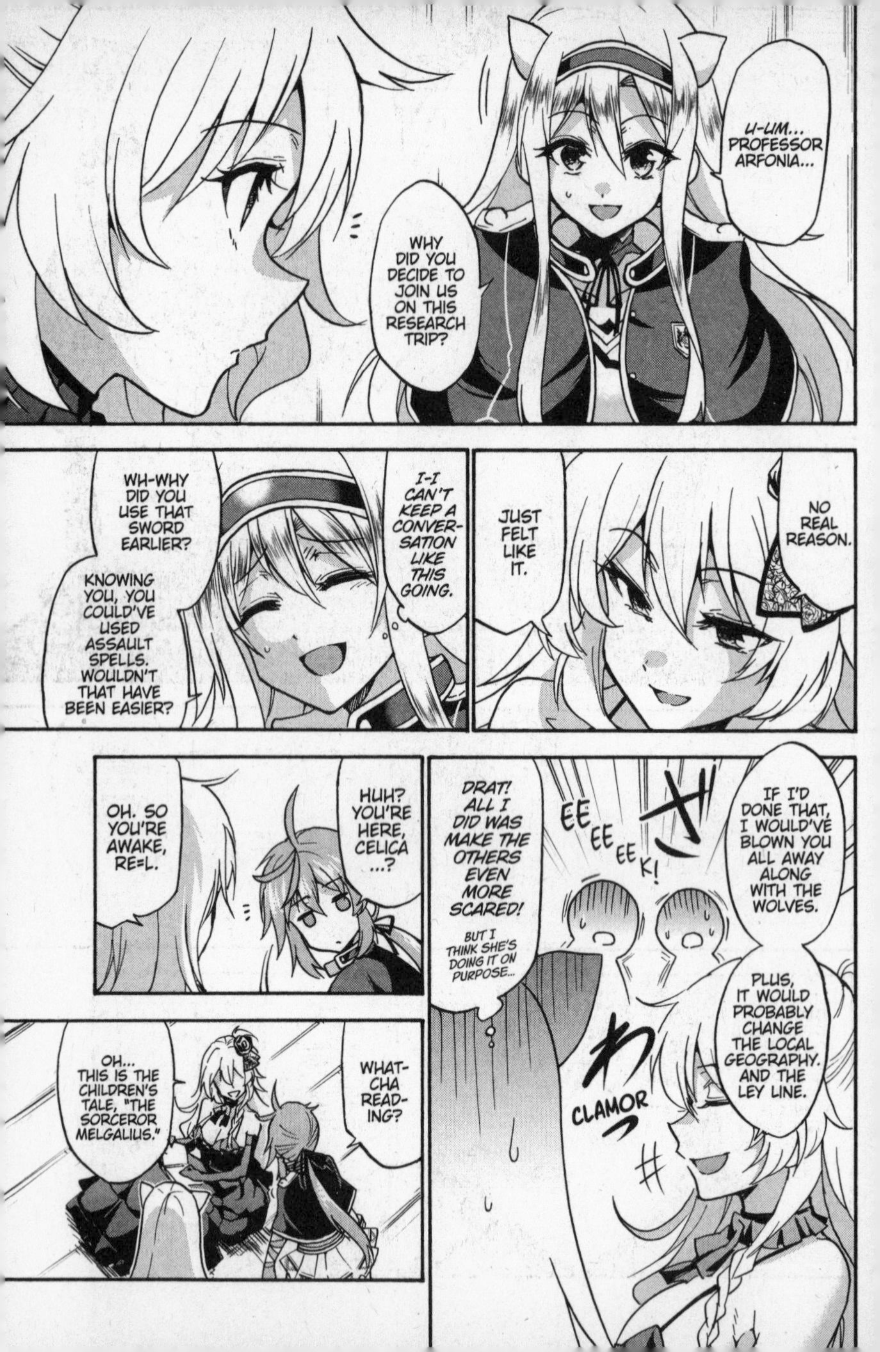
U-UM... PROFESSOR ARFONIA...
WHY DID YOU DECIDE TO JOIN US ON THIS RESEARCH TRIP?
NO REAL REASON.
JUST FELT LIKE IT.
I-I CAN'T KEEP A CONVER-SATION LIKE THIS GOING.
WH-WHY DID YOU USE THAT SWORD EARLIER?
KNOWING YOU, YOU COULD'VE USED ASSAULT SPELLS. WOULDN'T THAT HAVE BEEN EASIER?
IF I'D DONE THAT, I WOULD'VE BLOWN YOU ALL AWAY ALONG WITH THE WOLVES.
EE EE EE K!
DRAT! ALL I DID WAS MAKE THE OTHERS EVEN MORE SCARED!
BUT I THINK SHE'S DOING IT ON PURPOSE...
PLUS, IT WOULD PROBABLY CHANGE THE LOCAL GEOGRAPHY. AND THE LEY LINE.
CLAMOR
HUH? YOU'RE HERE, CELICA...?
OH. SO YOU'RE AWAKE, RE=L.
WHAT-CHA READ-ING?
OH... THIS IS THE CHILDREN'S TALE, "THE SORCEROR MELGALIUS."

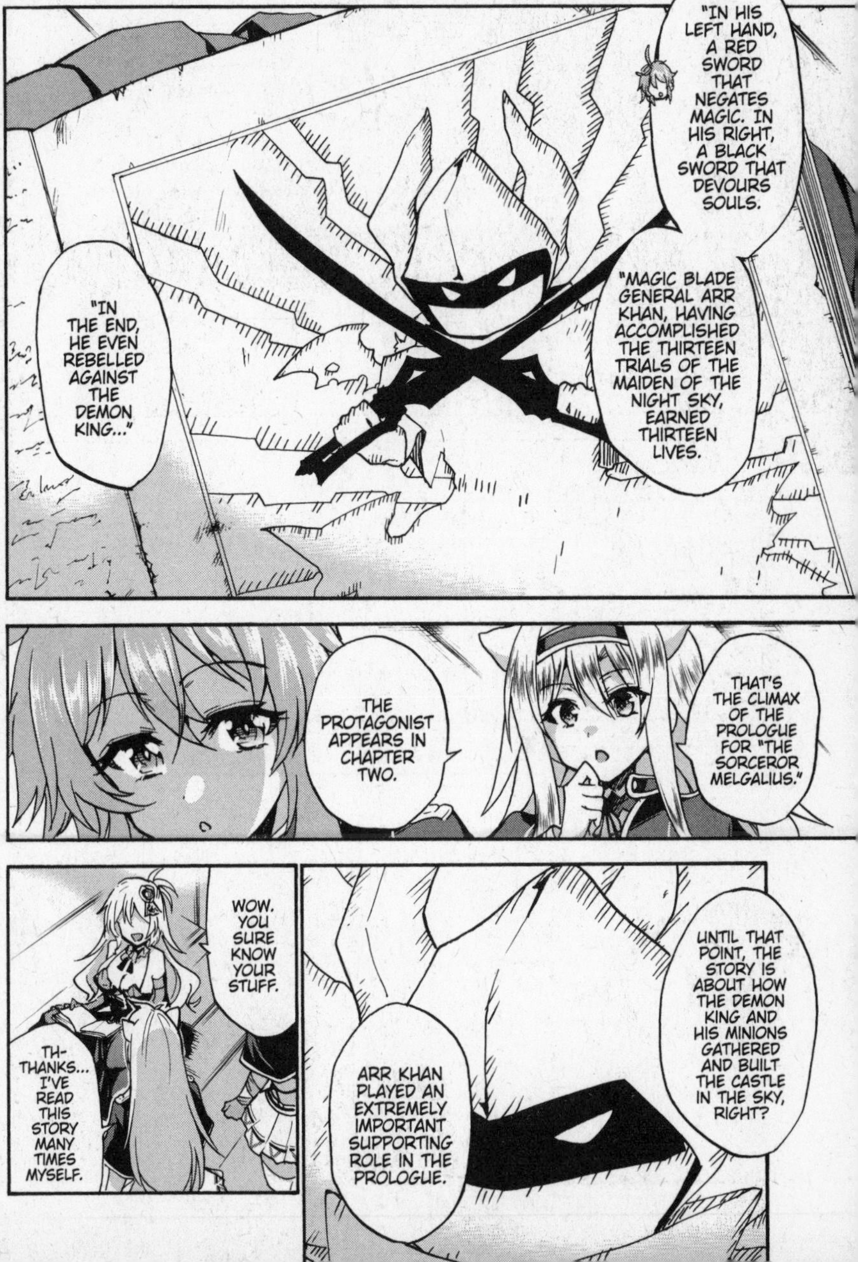
"IN HIS LEFT HAND, A RED SWORD THAT NEGATES MAGIC. IN HIS RIGHT, A BLACK SWORD THAT DEVOURS SOULS.
"MAGIC BLADE GENERAL ARR KHAN, HAVING ACCOMPLISHED THE THIRTEEN TRIALS OF THE MAIDEN OF THE NIGHT SKY, EARNED THIRTEEN LIVES.
"IN THE END, HE EVEN REBELLED AGAINST THE DEMON KING..."
THAT'S THE CLIMAX OF THE PROLOGUE FOR "THE SORCEROR MELGALIUS."
THE PROTAGONIST APPEARS IN CHAPTER TWO.
UNTIL THAT POINT, THE STORY IS ABOUT HOW THE DEMON KING AND HIS MINIONS GATHERED AND BUILT THE CASTLE IN THE SKY, RIGHT?
ARR KHAN PLAYED AN EXTREMELY IMPORTANT SUPPORTING ROLE IN THE PROLOGUE.
WOW. YOU SURE KNOW YOUR STUFF.
TH-THANKS... I'VE READ THIS STORY MANY TIMES MYSELF.

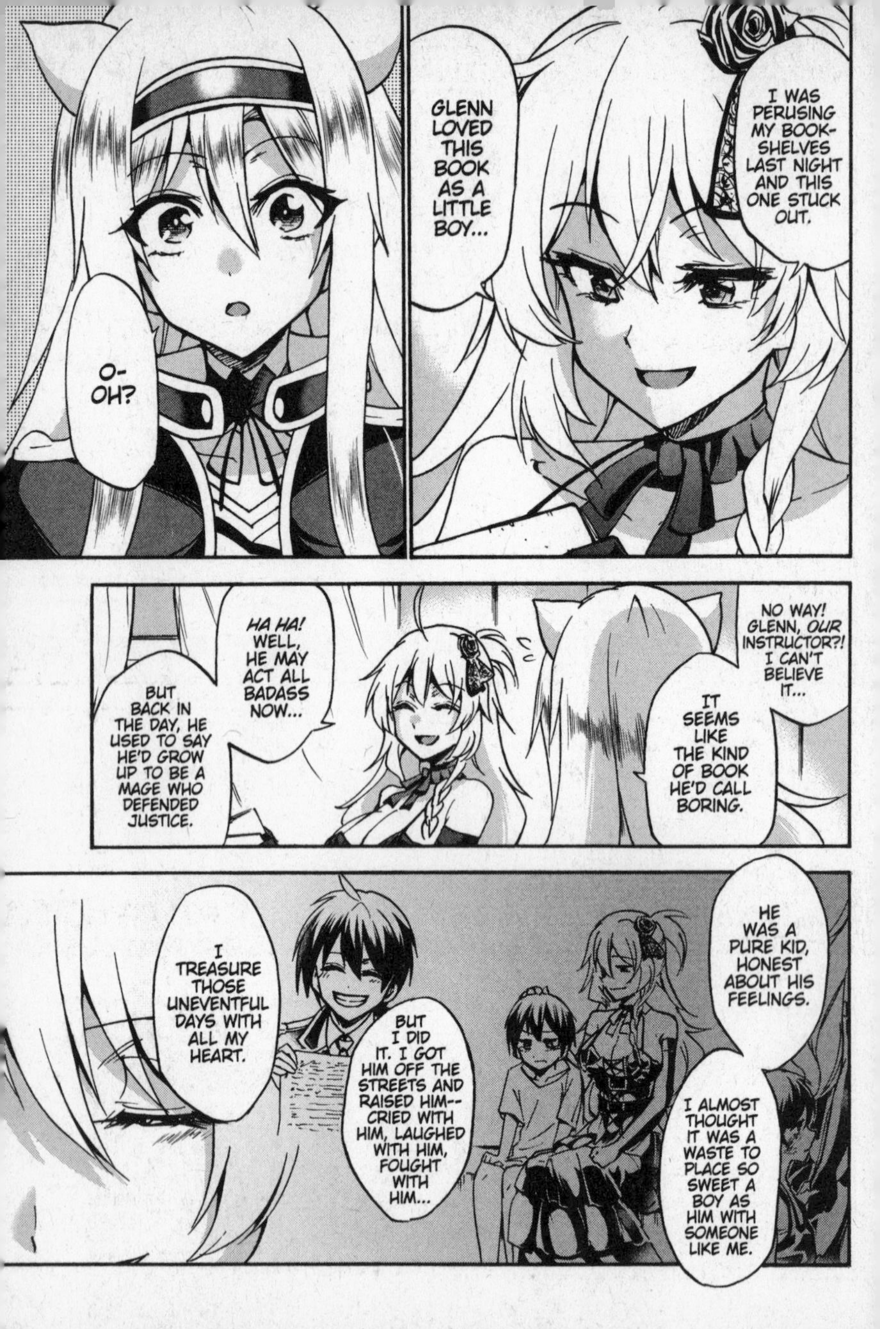
I WAS PERUSING MY BOOK-SHELVES LAST NIGHT AND THIS ONE STUCK OUT.
GLENN LOVED THIS BOOK AS A LITTLE BOY...
O-OH?
NO WAY! GLENN, *OUR* INSTRUCTOR?! I CAN'T BELIEVE IT...
IT SEEMS LIKE THE KIND OF BOOK HE'D CALL BORING.
*HA HA!* WELL, HE MAY ACT ALL BADASS NOW...
BUT BACK IN THE DAY, HE USED TO SAY HE'D GROW UP TO BE A MAGE WHO DEFENDED JUSTICE.
HE WAS A PURE KID, HONEST ABOUT HIS FEELINGS.
I ALMOST THOUGHT IT WAS A WASTE TO PLACE SO SWEET A BOY AS HIM WITH SOMEONE LIKE ME.
BUT I DID IT. I GOT HIM OFF THE STREETS AND RAISED HIM--CRIED WITH HIM, LAUGHED WITH HIM, FOUGHT WITH HIM...
I TREASURE THOSE UNEVENTFUL DAYS WITH ALL MY HEART.

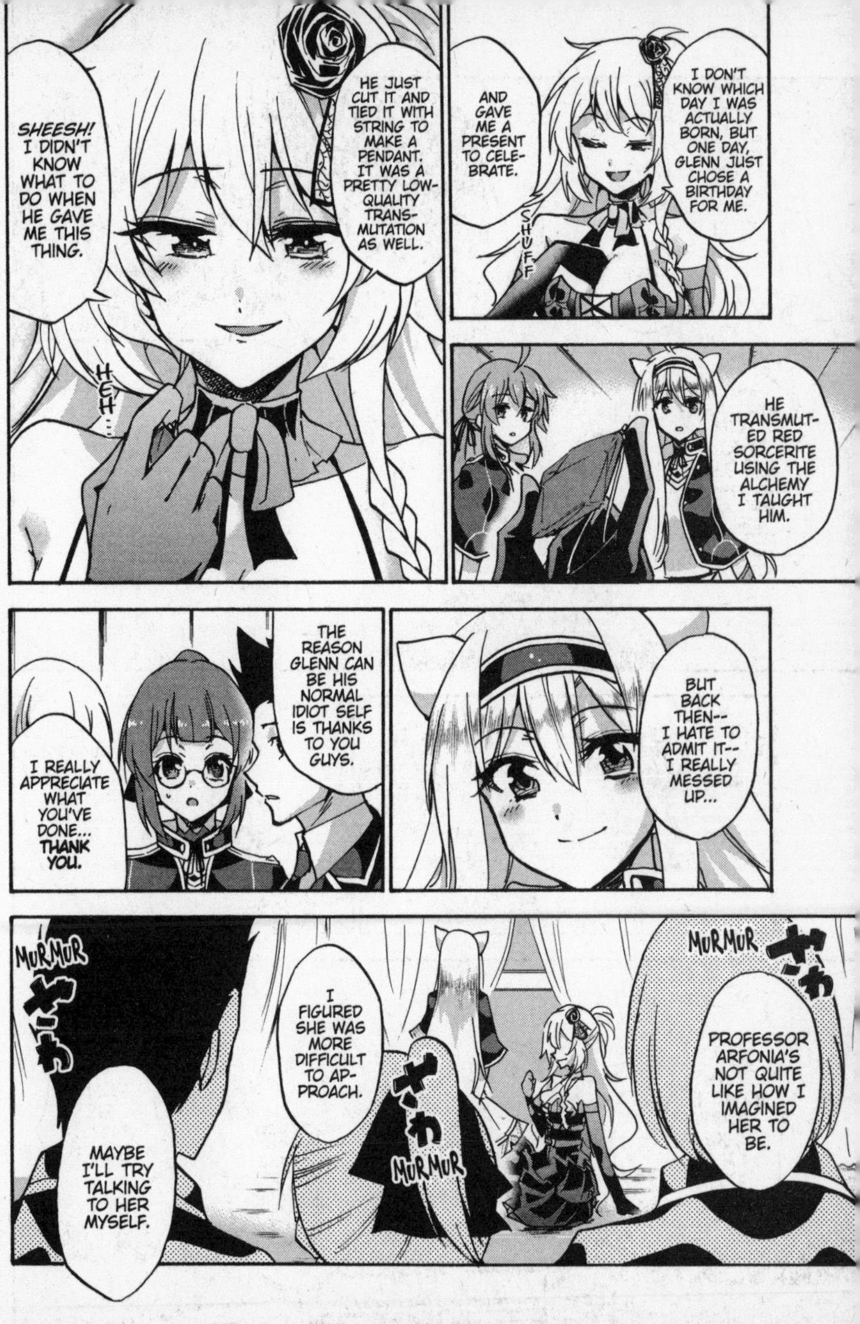

I DON'T KNOW WHICH DAY I WAS ACTUALLY BORN, BUT ONE DAY, GLENN JUST CHOSE A BIRTHDAY FOR ME.
AND GAVE ME A PRESENT TO CELE-BRATE.
SHUFF
HE TRANSMUT-ED RED SORCERITE USING THE ALCHEMY I TAUGHT HIM.
HE JUST CUT IT AND TIED IT WITH STRING TO MAKE A PENDANT. IT WAS A PRETTY LOW-QUALITY TRANS-MUTATION AS WELL.
SHEESH! I DIDN'T KNOW WHAT TO DO WHEN HE GAVE ME THIS THING.
HEH...
BUT BACK THEN-- I HATE TO ADMIT IT-- I REALLY MESSED UP...
THE REASON GLENN CAN BE HIS NORMAL IDIOT SELF IS THANKS TO YOU GUYS.
I REALLY APPRECIATE WHAT YOU'VE DONE... **THANK YOU.**
MURMUR
ざわ
PROFESSOR ARFONIA'S NOT QUITE LIKE HOW I IMAGINED HER TO BE.
I FIGURED SHE WAS MORE DIFFICULT TO AP-PROACH.
ざわ
MURMUR
MURMUR
ざわ
MAYBE I'LL TRY TALKING TO HER MYSELF.

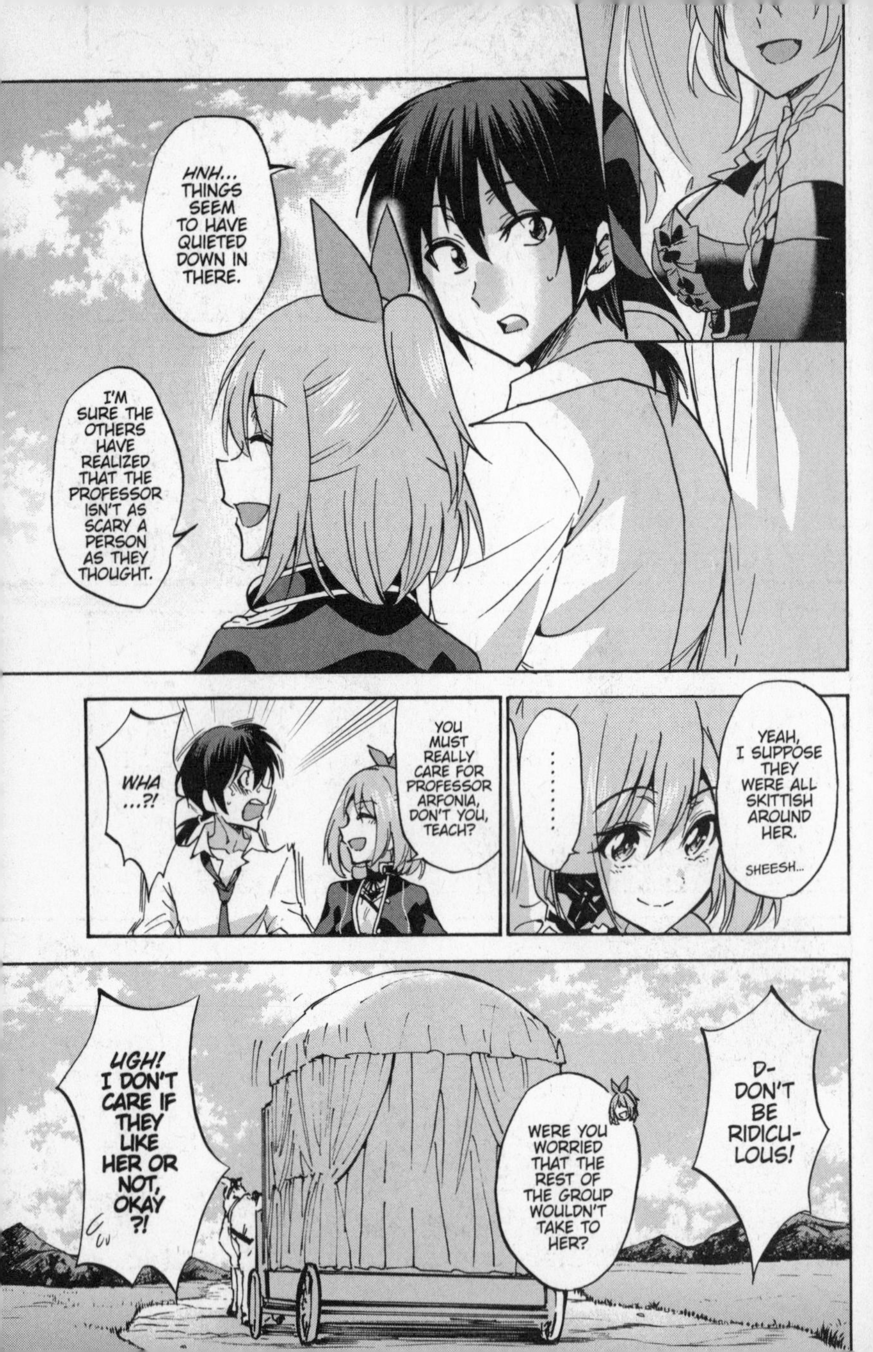
HNH... THINGS SEEM TO HAVE QUIETED DOWN IN THERE.
I'M SURE THE OTHERS HAVE REALIZED THAT THE PROFESSOR ISN'T AS SCARY A PERSON AS THEY THOUGHT.
YEAH, I SUPPOSE THEY WERE ALL SKITTISH AROUND HER.
SHEESH...
......
YOU MUST REALLY CARE FOR PROFESSOR ARFONIA, DON'T YOU, TEACH?
WHA...?!
D-DON'T BE RIDICULOUS!
WERE YOU WORRIED THAT THE REST OF THE GROUP WOULDN'T TAKE TO HER?
UGH! I DON'T CARE IF THEY LIKE HER OR NOT, OKAY?!

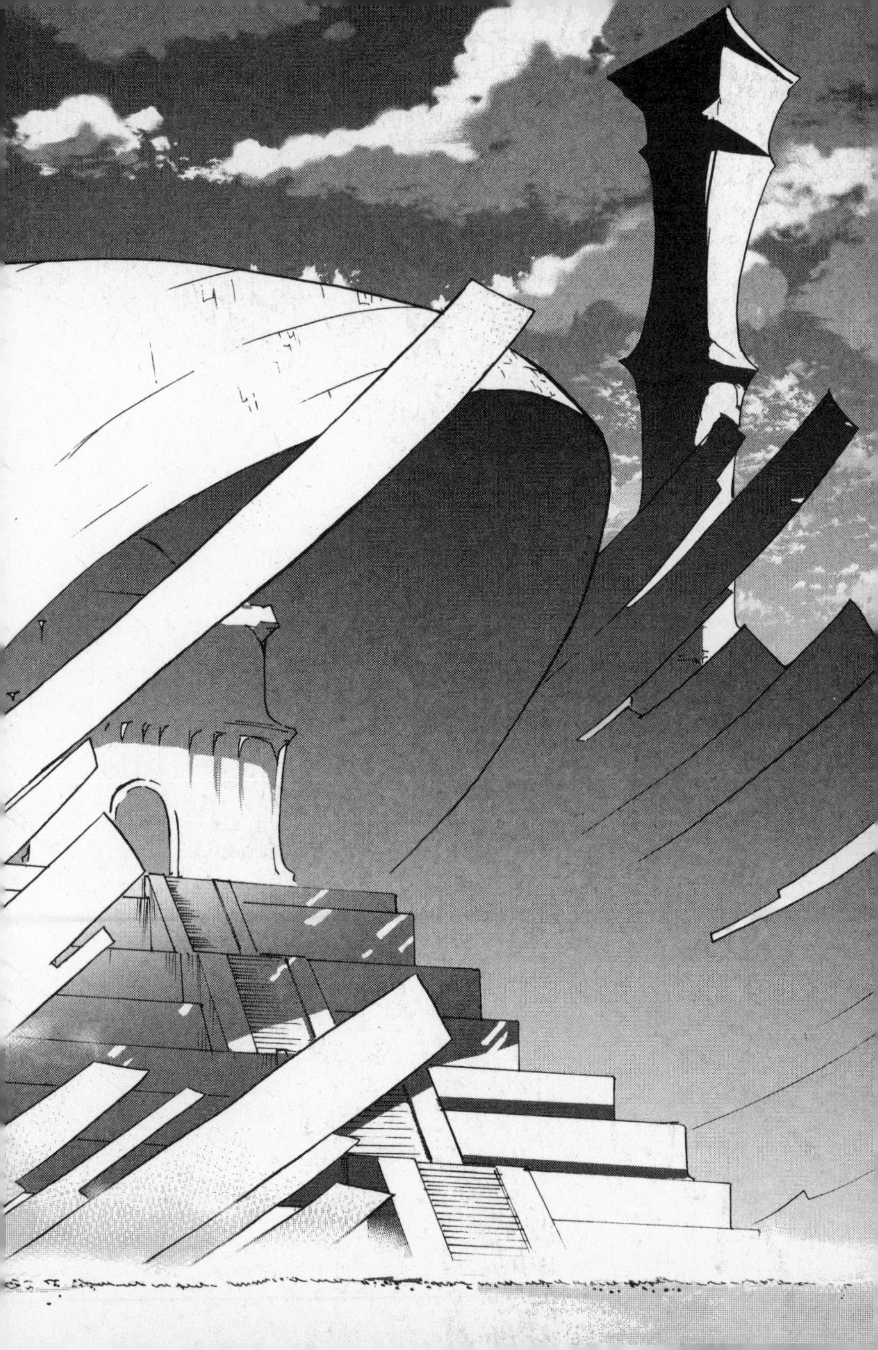

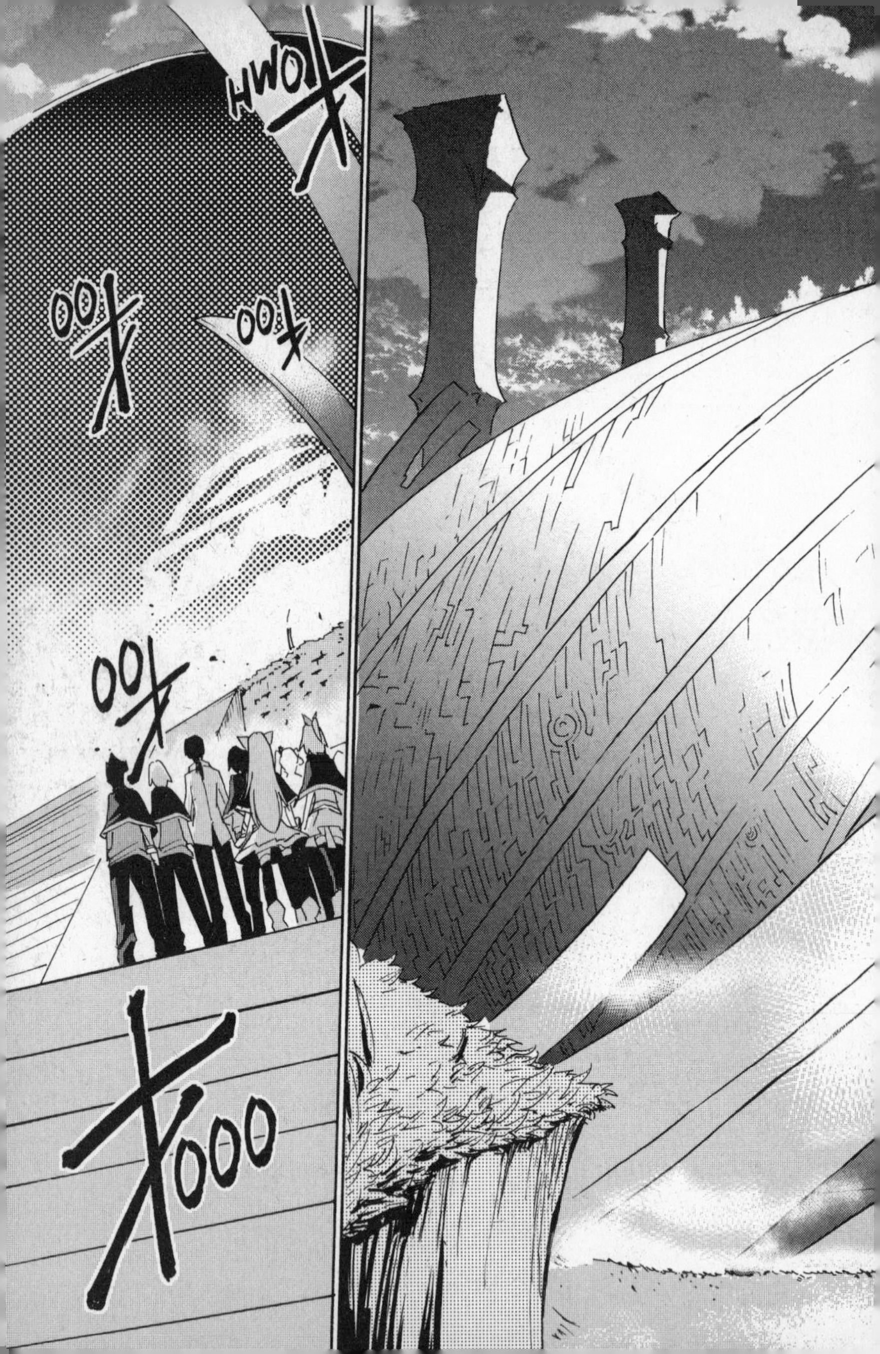
FOO
FOO
FOO
FOOO

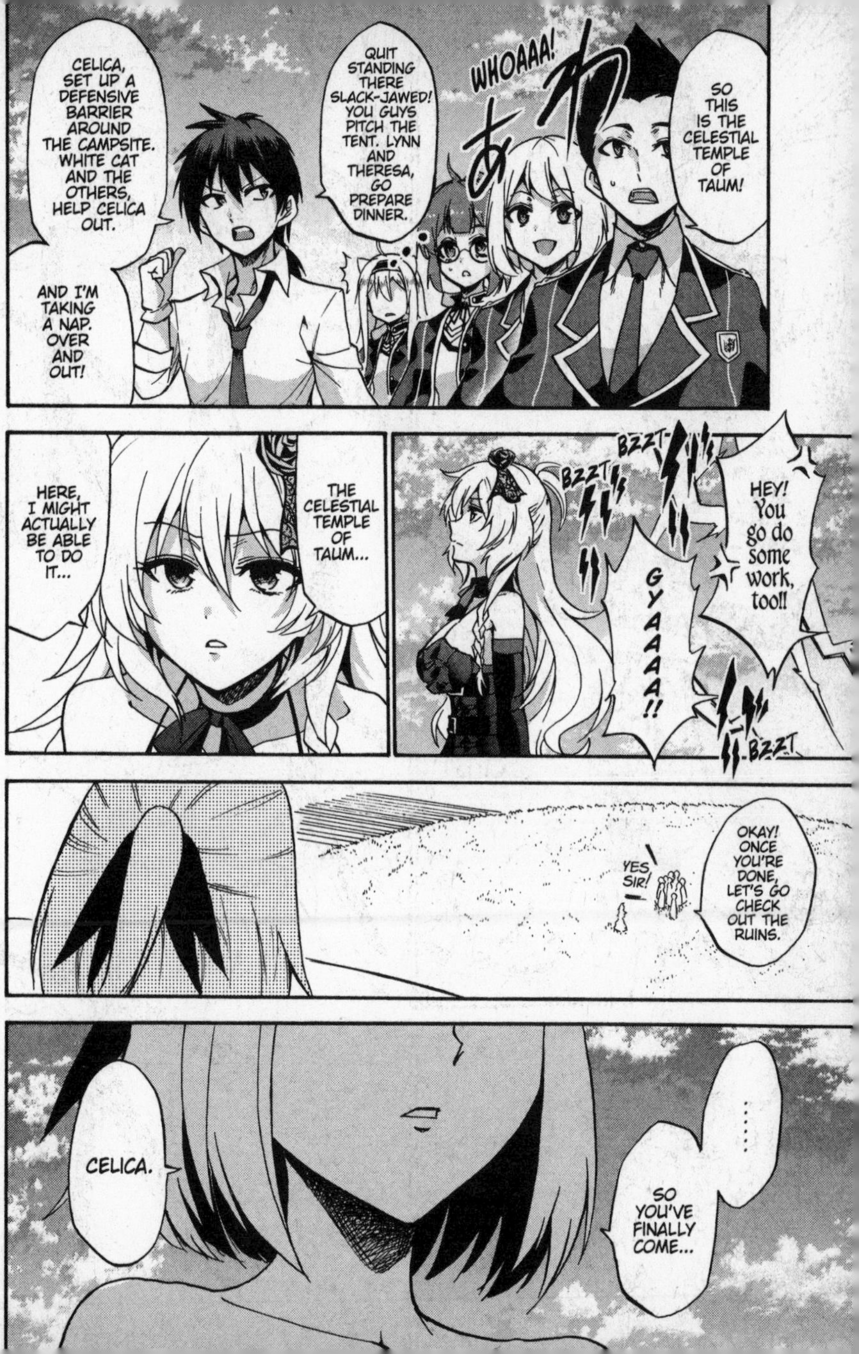

SO THIS IS THE CELESTIAL TEMPLE OF TAUM!
WHOAAA!
あわ
QUIT STANDING THERE SLACK-JAWED! YOU GUYS PITCH THE TENT. LYNN AND THERESA, GO PREPARE DINNER.
CELICA, SET UP A DEFENSIVE BARRIER AROUND THE CAMPSITE. WHITE CAT AND THE OTHERS, HELP CELICA OUT.
AND I'M TAKING A NAP. OVER AND OUT!
BZZT-
BZZT
HEY! You go do some work, too!!
GYAAAAA!!
BZZT
THE CELESTIAL TEMPLE OF TAUM...
HERE, I MIGHT ACTUALLY BE ABLE TO DO IT...
OKAY! ONCE YOU'RE DONE, LET'S GO CHECK OUT THE RUINS.
YES, SIR!
......
SO YOU'VE FINALLY COME...
CELICA.

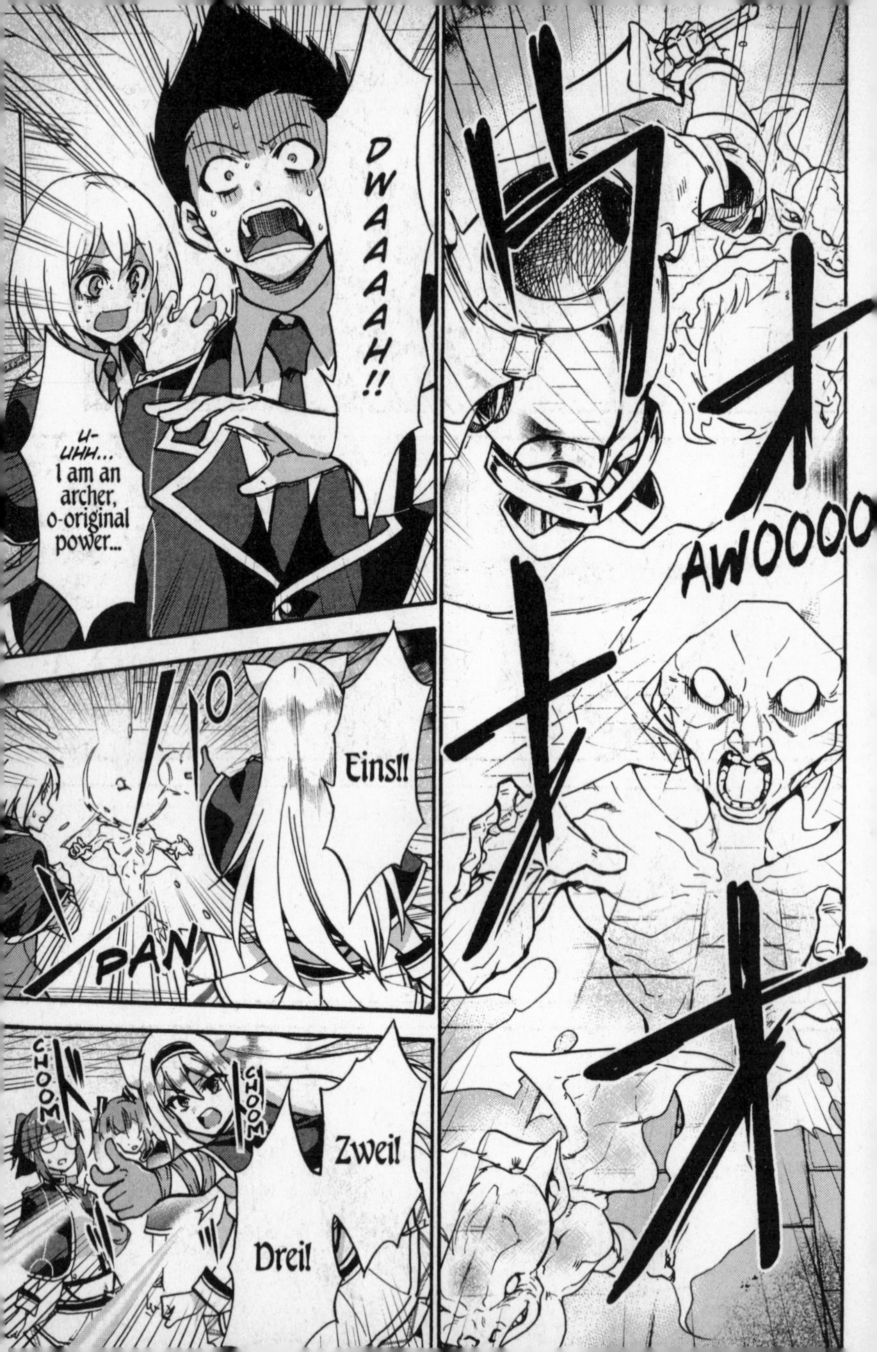
AWOOOO
DWAAAAAH!!
U-UHH... I am an archer, o-original power...
Eins!!
PAN
Zwei!
CHOOM
CHOOM
Drei!

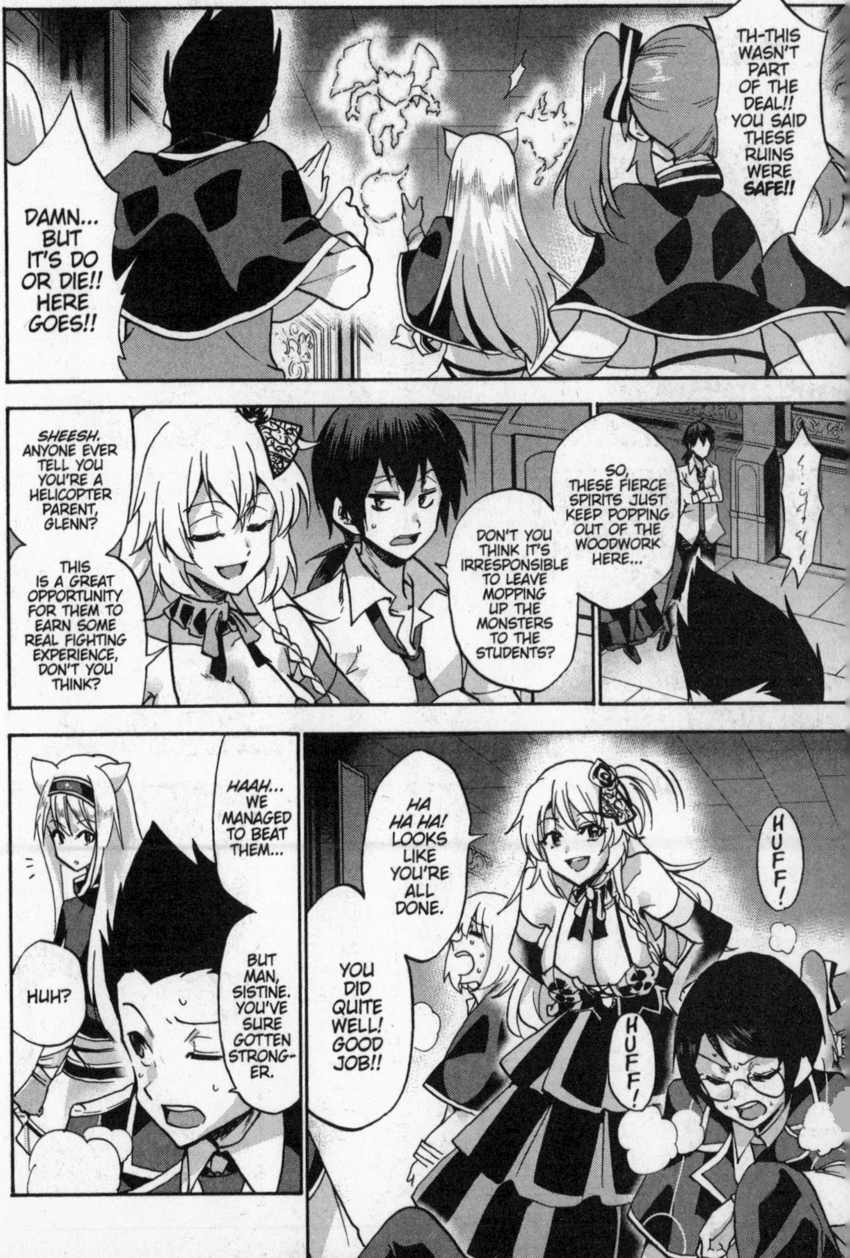
TH-THIS WASN'T PART OF THE DEAL!! YOU SAID THESE RUINS WERE **SAFE!!**
DAMN... BUT IT'S DO OR DIE!! HERE GOES!!
SO, THESE FIERCE SPIRITS JUST KEEP POPPING OUT OF THE WOODWORK HERE...
DON'T YOU THINK IT'S IRRESPONSIBLE TO LEAVE MOPPING UP THE MONSTERS TO THE STUDENTS?
*SHEESH.* ANYONE EVER TELL YOU YOU'RE A HELICOPTER PARENT, GLENN?
THIS IS A GREAT OPPORTUNITY FOR THEM TO EARN SOME REAL FIGHTING EXPERIENCE, DON'T YOU THINK?
HUFF!
HUFF!
HA HA HA! LOOKS LIKE YOU'RE ALL DONE.
YOU DID QUITE WELL! GOOD JOB!!
*HAAH...* WE MANAGED TO BEAT THEM...
BUT MAN, SISTINE. YOU'VE SURE GOTTEN STRONGER.
HUH?

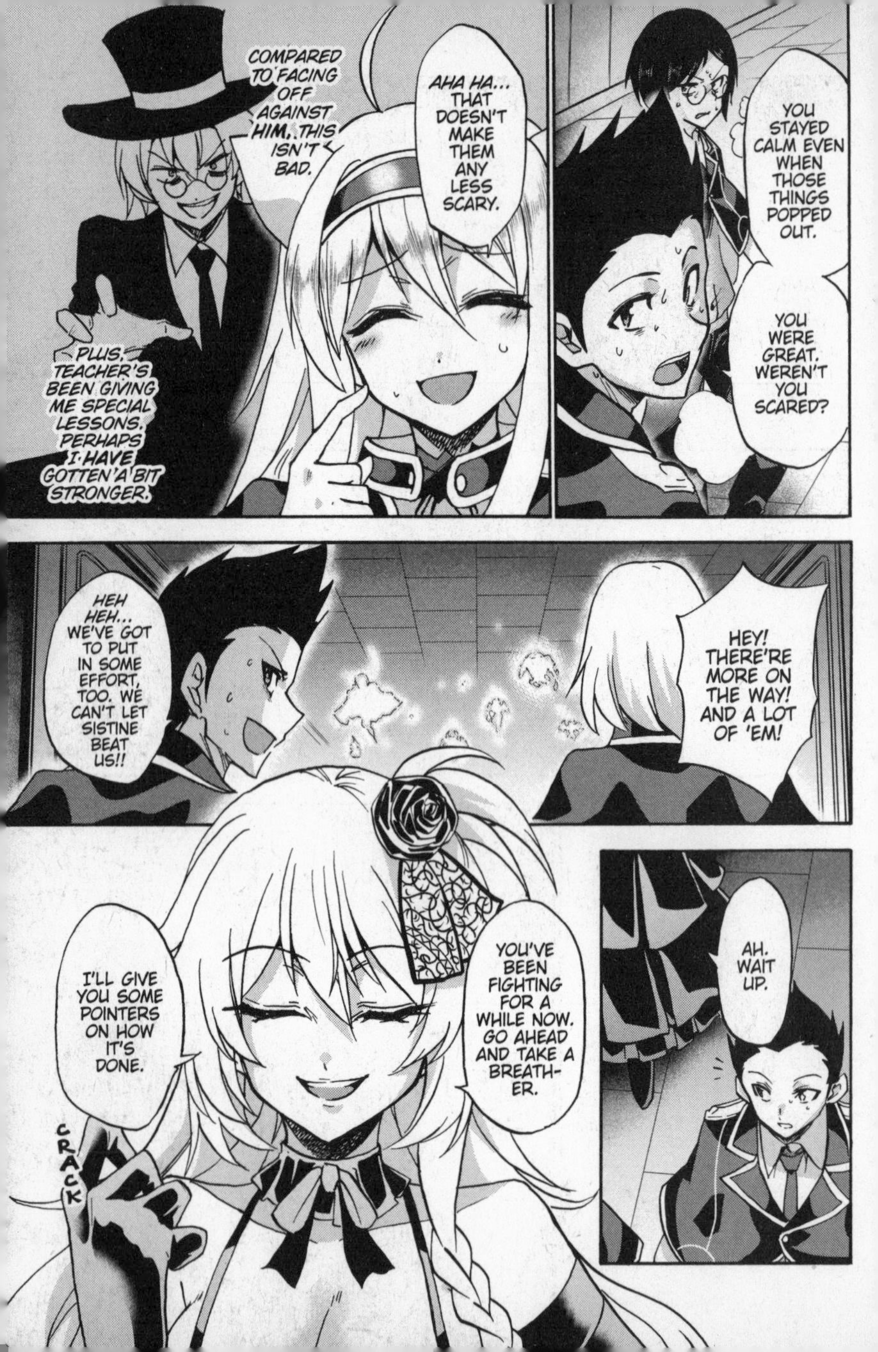

YOU STAYED CALM EVEN WHEN THOSE THINGS POPPED OUT.
YOU WERE GREAT. WEREN'T YOU SCARED?
AHA HA... THAT DOESN'T MAKE THEM ANY LESS SCARY.
COMPARED TO FACING OFF AGAINST HIM, THIS ISN'T BAD.
PLUS, TEACHER'S BEEN GIVING ME SPECIAL LESSONS. PERHAPS I HAVE GOTTEN A BIT STRONGER.
HEY! THERE'RE MORE ON THE WAY! AND A LOT OF 'EM!
HEH HEH... WE'VE GOT TO PUT IN SOME EFFORT, TOO. WE CAN'T LET SISTINE BEAT US!!
AH. WAIT UP.
YOU'VE BEEN FIGHTING FOR A WHILE NOW. GO AHEAD AND TAKE A BREATHER.
I'LL GIVE YOU SOME POINTERS ON HOW IT'S DONE.
CRACK

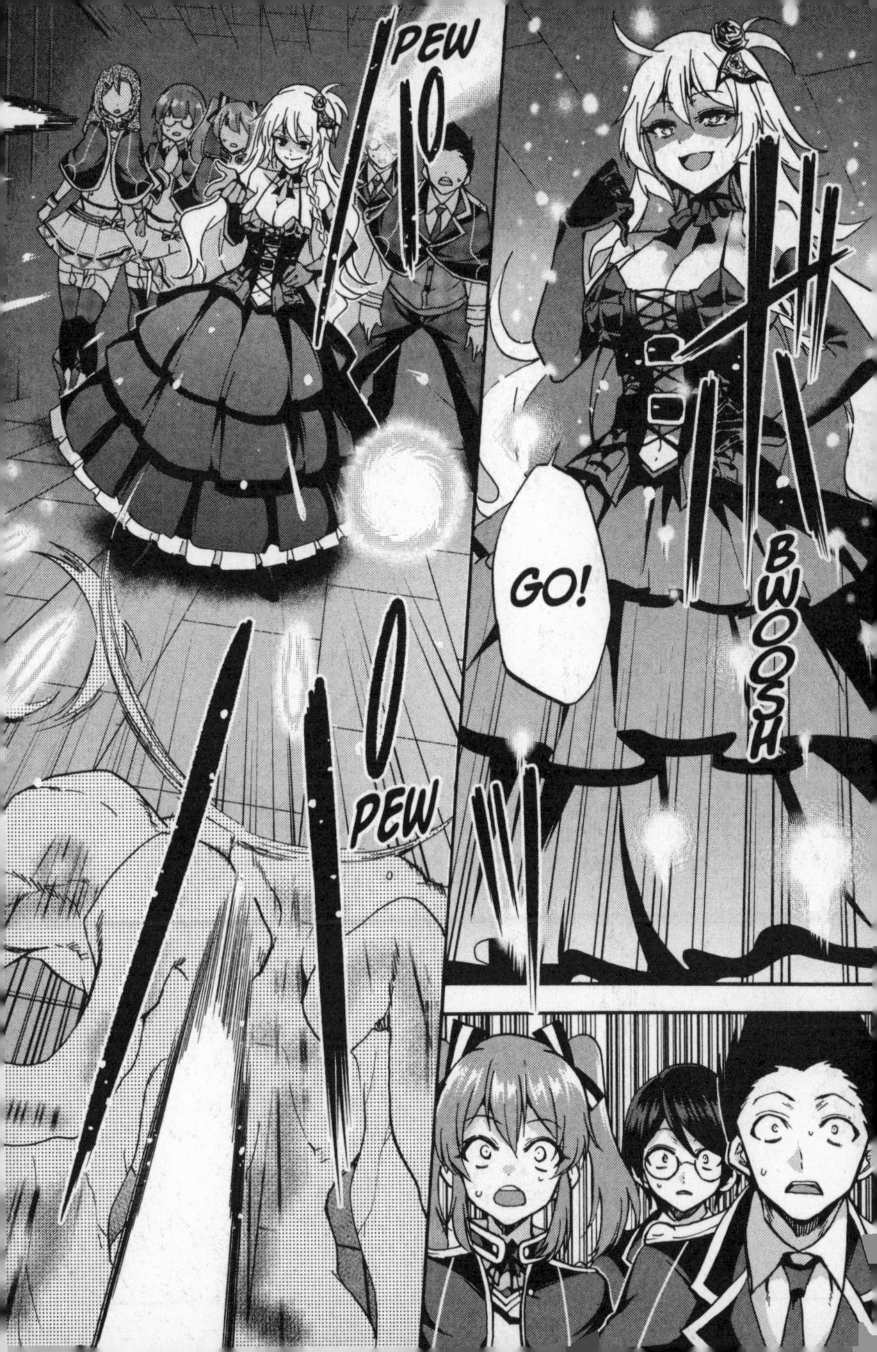
GO!
BWOOOSH
PEW
PEW

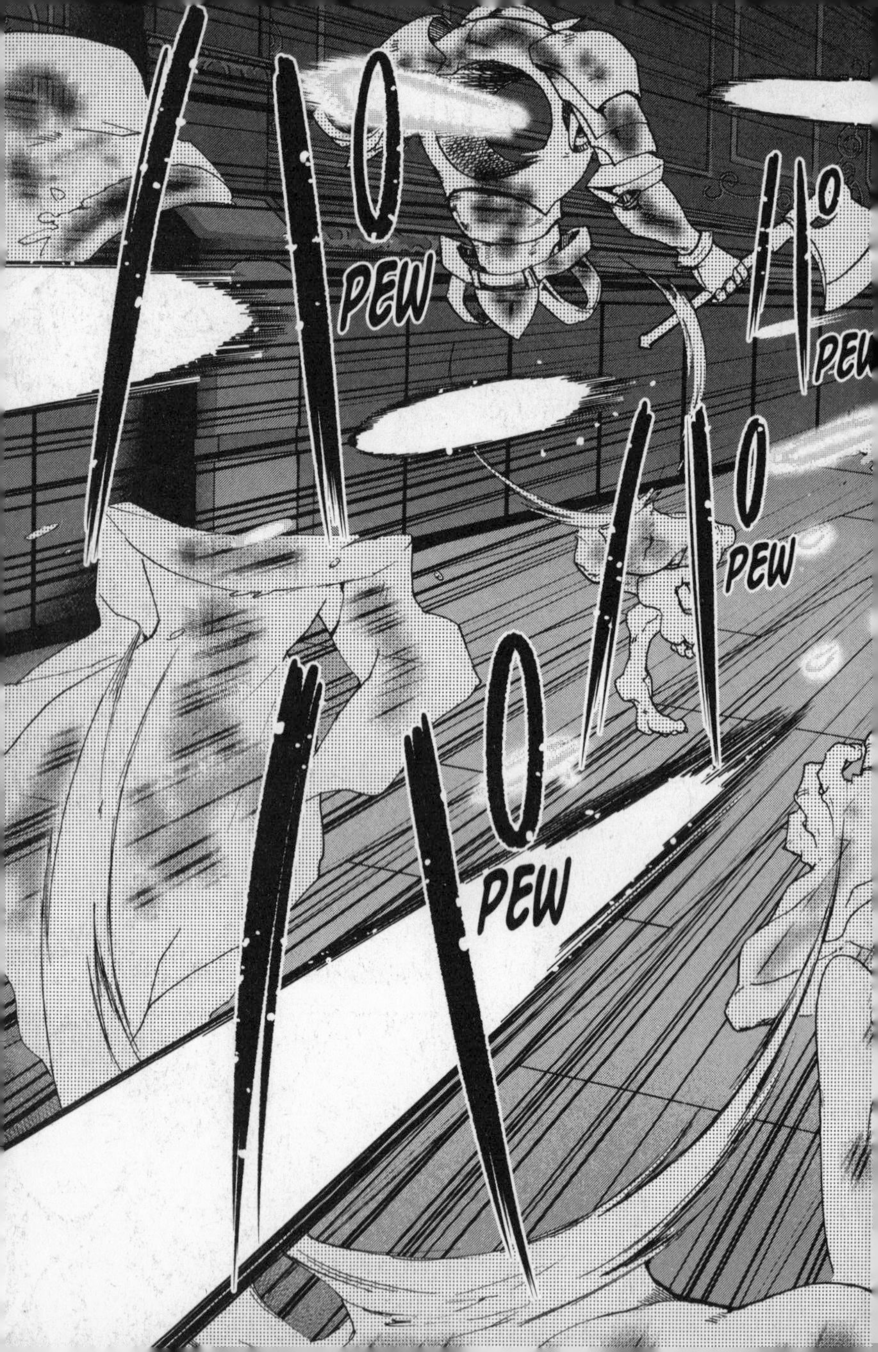
PEW
PEW
PEW
PEW

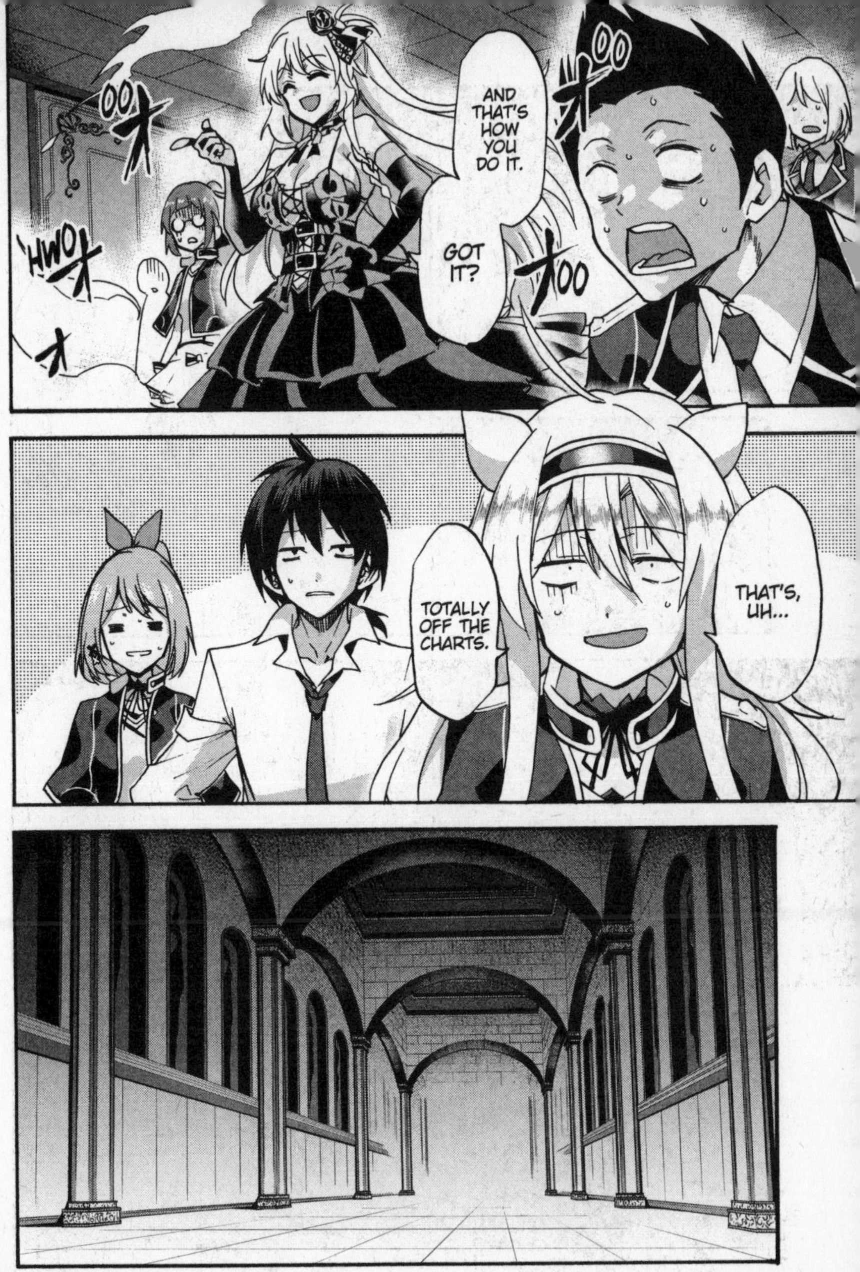
AND THAT'S HOW YOU DO IT.
GOT IT?
HWO
THAT'S, UH...
TOTALLY OFF THE CHARTS.

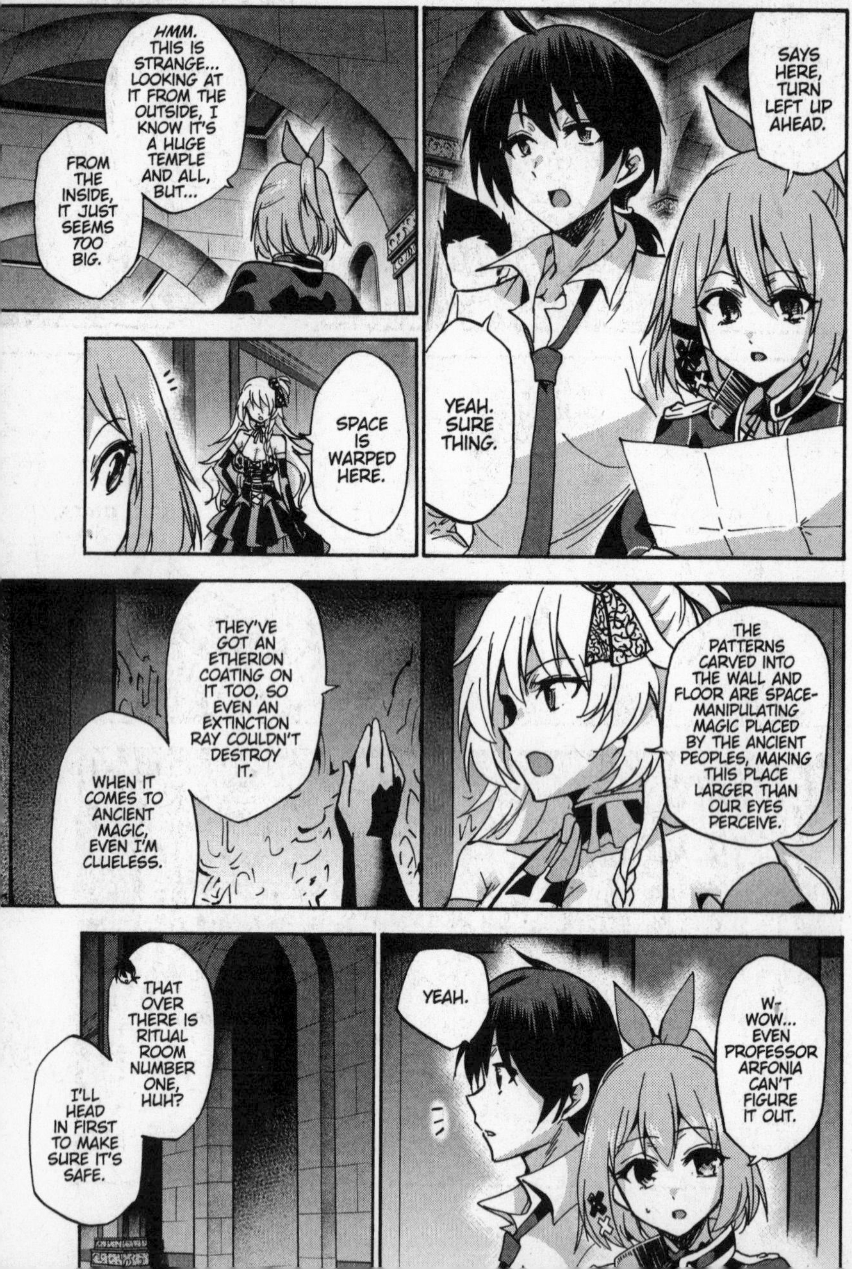
SAYS HERE, TURN LEFT UP AHEAD.
YEAH. SURE THING.
*HMM.* THIS IS STRANGE... LOOKING AT IT FROM THE OUTSIDE, I KNOW IT'S A HUGE TEMPLE AND ALL, BUT...
FROM THE INSIDE, IT JUST SEEMS *TOO* BIG.
SPACE IS WARPED HERE.
THE PATTERNS CARVED INTO THE WALL AND FLOOR ARE SPACE-MANIPULATING MAGIC PLACED BY THE ANCIENT PEOPLES, MAKING THIS PLACE LARGER THAN OUR EYES PERCEIVE.
THEY'VE GOT AN ETHERION COATING ON IT TOO, SO EVEN AN EXTINCTION RAY COULDN'T DESTROY IT.
WHEN IT COMES TO ANCIENT MAGIC, EVEN I'M CLUELESS.
W-WOW... EVEN PROFESSOR ARFONIA CAN'T FIGURE IT OUT.
YEAH.
THAT OVER THERE IS RITUAL ROOM NUMBER ONE, HUH?
I'LL HEAD IN FIRST TO MAKE SURE IT'S SAFE.

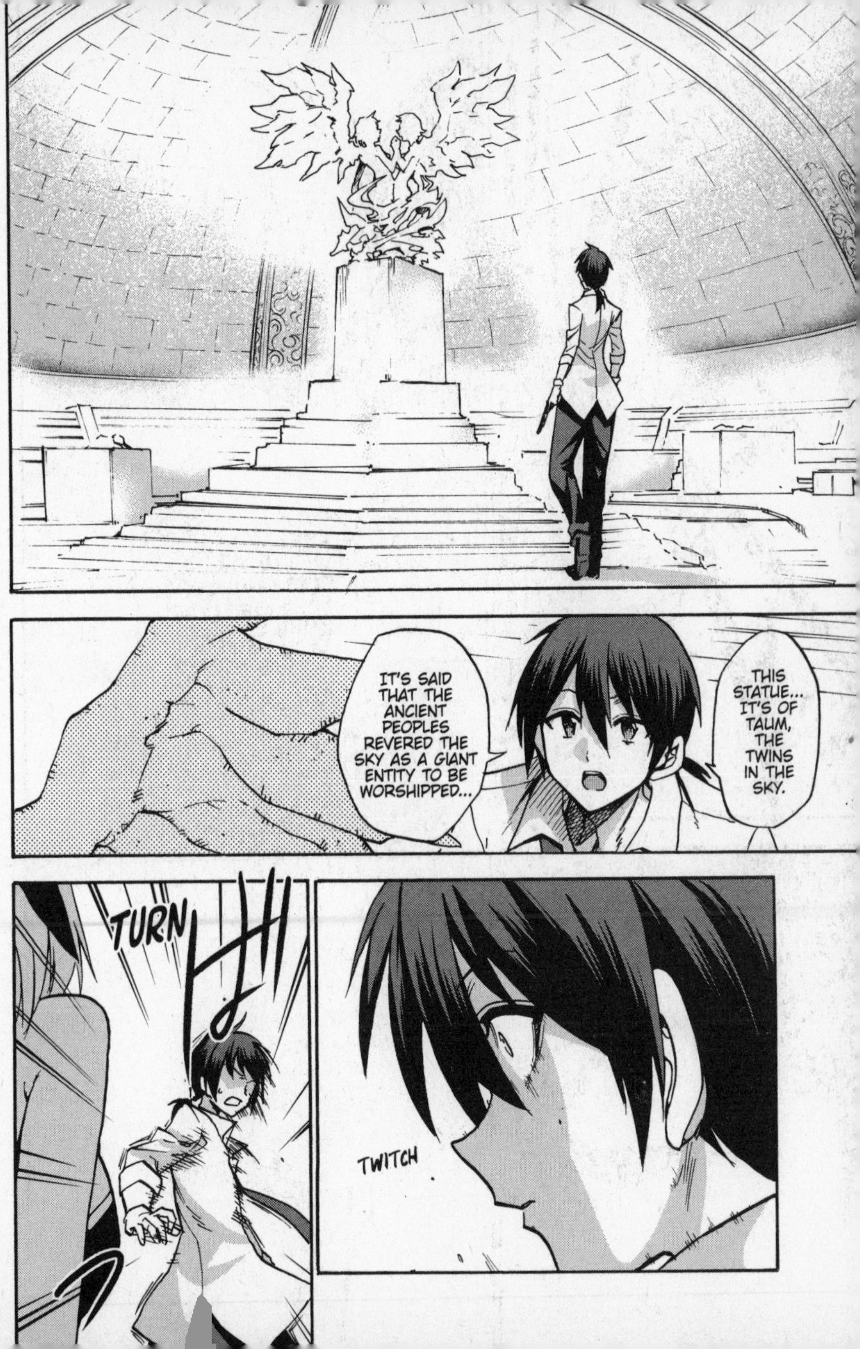
THIS STATUE... IT'S OF TAUM, THE TWINS IN THE SKY.
IT'S SAID THAT THE ANCIENT PEOPLES REVERED THE SKY AS A GIANT ENTITY TO BE WORSHIPPED...
TWITCH
TURN

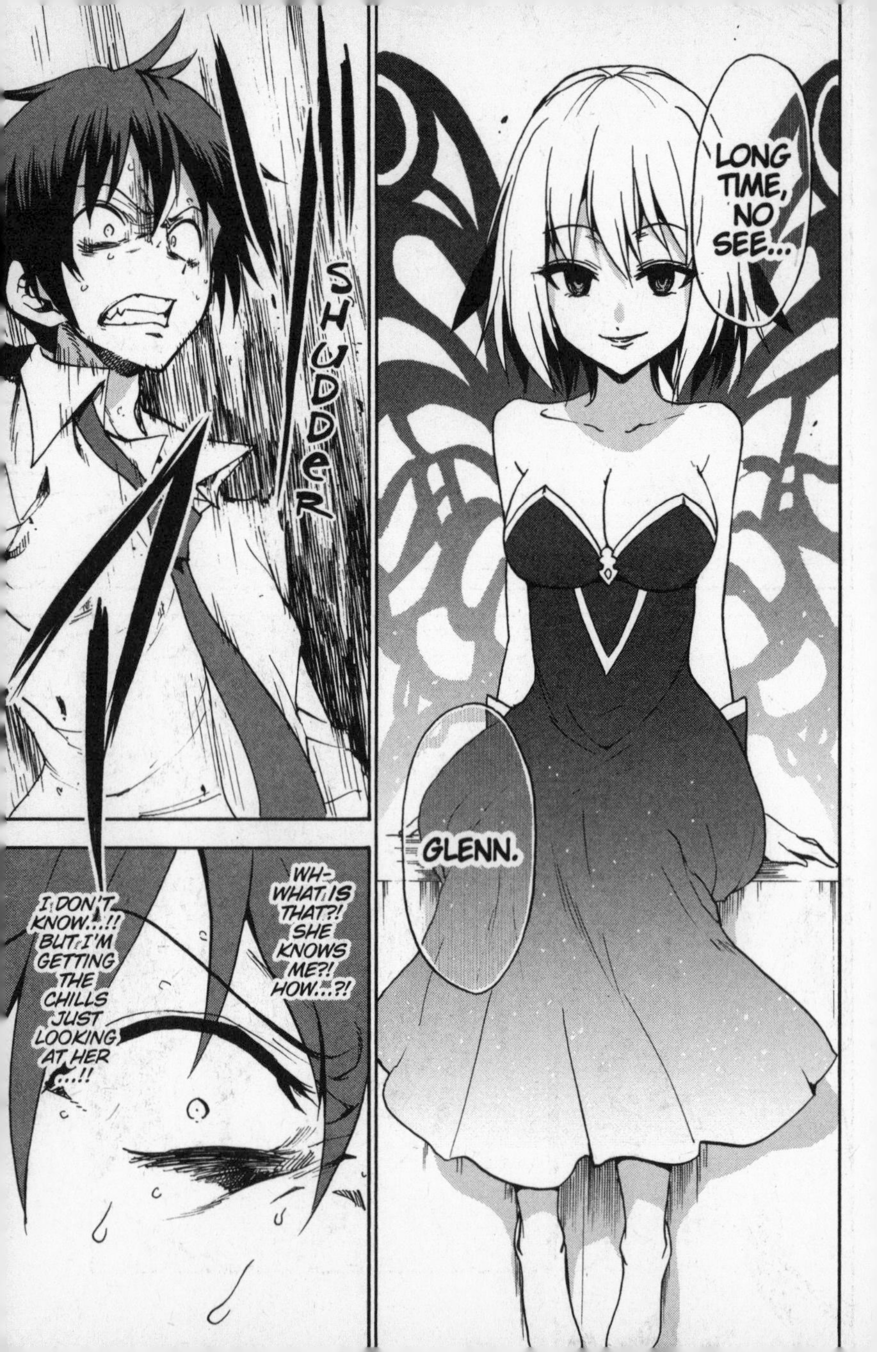
LONG TIME, NO SEE...
GLENN.
SHUDDER
WH- WHAT IS THAT?! SHE KNOWS ME?! HOW...?!
I DON'T KNOW...!! BUT I'M GETTING THE CHILLS JUST LOOKING AT HER ...!!

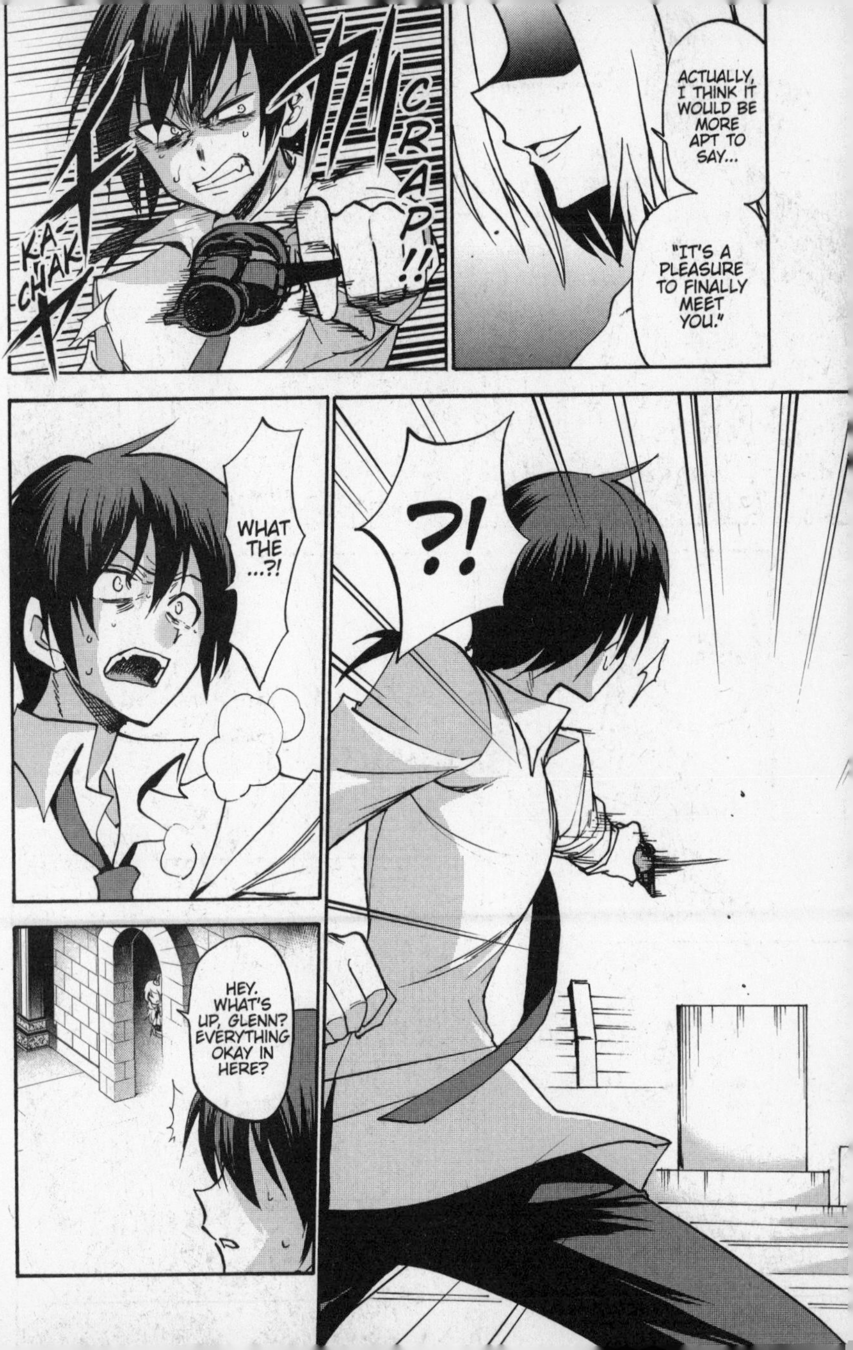
ACTUALLY, I THINK IT WOULD BE MORE APT TO SAY...
"IT'S A PLEASURE TO FINALLY MEET YOU."
CRAP!!
KA-CHAK
?!
WHAT THE ...?!
HEY. WHAT'S UP, GLENN? EVERYTHING OKAY IN HERE?

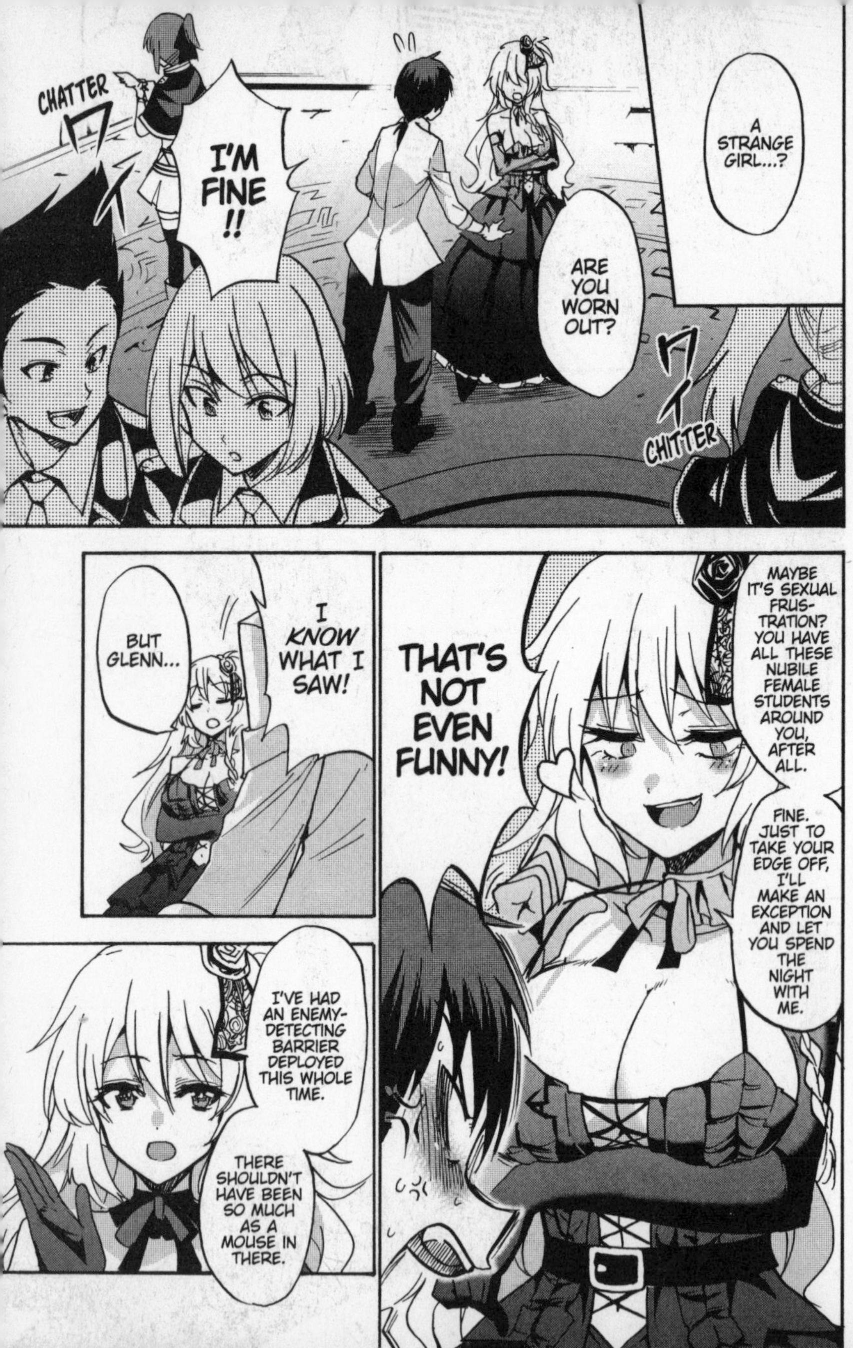

A STRANGE GIRL...?
ARE YOU WORN OUT?
CHITTER
I'M FINE!!
CHATTER
MAYBE IT'S SEXUAL FRUS-TRATION? YOU HAVE ALL THESE NUBILE FEMALE STUDENTS AROUND YOU, AFTER ALL.
FINE. JUST TO TAKE YOUR EDGE OFF, I'LL MAKE AN EXCEPTION AND LET YOU SPEND THE NIGHT WITH ME.
THAT'S NOT EVEN FUNNY!
I KNOW WHAT I SAW!
BUT GLENN...
I'VE HAD AN ENEMY-DETECTING BARRIER DEPLOYED THIS WHOLE TIME.
THERE SHOULDN'T HAVE BEEN SO MUCH AS A MOUSE IN THERE.

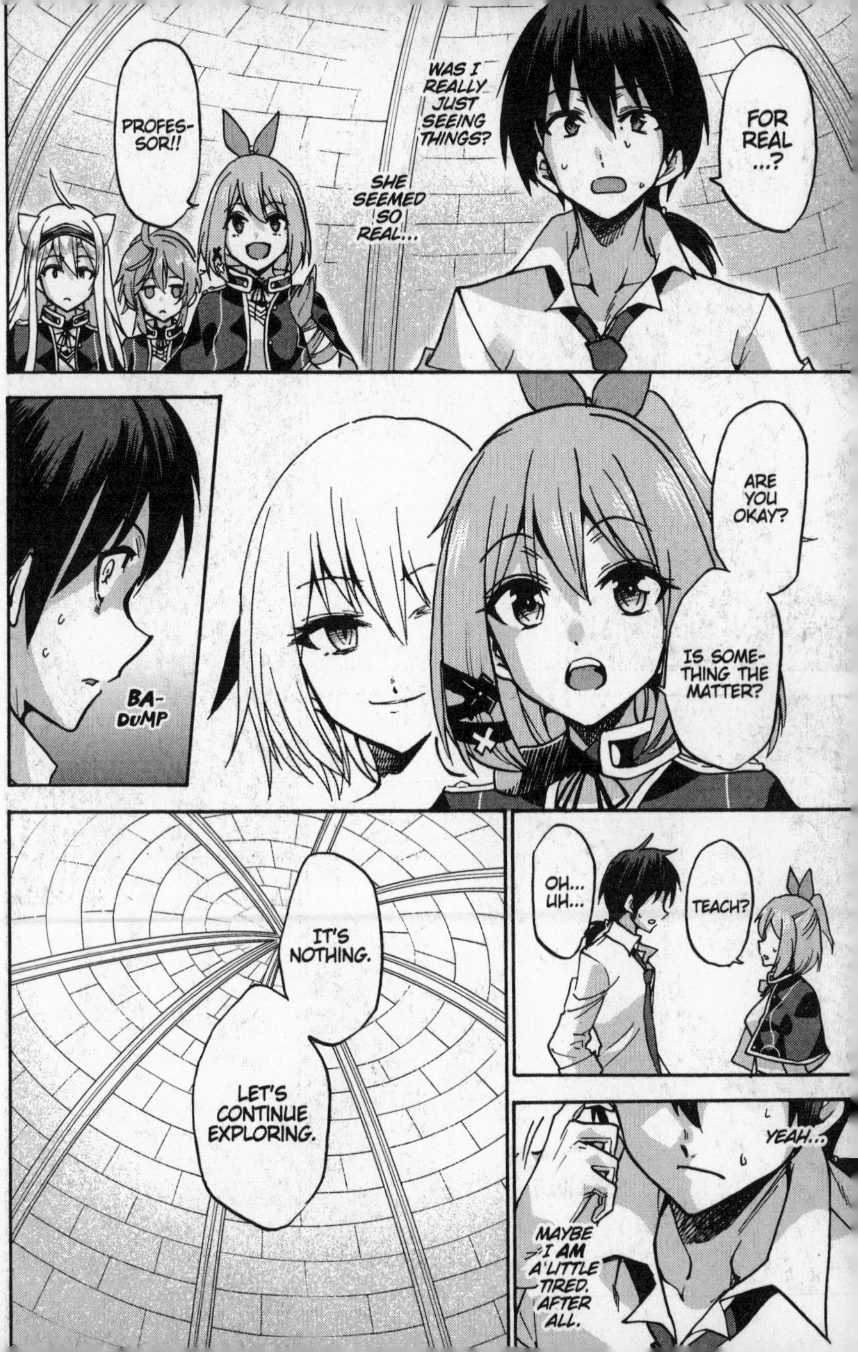
FOR REAL...?
WAS I REALLY JUST SEEING THINGS?
SHE SEEMED SO REAL...
PROFES-SOR!!
ARE YOU OKAY?
IS SOME-THING THE MATTER?
BA-DUMP
TEACH?
OH... UH...
YEAH...
MAYBE I AM A LITTLE TIRED AFTER ALL.
IT'S NOTHING.
LET'S CONTINUE EXPLORING.

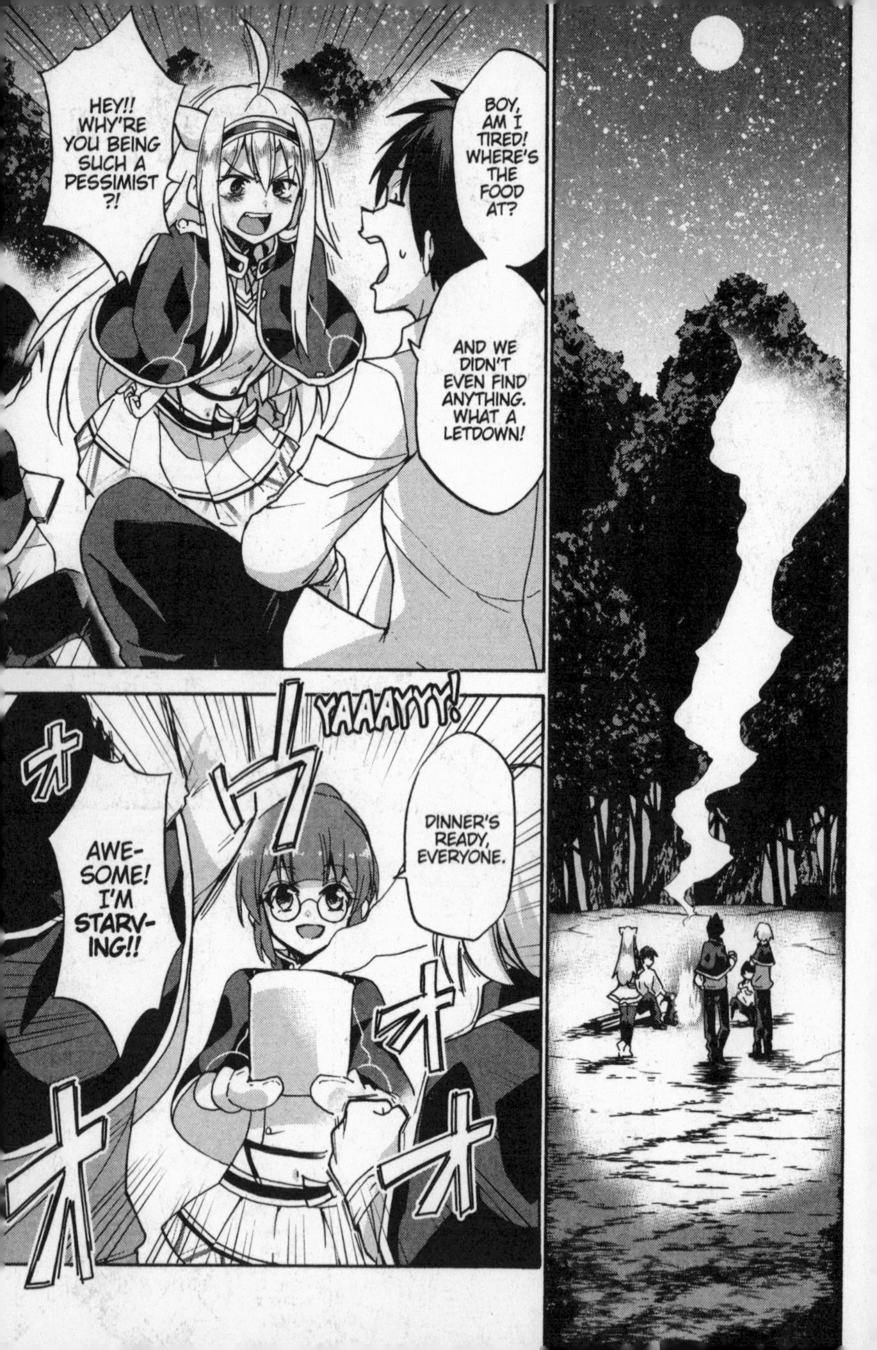
BOY, AM I TIRED! WHERE'S THE FOOD AT?
AND WE DIDN'T EVEN FIND ANYTHING. WHAT A LETDOWN!
HEY!! WHY'RE YOU BEING SUCH A PESSIMIST?!
DINNER'S READY, EVERYONE.
YAAAYYY!
AWE-SOME! I'M STARV-ING!!

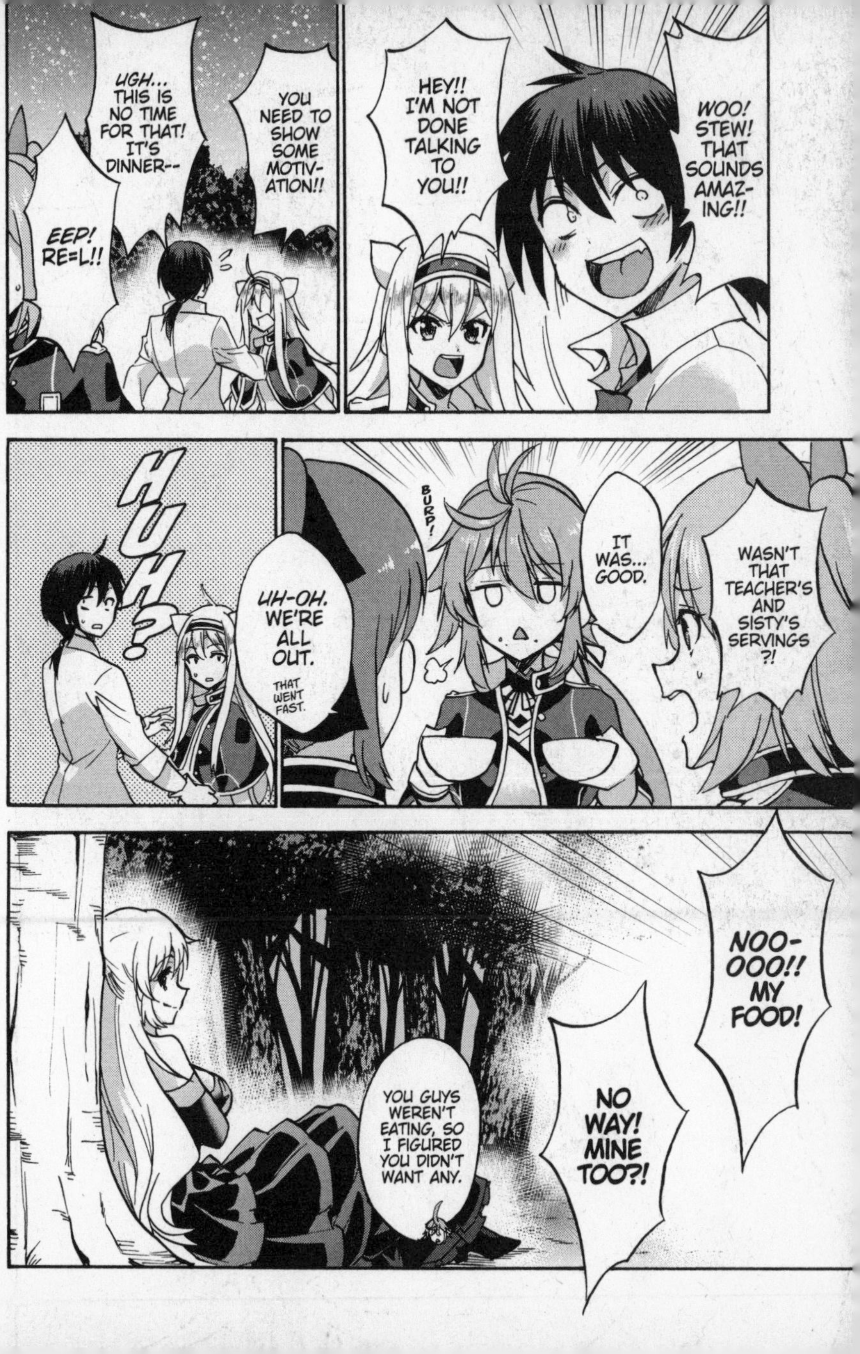
WOO! STEW! THAT SOUNDS AMAZING!!
HEY!! I'M NOT DONE TALKING TO YOU!!
YOU NEED TO SHOW SOME MOTIVATION!!
UGH... THIS IS NO TIME FOR THAT! IT'S DINNER--
EEP! RE=L!!
WASN'T THAT TEACHER'S AND SISTY'S SERVINGS?!
IT WAS... GOOD.
BURP!
UH-OH. WE'RE ALL OUT.
THAT WENT FAST.
HUH?!
NOOOOO!! MY FOOD!
NO WAY! MINE TOO?!
YOU GUYS WEREN'T EATING, SO I FIGURED YOU DIDN'T WANT ANY.

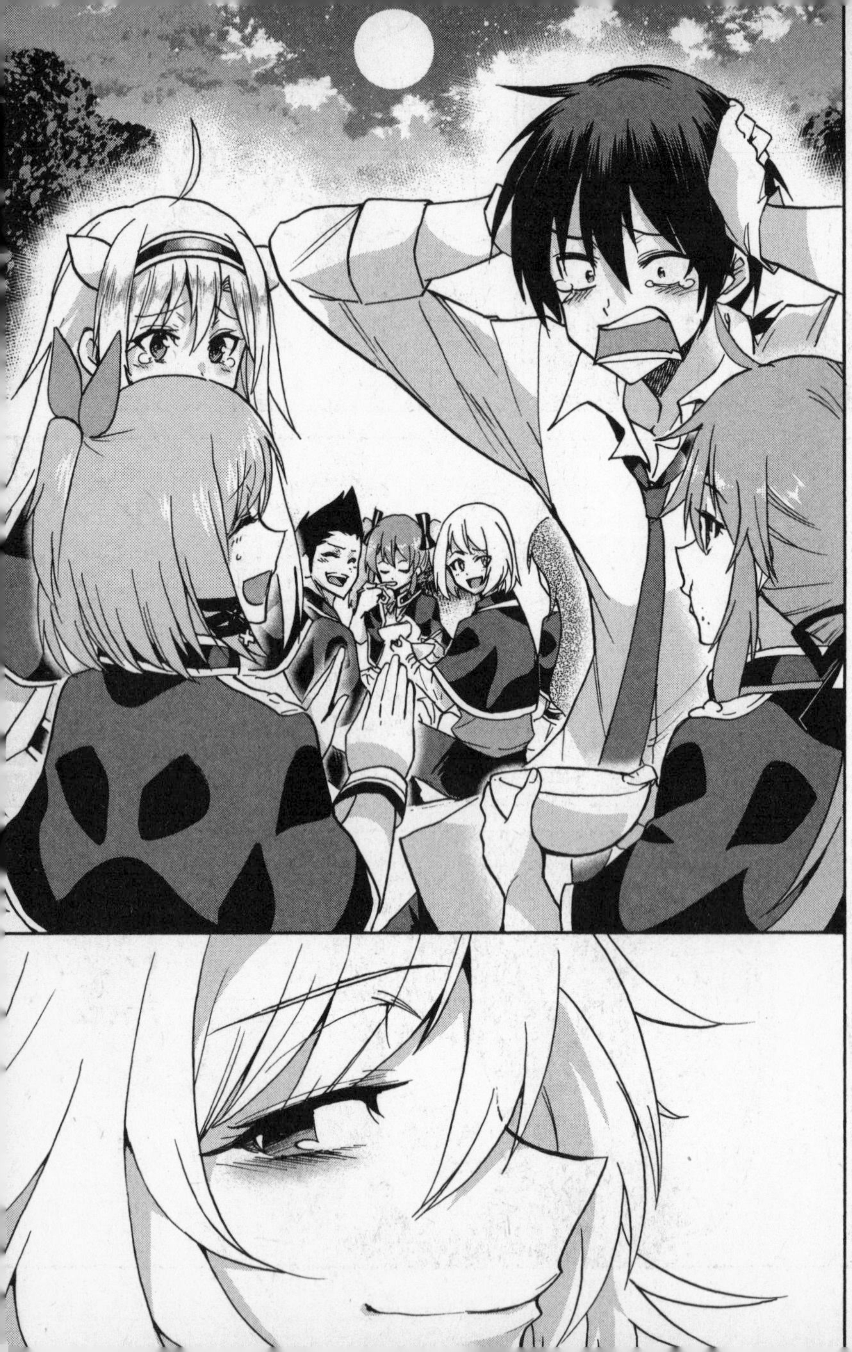

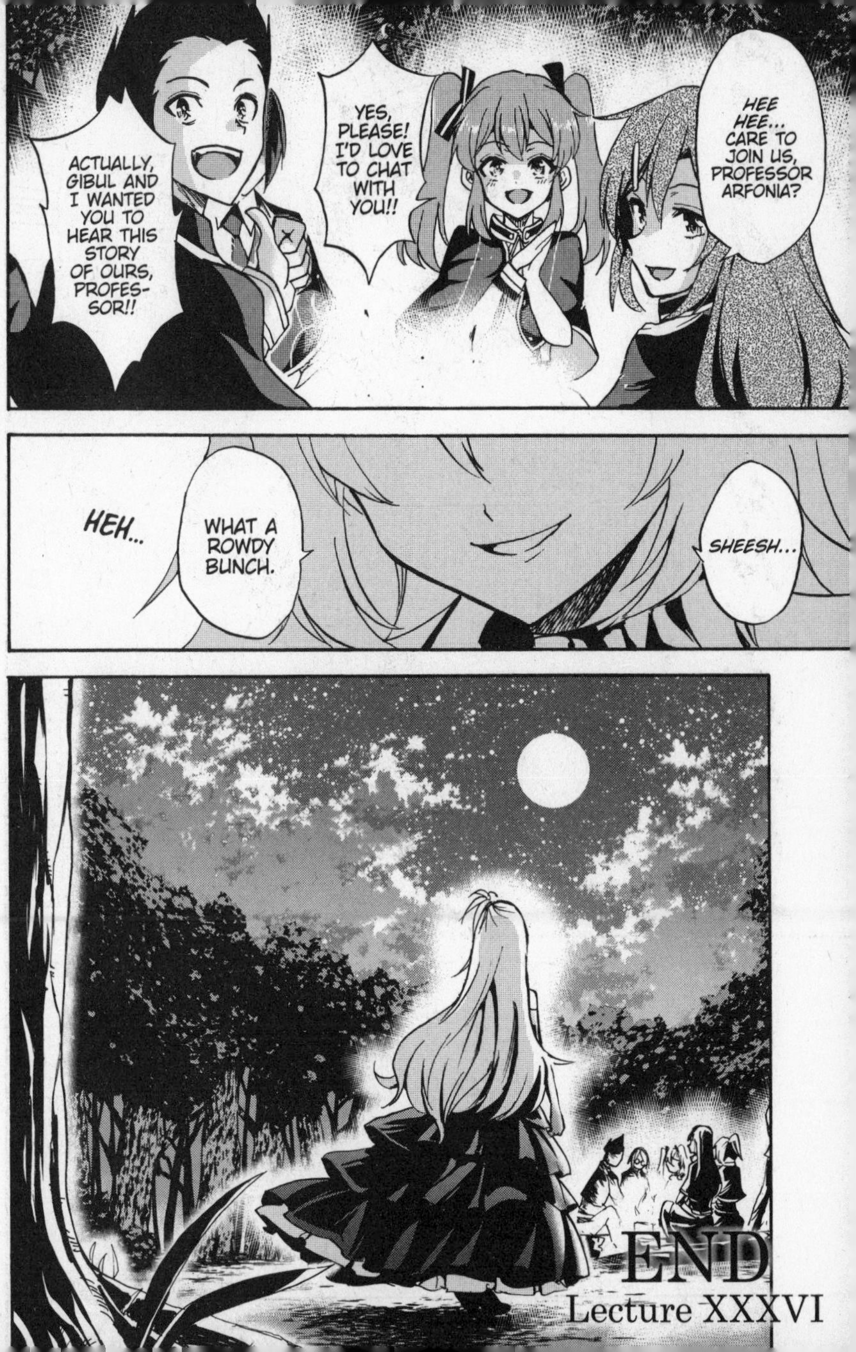
HEE HEE... CARE TO JOIN US, PROFESSOR ARFONIA?
YES, PLEASE! I'D LOVE TO CHAT WITH YOU!!
ACTUALLY, GIBUL AND I WANTED YOU TO HEAR THIS STORY OF OURS, PROFES-SOR!!
SHEESH...
WHAT A ROWDY BUNCH.
HEH...
END
Lecture XXXVI

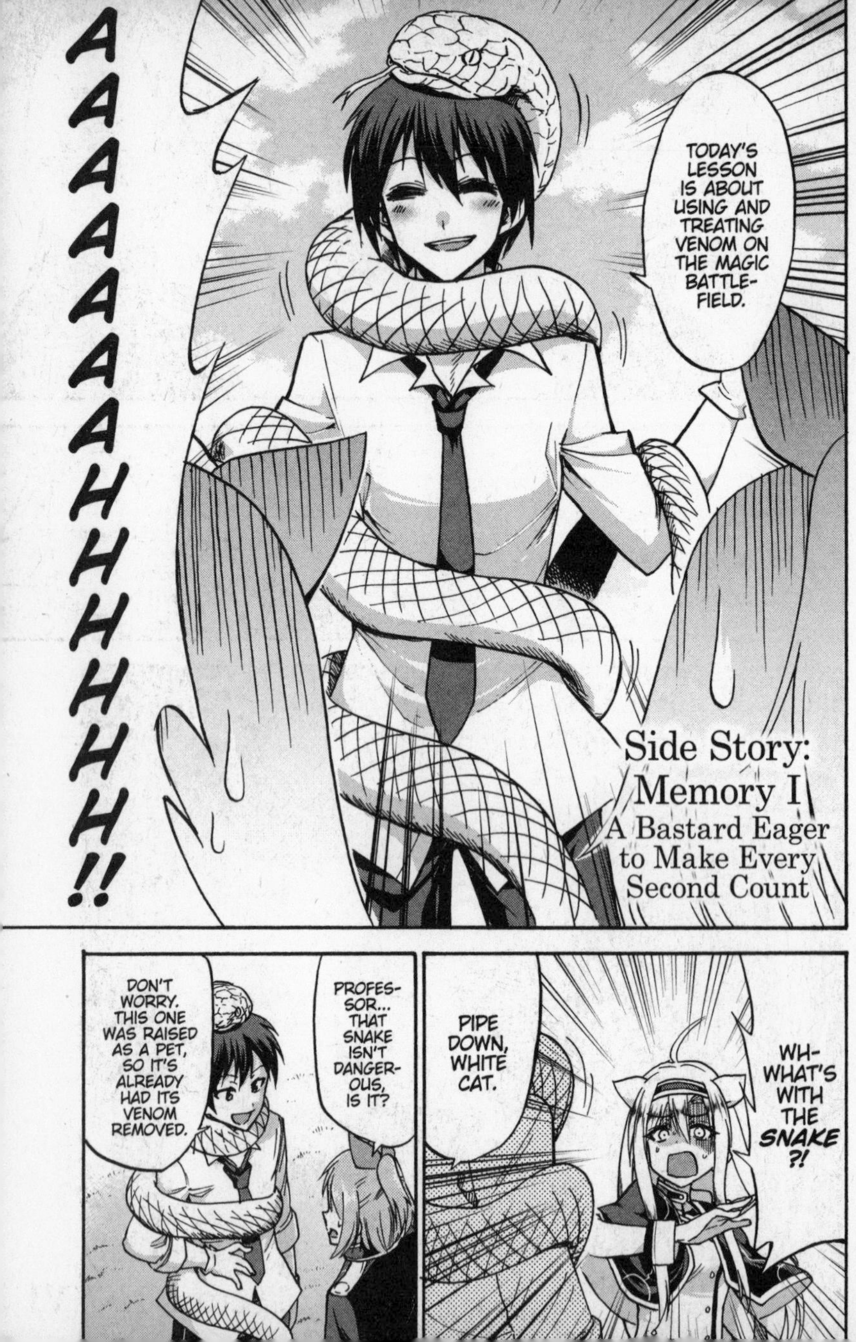
TODAY'S LESSON IS ABOUT USING AND TREATING VENOM ON THE MAGIC BATTLE-FIELD.
Side Story: Memory I
A Bastard Eager to Make Every Second Count
AAAAAAAHHHHHH!!
WH-WHAT'S WITH THE SNAKE?!
PIPE DOWN, WHITE CAT.
PROFES-SOR... THAT SNAKE ISN'T DANGER-OUS, IS IT?
DON'T WORRY. THIS ONE WAS RAISED AS A PET, SO IT'S ALREADY HAD ITS VENOM REMOVED.

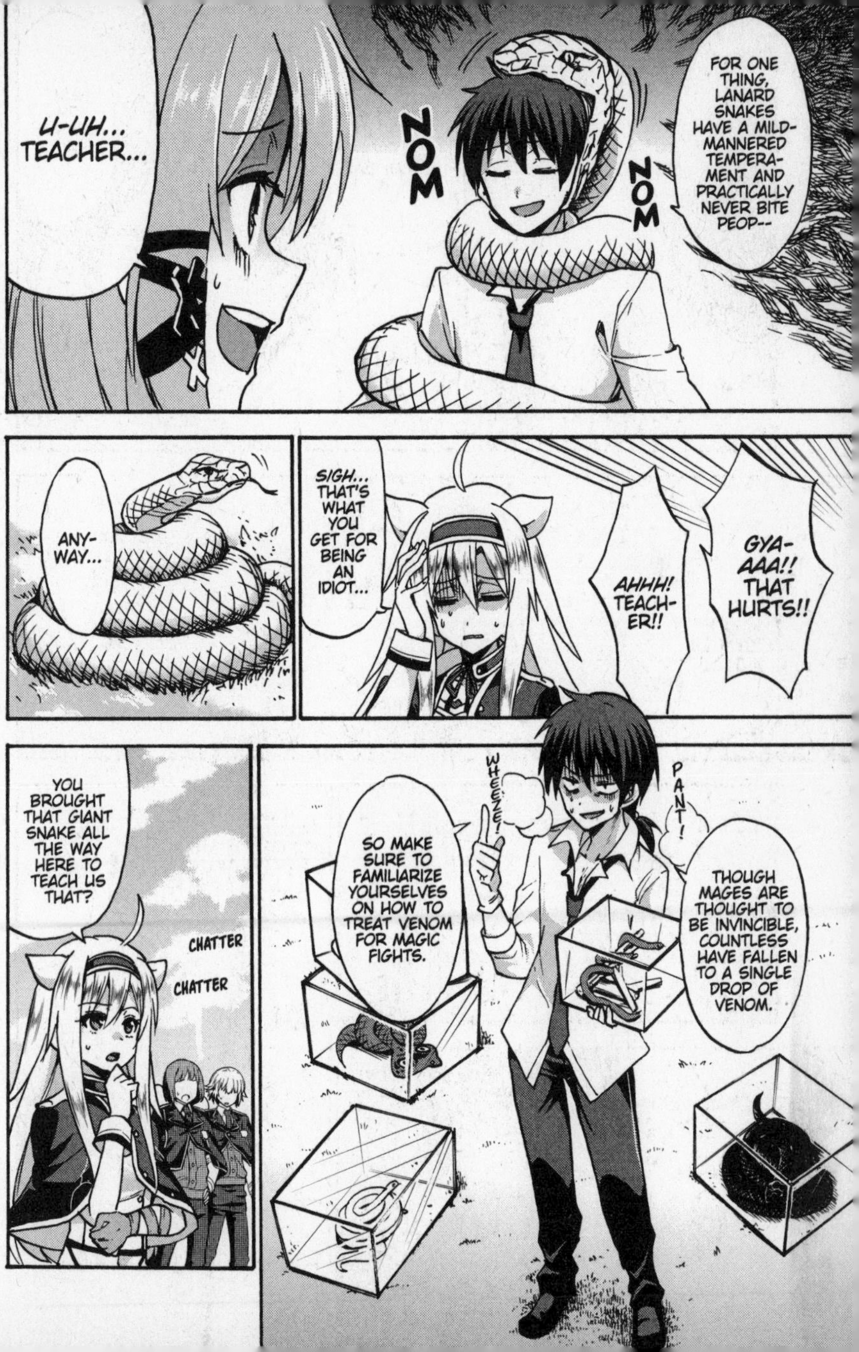
FOR ONE THING, LANARD SNAKES HAVE A MILD-MANNERED TEMPERAMENT AND PRACTICALLY NEVER BITE PEOP--
NOM
NOM
U-UH... TEACHER...
GYA-AAA!! THAT HURTS!!
AHHH! TEACHER!!
SIGH... THAT'S WHAT YOU GET FOR BEING AN IDIOT...
ANY-WAY...
THOUGH MAGES ARE THOUGHT TO BE INVINCIBLE, COUNTLESS HAVE FALLEN TO A SINGLE DROP OF VENOM.
PANT!
WHEEZE!
SO MAKE SURE TO FAMILIARIZE YOURSELVES ON HOW TO TREAT VENOM FOR MAGIC FIGHTS.
YOU BROUGHT THAT GIANT SNAKE ALL THE WAY HERE TO TEACH US THAT?
CHATTER
CHATTER

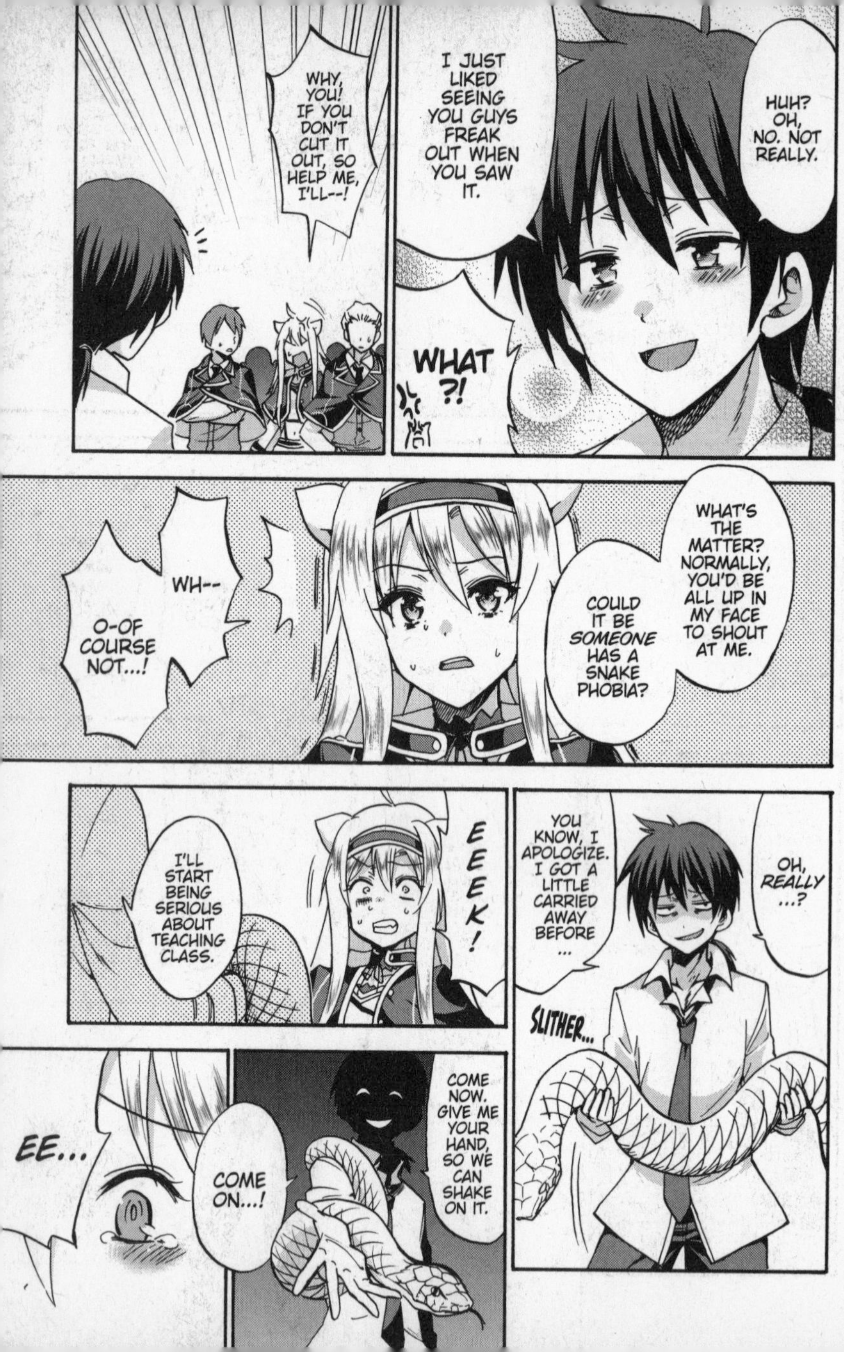
HUH? OH, NO. NOT REALLY.
I JUST LIKED SEEING YOU GUYS FREAK OUT WHEN YOU SAW IT.
WHAT ?!
WHY, YOU! IF YOU DON'T CUT IT OUT, SO HELP ME, I'LL--!
WHAT'S THE MATTER? NORMALLY, YOU'D BE ALL UP IN MY FACE TO SHOUT AT ME.
COULD IT BE *SOMEONE* HAS A SNAKE PHOBIA?
WH--
O-OF COURSE NOT...!
OH, *REALLY* ...?
YOU KNOW, I APOLOGIZE. I GOT A LITTLE CARRIED AWAY BEFORE ...
SLITHER...
EEEK!
I'LL START BEING SERIOUS ABOUT TEACHING CLASS.
COME NOW. GIVE ME YOUR HAND, SO WE CAN SHAKE ON IT.
COME ON...!
EE...

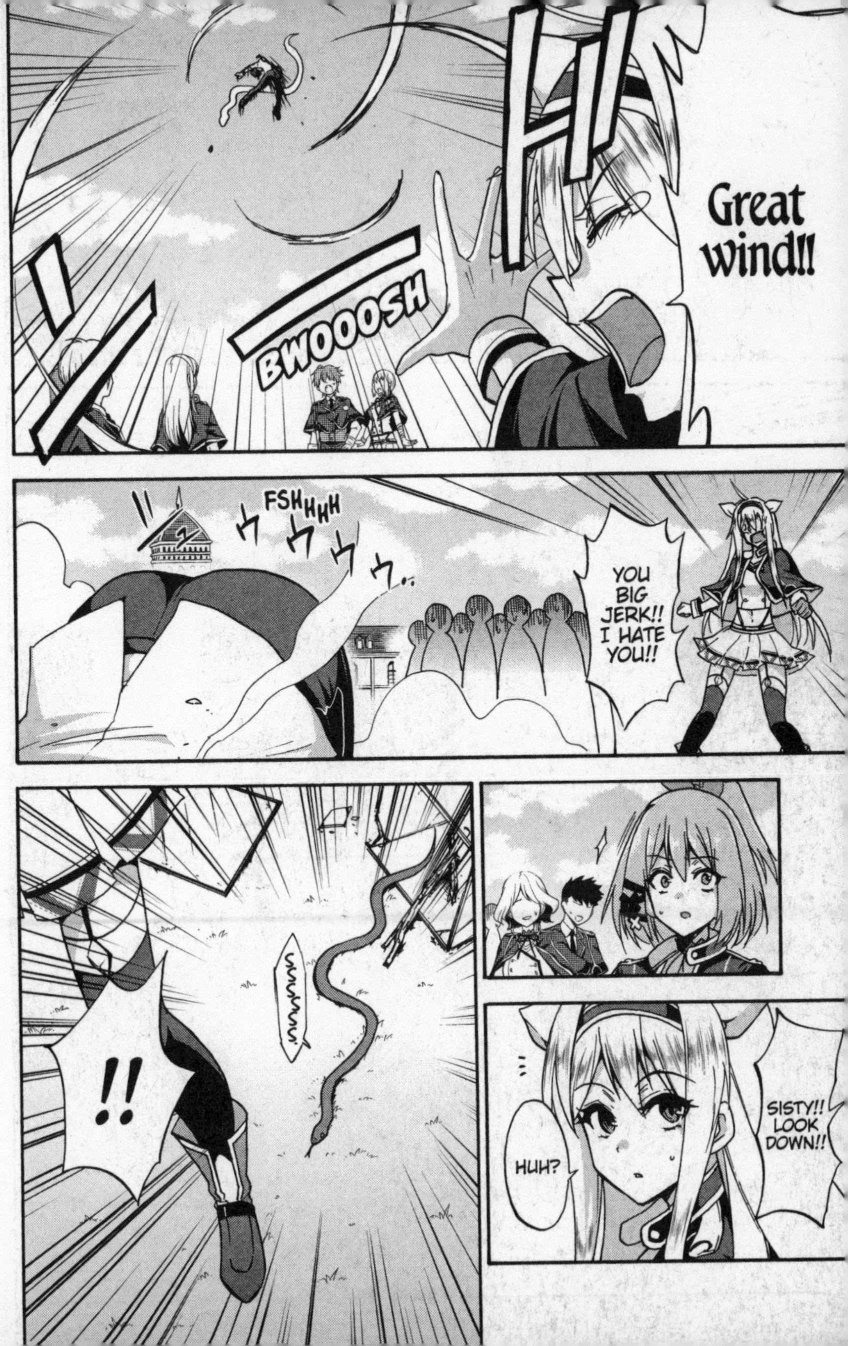
Great wind!!
BWOOOSH
YOU BIG JERK!! I HATE YOU!!
FSHHHH
SISTY!! LOOK DOWN!!
HUH?
!!

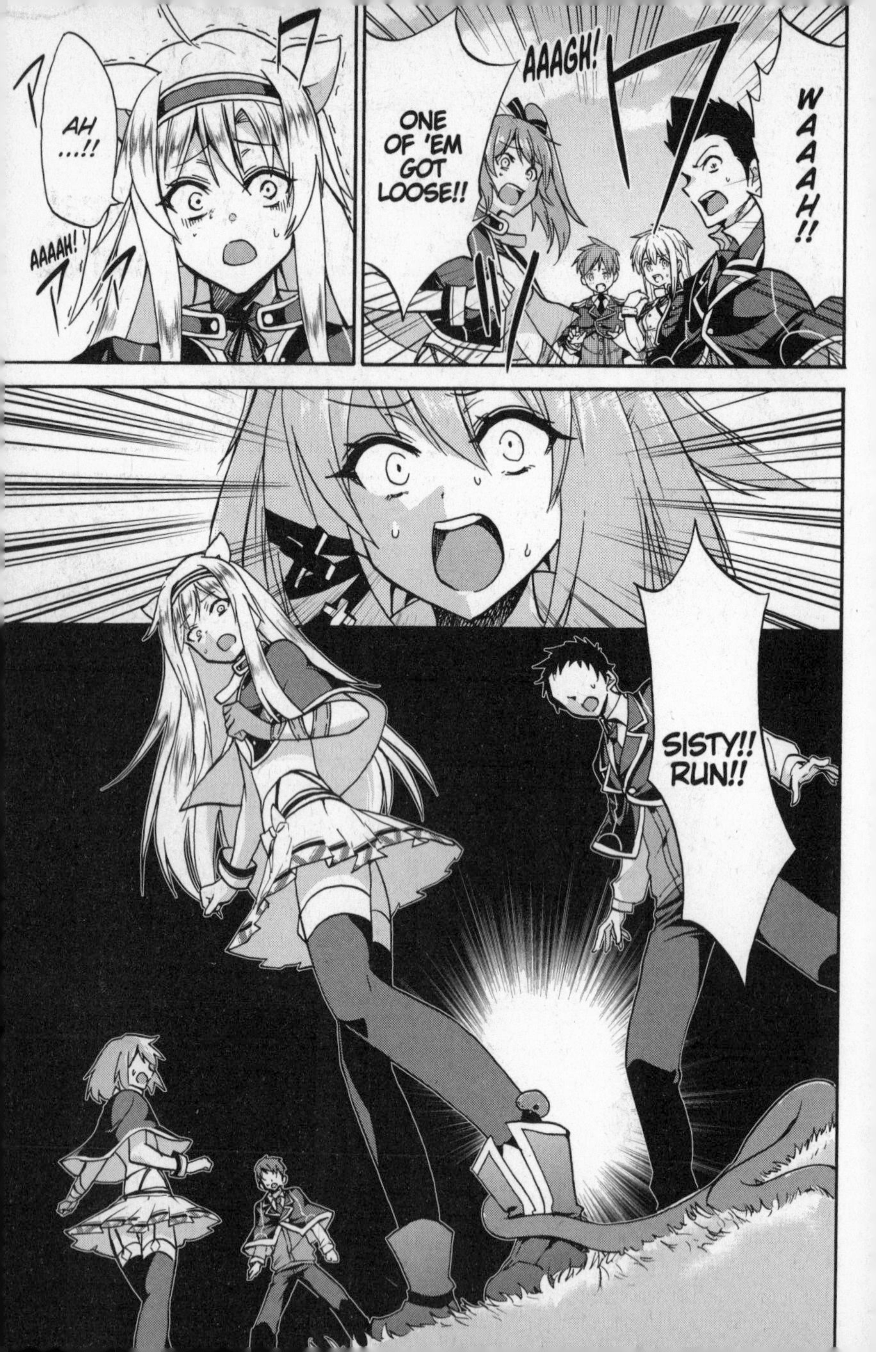
WAAAAH!!
AAAGH!
ONE OF 'EM GOT LOOSE!!
AH ...!!
AAAAH!
SISTY!! RUN!!

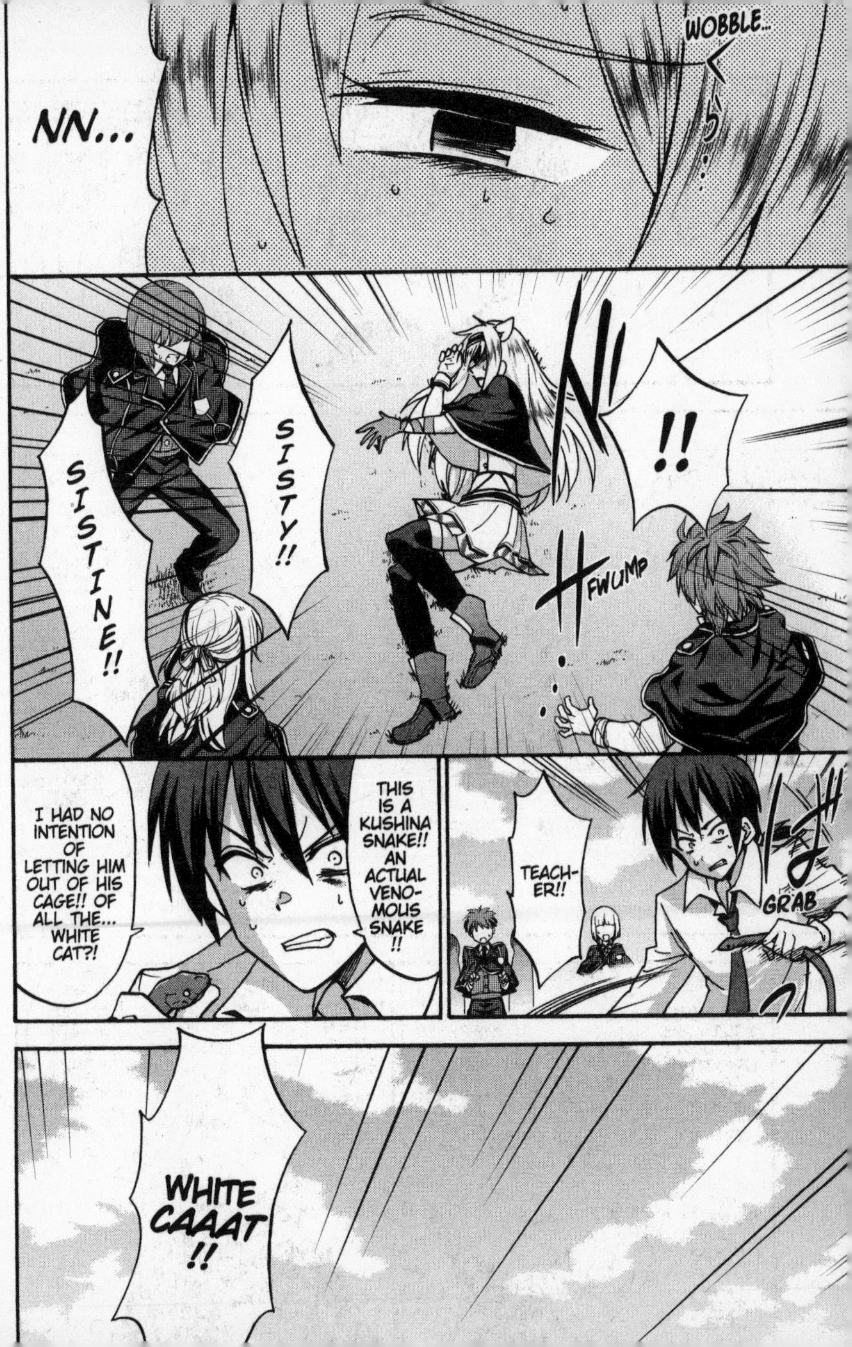
WOBBLE...
NN...
N!!
FWUMP
SISTY!!
SISTINE!!
GRAB
TEACHER!!
THIS IS A KUSHINA SNAKE!! AN ACTUAL VENOMOUS SNAKE!!
I HAD NO INTENTION OF LETTING HIM OUT OF HIS CAGE!! OF ALL THE... WHITE CAT?!
WHITE CAAAT!!

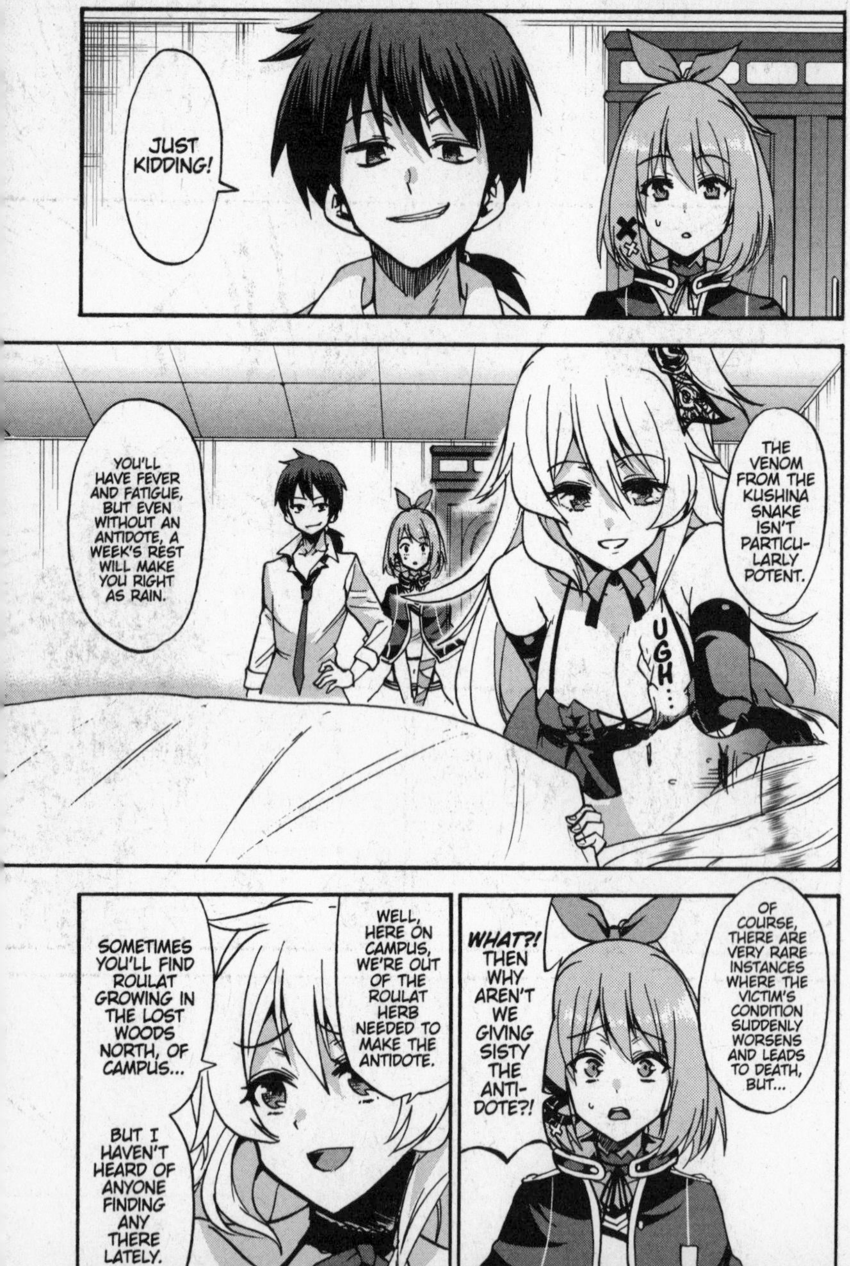
JUST KIDDING!
THE VENOM FROM THE KUSHINA SNAKE ISN'T PARTICULARLY POTENT.
UGH...
YOU'LL HAVE FEVER AND FATIGUE, BUT EVEN WITHOUT AN ANTIDOTE, A WEEK'S REST WILL MAKE YOU RIGHT AS RAIN.
OF COURSE, THERE ARE VERY RARE INSTANCES WHERE THE VICTIM'S CONDITION SUDDENLY WORSENS AND LEADS TO DEATH, BUT...
WHAT?! THEN WHY AREN'T WE GIVING SISTY THE ANTIDOTE?!
WELL, HERE ON CAMPUS, WE'RE OUT OF THE ROULAT HERB NEEDED TO MAKE THE ANTIDOTE.
SOMETIMES YOU'LL FIND ROULAT GROWING IN THE LOST WOODS NORTH, OF CAMPUS...
BUT I HAVEN'T HEARD OF ANYONE FINDING ANY THERE LATELY.

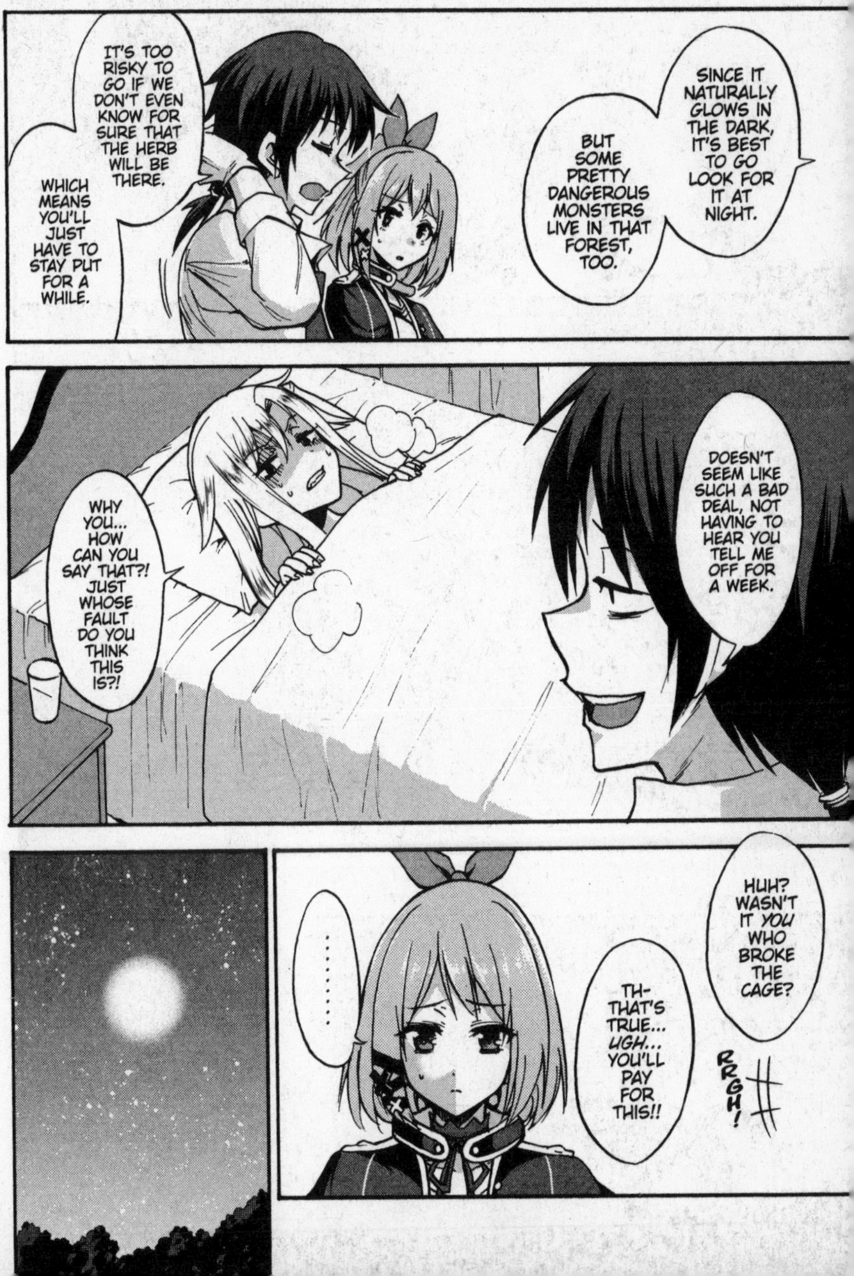
SINCE IT NATURALLY GLOWS IN THE DARK, IT'S BEST TO GO LOOK FOR IT AT NIGHT.
BUT SOME PRETTY DANGEROUS MONSTERS LIVE IN THAT FOREST, TOO.
IT'S TOO RISKY TO GO IF WE DON'T EVEN KNOW FOR SURE THAT THE HERB WILL BE THERE.
WHICH MEANS YOU'LL JUST HAVE TO STAY PUT FOR A WHILE.
DOESN'T SEEM LIKE SUCH A BAD DEAL, NOT HAVING TO HEAR YOU TELL ME OFF FOR A WEEK.
WHY YOU... HOW CAN YOU SAY THAT?! JUST WHOSE FAULT DO YOU THINK THIS IS?!
HUH? WASN'T IT *YOU* WHO BROKE THE CAGE?
RRGH!
TH-THAT'S TRUE... *UGH*... YOU'LL PAY FOR THIS!!
.......

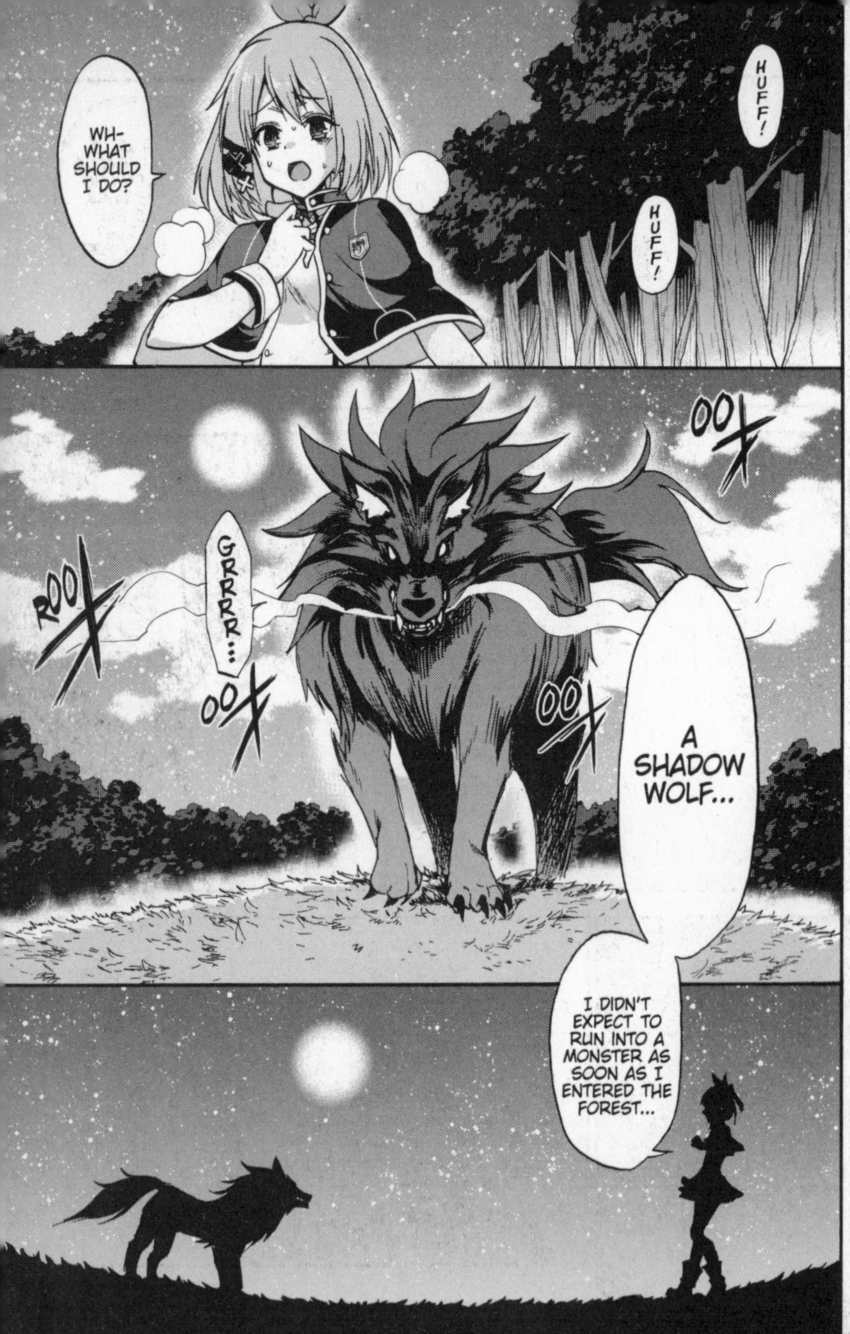
HUFF!
HUFF!
WH-WHAT SHOULD I DO?
OO
A SHADOW WOLF...
OO
GRRRR...
OO
ROO
I DIDN'T EXPECT TO RUN INTO A MONSTER AS SOON AS I ENTERED THE FOREST...

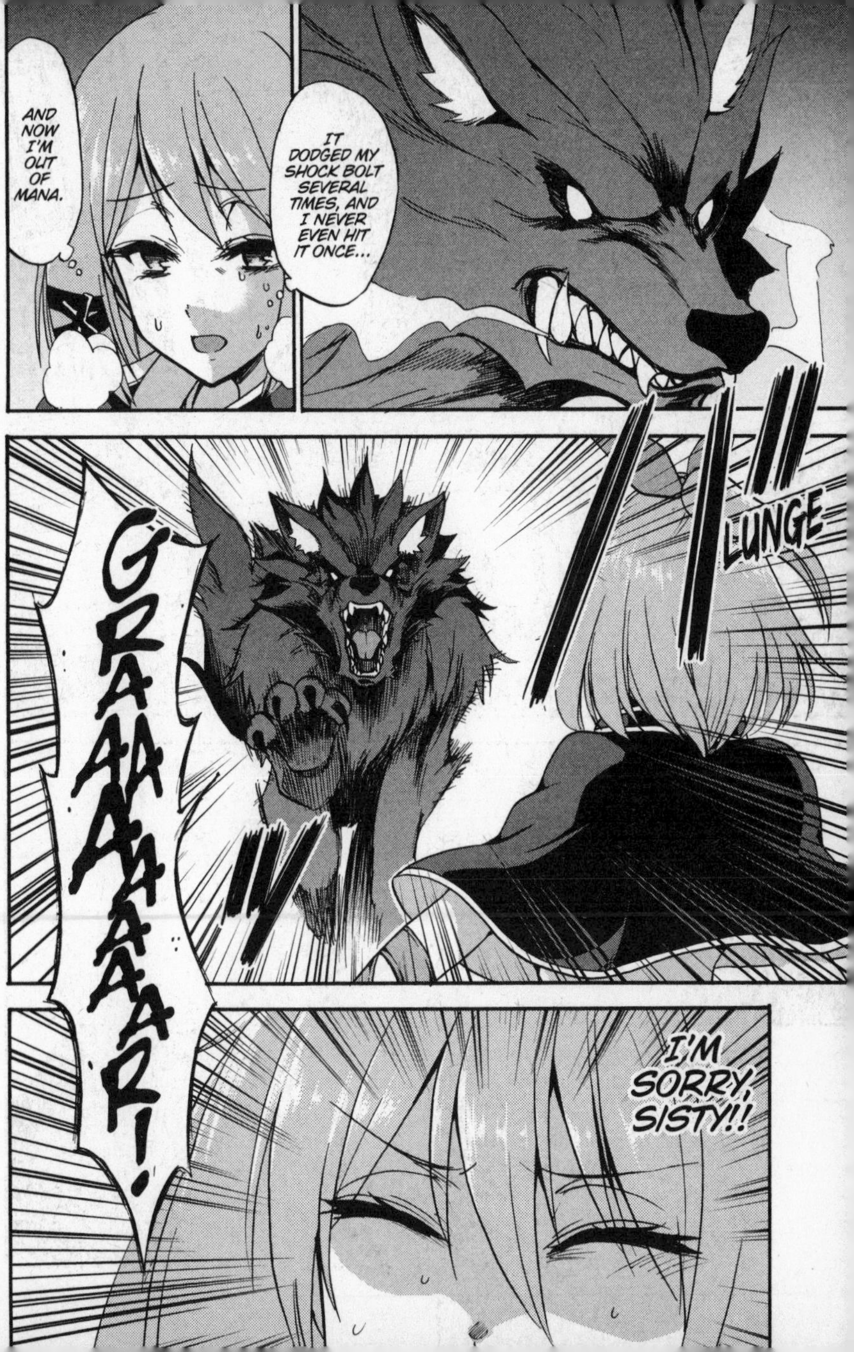
IT DODGED MY SHOCK BOLT SEVERAL TIMES, AND I NEVER EVEN HIT IT ONCE...
AND NOW I'M OUT OF MANA.
LUNGE
GRAAAAAAAR!
I'M SORRY, SISTY!!

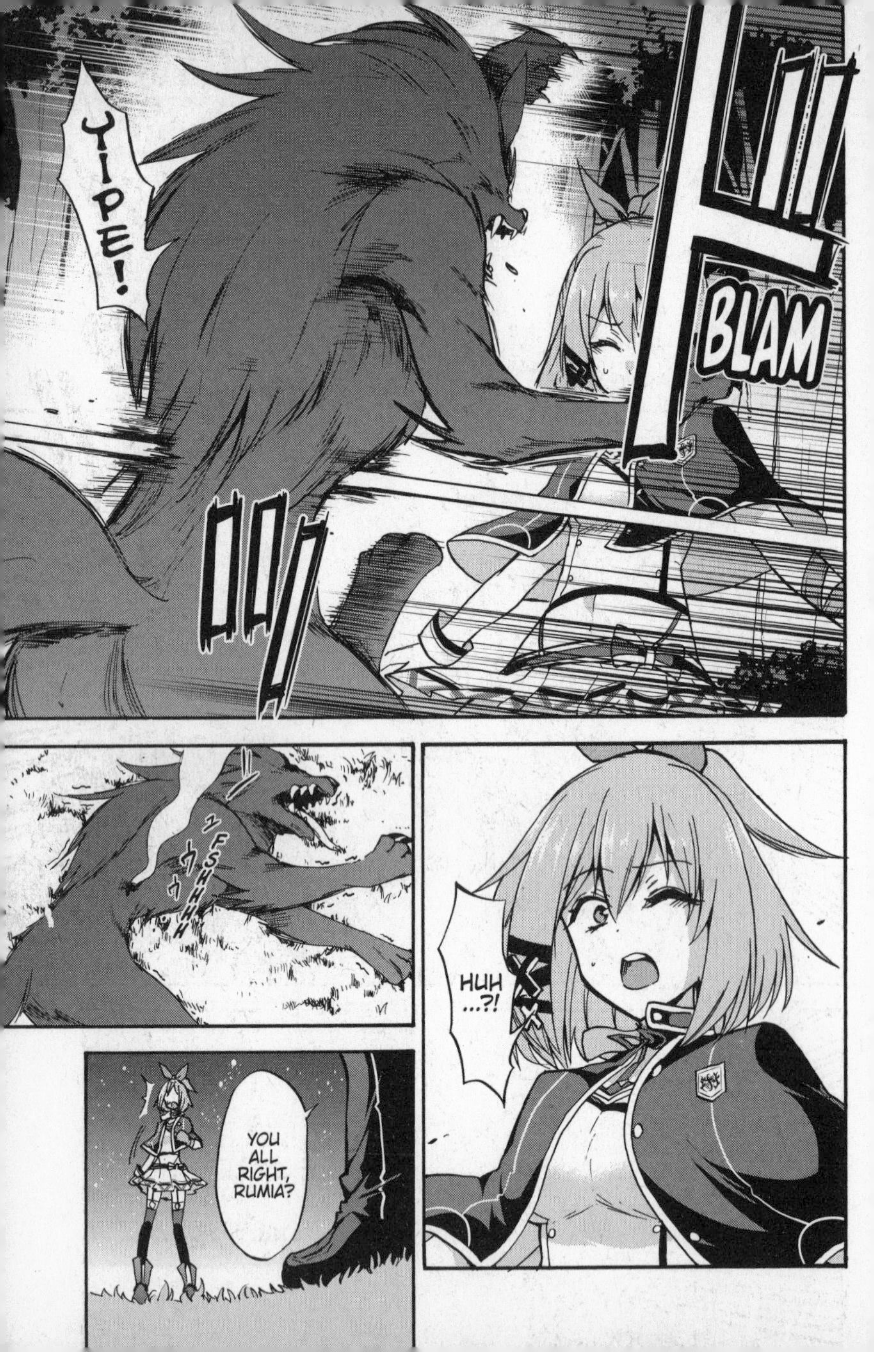
BLAM
YIPE!
HUH ...?!
FSHHHH
YOU ALL RIGHT, RUMIA?

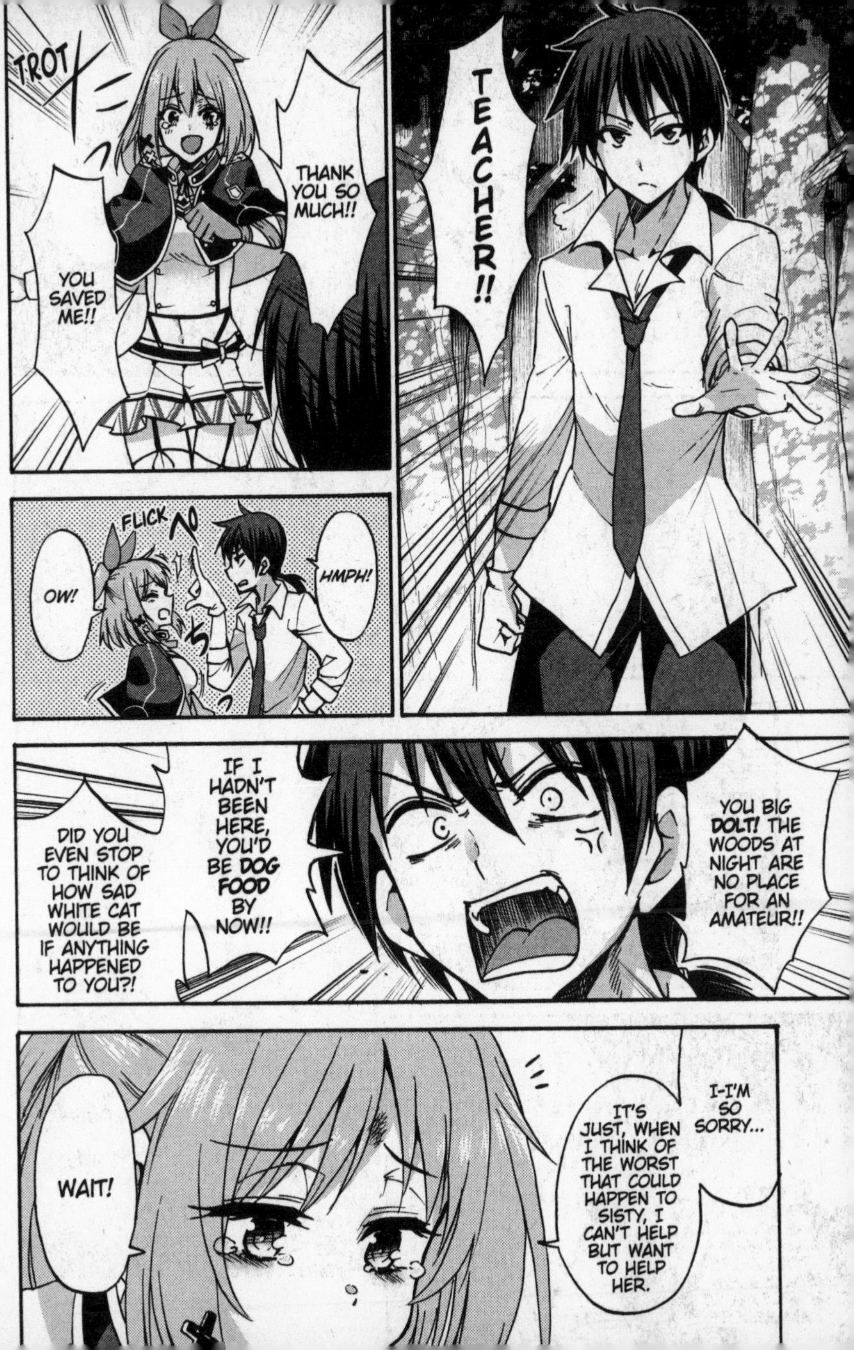
TEACHER!!
TROT
THANK YOU SO MUCH!!
YOU SAVED ME!!
FLICK
HMPH!
OW!
YOU BIG DOLT! THE WOODS AT NIGHT ARE NO PLACE FOR AN AMATEUR!!
IF I HADN'T BEEN HERE, YOU'D BE DOG FOOD BY NOW!!
DID YOU EVEN STOP TO THINK OF HOW SAD WHITE CAT WOULD BE IF ANYTHING HAPPENED TO YOU?!
I-I'M SO SORRY...
IT'S JUST, WHEN I THINK OF THE WORST THAT COULD HAPPEN TO SISTY, I CAN'T HELP BUT WANT TO HELP HER.
WAIT!

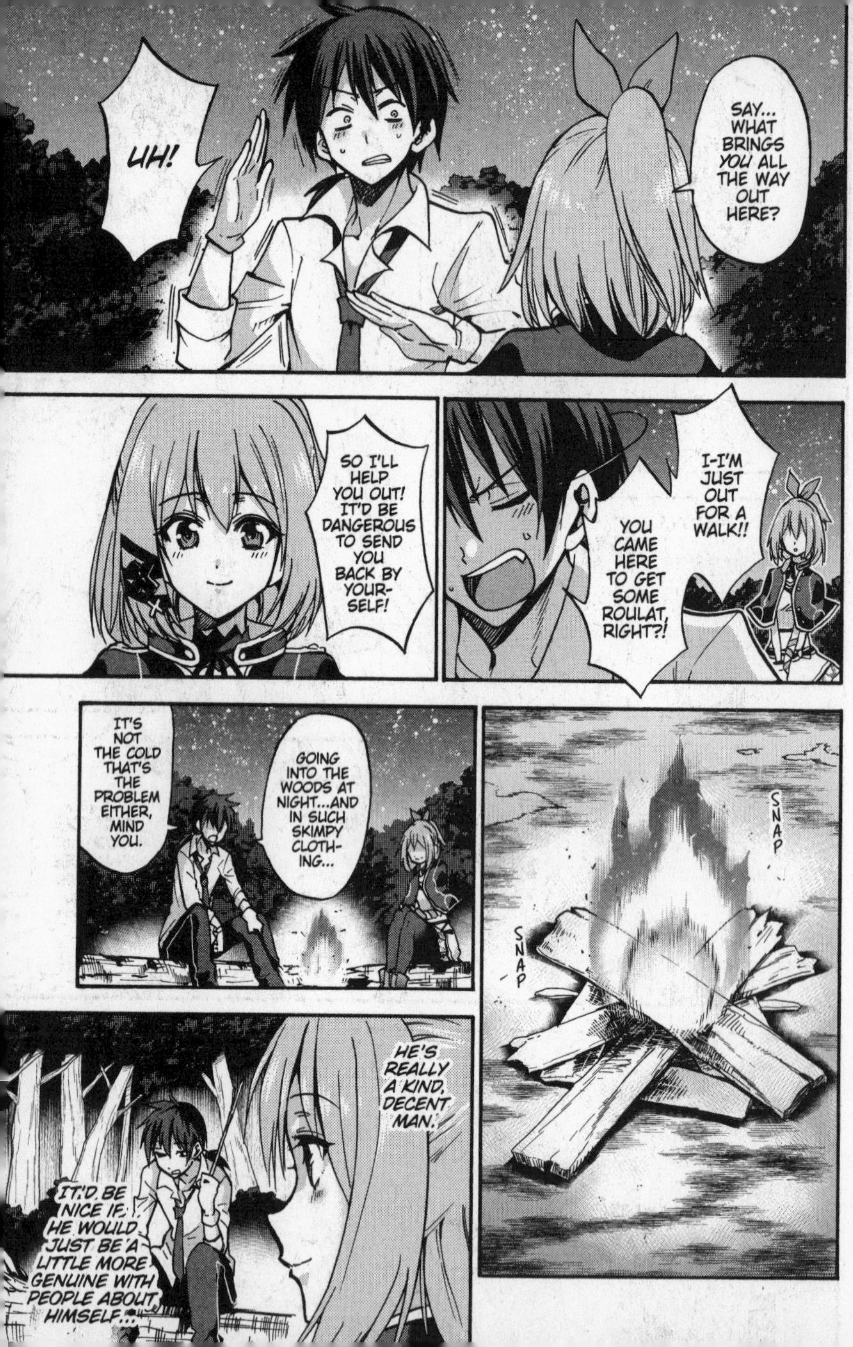
SAY... WHAT BRINGS YOU ALL THE WAY OUT HERE?
UH!
I-I'M JUST OUT FOR A WALK!!
YOU CAME HERE TO GET SOME ROULAT, RIGHT?!
SO I'LL HELP YOU OUT! IT'D BE DANGEROUS TO SEND YOU BACK BY YOURSELF!
SNAP
SNAP
GOING INTO THE WOODS AT NIGHT...AND IN SUCH SKIMPY CLOTHING...
IT'S NOT THE COLD THAT'S THE PROBLEM EITHER, MIND YOU.
HE'S REALLY A KIND, DECENT MAN.
IT'D BE NICE IF HE WOULD JUST BE A LITTLE MORE GENUINE WITH PEOPLE ABOUT HIMSELF...

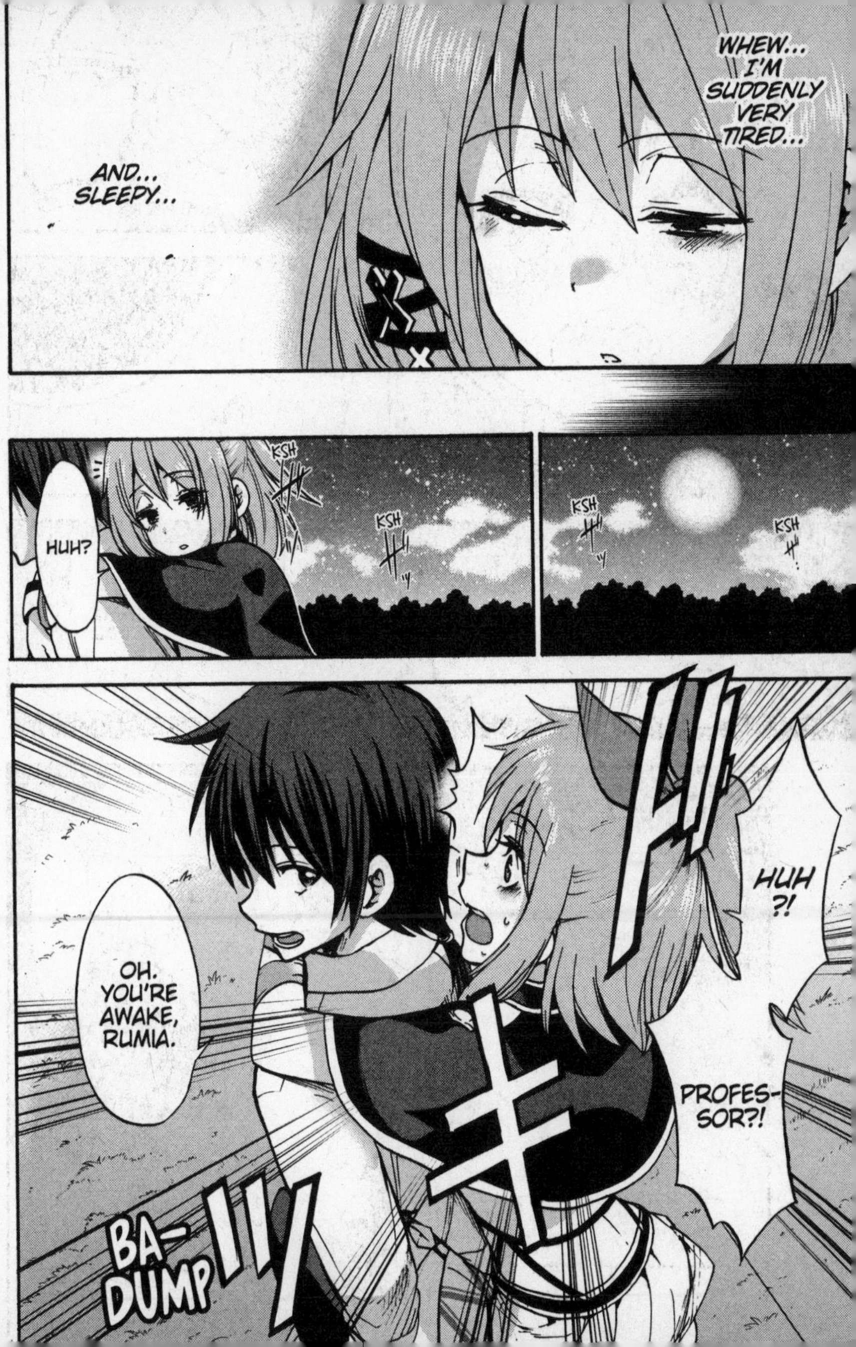
WHEW... I'M SUDDENLY VERY TIRED...
AND... SLEEPY...
KSH
KSH
KSH
KSH
HUH?
HUH?!
PROFES-SOR?!
OH. YOU'RE AWAKE, RUMIA.
BA-DUMP

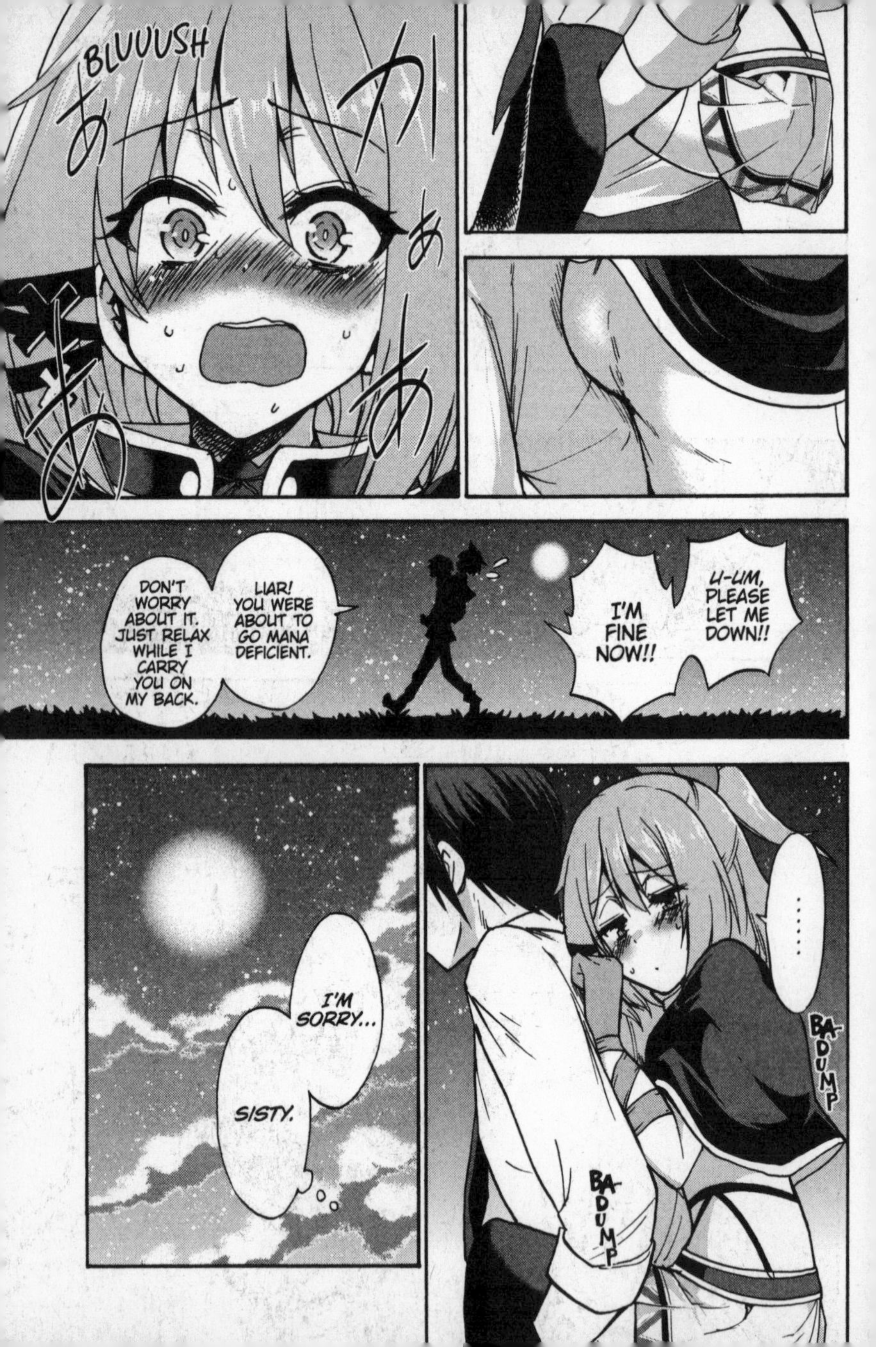
BLUUUSH
U-UM, PLEASE LET ME DOWN!!
I'M FINE NOW!!
LIAR! YOU WERE ABOUT TO GO MANA DEFICIENT.
DON'T WORRY ABOUT IT. JUST RELAX WHILE I CARRY YOU ON MY BACK.
......
BA-DUMP
BA-DUMP
I'M SORRY...
SISTY.

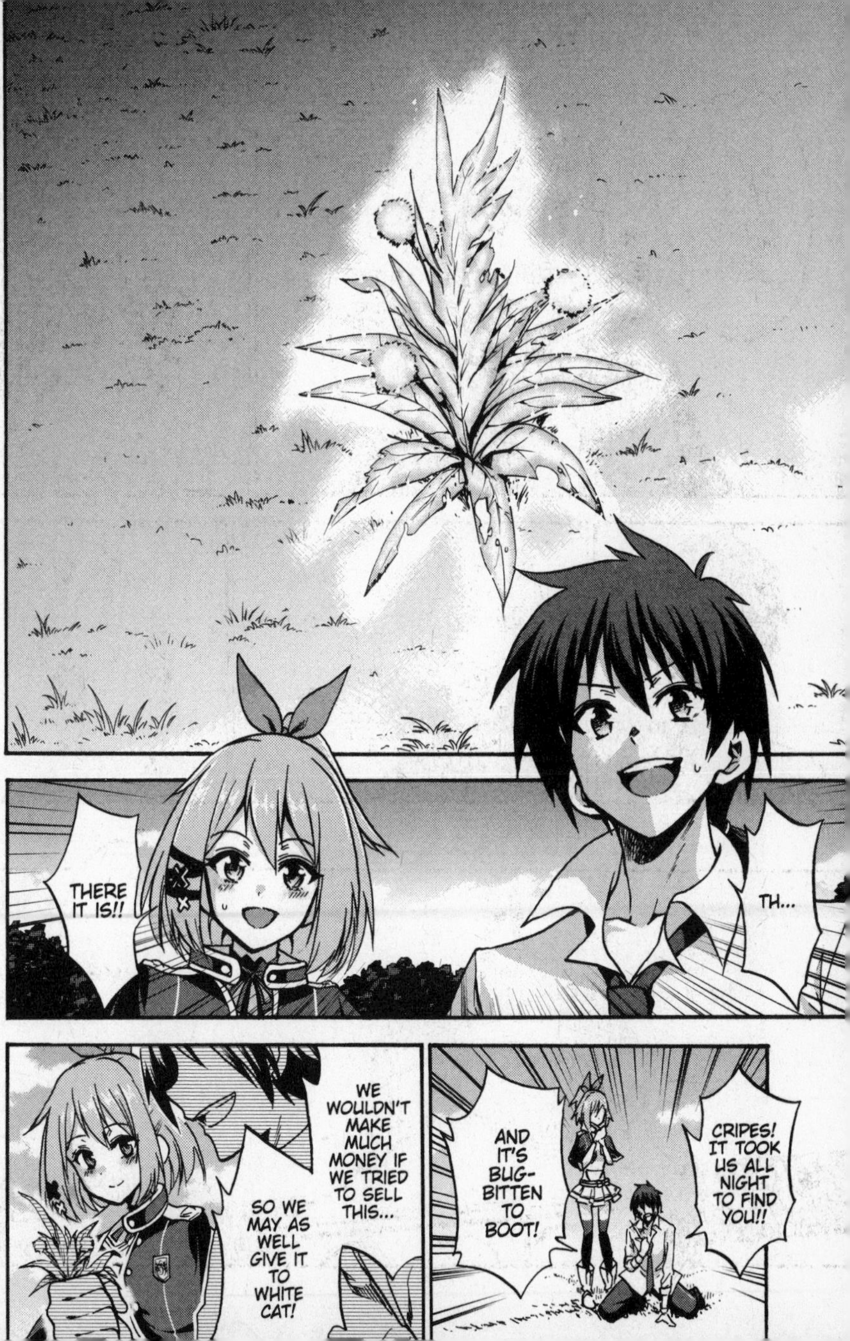
TH...
THERE IT IS!!
CRIPES! IT TOOK US ALL NIGHT TO FIND YOU!!
AND IT'S BUG-BITTEN TO BOOT!
WE WOULDN'T MAKE MUCH MONEY IF WE TRIED TO SELL THIS...
SO WE MAY AS WELL GIVE IT TO WHITE CAT!

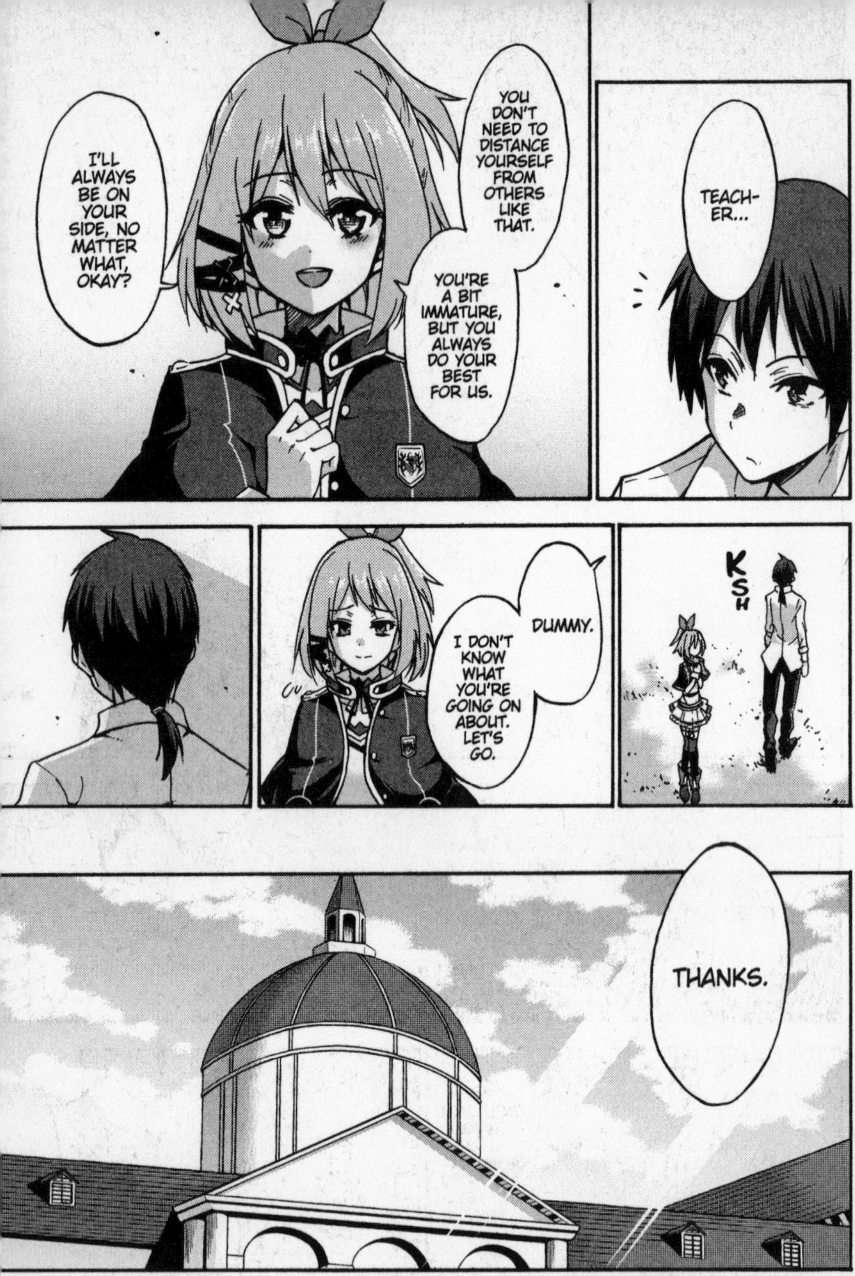
TEACHER...
YOU DON'T NEED TO DISTANCE YOURSELF FROM OTHERS LIKE THAT.
YOU'RE A BIT IMMATURE, BUT YOU ALWAYS DO YOUR BEST FOR US.
I'LL ALWAYS BE ON YOUR SIDE, NO MATTER WHAT, OKAY?
KSH
DUMMY.
I DON'T KNOW WHAT YOU'RE GOING ON ABOUT. LET'S GO.
THANKS.

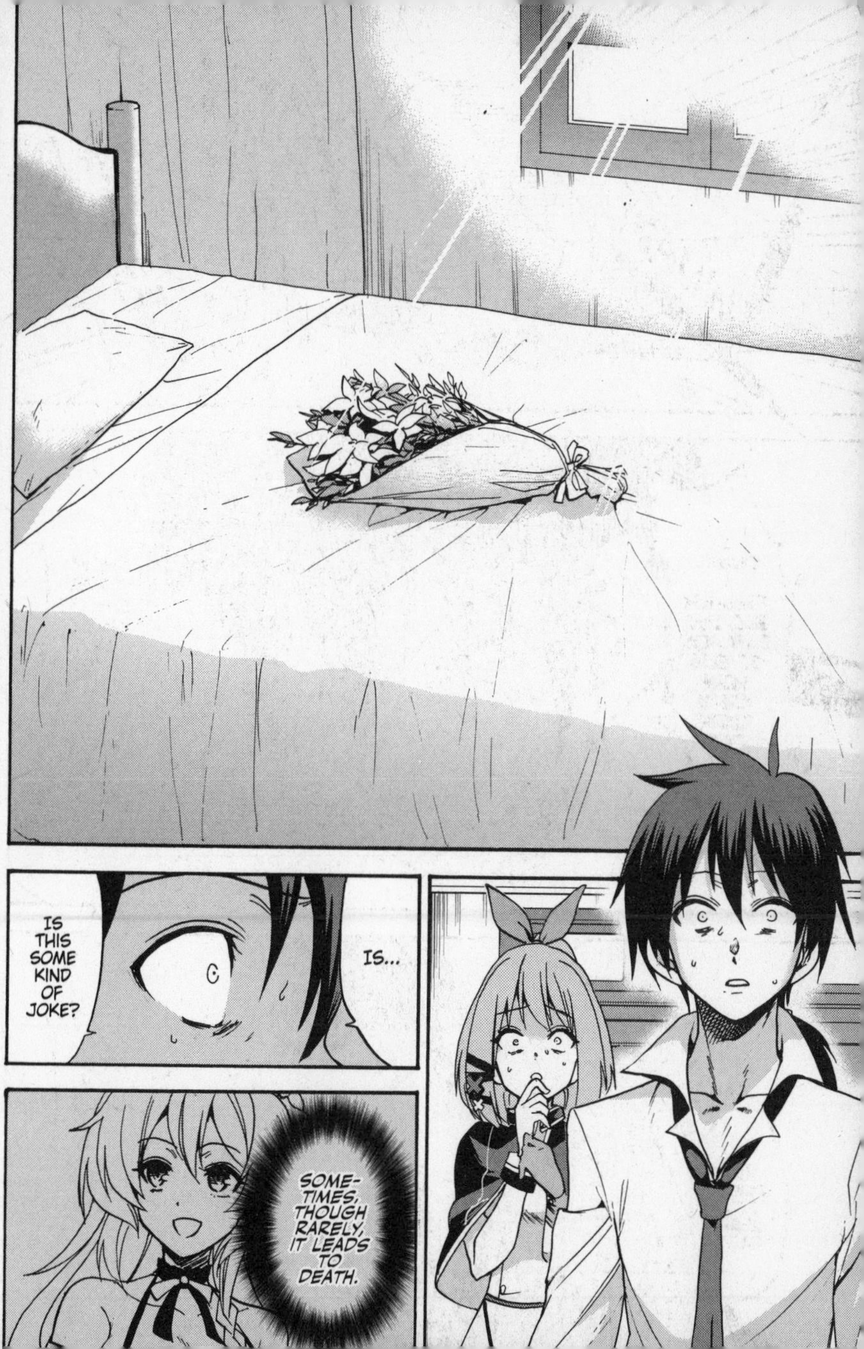
IS...
IS THIS SOME KIND OF JOKE?
SOME-TIMES, THOUGH RARELY, IT LEADS TO DEATH.

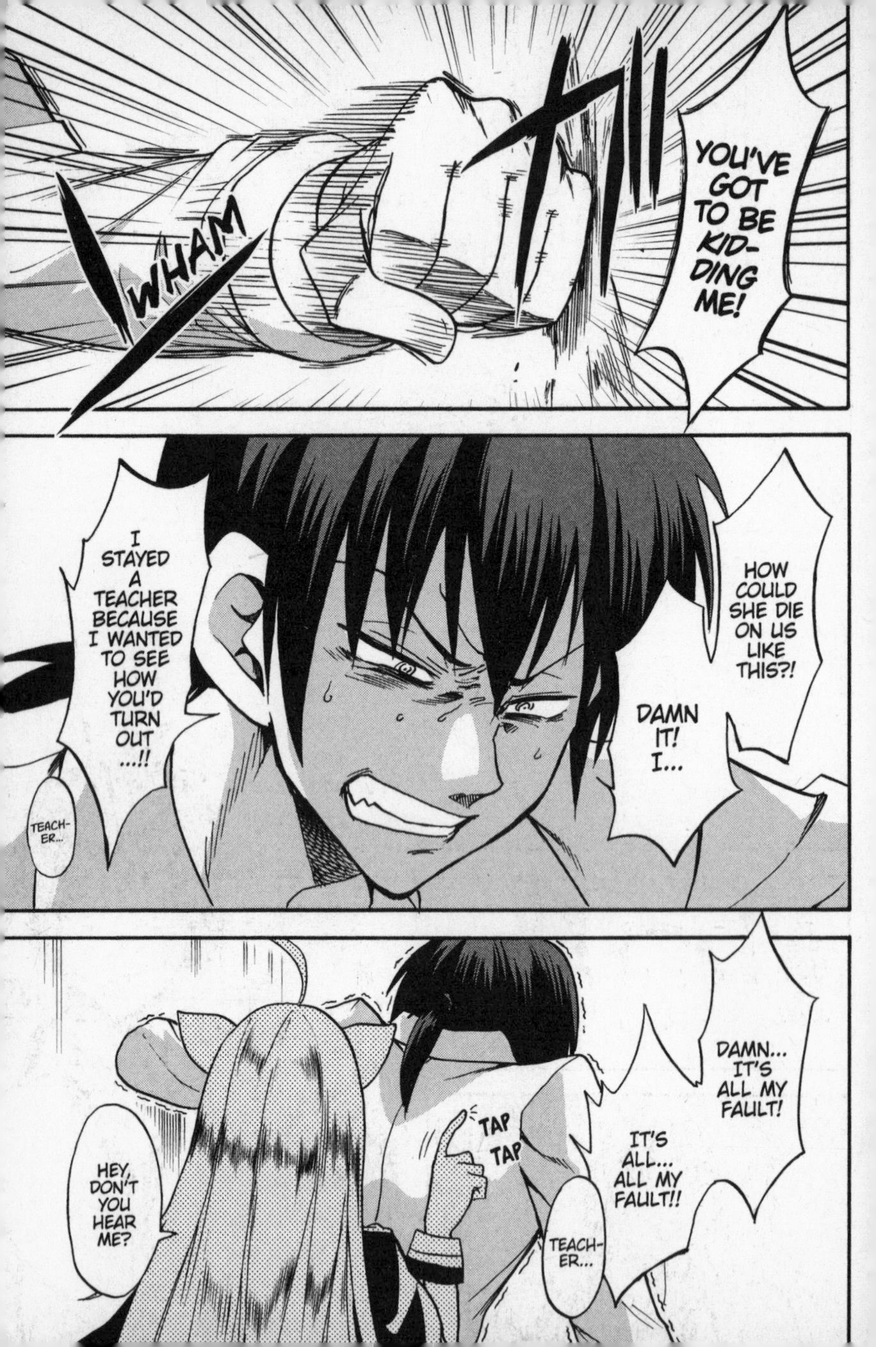
YOU'VE GOT TO BE KID-DING ME!
WHAM
HOW COULD SHE DIE ON US LIKE THIS?!
DAMN IT! I...
I STAYED A TEACHER BECAUSE I WANTED TO SEE HOW YOU'D TURN OUT ...!!
TEACHER...
DAMN... IT'S ALL MY FAULT!
IT'S ALL... ALL MY FAULT!!
TAP TAP
TEACHER...
HEY, DON'T YOU HEAR ME?

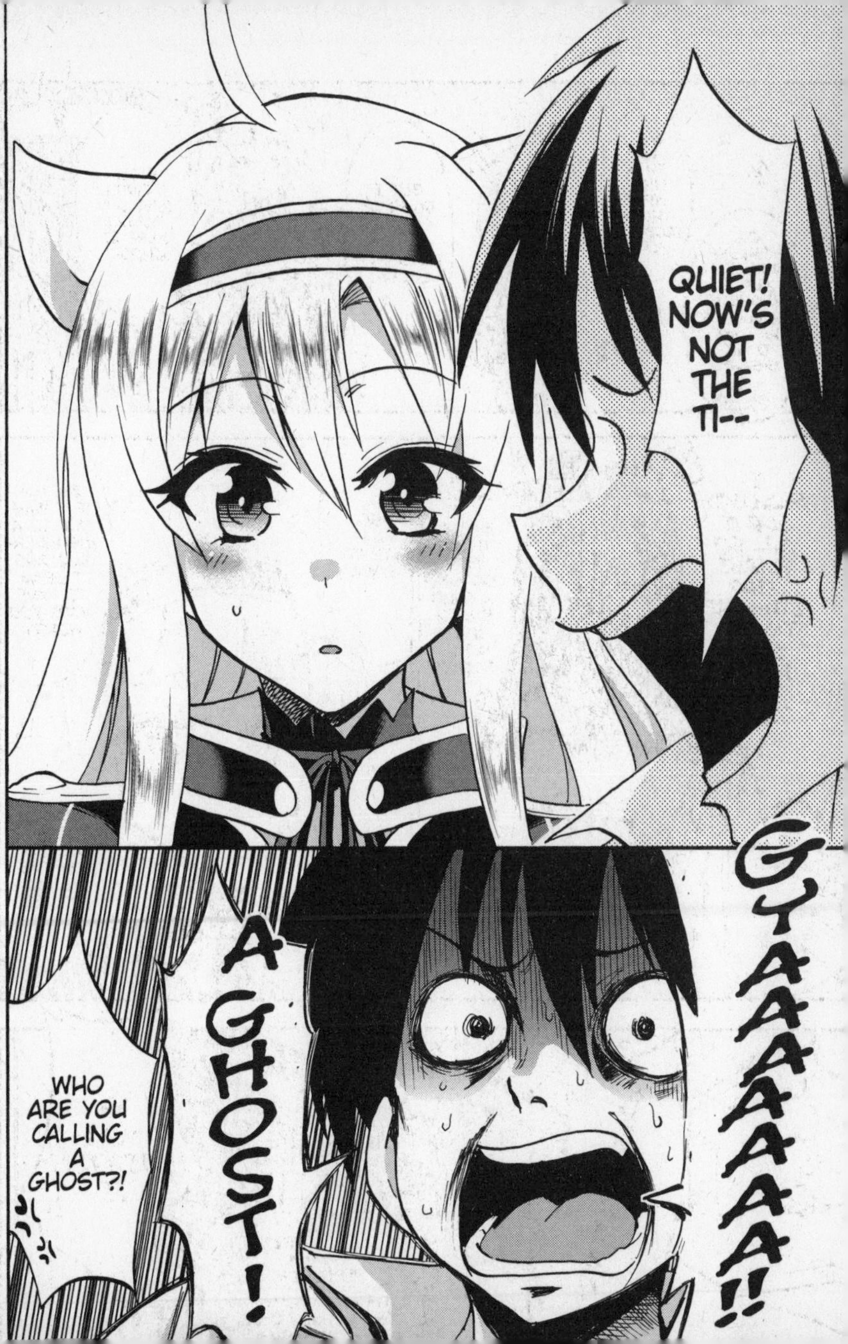
QUIET! NOW'S NOT THE TI--
GYAAAAAAA!!
A GHOST!
WHO ARE YOU CALLING A GHOST?!

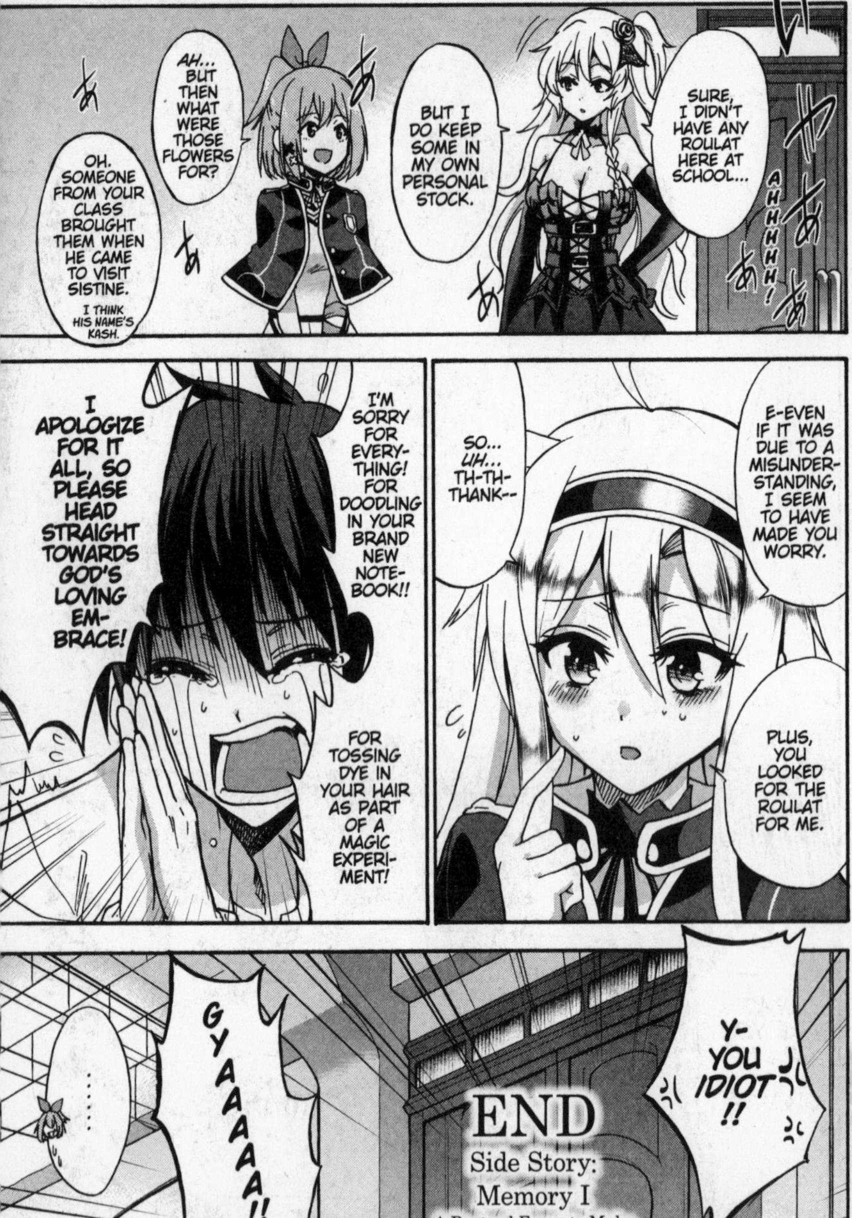
SURE, I DIDN'T HAVE ANY ROULAT HERE AT SCHOOL...
AHHHHHH!
BUT I DO KEEP SOME IN MY OWN PERSONAL STOCK.
AH... BUT THEN WHAT WERE THOSE FLOWERS FOR?
OH. SOMEONE FROM YOUR CLASS BROUGHT THEM WHEN HE CAME TO VISIT SISTINE.
I THINK HIS NAME'S KASH.
E-EVEN IF IT WAS DUE TO A MISUNDER-STANDING, I SEEM TO HAVE MADE YOU WORRY.
PLUS, YOU LOOKED FOR THE ROULAT FOR ME.
SO... UH... TH-TH-THANK--
I'M SORRY FOR EVERY-THING! FOR DOODLING IN YOUR BRAND NEW NOTE-BOOK!!
FOR TOSSING DYE IN YOUR HAIR AS PART OF A MAGIC EXPERI-MENT!
I APOLOGIZE FOR IT ALL, SO PLEASE HEAD STRAIGHT TOWARDS GOD'S LOVING EM-BRACE!
Y-YOU IDIOT!!
END
Side Story: Memory I
A Bastard Eager to Make Every Second Count
GYAAAAA!!
......

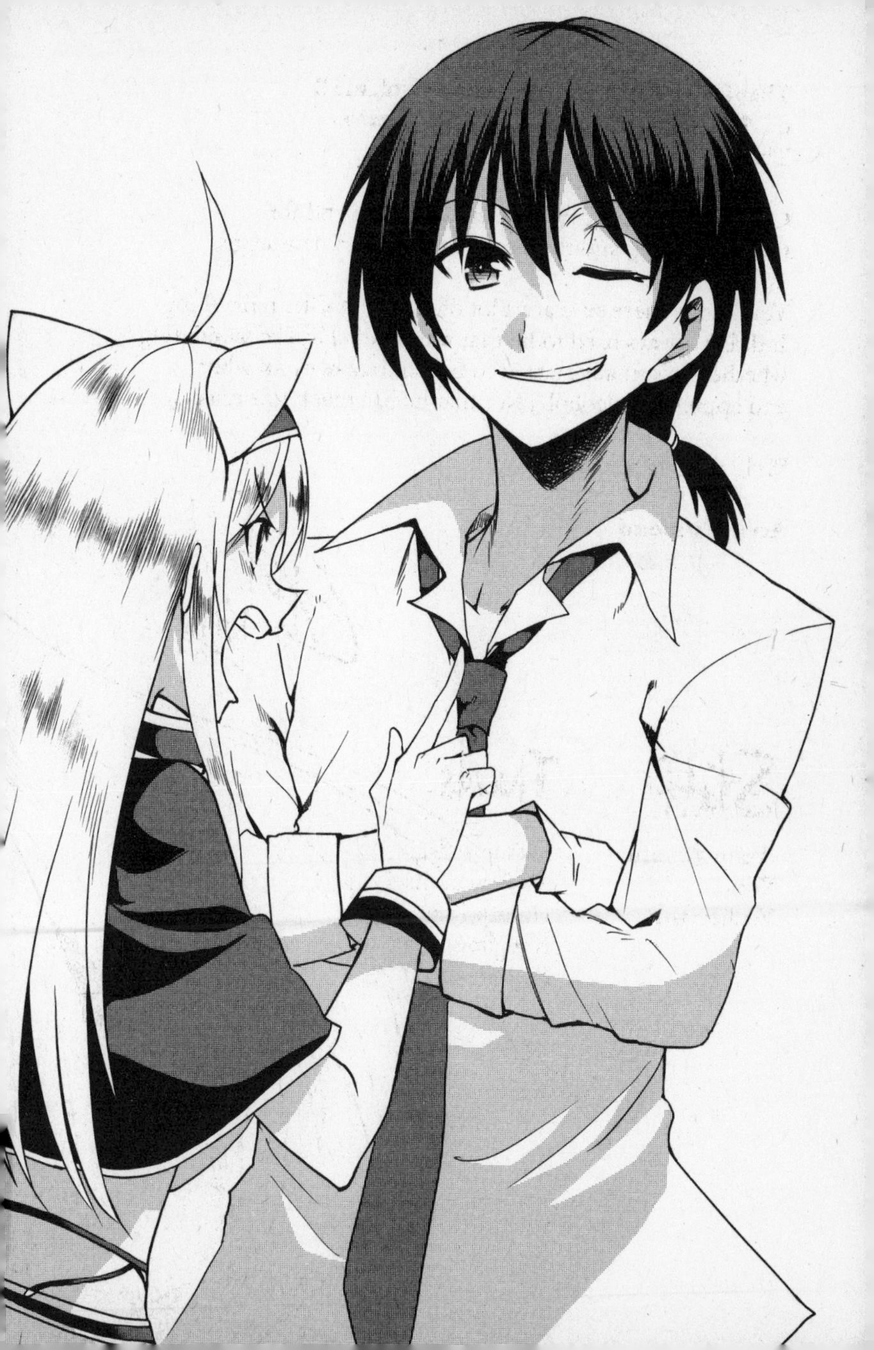

Thank you so much for picking up volume 8 of *Akashic Records of Bastard Magic Instructor.* This is Aosa Tsunemi.

One of Glenn's big fights has come to an end for the time being, and the story has entered a new stage.

You know, there sure are a lot of scenes of Glenn drinking. It didn't always used to be that way, but lately, I'm wondering whether he's finally started to become more of an adult and appreciate alcohol. (Not that he has much tolerance...)

Well, see you next volume!

**Aosa Tsunemi**

## Staff

Asahi Ruyoru
Piko
Yoshimaru

## Thanks

Hitsuji-sensei
Mishima-sensei
Hatusko-san
Katsumura-san
Kishida-san

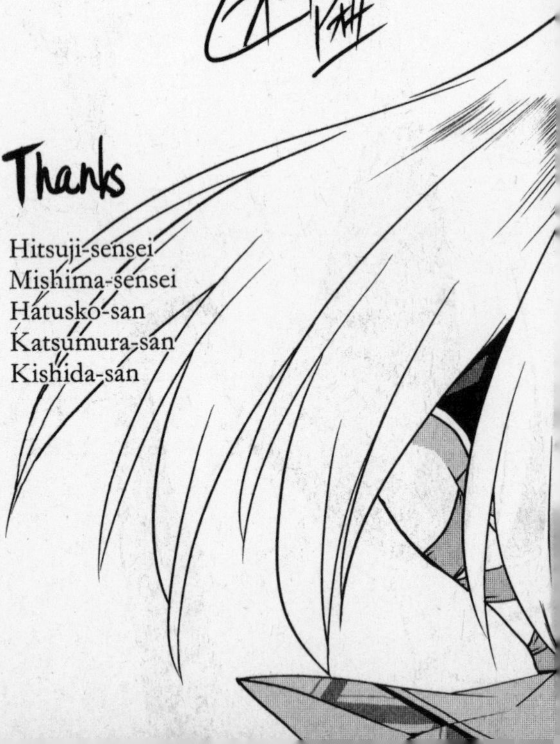

# Akashic Records
## o f *Bastard* Magic *Instructor*

SEVEN SEAS ENTERTAINMENT PRESENTS

# Akashic Records of Bastard Magic Instructor VOLUME 8


story by TARO HITSUJI art by AOSA TSUNEMI original character designs by KURONE MISHIMA



TRANSLATION
Ryan Peterson

ADAPTATION
Bambi Eloriaga-Amago

LETTERING
Brandon Bovia

COVER DESIGN
KC Fabellon

PROOFREADER
Danielle King
Janet Houck

EDITOR
J.P. Sullivan

PREPRESS TECHNICIAN
Rhiannon Rasmussen-Silverstein

PRODUCTION MANAGER
Lissa Pattillo

MANAGING EDITOR
Julie Davis

ASSOCIATE PUBLISHER
Adam Arnold

PUBLISHER
Jason DeAngelis





Seven Seas press and purchase enquiries can be sent to Marketing Manager Lianne Sentar at press@gomanga.com. Information regarding the distribution and purchase of digital editions is available from Digital Manager CK Russell at digital@gomanga.com.





ISBN: 978-1-64505-182-4

Printed in Canada

First Printing: January 2020

10 9 8 7 6 5 4 3 2 1




## READING DIRECTIONS

This book reads from ***right to left***, Japanese style. If this is your first time reading manga, you start reading from the top right panel on each page and take it from there. If you get lost, just follow the numbered diagram here. It may seem backwards at first, but you'll get the hang of it! Have fun!!

1
2
3
4
5
6
7
8
9

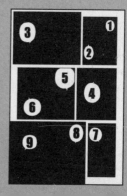

# YOU'RE FIRED!

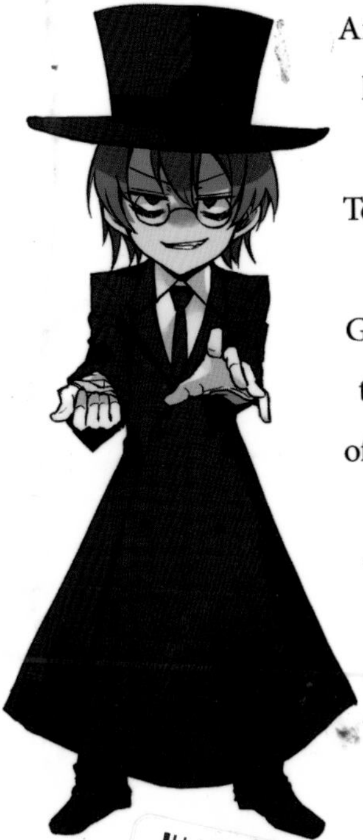

After the climax of a fierce battle with his old rival Jatice, Glenn's reward is maybe getting fired from his job. Teachers at the academy are expected to conduct original research, and Glenn's been so lazy and preoccupied that he hasn't done so much as a lick of it. So it's time for another field trip, this time to the Celestial Temple of Taum. Together, he and his students seek to uncover the secrets of an ancient ruin—and maybe save his career in the process!



TEEN
$12.99 USA
($15.99 CAN)
ISBN 978-1-64505-182-4
51299>
9 781645 051824

Seven Seas Entertainment
sevenseasentertainment.com

# Lecture XXXIII

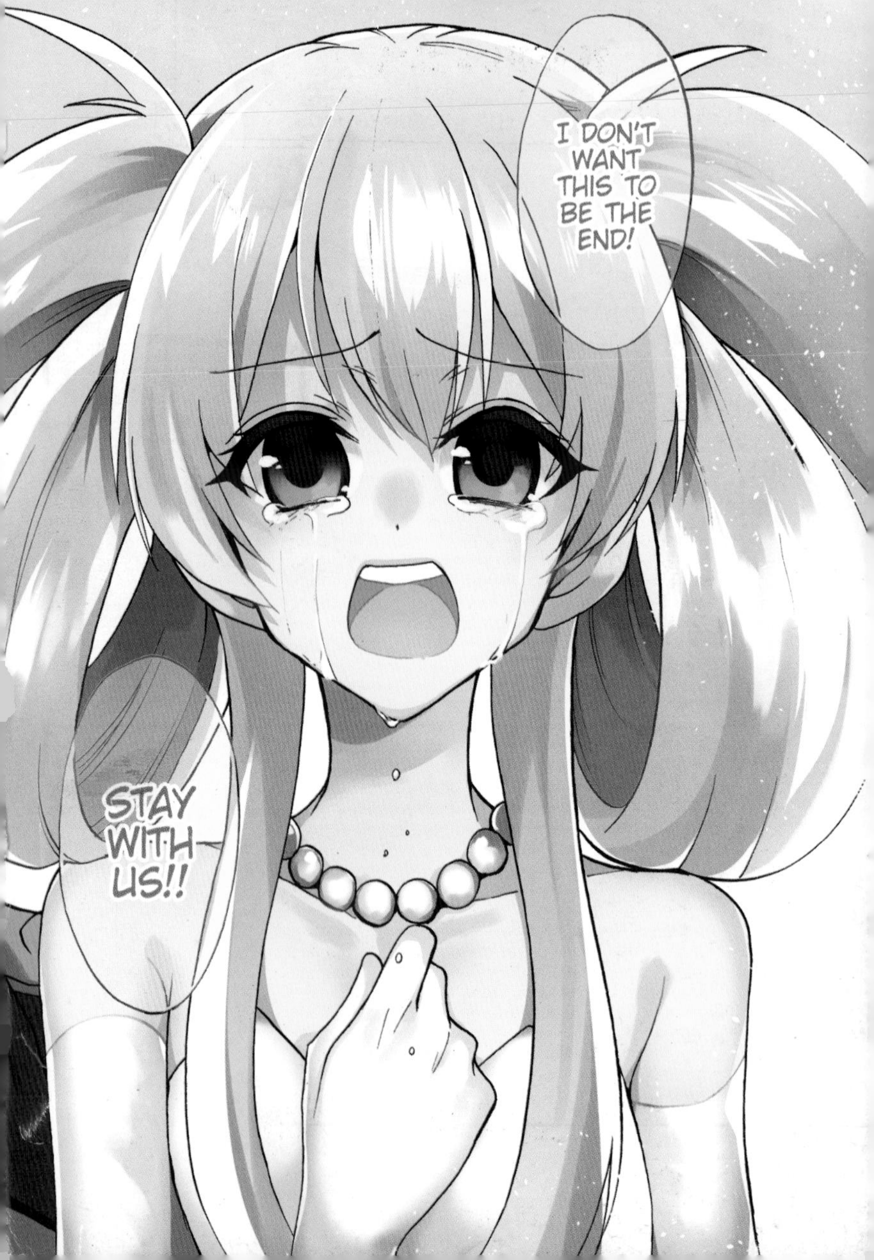
I DON'T WANT THIS TO BE THE END!
STAY WITH US!!

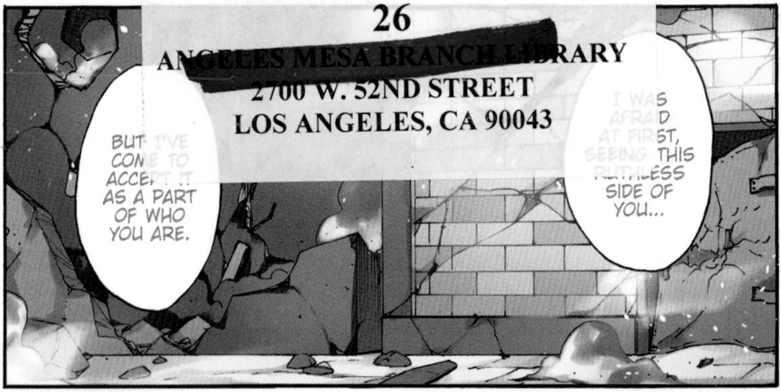
I WAS AFRAID AT FIRST, SEEING THIS RUTHLESS SIDE OF YOU...
BUT I'VE COME TO ACCEPT IT AS A PART OF WHO YOU ARE.

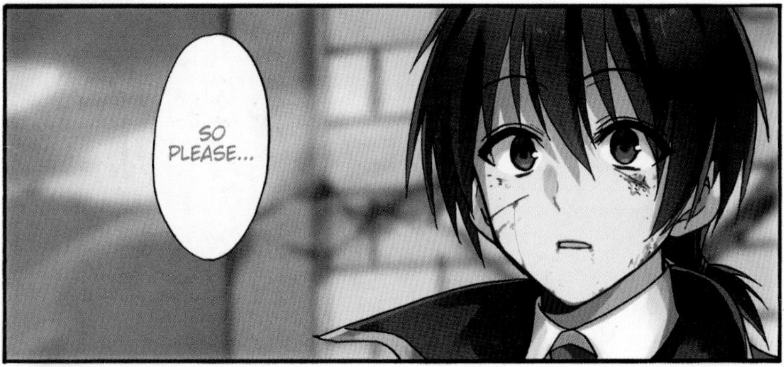
SO PLEASE...

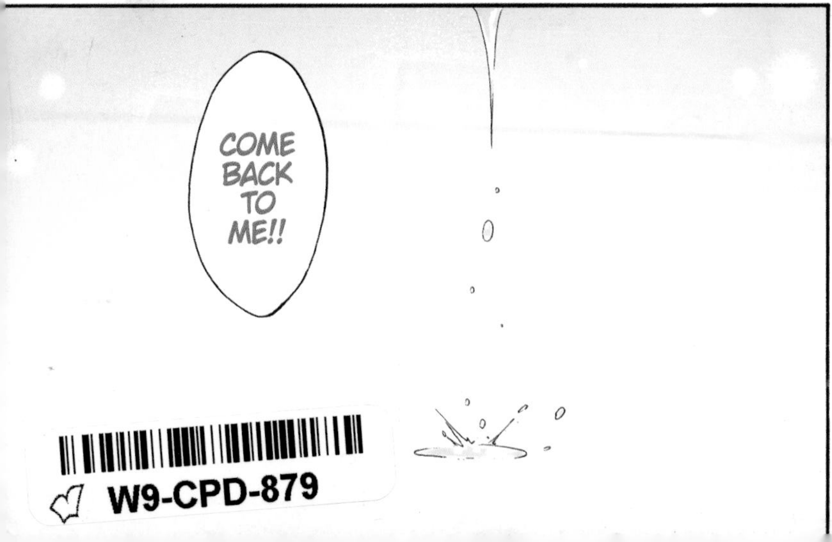
COME BACK TO ME!!